Manliness and Its Discontents

Gender and American Culture

Manliness

The University of North Carolina Press CHAPEL HILL & LONDON

and Its Discontents

**The Black
Middle Class
and the
Transformation
of Masculinity,
1900–1930**

Martin Summers

Set in Quadraat and Gill types by Tseng Information Systems, Inc.
Manufactured in the United States of America

Publication of this work was aided by a generous grant from the Z. Smith
Reynolds Foundation.

The paper in this book meets the guidelines for permanence and durability
of the Committee on Production Guidelines for Book Longevity of the
Council on Library Resources.

Library of Congress Cataloging-in-Publication Data
Summers, Martin Anthony.
Manliness and its discontents: the Black middle class and the transformation
of masculinity, 1900–1930 / Martin Summers.
     p.   cm. — (Gender and American culture)
Includes bibliographical references and index.
ISBN 0-8078-2851-3 (cloth: alk. paper) — ISBN 0-8078-5519-7 (pbk.: alk. paper)
1. African American men — Social conditions — 20th century.
2. Immigrants — United States — Social conditions — 20th century. 3. Men —
United States — Identity — History — 20th century. 4. Masculinity — United
States — History — 20th century. 5. Sex role — United States — History — 20th
century. 6. Middle class — United States — History — 20th century. 7. African
Americans — Social conditions — To 1964. 8. United States — Race relations.
9. United States — Social conditions — 20th century. I. Title. II. Gender &
American culture.
E185.86.S865   2004
305.38'896073'009041 — dc22   2003028252

cloth   08 07 06 05 04   5 4 3 2 1
paper   08 07 06 05 04   5 4 3 2 1

To my parents,
Ann L. Summers (1936–1999)
and
Charles E. Summers

Contents

Illustrations

Acknowledgments

This project began in my first year of graduate school. In a seminar entitled "Race and Sex in America," I, along with several other eager first-year students (and no doubt some jaded second- and third-years as well), read fascinating material dealing with the historical intersections of race, gender, and sexuality, and the sociohistorical constructions of African American womanhood. After one particular class, the professor, Deborah Gray White, casually asked me what I thought about the ways that African American men historically experienced their gender identity. Probably neither of us thought at the time that her question would result in a book-length answer twelve years later. I am grateful to her for asking it.

Over the course of the last twelve years, I have benefited enormously from the guidance and assistance of a number of individuals and institutions. First and foremost, David Levering Lewis, Deborah Gray White, Alice Kessler-Harris, and Wilson Moses oversaw the development of this project as a dissertation at Rutgers University. I want to thank David in particular for believing both in the project and in my ability to undertake it, for encouraging me to think about this subject in more complicated and nuanced ways, and for always pressing me to work harder (and faster). Deborah's initial and subsequent questions, along with her feedback over the years, have significantly shaped this end product. Past and present colleagues have contributed tremendously to my growth as a scholar. At Rutgers University, I benefited greatly from sharing my work with other "dissertators"—especially Michelle Brattain, Glen Keucker, the late Ron McGee, Peter Messer, and Colleen O'Neill. On two separate occasions—1994–95 and 1998–99—graduate and faculty fellows at the Rutgers Center for Historical Analysis offered a collegial and intellectually stimulating environment in which to develop my ideas. Among these fellows, I would like to single out for special thanks Jon Aveni, Herman Bennett, Jennifer Brier, Carolyn Brown, Christopher Brown, Patrick McDevitt, Jason McGill, and Jennifer Morgan. At the New Jersey Institute of Technology, my colleagues in the Federated Department of History of NJIT and Rutgers University–Newark—particularly Lauren Benton, Jon Cowans, Beryl Satter, Chris Sellars, and Richard Sher—provided invaluable support for me as a new assistant professor. I need to extend extra thanks to Clement Price. His generosity of spirit and his commitment to breaking down the ivory walls that so often separate urban campuses from their surrounding communities are an inspiration. He truly deserves the appellation "public intellectual." My current colleagues at the University of Oregon have contributed greatly to the final stages of this project. Past, present, and future chairs—Jim Mohr, Daniel Pope, and Jeff Ostler—have provided invaluable intellectual and logistical support. The advice and support of Peggy Pascoe and Ellen Herman is also greatly appreciated. I could not imagine existing and thriving here without the friendship and support of the "ES crew": Jayna Brown, Anthony Foy, Lynn Fujiwara, Matt Garcia, Shari Huhndorf, Steve Morizumi, Consuela Perez, and Jianbinn Shiao. They have been an incredible lifeline and I am extremely grateful for that.

Several people read the manuscript—either in whole or in part—and at various stages of its evolution. I am indebted to Mia Bay, Erika Bsumek-Hannon, Jennifer Brier, Beatrix Hoffman, Scott Sandage, and Beryl Satter for their comments on drafts of various chapters. Commentators and audience members at a number of different conferences provided much-needed feedback that helped me sharpen often inchoate ideas. The comments of Elsa Barkley Brown and Devon Carbado were particularly helpful. David Levering Lewis and Peggy Pascoe read the entire manuscript and I am grateful for their comments. Glenda Gilmore and E. Anthony Rotundo reviewed the manuscript for the University of North Carolina Press and their suggestions for revision have truly made this a better book.

The staffs at the Moorland-Spingarn Research Center, the Schomburg Center for Research in Black Culture, and the Beinecke Rare Book and Manuscript Library provided able assistance. I am particularly grateful to Beth Howse, Special Collections librarian at Fisk University Franklin Library, for her tireless work in helping me scour the university's archives during the summer of 1998 and for tracking down a photograph at the last minute. The interlibrary loan staffs at NJIT's Van Houten Library and the University of Oregon's Knight Library secured important material for me at critical moments. I am also thankful for the work of several research assistants. At Rutgers University, James Foglio's work generating a bibliography was indispensable while the last chapter could not have been written without Stephanie Sims's excellent archival work. Jurgen Ruckaberle at the University of Oregon provided much needed and very capable assistance in the final manuscript's preparation.

This project would not have been accomplished without the generous assistance of a number of institutions. The Rutgers University Minority Advancement Program provided key funding in the first four years of graduate school, and a graduate fellowship at the Rutgers Center for Historical Analysis, under the able direction of John W. Chambers II, gave me the opportunity to begin the process of writing the dissertation. Postdissertation funding was provided by two Separately Budgeted Research grants from NJIT's Office of Sponsored Programs and a New Faculty Award from the University of Oregon. Finally, I would like to extend my eternal gratitude to the Ford Foundation, which awarded me a postdoctoral fellowship in 1998–99. I was able to use that fellowship to fund a year as an associate fellow at the Rutgers Center for Historical Analysis. The theme of the center that year, "The Black Atlantic: Race, Nation, and Gender," under the adept direction of Mia Bay and Deborah Gray White, led to the assembly of a group of scholars which, to this day, composed the most intellectually stimulating and inspiring environment of which I have been fortunate to be a part.

My experiences with UNC Press have been nothing short of gratifying. My thanks go to the project editor, Pamela Upton, copyeditor Laura Cotterman, and especially my acquiring editor, Sian Hunter, whose excitement about this project has been as infectious as her advice has been sage.

Finally, these acknowledgments would not be complete without a tribute to my friends and family. Over the past decade, and beyond in some cases, I have been enriched by the friendship of Franklin "Earl" Parrish, Erika Bsumek-Hannon, Jayna Brown, and Kelvin Dickerson. Much love and appreciation go to my sister Carla, my brother Scott, my sister-in-law Wendy, my niece Lauren, my nephew Christian, my grandmothers Louise Summers and Elizabeth Mead, and aunts and cousins too numerous to mention individually. I hope they realize how much their support has meant to me over the years. I cannot adequately express my love and gratitude for my parents, Charles and Ann, who gave me the opportunities and, in fact, gave me no alternative but to succeed in life. I can only hope that the dedication of this book partly repays them for all of the dedication that they have shown me. Finally, I owe Karl Mundt thanks for a great many things, of which his support during the writing of this book is only one. His emotional care and offbeat humor continue to sustain me.

Manliness and Its Discontents

Introduction

In America, at the turn of the twentieth century, manhood seemed to be a national preoccupation. From individual concerns about one's own masculine character to larger collective anxieties over the nation's manliness, definitions of manhood—ones that were fundamentally racialized and class bound—pervaded everyday discourse. Everything from definitions of success and citizenship to national conversations over expansion and empire was shaped, in part, by a gendered set of ideas that also informed the identity formation of white middle-class men. The overarching question of what constituted manhood, in other words, dominated the ways in which most men and women in the United States conceptualized, among other things, economic prosperity, national belonging, and, for many, their position within racial, ethnic, and class hierarchies.

Turn-of-the-century notions of success and failure were rooted in the gendered mythology of the "self-made man." A product of the market revolution and the emergence of liberalism in the early nineteenth century, the ideal of the self-made man articulated a formula for success that was dependent upon the cultivation of one's "character." A catchall term that at once meant nothing and everything, character might best be described as the collection of individual traits that rendered one a virtuous member of the community. In the context of Victorian America, character included honesty, piety, self-control, and a commitment to the producer values of industry, thrift, punctuality, and sobriety. Individuals cultivated their character through a number of different mediums: the family, the church, the school, the fraternal organization, and the military. Although character was important in terms of the private lives of people, it was most often invoked as an indispensable quality when considering the public lives of individuals, specifically the individual's relationship to, and interactions in, the marketplace. The idea that one's character was crucial to one's success was axiomatic in the United States in the nineteenth and early twentieth centuries, giving rise to the literary genre of the success manual between 1870 and 1910. The qualities that constituted character also constituted manhood by dominant cultural standards. Indeed, the self-made man as the epitome of success depended upon, and reinforced, the coupling of manhood and character. As one historian argues, the Gilded Age "definition of success not only excluded women, it equated success and manhood in a way that depended on the corollary equation of failure and the feminine."[1]

As economic success and manliness were conflated in the minds of turn-of-the-century Americans, so too were manhood and citizenship. Defined primarily by the right to vote and the ability to participate in party politics, citizenship, by the 1830s, signified access not only to the levers of government, but also to the status of manhood, for white men of all classes. Throughout the remainder of the nineteenth century, and particularly in the middle decades, women challenged the gender-exclusive definition of citizenship through their campaigns to obtain suffrage. Women also asserted their own sense of *civitas* through their participation in various reform movements. By the turn of the century, women's activism in the areas of prohibition, education, consumer rights, and social welfare began to blur the distinction between the public sphere of electoral and party politics and the private sphere of middle-class reform. The public-private split was completely obliterated by the successful suffrage campaign that produced the Nineteenth Amendment, as well as the significant advances made by women in the area of education and fields of employment that had previously been reserved for men. Even with the female assault on exclusively male domains, however, turn-of-the-century Americans still imagined the public citizen within a masculinist paradigm.[2]

The turn of the twentieth century also witnessed the emergence of the United States as a world power. Beginning in the 1890s with the final Indian Wars and the "closing" of the frontier, and culminating in its intervention in the First World War, the United States positioned itself as a first-rate power alongside Great Britain, France, and Germany. The United States' defeat of long-time colonial power Spain in the Spanish-American-Cuban-Filipino War in 1898 solidified its own status as an imperial power. Similar to the ways in which Americans conceived of engagement in the marketplace and the arena of electoral and party politics, discussions over domestic and imperial expansion were grounded in masculinist discourses. Moreover, these discourses were shaped by social Darwinism, the theory that, like biological organisms, nations—conceptualized in racial and cultural terms—evolved into higher civilizations through a process of competition with other nations. Thus, the evolution and expansion of the American nation, argued proponents of empire, involved the vanquishing of the "savage" Indian and ultimately the Spanish, who were alternately represented as savage and effeminate. At the center of this narrative of American ascendancy lay the "manly" frontiersman and soldier. Indeed, this formula was so ingrained in the American imagination that debates over military intervention in Cuba's war of independence against Spain, and later the virtual colonization of Cuba and the Philippines, were cast in explicitly gendered terms. Pro-imperialists claimed the mantle of manliness by, on the one hand, arguing that the childlike Cubans and Filipinos needed the "civilized" hand of white American men to prepare them for eventual self-government and, on the other, by attacking contrary arguments by anti-imperialists as being fundamentally effeminate in nature. The maturation of the United States as an industrial power, and the expansionist and imperial implications of that maturation, then, were articulated within a gendered framework.[3]

For black men in the United States, manhood was equally a matter of some consequence. The arrival of the twentieth century marked the maturation of Jim Crow in the South, a complex of legal, economic, political, and social practices whose logic and mechanisms of oppression were primarily based on race but which also shaped the gender identity formation of blacks and gender relations within black communities. Disfranchisement, implemented at the state level and upheld by state and federal judiciaries between 1890 and the first decade of the twentieth century, attenuated the links between manhood and citizenship for blacks. Economic discrimination and the inability of most black families to survive solely on a male breadwinner's income militated against the patriarchal organization of the black household, further making it difficult to obtain manhood by dominant cultural standards. The ever-present threat of lynching and mob violence, which purportedly sought to police an aggressive black male sexuality and often incorporated the horrific act of castration, made any assertion of independence or brazen behavior a potentially perilous action. Additionally, the legal and customary practice of segregation functioned to produce a precarious sense of manhood among blacks in at least two ways. On the one hand, black men often criticized the substandard nature of segregated facilities—in terms of both physical condition and resources—as an insult to their collective manhood. Weldon Victor Jenkins, a black correspondent for the *Chattanooga Times*, for instance, framed the inferior conditions of black residential areas, and the role that these conditions were playing in blacks' decisions to move out of the South, in masculinist terms. "One of our grievances," he wrote, "is that in colored localities we have very bad streets, no lights, no sewerage system, and sanitary conditions are necessarily bad. Give the negro the right kind of a show, living wages, consider him as a man, and he will be contented to remain here."[4] On the other hand, in as much as segregated spaces were reflective of, and enforced, racial distinctions, they tended to collapse intraracial distinctions.

For instance, while middle- and upper-class white women passengers enjoyed a separate ladies' train car—presumably to protect them from the edgier and potentially vulgar world of men—black men and women of all classes rode together in the Jim Crow car. Moreover, they generally had to share one uni-sex lavatory. Segregation, in other words, not only blurred class distinctions within the black community; it also had the potential of blurring gender conventions that were otherwise rigidly delineated within the dominant culture.[5]

Of course, all blacks within the United States did not suffer the daily indignities of Jim Crow.[6] Nor did all black men experience their gender identities solely in relation to their social, economic, and political marginalization. Black men constructed and staged a gendered self within a host of relationships and contexts—of which the state and white society were only two. Still, it is difficult to imagine race, and racism, not impacting the ways in which men of African descent in the United States experienced their gender identities. When early-twentieth-century activists articulated their grievances and couched their demands for remedies within a discourse of "manhood rights"; or when the intellectual W. E. B. Du Bois argued, in 1903, that "submission to civic inferiority . . . is bound to sap the manhood of any race in the long run"; or when black men sought to organize households and institutions within the black community, such as the church, along the lines of patriarchy; or when black leaders pointed to African Americans' involvement in the Spanish-American-Cuban-Filipino War and the missionary projects occurring in Africa as a badge of the race's manhood, they engaged in the same discourses that white men did—discourses that grounded manhood in, among other things, independence, citizenship, engagement in the marketplace, mastery over self and the environment, and patriarchy.[7]

This book is about how black men in the United States imagined and performed a gendered subjectivity in the first three decades of the twentieth century. Specifically, the book examines ideas of manhood as they were articulated by middle-class men within four distinct, yet interrelated and overlapping, social milieus: the fraternal environment of Prince Hall Freemasonry, the nationalist networks of the Universal Negro Improvement Association (UNIA), the modernist circles of the cultural production movement known as the Harlem Renaissance, and the post–World War I campuses of historically black colleges. It looks at the ways in which African American and African Caribbean immigrant men constructed a gendered self through rhetoric, organizational activities, literature, and daily public rituals of performance. It explores how these men formed their gender identities in relation, and in opposition, to the gender identities of white men, black women and youth, and the dominant cultural representations of black manhood. Finally, it charts the changing ideas of manhood within the black middle class from the turn of the century to the Great Depression. The scope of this examination—roughly 1900 to 1930—provides a window through which we can look at constructions of black manhood and particularly how they were shaped by at least three historical developments: migration (both by rural southern blacks and African Caribbeans) and urbanization, class formation within black communities, and changing ideas of manhood within the dominant culture.

The first three decades of the twentieth century witnessed an increased migration of African Americans and African Caribbeans to northern and midwestern urban areas. Between 1899 and 1937, more than 140,000 black immigrants made their way to the United States; the vast majority of these immigrants were from the Caribbean. Intraregional and international migration of African Caribbeans—like that of southern and eastern Europeans during much of the same period—was driven by economic dislocation, natural disasters, and political marginalization. The decline of the sugar economy, coupled with the increasing consolidation of land in the hands of fewer planters and agricultural corporations, adversely affected the peasant populations on the islands. As the rural sugar industry collapsed and the amount of land available to blacks decreased, most Caribbean colonies experienced rapid urbanization. Without a parallel process of industrialization, a growing proportion of African Caribbeans were relegated to the margins of the economy, mainly in the areas of domestic service, unskilled labor, and minor trade. Further, the importation of indentured "coolie" labor from East and South Asia pressed the existing low wages of African Caribbeans further downward. Accompanied by a succession of natural disasters, from alternating droughts and floods to hurricanes and earthquakes, between the 1870s and 1910s, the economic dislocation suffered by African Caribbeans prompted many to search for a livelihood elsewhere. Labor shortages in other parts of the Caribbean and Central America opened up new possibilities for prospective emigrants. Blacks from Jamaica, Barbados, St. Kitts, Nevis, Antigua, Montserrat and, to a lesser extent, Trinidad and Guyana, pulled up stakes and sought better economic opportunities as agricultural laborers in Cuba, Dominican Republic, and Costa Rica; as dock workers and teamsters in Bermuda; and as construction workers in Panama. Racial discrimination, in the form of segregation in countries such as Panama, and wage disparity led to further out-migration, either back to their home islands or on to the United States. African Caribbean immigrants settled primarily in New York, Boston, and southern Florida.[8]

These African Caribbean immigrants joined a much larger stream of African Americans leaving the rural South for northern and midwestern urban areas. Several factors contributed to the mass exodus: depressed cotton prices resulting from overproduction, the devastation of the cotton crops of 1915 and 1916 by the boll weevil, droughts and floods, and the increased demand for labor in the emerging war industries coupled with the near cessation of southern and eastern European immigration. The social factors that worked to "push" African Americans northward and toward southern cities included disfranchisement, segregation, and the widespread threat of racial violence. Between 1910 and 1920, and particularly during the years surrounding World War I, more than 500,000 blacks moved from rural southern areas to the industrial and commercial centers of New York, Philadelphia, Chicago, Pittsburgh, Detroit, Milwaukee, and Cleveland. During that same period and the next decade, an additional 750,000 or more southern blacks migrated to urban areas within the region. Those who migrated comprised only a fraction of the entire African American population, but the overall movement was, by far, the most rapid change in black demographics that had ever occurred.[9]

Accompanying migration was the emergence, in the United States, of a "new" black middle class, a socioeconomic stratum that was defined by occupation, wealth, and skill, as much as it was by the subjective markers of ancestry, culture, and education that had constituted the parameters of the old nineteenth-century black elite. By the second and third decades of the century, a new elite composed of entrepreneurs, professionals, and skilled workers, and whose existence was tied to the segregated world of consumer capitalism, vied with the traditional black aristocracy for the economic, political, and moral leadership of the race.[10] To be sure, discerning a black middle class using the objective measurements of occupational status and income is problematic, given that the opportunities for social mobility were limited for blacks in ways that they were not for white middle-class aspirants. According to one scholar, the entrepreneurs and professionals of the "new" black middle class, as a social group, resembled the "nineteenth-century petit bourgeoisie" more than it did the bureaucratic and managerial workforce that constituted the bulk of the white middle class in the early twentieth century. And, as Kevin Gaines argues, it is far easier to talk about the black middle class as a collection of individuals sharing an ideological preoccupation with "bourgeois status" than it is to talk of them as a group sharing the material benefits of the larger American middle class.[11] In this sense, the black middle class is defined more by its self-conscious positioning against the black working class—through its adherence to a specific set of social values and the public performance of those values—than by real economic and occupational differences. Indeed, the boundaries of the black middle class were quite expansive—in terms of occupation and income at least—and managed to accommodate workers who commanded steady incomes, including skilled laborers and service employees. Entrance into the middle class was determined as much by subjective criteria as it was by objective economic indicators.

Although it is certainly true, to a degree, that the black middle class was an ideological self-invention, there were also palpable changes that differentiated it from the working class, particularly given the consumer economy that characterized the early twentieth century. In addition to the older elite positions of journalists, ministers, educators, and entrepreneurs who catered to a white clientele, the "new" middle class included professionals, such as social workers, lawyers, doctors, and dentists; small entrepreneurs who increasingly serviced segregated communities, such as grocers, retailers, beauticians, restaurateurs, hoteliers, real estate agents, and undertakers; and individuals engaged in larger financial ventures such as banks, building and loan associations, and insurance companies.[12]

Similarly, African Caribbean immigrants came from communities with malleable concepts of class. The "middle stratum" in Caribbean colonies, particularly those of the British and the French, did not necessarily achieve a qualitatively higher standard of living than the rural and urban working class. Rather, members of this stratum laid claim to a bourgeois status partly through respectability, which historian Bridget Brereton has defined as "subscribing more or less to middle-class British/French norms of organization, sexual behavior, and life-styles" and "stress[ing] the importance of educational advancement for their children."[13] In the early twentieth century, however, those few avenues of social mobility—especially through particular forms of employment—began to narrow. Entry to the civil service and other professional fields became increasingly difficult for the majority of African Caribbeans. The cessation of competitive civil service exams in Jamaica in 1911, for instance, reduced the number of blacks, particularly darker-skinned ones, entering the colonial bureaucracy. Even those who managed to circumvent these barriers eventually butted up against glass ceilings. This contributed to the phenomenon of the smallest socioeconomic group—as little as 2 percent of the entire black population on most islands according to one scholar—providing a disproportionate amount, along with skilled workers, of the migrating population to the United States. Moreover, migrants with professional backgrounds, or those who possessed some type of skill, were less likely to return to their home islands on a permanent basis.[14]

The migration of African Americans and African Caribbean immigrants and the class formation that was beginning to take place within those communities paralleled a shift in the dominant cultural ideas of manhood. As the United States underwent a transformation from a producer-oriented to a consumer-oriented society in the first three decades of the twentieth century, Americans began to articulate fundamentally different understandings of what it meant to be a man by dominant cultural standards. A modern ethos of masculinity supplanted earlier nineteenth-century notions of manliness that characterized a society dominated by Victorian values. Manhood became less defined by production (or engagement in the marketplace), character, respectability, and the producer values of industry, thrift, regularity, and temperance. Rather, middle-class Americans increasingly unlinked manhood from the market, at least from the orientation of the producer, and began to define it in terms of consumption. One's manhood became more and more defined by the consumer goods one owned, the leisure practices one engaged in, and one's physical and sexual virility. Respectability, or the public performance of producer values, also became less important in middle-class constructions of masculinity.[15]

The central argument of this book is that the black middle class experienced a similar transformation in its conceptualizations of manhood. The shift from Victorian manliness to modern masculinity as the hegemonic model of manhood also guided middle-class black men's constructions and performances of their gender identity. This can clearly be seen in the ideas about manhood circulated among, on the one hand, older men affiliated with Prince Hall Freemasonry and the UNIA and, on the other, younger men who, coming of age either during or after World War I, composed the modernist vanguard within the Harlem Renaissance and populated the campuses of historically black colleges. In many ways, black Masons and Garveyites articulated similar investments in Victorian gender conventions. Men within both organizations placed an emphasis on the productive character of manhood. The centrality of the marketplace, the importance of character and respectability, and the indispensability of producer values lay at the heart of an idealized Victorian manhood to which these men aspired. The public-private organization of gender roles—within their homes, their organizations, their communities, and, for Garveyites, the nascent black nation—also informed the ideas of manhood held by these men, although, as we will see, their patriarchal "prerogative" was often contested by women affiliated with the movements. By the mid-1920s, the Jazz Age, as a manifestation of the confluence of postwar youth and consumer cultures, offered more modern ideas of manhood to all Americans. Black youth in urban areas and college campuses alike began rejecting earlier generations' emphasis on respectable bourgeois manliness. In the jazz culture created in New York, Chicago, and Kansas City, in the literature produced by the younger Harlem literati, and in the uprisings that erupted at black colleges throughout the decade, black men were articulating fundamentally different notions of masculinity—notions that were not dependent upon one's relationship to the marketplace, that did not rely upon a patriarchal and hetero-normative posture, and that revolved around consumption and the body.

This story, then, is one of generational change. It is about the transition in definitions of manhood—from production to consumption, from character and respectability to the body and personality, from manliness to masculinity—and how that transition played out within the black middle class intergenerationally. But it is not a story of seamless change. It is not as if there was a perfectly unalloyed model of manhood, based on production and character, that completely gave way to a model that was unambivalently dependent on consumption and the body. Indeed, the physical capacity of male bodies was important to constructions of Victorian manliness, and many young men who came of age in the postwar era continued to invest a great deal of importance in the concepts of character and respectability. The tentacles of consumer capitalism insinuated themselves into the gender identity formation of many men who proudly subscribed to Victorian ideals of manhood, while a producer ethos continued to undergird the gender identities of many men caught up in the modern jazz and youth cultures of the 1920s. To put it more directly, this examination of manhood operates on the premise that gender identity is not a fixed, immutable essence that one possesses but, rather, a process—a means of becoming—that is marked by ambiguity, contradictions, and uncertainty.

In treating gender as a process, this book has been deeply influenced by work in history, sociology, literary criticism, and cultural studies that posits gender as a socially constructed category of identity. Social constructionists argue that gender is far from being a collection of innate qualities and characteristics. Rather, the ways in which women and men think about themselves as gendered subjects—and perform that gendered subjectivity—are socially defined, constantly reproduced through the social meaning of language, and embedded within specific economic, political, and cultural institutions. People have gender identities, whereas societies or cultures produce gender conventions. Conventions are essentially how society positions and regulates men and women within a framework of hierarchical social relations. They are, furthermore, historically and culturally specific. Gender identities are not only the aggregation of specific values and attributes that society imposes on an individual's physical, "sexed body"; they are also the individual acts of conforming to, contesting, or negotiating the gender conventions of a particular society. In this sense, gender is not a fixed, stable condition of existence; rather, it is a dynamic process.[16] The social constructionist approach also emphasizes the relationality of gender. Like other characteristics that constitute an individual's selfhood, masculinity is relational. In the process of defining oneself as masculine, individuals within specific historical contexts use identifiable characteristics against which to construct their manhood. These qualities are not only determined by sex (male against female), but also by class and skill level (middle-class manliness against working-class, "rough" masculinity), age (men against boys), sexuality (heterosexual against homosexual), and race and ethnicity (white, "civilized" manliness against nonwhite and non-Western "savage" masculinity).[17] Thus, gender functions not only as a category of identity that mediates, and is mediated by, other categories of identity; it also functions as a discourse in that it signifies power relations, not only between men and women, but also relations based on class, race and ethnicity, nationality, and sexuality.[18]

Social constructionism has led to an explosion in scholarship on men's history. In the past fifteen years, historical scholarship on masculinity has abandoned the earlier paradigms of sex role theory and psychoanalytic theory —both of which, according to their critics, failed to address the disparities of power that inhere in gender relations and neglected the complexity of different male experiences—and, instead, has focused more on gender identity as a historically specific process that is structured by race, ethnicity, class, age, and sexuality.[19] Although there is acknowledgment that race is a prominent category through which this formative process occurs, most social constructionist studies treat black masculinity mainly as a negative referent. The importance of race, in other words, is acknowledged primarily to the extent that it shapes how white men have historically constituted their gender identities through a negation, or in some cases, an appropriation, of blackness. Black men are rarely agents in the "new" men's history.[20]

Another way in which social constructionists address race and ethnicity without really granting agency to nonwhite men is by utilizing a theoretical framework of hegemony. Drawing on Antonio Gramsci's theory of how a ruling group wields power through a normativization of its ideology, scholars have used hegemony to illustrate the power relationships that are constitutive of the social construction of masculinity. "Hegemonic masculinity," writes sociologist R. W. Connell, "can be defined as the configuration of gender practice which embodies the currently accepted answer to the problem of the legitimacy of patriarchy, which guarantees (or is taken to guarantee) the dominant position of men and the subordination of women." Hegemonic masculinity, the dominant ideas of manhood that hold the greatest cultural currency in any given historical period, is not an unchanging, transhistorical "configuration of gender practice"; rather, it is a "historically mobile relation." In addition to structuring the relations of dominance/subordination between men and women, hegemonic masculinity also rests upon an exclusion of subordinated or marginalized masculinities: those of working-class men, nonwhite men, and gay men.[21]

This theoretical model of hegemony and marginalization has value in that it does not, unlike sex role and psychoanalytic theories, neglect issues of power. However, by reducing gender identity to the expression of power, it threatens to render marginalized social groups invisible. Or it allows them visibility only to the extent that they validate hegemonic masculinity. An example of this type of scholarship is the historical sociological work by Michael Kimmel, *Manhood in America*. "What it means to be a man in America," Kimmel writes, "depends heavily on one's class, race, ethnicity, age, sexuality, region of the country. To acknowledge these differences among men, we must speak of *masculinities*. At the same time, though, all American men must also contend with a singular vision of masculinity, a particular definition that is held up as the model against which we all measure ourselves."[22] Kimmel recognizes the importance of differentiated social experience even as he stresses the necessity of understanding the primacy of hegemonic masculinity. However, the extent to which he legitimizes the experiences of men outside of the dominant social group—primarily black men and gay men—is the extent to which they operate, again, as negative referents. Or, because of these marginalized social groups' exterior position to the larger configuration of social structures and practices in which hegemonic masculinity is constituted, if black men and gay men are not solely negative referents in Kimmel's study, their masculinity, or their lack thereof, is always discussed in relation to their social, political, and economic marginalization. So, for example, Kimmel consistently argues that "[black men] remained excluded from full manhood" by virtue of their absence from the United States' exhibits at the 1893 Chicago World's Fair; or that the black cultural production of the 1940s by writers such as Richard Wright was an "attempt to reclaim their manhood"; or that the Black Panther Party represented a "growing preoccupation with proving a manhood long suppressed and denied by racism."[23] Certainly, black men often expressed their alienation from the dominant culture in gendered terms. And, to be sure, political, economic, and social marginalization in the United States have influenced the ways in which black men have experienced their gender identities. Black male subjectivity, however, cannot be reduced to these relationships or else it becomes a solely reactive process. It also becomes a relatively static concept with which to analyze not only masculinity as a socially constructed category, but also how gender and power organize relationships *within* black communities.

There is an ample amount of scholarship that situates men of African descent at the center of any investigation of masculinity and it has grown over the past decade. In the aggregate, this scholarship provides a much-needed corrective to earlier historiographic and theoretical paradigms in which black men function primarily as negative referents for the construction of hegemonic masculinity. Much of this work has been in the fields of sociology, cultural studies, and critical race theory, although there have been several historical treatments as well. This work might be grouped into three conceptual paradigms. First, there is the hard social science and social theory scholarship that discusses black masculinity primarily in relation to interrelated "structures of oppression"—such as schools, a discriminatory labor market, the criminal justice system, technologies of surveillance—that result in the "institutional decimation of black males."[24] Through this scholarship, replete with staggering statistical and anecdotal evidence of unemployment and underemployment, high incarceration and high school dropout rates, and broken homes, we are constantly reminded of the "crisis" of black manhood, of black men as victims of institutional racism. The second paradigm in which critical examinations of the construction of black masculinity cohere is discursive in its epistemological approach. Centered primarily in the softer social sciences and humanities—particularly in the fields of cultural studies and literary criticism—this discursive approach examines black masculinity through its representations within the dominant culture and the ways in which those representations constitute, and are reflective of, the power relationships between blacks and whites.[25] The third paradigm provides an understanding of black masculinity that is rooted in larger historical narratives. Not limited to the efforts of historians, the works that fall under this paradigm tend to overlay a history of black masculinity onto a traditional narrative of African American history. Thus, the history of black masculinity becomes merely the staples of black history read through a gendered lens. That is, the history of black masculinity becomes the adverse effects of slavery and Jim Crow on black men; the history of black masculinity is played out in the Washington–Du Bois debate; and the history of black masculinity is unearthed in the masculinist political agendas of civil rights activism and various nationalist movements.[26]

Of course, all three approaches are valuable. The hard social science approach reminds us, in the academic community, that—given the realities of institutional racism in the United States (or the West for that matter)—this is one subject we can not afford to sequester within disciplines or lines of inquiry that are dominated by theory. The discursive paradigm, however, allows us to think about the connections between cultural representations of black masculinity, the importance of those representations in the production and maintenance of white male power and privilege, and the real institutional practices that marginalize men of African descent. Finally, the historical narrative approach reminds us of the importance of historicity—of recognizing that the ways in which men imagine and perform their gender identities are historically contingent, and marked by change and continuity. Notwithstanding the various advantages of these paradigmatic approaches, they all share a fundamental deficiency with the model of hegemonic masculinity: they tend to reduce black male subjectivity to its subordinated status within dominant cultures. In this sense, they tend to reproduce the notion of the black male as "social problem." Moreover, very little of this scholarship examines how black men engage in their gender identity formation through quotidian practice: work, leisure, organizational life, interaction with families and communities, and so forth. As such, much of the work within these three paradigms neglects the complexity of black male subjectivity. Through their emphasis on the marginalization of a black masculinity, they fail to consider the way in which the construction and performance of black masculinities occur outside of black men's relationship to the state and how they alternately, or even simultaneously, shape resistance to the dominant culture and create conflict within the subordinated communities. As sociologists Andrea Hunter and James Earl Davis suggest, "It is important to note . . . that the dynamics of race, culture, and class have forged varied constructions of manhood whose contours and shades are not limited to the hegemony of masculinity or the politicized images of Afro-American men."[27]

This study attempts to reconcile these two approaches. On the one hand, it seeks to recognize black men's agency while also taking the hegemonic power of white, middle-class masculinity seriously. On the other hand, it seeks to do so without reducing the gender identity formation of black men to an act of resistance. That is, one thing I want to do in this book is to keep a model of hegemony that acknowledges the role that power plays in the social construction of masculinity; yet I also recognize that the construction of gender occurs across a range of relationships, of which hegemonic masculinity versus marginalized masculinity is only one. In order to do this, I have relied heavily on Raymond Williams's notion of hegemony. In *Marxism and Literature*, he defines it as "a lived system of meanings and values—constitutive and constituting—which as they are experienced as practices appear as reciprocally confirming. It thus constitutes a sense of reality for most people in the society, a sense of absolute because experienced reality beyond which it is very difficult for most members of the society to move, in most areas of their lives. It is, that is to say, in the strongest sense a 'culture,' but a culture which has also to be seen as the lived dominance and subordination of particular classes." Hegemonic masculinity—or the dominant cultural ideals of what it means to be a man—becomes the terrain on which all marginalized, or subordinated, masculinities are constructed and performed. However, since cultural hegemony operates through the normativization of a historical bloc's worldview and the consent of marginalized communities to that normativization, the relationship between these masculinities is not always one of antagonism. Thinking of hegemonic masculinity in this way allows us to treat black men as subjects in a process of gender identity formation that, although ultimately shaped by the dominant culture, is not merely reactive, responsive, or resistant to the dominant culture. As hegemonic masculinity relies on negative referents for its construction and contributes to relations of domination and subordination *between* men in dominant and subordinated social groups, so too does the social construction of masculinity contribute to relations of power *within* those marginalized communities.[28] Using a model of hegemony also allows us to think about the influence of marginalized masculinities on the culturally dominant gender conventions—black masculinity as "counter-hegemonic." As Williams reminds us, hegemony "does not just passively exist as a form of dominance. It has continually to be renewed, recreated, defended, and modified. It is also continually resisted, limited, altered, challenged by pressures not at all its own."[29]

Hegemonic discourses of manliness clearly shaped how black men in the early twentieth century thought about themselves as men. This was, as I will show in part I, a central dynamic in the gender identity formation of Prince Hall Freemasons and male Garveyites. These men found it difficult to move beyond the definitions of manhood as they were articulated by the dominant culture of late-Victorian society. African Americans and African Caribbeans who matured to adulthood in the years during and following World War I developed a fundamentally different relationship to the hegemonic gender conventions of the American middle class. On the one hand, their participation in jazz culture and postwar cultural production constituted one of the "pressures" that ultimately undermined the power of Victorian manliness. Still, as we will see in part II, even as younger blacks in the 1920s constructed a modern ethos of masculinity that was antithetical to an older generation's ideals of manhood, many of them clung—some unconsciously and others very deliberately—to many of the constitutive values of manliness such as production and independence.

Ultimately, this book is about the ways that African American and African

Caribbean immigrant men engaged in their own gender identity formation, a process that was shaped not only by their race and ethnicity, but by their class, age, and sexuality as well. It is about the relationships that the process of gender identity formation created and relied upon: relationships between black men and the dominant culture, between black men and black women, between black men and black youth, and between black men themselves.

Manliness

The Death and Life of Sir John E. Bruce

On a somber afternoon in August 1924, the residents of Harlem witnessed what amounted to a state funeral for John Edward Bruce. A prominent Prince Hall Freemason and member of the Universal Negro Improvement Association (UNIA), Bruce was a veritable institution within the African American and African Caribbean community. Born into slavery in Maryland in 1856 and emancipated in 1860, the self-educated Bruce became a noted journalist and political activist. He wrote for over a score of newspapers and published at least four, short-lived ones of his own. Bruce was also active in several civil rights organizations around the turn of the century, including the Afro-American League—which he founded along with African Methodist Episcopal Zion bishop Alexander Walters and journalist T. Thomas Fortune in 1890—and its successor, the Afro-American Council, founded in 1898. A staunch believer in the importance of historical knowledge of self for individual and collective self-esteem, Bruce cofounded the Negro Society for Historical Research with Afro–Puerto Rican bibliophile Arthur A. Schomburg in 1911. Like other blacks during the post–World War I period who became disillusioned by the nation's failure to live up to its democratic creed, Bruce's congenital militancy found a new home in the Garvey movement. From 1920 to 1924, he wrote a column for, and was contributing editor to, the UNIA's newspaper, the *Negro World*. He also held two of the most prestigious titles in the organization: Knight Commander of the Order of the Nile and Duke of Uganda.[1]

By all accounts, Bruce's funeral was quite an elaborate affair. It began with a "gorgeous procession" to the UNIA's Liberty Hall on 138th Street. "Virtually the entire assemblage was in uniform except [Marcus] Garvey, who was dressed in black as a symbol of the grief of the organization of which he is President General," one article reported. The service itself consisted of three separate funeral rites. The first was conducted by Reverend Charles D. Martin, pastor of the Fourth Moravian AME Zion Church and member of Prince Hall Lodge No. 38. Reverend George Emonei Carter, the UNIA's secretary-general, presided over the second part, in which Garvey and William Sherrill, second assistant president-general, gave eulogies. Resolutions drafted by the UNIA, the Negro Society for Historical Research, and the American Negro Academy, were also read. The nationalist overtones of the funeral were present in the performance of the UNIA's Universal Choir, the bearing of floral arrangements by the UNIA's Black Cross Nurses, and the stationing of the Universal African Legionnaires by the casket.[2]

The third part of the service was in keeping with Bruce's status as a Master Mason. Although the journalistic accounts' brief mention of the funeral's Masonic rites do not provide great detail, this section of the service most likely conformed to standard Prince Hall ritual.[3] Bruce's fellow Masons adorned their dark suits with black top hats, white gloves, a white lambskin apron, a black crepe brand around the left arm, and an evergreen sprig in their left breast pocket. Lodge officers wore their fraternal jewels. The lodge's tiler, with a drawn sword, and stewards carrying white rods led the procession into Liberty Hall. The procession itself was hierarchically organized, with Master Masons at the forefront, followed by lodge officials, Past Masters, the lodge chaplain, and finally the Most Worshipful Master. Members of the procession also carried the Bible, the Book of Constitution, and the Marshal's baton, all of which were trimmed with black crepe. Once inside, the highest officer opened the service in the Third Degree, that of the Master Mason. The Most Worshipful Master led the liturgy, and, upon conclusion, the coffin was closed and carried to the interment site. At the cemetery, Bruce's fellow Masons circled his coffin and engaged in scriptural call and response and prayer. After the coffin was lowered into the vault, the Most Worshipful Master deposited into the grave Bruce's lambskin apron and a parchment with his name and age inscribed upon it. The brothers then passed the plot and dropped their evergreen sprigs on top of the coffin. The burial rite ended with a prayer and a dirge.

Bruce's funeral provides an important illustration of the interrelatedness of the UNIA and Prince Hall Freemasonry. The two organizations intersected at a number of different levels. In terms of personnel, there was crossover membership between the two groups. Indeed, one of the reasons that Garvey may not have worn a UNIA uniform to the funeral is that he himself had become a Freemason at Bruce's encouragement.[4] In organizational terms, the two were also similar. Several historians have pointed out, for instance, that the structure and operation of the UNIA resembled fraternal and benevolent associations.[5] But Garveyites and Prince Hall Freemasons were similar in an-

Funeral of John Edward Bruce, 1924. Arthur Schomburg and Marcus Garvey are second and third from the right. (Courtesy of Marcus Garvey Portrait Collection, Photographs and Prints Division, Schomburg Center for Research in Black Culture, New York Public Library, Astor, Lenox and Tilden Foundations)

other crucial respect. That is, they shared similar commitments to bourgeois gender conventions, particularly in their adherence to the ideals of manliness.

Officially designated Free and Accepted Masons, Prince Hall Freemasons trace their history—and their legitimacy as descendants of ancient Free-masonry via their relationship to English lodges—back to 1784, when Prince Hall, a black artisan and Revolutionary War veteran, organized the African Lodge in Boston. Although little is known about Hall's early life, his instru-mentality in introducing Freemasonry to people of African descent in the Americas is clear. In March 1775, Hall and fourteen other free blacks were initiated into Irish Military Lodge No. 441, a lodge chiefly made up of Irish soldiers attached to the British regular army based in Boston. After being raised to the degree of Master Mason, the fifteen received a temporary permit to meet as a lodge. The permit allowed the members of Provisional African Lodge No. 1 to meet and conduct Masonic rites—including funerary rituals—but it did not give them authority to grant degrees. For this, they needed a charter or warrant from a Grand Lodge. Hall submitted a petition to the Pro-vincial Grand Master of Massachusetts, head of the governing body of white Masons in the New England colony, but he failed to act upon it. The objective of constituting a "Regular Lodge" was put on hold for the next several years, a period in which Hall joined the colonial movement for independence. After the war, Hall petitioned the Grand Lodge of England for a warrant. In 1784, the Grand Lodge recognized that "Prince Hall, Boston Smith, Thomas Sanderson, and several other brethren residing in Boston, New England, in North America, do hereby constitute . . . a Regular Lodge of Free and Accepted Masons, under the title or denomination of the African Lodge," although Hall did not receive the actual charter until 1787.[6]

In 1791, African Lodge No. 459 achieved the status of a Grand Lodge, with Hall as its Most Worshipful Grand Master. This new status gave the African Lodge the power to create subordinate lodges throughout North America. New lodges were formed in Philadelphia and Providence, Rhode Island, in 1797. In 1808, one year after Hall's death, the African Grand Lodge was renamed Prince Hall Grand Lodge. Throughout the first half of the nineteenth century, Prince Hall Freemasonry spread rapidly along the eastern seaboard and westward. By the turn of the twentieth century, black Masons in every state and territory—except Vermont, New Hampshire, Maine, and South Dakota—had Grand Lodges or were in the process of forming them.[7]

By the time African Lodge No. 459 was chartered, Freemasonry in Great Britain, continental Europe, North America, and elsewhere was largely "speculative," or symbolic, in nature. As opposed to the "operative" masonry that defined membership in the guildlike lodges of medieval Europe, Freemasonry in colonial North America consisted largely of merchants and professionals. Skilled artisans did not become regular habitués of Masonic lodges until the late eighteenth century, and by the early nineteenth century "the order increasingly attracted an emerging middle class of lawyers, prosperous farmers, and independent tradesmen."[8]

Throughout the nineteenth century, Freemasonry, in its celebration of producer republicanism[9] (through its symbolic association with the master craftsman) and its emphasis on understanding the physical and spiritual world through reason and science, became a prominent institution in which both individual and collective, middle-class, male identities were produced. Since its inception, Prince Hall Freemasonry has been an important social institution within black communities in North America, the Caribbean, and Africa. In its various capacities, it has served as a voluntary charitable association, an entrepreneurial and professional network, and a seedbed of black middle-class leadership. Along with churches, benevolent associations, and political clubs, Masonic orders played a significant role in the political and reform activities of free black communities in the antebellum period and continued to form the spine of the institutional life of post-emancipation communities until at least the middle of the twentieth century. Although it has concerned itself with the larger social, economic, and political issues confronting black people, Freemasonry has also fulfilled the narrower responsibilities of providing financial assistance, business opportunities, and a putative middle-class status to its members and their families.

In many ways, the objectives of the UNIA fundamentally diverged from those of Prince Hall Freemasonry. Although initiated in Jamaica in 1914, it quickly became an international organization. After several years of haltingly erratic growth, the association, by the mid-1920s, was arguably the largest secular organization for people of African descent in the world. Most of its chapters were located in the United States. Thirty-eight states contained UNIA chapters, with the southern states boasting the largest number. The Caribbean, and particularly the islands of Cuba and Trinidad, was also a stronghold of Garveyite activity. UNIA chapters existed in Central and South America, Africa, Great Britain, and even Australia. By the late 1920s, the organization consisted of nearly a thousand chapters and several hundred thousand members.[10] In the North American context, the UNIA was part of a longer tradition of community development. The work done by UNIA chapters and their various auxiliaries resembled self-help organizations such as black fraternal associations and benevolent societies, while the *Negro World* functioned in a similar manner to antebellum black newspapers and later national publications in its communication of political, economic, and social events and trends that were deemed significant to blacks. The UNIA was a nationalist organization and, as such, it advocated group solidarity, racial chauvinism and race purity, and the development of a "modern" state in Africa that would be economically and politically powerful enough to protect the interests of blacks worldwide. The prevailing ethos of the Garvey movement was its emphasis on entrepreneurship as the means to racial advancement. Economic empowerment, through restaurants, clothing factories and stores, cooperative markets and financial institutions, laundries, hotels, and printing presses, was the priority of the UNIA's central leadership and local membership. The most organized economic venture undertaken was the Black Star Line, the organization's shipping company. Launched in 1919, the UNIA conceived of the Black Star Line as a commercial link between black entrepreneurs in North America, the Caribbean, Latin America, and Africa. Financial mismanagement by individuals within the company and the zealous efforts of various U.S. government agencies, however, led to Garvey's arrest, conviction, incarceration, and deportation on mail fraud charges between 1923 and 1927.

Despite their differences — the desire of Garveyites to politically and economically unify the African diaspora through a concrete entrepreneurial agenda versus the desire of Freemasons to unify like-minded men through the esoteric teachings of the Craft—men who joined the UNIA and Prince Hall shared fundamental ideas about what it meant to be a man in the early twentieth century. Both subscribed to bourgeois ideals of manliness that rested upon production—or an active engagement in the marketplace and an adherence to the producer values of industry, thrift, regularity, and sobriety—and respectability. Male Garveyites and black Masons also positioned themselves as providers for, and protectors of, black women and children. Through rhetoric and prescriptive literature, men within these organizations produced and reproduced a black, middle-class male subjectivity. But as Bruce's funeral suggests, these men also performed their subjectivity. Indeed, the daily performances engaged in by male Garveyites and Prince Hall Freemasons reveal the ways in which gender identity functioned in the lives of these men as a dynamic *process* as opposed to a stable condition of existence. At their most basic, the rituals performed by black Masons and Garveyites bound individuals together in, respectively, an ancient fraternal order rooted in the tradition of artisanal labor and a modern political movement preoccupied with the exigencies of black nation building. In the sense that these performances produced "social cohesion" among individuals, a sense of shared community based on a "continuity with a suitable historic past," they conformed to what historian Eric Hobsbawm and others refer to as an "invention of tradition." This "invention of tradition," moreover, was coded in terms of gender. As historian Mary P. Ryan notes, "public rituals can serve to identify and evaluate differences within a community, including the distinctive places of male and female."[11]

The gender identity formation of black middle-class men, then, operated through a variety of modalities: rhetorical oratory, prescriptive literature, intraorganizational relationships, and public and private rituals of performance. When African American and African Caribbean men were inducted into Prince Hall Freemasonry and raised up the ranks through cryptic rituals, donned attire that was reflective of respectability and symbolic of craftsmanship, participated in elaborate foundation-laying ceremonies, and heard speeches about their role as patriarchs within the community, they articulated a gendered self full of multiple meanings. It was both public and private. It was specific to the world of Freemasonry yet emblematic of larger middle-class gender conventions. When African American and African Caribbean men joined a UNIA chapter, engaged in daily conversations and read weekly articles about the black man's role in Africa, were inducted into the organization's pseudo-aristocracy, or marched down Lenox Avenue in Harlem with the militaristic African Legion, they were involved in a similar gender identity formation—one that occurred within both the confines of Liberty Hall and the openness of public space. This gender identity was at once at the center of the UNIA's racial consciousness yet not very dissimilar to Anglo-American middle-class ideals of manliness. The imagining and performance of a black, middle-class male subjectivity for these men was a complex process—a process that signified their agency yet was ultimately overshadowed by the hegemonic power of dominant cultural constructions of manhood.

I

Does Masonry Make Us Better Men?

Much to their delight, individuals who joined a Prince Hall lodge could claim membership in a fraternal order that stretched across the diaspora and included prominent men in the fields of politics, business, science, and the arts. When Masons invoked the history of their organization, they took pride in pointing to the men of various backgrounds who hailed from North America, the Caribbean, and Africa. Indeed, Prince Hall Freemasonry and its many branches—Scottish Rite, Royal Arch, Knights Templar, Order of Nobles of the Mystic Shrine—assumed a diasporic character from the beginning.[1] Black seaman from British North America and the French West Indian colonies, after having been initiated in lodges in Liverpool and London, introduced the Royal Arch Masonic and Knights Templar degrees to black Masons in Philadelphia in the late eighteenth and early nineteenth centuries. These forms of Masonry spread into other states throughout the antebellum era.[2] Moreover, Prince Hall lodges existed in virtually every country in the Western Hemisphere in which blacks lived, and lodges within American cities with large black immigrant populations tended to be ethnically diverse.

Equally as important as the ethnic and national diversity of the Freemason order was its class composition. Official historians and regular members regularly pointed to a roster that included active and former Masons such as James Forten, a sail maker and patriarch of one of Philadelphia's elite black families; Richard H. Gleaves, the son of a Haitian man and English woman, who held several positions in the United States civil service and, from 1873 to 1877, was the lieutenant governor of South Carolina; James B. Dudley, a North Carolina journalist and businessman who became the principal of the state's black land grant school; and Robert H. Terrell, the Harvard-educated teacher, civil servant, judge, and overall Washington aristocrat.[3] In addition to the list of celebrated Masons that appeared in the histories of the order, Masons boasted of the general quality of the membership of lodges throughout the country. Shortly after the Civil War, for instance, John F. Cook, the grand master of Washington, D.C., pointed to the simultaneous growth of the order and the expansion of opportunities for blacks in the federal government. Increasing numbers of black civil servants were either already, or seeking to become, members of Prince Hall. "Again, nearly all of the officers of this Grand Lodge are in public places of some kind," Cook declared, "and they are not to be overlooked." High Marine Lodge No. 12, founded in 1890, was, according to William Grimshaw, "composed of the best citizens of Salt Lake City." G. W. Alexander of the Acme Temple of the Mystic Shrine, located in Montana, made similar assessments about the Masons of that state in 1902. Although there was a high turnover of membership—due to the transient nature of residency caused by the "depression of business"—Alexander was encouraged by the "devotion to the order." "The members realize that the badge of a Mason carries with it character and respectability," he noted. "Hence, they keep in touch with their Lodges wherever they go. None but the very best men are accepted in our Lodges."[4]

Although not the largest fraternal order among blacks, Prince Hall Freemasonry is a prestigious tradition that has attracted many black men, particularly during the first half of the twentieth century. According to one scholar, between 1904 and 1955, membership in the order went from 46,000 to over 300,000, with most of the gains occurring prior to 1930.[5] Despite the fact that it has been such an important institution, Prince Hall Freemasonry has attracted surprisingly little scholarship. Black Masonic orders are usually discussed as far as their relation to the civic and political lives of black communities is concerned.[6] The most extensive, and definitive, studies of Prince Hall Freemasonry as a social institution focus on the ways in which fraternalism worked to produce a middle-class subjectivity among its participants.[7] Yet Freemasonry was also instrumental in contributing to the gender identity formation of large numbers of middle-class black men. It is this fundamental aspect of Masonic orders with which this chapter concerns itself. By examining the fraternal order in general—and one lodge in particular—I explore how African American and African Caribbean men in the United States in the early twentieth century used the philosophy, symbolic trappings, and organizational framework of fraternalism to constitute themselves as middle-class male subjects.[8]

As members of a fraternal organization that conferred an ideological bourgeois status, Prince Hall Freemasons concretely and symbolically constructed their gender identities within the paradigms of providership, production, and respectability. In the case of their charity work and the networking capacity of the order, black men articulated a gendered subjectivity by assuming the role of protectors of women and children and through a productive engagement with the marketplace. Symbolically, Masonry provided black men with an imaginary claim to traditional, nineteenth-century notions of manhood. Through the collective and symbolic ownership of property—as realized in the building of temples—and through the ritual celebration of artisanship, Prince Hall Freemasons invented a collective masculine self during a period when owning land, becoming a proprietor, or earning a living through skilled labor was difficult for large numbers of black men. As African American and African Caribbean men moved into urban areas within the United States, the prospects of owning property or participating in the skilled labor sector of the economy—particularly with the exclusionary policies of most unions—diminished even more. In societies that equated these achievements with social adulthood, Masonry fulfilled a role in the lives of men who were increasingly excluded from realizing these goals as individuals.

Gender identity formation for these men involved a relational process that was organized around gender, class, status, and age. As devotees to an all-male organization that placed a premium on character and respectability, Prince Hall Freemasons arrogated for themselves leadership status based on class superiority and, as Mary Ann Clawson writes concerning white Masons, "the assertion of masculine privilege and authority."[9] In assuming a role as an important institution in black communities, the order drew links between production, providership, respectability, and racial progress and conflated them with manhood. Moreover, Masons framed these relationships as natural and transhistorical. Women became subordinated within this gendered framework of racial progress, as did men who did not conform to middle-class producer values and respectability. Because it was an organization that only accepted individuals who had reached the age of majority, Prince Hall Freemasonry also established age as a central category through which black men constituted themselves as gendered subjects. This was further accomplished through the creation of juvenile arms of the order, in which young men were inculcated with the values needed to achieve, and maintain, a "manly" status. Race also figured prominently in the gender identity formation of black Masons. As members of Prince Hall sought to lay claim to an authentic Masonic heritage, they consistently had to deal with the general white Masonic policy of nonrecognition. Although they recognized social and cultural differences of race within the profane world, African American and African Caribbean men continually asserted their equality with whites in the sacred world of Freemasonry. Since definitions of manliness were rooted in dominant Anglo-American ideas of gender and power, black men who joined Prince Hall Freemasonry reproduced a gender identity that was grounded in, and unable to transcend, the gender conventions of late-Victorian white America.

■ "Fate, that unknown quantity among mortals, decreed a call from some young gentlemen of Brooklyn, N.Y., whose progressive and uplifting minds made anything possible, and this call was to form a Club, with the full purpose of making it a representative Masonic Lodge." So recalled Louis Alexander Jeppe, the inaugural "worshipful master" of Carthaginian Lodge No. 47, of its auspicious beginnings.[10] Jeppe's use of the descriptors "gentlemen," "progressive," and "uplifting" typifies the investment that Masons had in defining the order as a respectable body of men. Jeppe's representations of Carthaginian's founders, along with the ways that Masons in general referred to the character of members of the Craft, illustrate the "slippery" definitions of class that characterized the black experience in the late nineteenth and early twentieth centuries. As I discussed in the introduction, entrance into the middle class was determined as much by subjective criteria as it was by objective economic indicators. Even as income and occupation became central avenues of access to the "new" middle class, personal qualities and public behavior remained critical components of upward mobility within black communities. Or, perhaps more accurately, standards of personal character and public behavior were the means by which a self-conscious black middle class policed its borders. Respectability, character, aspirations to the ownership of property, conscientious modes of consumption and leisure were qualities and behavioral patterns that one was expected to possess before assuming a place in the black bourgeoisie. Involvement in Masonry, which stressed property ownership, respectable public behavior, and producer values, was one of the many associational routes into the black middle class.[11] Since Freemasonry was one of the agents of class formation, then how did it socialize African American and African Caribbean men into bourgeois gender conventions? What are the relationships between class formation, acculturation, and gender identity formation? These are questions we can begin to answer by examining Carthaginian No. 47, in detail.

Carthaginian dates back to the spring of 1904, when several black Masons who had been initiated and raised to the level of Master Mason in Manhattan lodges decided to petition the Grand Lodge of New York for a charter in central Brooklyn. Starting out as merely a club of Masons and those interested in the order, the group received a dispensation, or an authorization to practice Freemasonry on a probationary basis, in October 1904 and an official charter a year later. The inaugural class of initiates numbered twenty-three, which, in addition to those seven who had already become Masons in other lodges in order to petition for a warrant in the first place, brought the total number in the lodge to thirty.[12]

Who joined, or attempted to join, Carthaginian Lodge No. 47? Over a sixteen-year period between 1904 and 1930, at least 186 individuals were proposed for membership. Based on an analysis of the lodge's minutes, it appears to have been an ethnically diverse group.[13] Of the eighty-two individuals for whom there is sufficient biographical information, fifty-six were listed as having been born in the United States. The birthplaces of twenty-four prospective initiates were located in the British West Indies. The remaining two listed their place of birth as Bombay, India, and St. Thomas, Virgin Islands. If this last individual is added to those from the British West Indies, twenty-five of the eighty-two proposed members — or roughly 30 percent — were from the English-speaking Caribbean. The majority of African Caribbeans who applied for membership in Carthaginian were Barbadian.[14]

Looking at the occupational information of the applicants, the malleable character of the "new" middle class becomes fairly apparent. The two occupational categories that formed the core of the black bourgeoisie in the early twentieth century, entrepreneurial and professional, were underrepresented among those who applied for membership. Nine of the prospective initiates can be classified as professionals; the same number of individuals can be considered entrepreneurs. Combined, they represent slightly less than 22 percent of the sample.[15] The greatest number of proposed members (twenty-four of eighty-two, or 29.2 percent) engaged in white-collar or managerial employment. Of those twenty-four, eight were messengers, five were postal employees (both clerks and letter carriers), four worked as clerks in both the public and private sectors, and two were inspectors.[16] A building superintendent, a traveling salesman, a shop foreman, an operator, and the general secretary of the Colored Branch of the Young Men's Christian Association in Brooklyn comprised the rest of the white-collar/managerial group. The next largest contingent was employed in the service sector of the economy. Eleven applicants listed their occupations as chauffeurs, making it the most common form of employment among the eighty-two prospective members. Combined with four porters, one butler, one waiter, and one steward, the number of individuals engaged in service made up 21.9 percent of the total applicants. Semiskilled and unskilled laborers constituted almost 16 percent of those who were proposed, and the seven skilled laborers, artisans, and artists made up the smallest percentage at 8.5.[17] At least one student — although in his twenties — attempted to join the lodge as well.

Only one significant pattern emerges when an occupational breakdown of the applicants according to ethnicity is made. A plurality of the African Caribbean applicants was engaged in personal service employment (ten of twenty-five, or 40 percent), while a plurality of prospective African American members consisted of white-collar employees (twenty of fifty-six, or 35.7 percent). Conversely, those African Americans employed as service workers only made up 14 percent of the total African American candidates (eight of fifty-six), and there were only four African Caribbeans who worked in white-collar jobs (or 16 percent of the total). The disparity might be partly explained by considering the possibility that African Americans were more likely than black immigrants to secure employment in municipal, state, and federal agencies. No African Caribbeans among the sample, for instance, were postal employees or city clerks, which explains, in part, their lower numbers among the white-collar/managerial group.[18]

Although Carthaginian accepted applications from people of various occupational backgrounds, the majority of those who, certainly from their perspective, were fortunate enough to be considered for membership tended to fall within the economic parameters of the middle class. Grouping together those individuals who were entrepreneurs, professionals, or white-collar workers, just over half (51.2 percent) of those applying for admission into Carthaginian could be considered middle class by the objective measurements of occupation and income. Significantly, very few people who were clearly unskilled workers—day laborers, janitors, and elevator operators—were proposed for admission to the lodge.

Given this predisposition toward accepting applications from entrepreneurs, professionals, and white-collar employees, however, there are no discernible patterns in terms of correlation between occupation and admission. The minute books do not provide comprehensive data on whether or not these applicants were admitted. Out of the sample of eighty-two, there are only sixty-three confirmations on the admission or rejection of the candidates. Of the entrepreneur-professional-white-collar group of candidates, thirty-two of the forty-two were admitted while three were rejected. Four of the seven skilled laborers or artisans were admitted while one was rejected. Among the semi- and unskilled labor group, nine survived the strenuous admission process while one did not. Ten of the eighteen individuals employed in service were deemed worthy and one was indicated as having been rejected. Similarly, there was no correlation between nationality and admission. Of the six rejected over the fourteen-year period for which there are records, four were African American and two were African Caribbean.

The lack of any apparent pattern is most likely due to the subjective nature of the selection process. To begin with, an individual had to be proposed by a master mason of the lodge. The candidate had to file an application, along with a fee and a doctor's certificate testifying that he was in good physical condition. The application packet was then turned over to an investigative committee, which inquired into the individual's personal background. The committee made a recommendation to the lodge's master masons, who then voted, usually according to the committee's report. It took only one negative vote, however, or a blackball, to sink a candidacy.[19] Individuals who were rejected may have been so for a number of reasons. Their relatives, neighbors, or employers may have given less than flattering assessments to the investigating committee. In the case of two, both of whom were fifty, their age may have worked against them in the sense that many lodges were reluctant to offer membership to someone who they felt might benefit from the mutual aid features disproportionately to his contributions. Personal histories between the applicant and one or more lodge members may have also led to the applicant's rejection.

What is striking about the prospective membership of Carthaginian, based solely on the biographical information of candidates, is its expansiveness in terms of occupation and ethnicity. Indeed, African Caribbeans appear to have applied in numbers that were disproportionate to their total population in Brooklyn. Men of Caribbean origin represented almost a third of the prospective initiates during a period when, according to the best estimate, the number of foreign-born blacks in Brooklyn constituted from 11 to 19 percent of the borough's total black population.[20] This should not be entirely surprising given that black immigrants often formed, or reconstituted, mutual aid societies and benevolent associations upon their arrival. There were also many African Caribbeans who were already Masons before migrating to the United States. According to an article in the New York World, some black Masons who had been initiated in British West Indian lodges, upon arriving in the states, attempted to visit white Masonic lodges but were turned away because of most white lodges' policies of nonrecognition. "West Indians aver there are times when the white Masons endeavor to hurdle a delicate situation," the article stated, "by sending them with credentials to lodges under the Prince Hall jurisdiction."[21]

While some African Caribbean Masons attempted to affiliate with their white "brethren," others either joined existing Prince Hall lodges or developed new lodges along the lines of national identity, language, and color. El Sol de Cuba Lodge No. 38, for instance, was created in 1881 in order to provide a fraternal environment for, and Masonic instruction to, Spanish-speaking blacks. It emerged out of a desire on the part of several African Cuban Masons in New York City to establish a lodge, "the work of which could be conducted in the Spanish language." The individuals were already members of two Prince Hall lodges in New York, so the Grand Lodge of New York granted the warrant for El Sol de Cuba. The membership of this lodge was largely Cuban although it also attracted Puerto Ricans who were fleeing to New York "because of persecution by the Spanish authorities." Following the Spanish-American-Cuban-Filipino War, the numbers of Masons emigrating from Cuba and Puerto Rico decreased, which led to the ascendancy of an English-speaking membership. In 1914, the lodge changed its name to Prince Hall Lodge No. 38 and received a new warrant. Hijos del Caribe Lodge, an interracial lodge of Puerto Rican and Cuban Masons who had emigrated to New York City, is another example of the way in which language and color contributed to the creation, or reconstitution, of new Masonic bodies in new environments—bodies which utterly flummoxed white Masonic authorities. When the white Grand Lodge suggested that the lodge disband and have its members affiliate with lodges of their own color, Hijos del Caribe brothers rejected this proposal and applied for a dispensation from the Prince Hall Grand Lodge of New York.[22]

Prince Hall Freemasonry was more inclusive, in terms of ethnicity, than white American Masonry. This inclusiveness went beyond language and national identity and involved accepting members of different racial groups. One of the charter members of Carthaginian, for example, was Fred M. Holzworth, a twenty-nine-year-old butcher who was white.[23] Other lodges accommodated members of other racial groups, individuals who may have sought the business and professional networks and middle-class respectability that the lodge afforded. Prince Hall lodges in California and Washington State, for instance, apparently counted Filipinos among their membership.[24] This practice of racial and ethnic inclusiveness was far different from the nativism that characterized white Masonry. As Lynn Dumenil points out, although official Masonic doctrine did not countenance, and indeed discouraged the circulation of, ideas of racial superiority, anti-immigrant, anti-Catholic, and anti-Semitic sentiments existed in white Masonic lodges at the local level, particularly during the 1920s. Even as Freemasonry was practiced in urban lodges that were solely, or primarily, made up of immigrants, most white Masons continued to equate the Craft with native-born, Protestant "Americanism."[25]

Although Prince Hall lodges did not draw racial boundaries as rigidly as white Masonic lodges, they were clearly geared toward providing African American and African Caribbean men a fraternal environment. One scholar has suggested that, upon arriving in the states, some black immigrants joined "native-black-run fraternal orders" that "tended to de-emphasize one's ethnic background while promoting racial solidarity, self-help, and self-reliance."[26] In the case of Carthaginian (as well as many other lodges in areas with high concentrations of foreign-born blacks), such a large presence of African Caribbean men suggests that ethnic ties and racial solidarity were not necessarily in tension. Indeed, the idea that Prince Hall lodges were "native-black-run" is only true to the extent that certain urban areas and rural regions had a preponderance of African Americans. Prince Hall Freemasonry was an international movement with lodges in North America, the Caribbean, and parts of Africa. These lodges were institutions within communities made up of African Americans, African Canadians, African Caribbeans, and Africans. When a black Barbadian migrated to Brooklyn and joined Carthaginian, he probably thought of himself as an individual who was joining an institution that had a history and a presence throughout the diaspora rather than as an African Caribbean who was joining an African American institution.

If Prince Hall Freemasonry contained many ethnicities, however, it was less accommodating to multiple, or divergent, articulations of class. From an economically objective standpoint, it would be inaccurate to say that Prince Hall Freemasons were exclusively middle class. Harry A. Williamson, a member of Carthaginian, judged that an overwhelming majority (98 percent) of Freemasons in New York were "merely wage earners" who "have to be assisted by their wives going to work."[27] Given the occupational composite of those who applied for membership to Carthaginian, Williamson's assessment seems exaggerated. Class took on both an objective and subjective, or material and representational, quality in the case of Prince Hall Freemasons. On the one hand, men who joined a Prince Hall lodge either already enjoyed a certain bourgeois status or were attempting to achieve that status. In this case, Freemasonry provided these men with a certain subjective claim to being middle class through their adherence to a worldview that was shaped by respectability and producer values. On the other hand, real material factors determined whether or not these men could even hope to enter the world of the Craft. One of these factors was gainful employment. Another was the cost, often prohibitive, of joining a lodge. To even apply for membership, one had to pay a five-dollar fee. Once accepted, an initiate had to pay a twenty-five-dollar fee. Masons had to pay regular dues and fees upon receiving degrees, contribute to the lodge's charity fund, and purchase the necessary clothing that comprised the Masonic uniform.[28] Becoming a Freemason was no inexpensive undertaking. Ultimately, black men of both the old elite and the "new" middle class joined the order in the first three decades of the twentieth century. More importantly, they all shared a certain bourgeois consciousness—and adhered to its attendant gender conventions—that appears to have transcended ethnic and national difference.

■ In 1893, Captain R. R. Mims, the grand master of Alabama, took to a stage in Chicago to deliver an address before the National Congress of Free and Accepted Masons. Presumably inspired by the World's Columbian Exposition, which was occurring in the city at the same time, the purpose of the National Congress, Mims pointed out, was "to deliberate, not to make laws, but to suggest plans whereby we may better understand each other and become better acquainted." Like the "millennial perfection" discourse of much of the world's fair, Mims's short speech extolled American civilization's strides in the sciences, politics, and arts. He suggested that a real measure of civilization would entail an examination of how far African Americans had come since emancipation three decades earlier when he told his fellow Masons that "we can see what progress has been made by us as a people, and by our noble and grand institution, with all the obstacles, drawbacks and disadvantages that we are placed under and we continue to go onward and upward." [29]

Although Mims located Prince Hall Freemasonry within the narrative of progress from slavery to freedom, his speech's emphasis on racial uplift conformed more to the elite uplift ideology identified by historian Kevin K. Gaines. According to Gaines, uplift ideology among African Americans around the turn of the twentieth century assumed both popular and elite forms. Popular discourses of uplift, present before emancipation, evoked the historical memory of slavery and espoused general racial advancement. Elite forms of uplift ideology, however, were wielded most consistently by an emergent black bourgeoisie that equated racial progress with class stratification and the realization of Victorian gender conventions within the black family. [30] Mims participated, as did other Masons, in this latter discourse. Indeed, he reminded his brethren that they were a fraternity in its most exclusive sense. While he suggested that Freemasonry was reflective of the progress of African Americans, he attempted to disabuse the audience of the notion that they were responsible for the collective race. "I am of the opinion," he declared:

> that it cannot be too strongly impressed upon the minds of all that Masonry is not a reformatory society. No one ought to be admitted who is unqualified, or who possesses negative qualifications only, but his standing and good qualities ought to be such as would add to the moral character of our institution, instead of being a lifeless and therefore heavy load to carry. No candidate ought to receive a clear ballot in the hope that his admittance to the order would be the means of leading him into the ways

of morality and virtue when his previous life and character have given evidence that his walk in life has not been in accordance with the tenets and profession of the cardinal virtues.[31]

Mims's articulation of an elitist class consciousness was perhaps more extreme than that of other Masons. As historian William Muraskin points out, Masonry provided many middle-class blacks the means with which to distinguish themselves from the working class while simultaneously propping themselves up as models of progress. Through their emphasis on producer values and respectability, Masonic orders not only ensured that their members would be upright, conscientious men; they also hoped that the transmission of bourgeois values would improve the lives of working-class blacks, thereby elevating the entire community. As the grand master of New York exclaimed in 1920, "Let other organizations parade the necessity of a big time, how much liquor can be drunk by the members thereof, and how much noise they can make, it is our place to be so temperate in all that we do that we may be the criterion by which they regulate their being."[32] Still, when Mims defined the order's ideal membership, he invoked specific notions of class and status, as subjective as those notions may have been. Given that gender was the other primary category through which Masons maintained an exclusive fellowship, it is important to examine the ways in which class and gender intersected in the identity formation of Prince Hall Freemasons. In other words, gender identity among black Masons was constructed through the relational nature of class and, conversely, their class consciousness was expressed through their claims to achieving, and maintaining, manhood.[33]

The fraternal boundaries of Masonry were demarcated by relationships of class and gender. Women were prevented from joining the order—although lodges had women's auxiliaries—as were men who had questionable reputations. In this sense, the gender identity of Freemasons was not only defined by biological difference. Class-bound discourses of production and respectability were indispensable to Masonic constructions of manliness. This is clear from the guidelines for membership that Masons followed. "The necessary qualifications for a candidate for admission into a Lodge," the *Masonic Handbook* for the state of Arkansas detailed, "are that he be free-born and no bondsman, of good report, hale and sound, so as to be capable of earning a livelihood for himself and family, and to perform the work of a member of the Lodge, and he must have some visible means of gaining an honest livelihood."[34] An engagement in an "honest livelihood" could not be stressed enough. In 1890, the Grand Lodge of Illinois, for instance, passed a resolution preventing subordinate lodges from accepting "any man who keeps a saloon, grogshop or any place for selling intoxicating liquors, or a liquor dealer."[35]

For Masons, production went beyond merely playing an active role in the marketplace as producers rather than as consumers. It also included internalizing the self-ascribed values of the bourgeoisie: thrift, regularity, and sobriety. Of course, the producer republicanism evident in Masonic rhetoric and organizational framework was not identical to that of the antebellum ideology of small, independent, white farmers, proprietors, and skilled artisans. Like those whites who flocked to Masonry in the late nineteenth and early twentieth centuries, the concept of production (and its association with the nineteenth-century craftsman) appealed to black Masons even as very few had access to entrepreneurial and skilled labor positions in the American economy. Still, the producer values did represent a commitment to middle-class notions of work ethic.[36]

As the foundation of Masonic constructions of manhood, production operated on both a symbolic and concrete level. The physical exclusion of women, for instance, reified the masculinist character of the organization. The single-sex nature of the fraternity was symbolically justified by invoking the Masonic tradition's ancient history. "As Masonry, at its origin," wrote William Grimshaw, "and through many centuries, was occupied solely with physical labors, in which females do not participate, the instructions of ancient Masonry are only suited to the male sex."[37] Similarly, a producerist manhood was symbolically present in the lives of these men through the language and rituals associated with Freemasonry. Metaphors of craftsmanship structured the meaning of the rituals and organizational work in which members engaged. When the worshipful master ended the refreshment period by calling lodge members back to "labor," or when members' initiation into the first three degrees was signaled by the presentation of the "working tools," Masons reaffirmed an imaginary link to a masculinist tradition of artisanship. More concretely, however, certain organizational aspects of Prince Hall Freemasonry, particularly the fraternity as both mutual aid society and professional and entrepreneurial network, provided more tangible markers of manhood than the symbolism represented by the nineteenth-century republican producer.

Mutual aid, charitable work, and providing a network for professional development constituted the bulk of the institutional features of Masonry. While these elements of fraternalism provided material benefits for the members, their families, and, to a lesser extent, the larger community in which a particular lodge was located, they also contributed to the gender identity formation of these men. Through financial assistance and charity, Masons sought to fulfill their gender roles as providers for the families of sick or deceased brethren and, in some cases, the less fortunate of the nonfraternal community. In the case of the business ties that were built and maintained, Masons affirmed, particularly in the early twentieth century, the links between manhood and the marketplace. In this sense, Masonry connected notions of manliness to the gendered mythology of the "self-made man," albeit a racialized one.[38]

Although Masons considered charity to be "one of the foundamentals [sic] of our ancient [and] honorable institution," the majority of financial aid and charitable work engaged in by the fraternity was carried out close to home.[39] Monetary assistance was dispensed primarily to lodge members and their families. This took the form of insurance policies, relief funds, payment for burial expenses, and economic assistance to widows and orphans. These payments were disbursed from the lodge treasury or specific charity funds. A typical example of the mutual aid engaged in by Masons was the burial of their fellow brethren. In addition, Masons were responsible for seeing the family through the transitional period of adjusting to the loss of a wage-earning member. Members of Carthaginian, for example, not only paid one hundred dollars for the burial of a fellow Mason, they were also concerned about the "destitute condition of his widow [and] family." As a result, "a motion was made and carried that $12 be drawn from the charity fund to make up $25 for Mrs. Benson's contribution." The mother of G. L. Smith was more fortunate, receiving seventy-five dollars after she appealed to Carthaginian for assistance after her son's death. Masons also distributed money to "distressed brethren" and their families. Brothers who were ill or otherwise incapable of making a living received assistance. Herbert Fitz Lewis, who was "in a very bad condition," received ten dollars "as charity." The lodge also voted to give $9.80 to the wife of one of its members who was "at present incarcerated."[40]

In order to administer the disbursement of economic assistance, lodges established standing committees to hear appeals for aid, to investigate the veracity of those appeals, and to allocate the monies accordingly. The Committee on Widows and Orphans and the Charity Bureau were responsible for this process in the Carthaginian Lodge. The Committee on Widows and Orphans consisted of ten lodge members who were responsible for keeping track of the families of deceased Masons. They were also responsible for collecting and distributing food to the families on the holidays. Upon determining that a widow or orphan was in need of assistance, the committee made a referral to the Charity Bureau, which would conduct its own investigation into the "worthiness" of the claim. The bureau's report was then passed on to the membership for consideration. If an application or a referral received an affirmative vote, the claimants could expect to receive "a sum of money not in excess to Ten Dollars on any one case." Mutual aid was not only the manifestation of a "brother's keeper" mentality; Masons also hoped that assisting the families of its members would enhance the public's perception of the order.[41]

While the kind of work carried out by the Committee on Orphans and Widows and the Charity Bureau was stopgap and local in nature, Masons mounted even larger assistance programs on the state level. Grand Lodges of certain states administered insurance plans for members of their subordinate lodges. These relief or benefit associations collected more money and were able to dispense larger sums to widows and orphans. Yearly assessments ranged anywhere from three to six dollars per member, and beneficiary claims could amount to as much as three hundred dollars.[42] Resistance to intricate systems of insurance, with their compulsory dues, existed in many quarters. Many Masons felt that being forced to pay premiums introduced a crass business ethic into a fraternal tradition that was based on selfless, brotherly acts of fellowship and mutual reciprocity. Moreover, because other fraternal orders such as the Elks and Odd Fellows made insurance an integral part of their raison d'être, Masons felt that elevating this particular type of assistance would link them to what they considered to be less than august organizations. According to one scholar, the reluctance with which Masons approached instituting an insurance system was partly the desire to "not want to appear to be competing for adherents, nor to be forced to lower their requirements in order to maintain the system."[43] How pervasive was this sentiment is not really known, particularly given the fact that there tended to be crossover membership among all of these fraternal orders. Still, many Masons were determined that the venerable institution of Masonry should not become just another business in segregated communities.

Masons provided other forms of financial assistance that were of a more expansive nature than merely paying for burial services and furnishing temporary economic relief for its members and their families. These other forms were both political and philanthropic. Politicized financial assistance included—among Carthaginians in any event—annual contributions to the local chapters of the Urban League and the National Association for the Advancement of Colored People, as well as progressive social service agencies. Masons also monetarily aided each other in their struggles against racial oppression. When a man belonging to a lodge in Staten Island had a long-running confrontation with the local Ku Klux Klan, which was evidently attempting to run him out of his neighborhood, he applied to the Grand Lodge for "fanancial [sic] aid from the fraternity in his legal battle against this wrong." The practice of soliciting this kind of assistance was somewhat rare—at least it does not show up frequently in the lodge minutes—but the Staten Island Mason felt that he was involved in "a case against the colored race [rather] than an individual one." The members of Carthaginian agreed and voted to contribute fifty dollars to the campaign.[44] Other forms of philanthropy and financial assistance characterized the activity of Masons, including the establishment of orphanages and homes for the elderly.[45] Although the various forms of aid provided tangible benefits to its recipients, the kind of service engaged in by Masons contributed to not only a group identity as members of a fraternal order; it also contributed to a collective gender identity—as providers and protectors—among these middle-class men.

While the mutual aid aspects of Masonry allowed these men to perceive themselves as fulfilling the role of community patriarchs (even at a time when black women engaging in employment outside of the home and organizational work in the public sphere was the norm), the professional and entrepreneurial features of the order evinced a somewhat more complicated relationship between manhood and the market. Prince Hall Freemasonry acted as a professional and business network for its members and their families and, therefore, represented an avenue of social mobility for those who, according to Masons, already demonstrated the requisite industry and character. Individuals used the organization as a reference for employment as when, for instance, Brother John M. Royall "request[ed] the lodge's endorsement for his application to position as Recorder of Deeds." Carthaginian honored Royall's request and wrote to President Warren G. Harding on his behalf. Members of the lodge who were entrepreneurial-minded envisioned their brothers as a significant consumer base. During one meeting, Brother Joseph Banks told Carthaginian "of his new enterprise and ask[ed] for the brothers['] patronage when in his vicinity." The lodge could also act as an incubator for business. Widow Rosa Jackson, for instance, asked the lodge to supply the overhead capital for her boardinghouse. Jackson "was found in dire circumstances for a start in her enterprise of subletting rooms. It was moved, sec[onded and] ordered that Carthaginian Lodge donate $35 to her."[46] As this last case suggests, Masons were attentive to the needs and desires of female entrepreneurs. In significant ways, however, the idea that entrepreneurship was crucial to racial progress was yoked to the persistent belief that Masons were the best shepherds of commercial development. The fact that Masonry was an all-male organization is not an insignificant one in this sense. Despite the fact that black women formed an important sector of the black business community—primarily as beauty parlor owners, restaurateurs, boardinghouse owners, and seamstresses—Masons continued to view entrepreneurship, and the ability to support entrepreneurial efforts, as one of the integral factors in the achievement of individual and collective male identity.[47]

This equation of manhood and entrepreneurship was particularly prevalent in the Masonic efforts to build temples and the discourses surrounding those efforts. Carried out on both the state and local level, the building of temples represented a combination of pure materialism and emphatic idealism. It embodied notions of commerce, property ownership, race progress, and manhood. "Temple Building fever," according to Muraskin, "has stemmed from the belief (not totally incorrect) that in capitalistic America neither a man nor a race is anything unless he owns property; and the bigger, the more prominent, expensive and gaudy the better."[48] Masons did invest the construction of temples with tremendous social significance, much of which was shaped by race and gender.

In the mid-1920s, New York's Grand Lodge launched a campaign to erect a two-story temple in Harlem. Plans for the temple included a basement with a dance floor, an auditorium on the main floor, and a second story with space for lodge rooms, an armory, and a library. The Grand Lodge expected to finance the construction by selling bonds to members of subordinate lodges. Discussion of the temple and appeals for financial contributions were often situated within a gendered framework of racial progress. To be sure, some Masons envisioned the temple as a collaborative effort between black men and women that would ultimately benefit the whole community. Joseph Sullivan, the grand master, declared: "The erection of this Temple will not only be a monument to Negro manhood and womanhood, but it will likewise be a safe investment that in time to come will make glad the hearts of those who at this time show that fidelity and highness of thought to do and dare." Others, however, saw the construction of a temple as a particularly "manly" feat. Reverend Charles D. Martin, of Prince Hall Lodge No. 38, situated the effort within a larger history of Prince Hall Masonic activity. "How grand to be a Mason charged with the fulfil[l]ment of the longings of our Masonic fathers—the erection of a Masonic Temple," he wrote. "Erect it and at once do honor to the past—show that we are not forgetful and ungrateful but intend to beautify and augment what has been bequeathed to us—prove that we are men who realize that the gains of the past can only be kept by the progressive advance of the present."[49] Black Masons also invested temples with a particularly racialized significance. On a trip to Carthaginian (possibly as part of a larger fund-raising tour), for instance, the "most worshipful grand master" of New York "explained to the bre[thre]n that non-completion of our temple would mean disgrace to our race [and] order, while completion would mean recognizion [sic]." He further couched his plea for money in terms that placed a great deal of importance on white perceptions of blacks. Building the temple, he told them, would "contradict the white man's saying that masonry is too big for the colored man."[50]

These somewhat idealistic notions that erecting a building would undermine racial prejudice seem fanciful and, indeed, much of it was rhetorical suasion. The temple represented concrete business opportunities and that was the crux of the matter. As Martin pointed out, the temple "means capital: it means revenue: it means safe investment."[51] Masons in Washington, D.C., realized the goal of erecting a temple that would have great utility for the larger community. At a cost of a half-million dollars, the six-floor temple contained a restaurant, retail space, and offices, in addition to an auditorium, lodge rooms, a library, an "exquisitely furnished lounge for ladies," and "a well appointed club room for men." Tenants of the temple included a dentist, a doctor, a brokerage firm, and a news agency.[52] In most cases, temples were the ultimate realization of Masonry as integral to the development, and maintenance, of a black business community. The construction of temples held emotional resonance for Prince Hall Freemasons: in the larger historical tradition, the building of temples was conducted solely by men. Temples were also psychologically important because they affirmed for Masons, in the contemporary moment, that they were participating in the marketplace as producers, not merely consumers.

Even as Masons integrated entrepreneurship into the process of class and gender identity formation, they did not blindly reduce the achievement of manliness to an active engagement in the marketplace. Indeed, there was pervasive suspicion among Masons of those seeking entrance whom, they felt, viewed the fraternal order solely as a professional and business network.[53] Mims expressed this concern in his Chicago speech. The order, he argued, should only accept businessmen, or men who were otherwise affluent, if they possessed a strong character. Education was important to the development of character, Mims suggested. "None should be accepted for their money alone, but for their internal qualifications; their moral and educational qualities. Education is power; it moves the great levers of nations; it makes men better citizens, better mechanics and better Masons; it prepares one for the race of life." Masons also looked askance at men who appeared to join the order simply to provide a financial safety net for their family. Forty years after Mims's speech, Georgia's grand master, John Wesley Dobbs, suggested that, in much the same way that Masons excluded uneducated men they should not initiate older men. "It is the object of Masonry to build character in men, and everybody knows that the character of men from 50 to 60 years old is fixed and sealed already," he stated. "Men of that age are not expected to live very long. They were bad risks to insure at any rate and could be expected to contribute but very little to the Masonic cause."[54] Mims's and Dobbs's rationale for the exclusion of certain individuals is different only in degree. Mims called for exclusion based on education and, in many ways, exposed his class bias. On the other hand, Dobbs's use of age as a major determinant revealed his concern about the ability of the order's insurance system to remain solvent. Underlying both of their positions was the idea that Masonry was a *process* that involved the *progress* toward perfection. Uneducated men were incapable of benefiting from this process, as were those who were already set in their ways, according to Mims and Dobbs. In this sense, a strong character—but one that was malleable as it related to receiving the "mysteries" of the Craft—was indispensable to the identity formation of these men. Ability to succeed in business was not enough.

In forming a collective class and gender identity, then, Masons understood manhood to have some relation to the capitalist ethos, but not to be entirely governed by it. Manliness, in other words, was forged within the marketplace but at the same time existed above it. It was configured along the lines of morality and ethics as much as it was constructed within the competitive world of commercial capitalism. According to Masons, this was the contribution of their fraternal tradition to human civilization. Commitment to virtue, character, and morality, cornerstones of the nineteenth-century ideology of producer republicanism, emerged most clearly in the ways in which Freemasons dealt with behavior they deemed "un-Masonic."

When black Masons invoked their positions as protectors of, and providers for, women and children, and spearheads of commercial development within the black community, they were engaging in the formation of a gender identity that was rooted in notions of production. Just as often—and, indeed, as a complement to the producer values that shaped middle-class constructions of manliness—black Masons employed the concept of respectability as an important marker of manhood. In the process of inventing itself, the black middle class exhibited an ambivalent relationship to respectability, defined here as a commitment to the producer values of thrift, temperance, cleanliness, and sexual continence, and the public display of those values. As Evelyn Brooks Higginbotham astutely argues, on the one hand, respectability represented for blacks a necessary tool to combat popular cultural images of their race as lazy, dirty, unintelligent, morally lax, and sexually rapacious. On the other hand, utilizing the concept of respectability to contest dominant stereotypes amounted to a capitulation to the hegemonic discourses of the dominant culture. Moreover, by using respectability to establish themselves as bourgeois, middle-class blacks constructed their own status against that of the black "unrespectable" poor.[55] Masonic adherence to the discourse of respectability was particularly manifest in the concept of "un-Masonic conduct." Through this ideal, the order regulated its membership and maintained an exclusive brotherhood along the parameters of class upon which Masonry was based. Using un-Masonic conduct as a correlative of improper behavior also allowed Masons to define what indeed was proper and "manly" behavior.

Masonic standards of propriety were grounded in, first and foremost, the Judeo-Christian tradition. No matter how often they dressed up their religious faith in secular language, Masons could not hide—nor did they want to—the pseudoreligious character of their order. A prerequisite for membership was the belief in God, who they often referred to as the Grand Architect of the Universe. One of the Craft's ancient landmarks, or the twenty-five immutable laws that governed the Masonic tradition, required that every lodge have a Book of the Law, or Bible, in plain sight. The very objective of Freemasonry was "the search for truth" that was embodied in an analytical understanding of God. Masons drew direct links between the tenets of the Craft, godliness, and respectability.[56] As such, unrespectable behavior was tantamount to a transgression against the ethical and moral tenets of the primarily Judeo-Christian belief system to which Masons conformed.

Un-Masonic conduct fell into primarily two areas: conduct that was considered dishonorable because it was harmful to the internal workings of the order itself, and conduct that was considered dishonorable because it was harmful to the order's image. Brothers were occasionally disciplined for engaging in activity such as the misuse of the lodge's money. In March 1912, the Grand Lodge of New York suspended a former grand secretary, and a member of St. John's Lodge No. 29, in New York City, for "misappropriating funds of the Grand Lodge." During that same year, the Grand Lodge heard an appeal from a member of Hiram Lodge No. 4. In this case, the individual had been found guilty of skimming money off of an application fee. The Commission of Appeals refused to overturn his conviction, stating "that instead of defrauding a brother as originally stated, he has defrauded the Lodge as the money placed in his hands was the property of th[e] Lodge. We characterize it a scandal and a disgrace to the Fraternity as well as a fraud, and respectfully beg to affirm the action of the Lodge." The year, 1912, was a busy one for expulsions. The Grand Lodge also expelled a former worshipful master of Widow Son's Lodge No. 21, in Brooklyn, for "assault with a weapon" upon another brother.[57] Such deeds impaired the functioning of the order and were the very antithesis of brotherhood. In misusing lodge funds, individual Masons placed their financial well being above that of the group, while a physical attack was seen as an inappropriate way of handling conflict. Both actions undermined trust within the lodge and, consequently, had to be dealt with forcefully.

While un-Masonic conduct on this level was dealt with in a swift and resolute manner, other inappropriate behavior was taken no less seriously. This latter kind of un-Masonic conduct often included "crimes" against the public, "crimes" against the family, and infractions of bourgeois standards of morality and respectability. These were not considered discrete categories of misconduct and, indeed, they are more my divisions than that of the Masons. Anything that threatened to undermine the image of Masonry could be considered un-Masonic conduct. The senior warden of Carthaginian in 1927 expressed his concern, for instance, for "the absolute necessity of being cautious about the selection of candidates in future as it is a reflection on the fraternity to have members before the court for assault [and] offenses of that kind." [58]

Actions that were considered crimes by the state could be grounds for dismissal. Conviction for manslaughter, for instance, resulted in the expulsion of one brother from Antioch Lodge No. 66, in New York City. [59] Less deadly, but no less weighty, were the crimes of gambling and facilitating traffic in liquor. The arrest and indictment of a grand officer who engaged in this activity prompted the Grand Lodge of New York to issue an official warning to its subordinate lodges. "The time has arrived," it began, "when the Executive Officers of this MOST WORSHIPFUL GRAND LODGE OF THE STATE OF NEW YORK should be men without reproach, pure men with nobler deeds, higher thoughts and loftier conceptions than to keep gambling houses and dance halls for the entertainment of lewd and licentious characters, which are liable at any time to be raided by the police[.]" In addition to the possibility that police raids of grand officers' homes might lead to the loss of the fraternity's archives, the issuers of the declaration felt that any arrest would "bring the Order into disrepute." To prevent this, they reminded lodge members, "in your selection of Grand Officers, let purity of character, and rectitude of conduct be the paramount beacon as to qualification for office." [60]

Masonic officials were not completely intractable when considering punishment for those who ran afoul of the law. There is evidence that Masons occasionally considered the context in which the crime was committed. In 1925, for instance, John C. Ellis, the most worshipful grand master of Illinois recommended that Lafayette Parker be reinstated in the order. Parker had been convicted of "supposed rioting" in the East St. Louis race riot in 1917.

After spending several years in prison, he petitioned the Grand Lodge for re-instatement and won Ellis's endorsement. "Because of conditions existing in this country I do not believe that we should expel a brother from the Frater-nity because of charges resulting from Race Riots," Ellis wrote.[61] Ellis's use of the term, "supposed rioting," suggests that he was either not convinced of Parker's guilt given the racial realities of the American judicial system or that he understood that most blacks in East St. Louis were victims, rather than perpetrators, of the rioting. Regardless of his reasoning, Ellis's action reveals that the definition of un-Masonic conduct was malleable and relative to the larger circumstances that surrounded the particular activity.

Inappropriate behavior in marital relationships illustrates the malleability of the concept of un-Masonic conduct. By most standards, Freemasons con-sidered adultery to be a violation of the moral tenets of the Craft, society, and civilization. New York grand master Harry Spencer regarded adultery to be a "flagrant violation . . . of the laws, traditions [and] obligations of free-masonry." Spencer made this declaration in response to a growing contro-versy in a subordinate lodge in the western part of the state. One of the "past masters" of Light of the West Lodge No. 42 had been accused of being an adulterer but the lodge had failed to bring charges against him. After two years of hearing such rumors, Spencer conducted his own investigation and "found that the rumors which had come to me had been common talk for years and that every brother in the lodge, from the master down, knew of such charges." Spencer felt that the lodge had been slow to act because of a "false fear of a public scandal . . . or from favoritism" and had allowed the situation to become "a cancerous sore which would have, ultimately, had for a result the disintegration of the lodge and a stumbling block to the wholesome progress of the jurisdiction." He understood, on some level, the hesitancy with which the lodge approached the accused, given that he was a well-liked and trust-worthy member of both the lodge itself and the Grand Lodge. Nevertheless, Spencer directed the lodge to conduct an "official trial." After a failed attempt by some members of the lodge to dismiss the charges, the past master was tried, found guilty, and sentenced to a ninety-nine-year suspension. Spencer concluded his assessment of the matter by elevating the image and state of the order over the reputation of one person. "My obligations to the fraternity," he declared, "were far more sacred than my personal freindship [sic] to the indi-vidual." As this example suggests, there were no uniform applications of the code of conduct. Even though Masons prided themselves on being models of decorum within the community, close friendships, personal reputations, and probably a certain willingness to tolerate sexual indiscretions clouded what otherwise should have been an obvious course in this case.[62]

Whether or not adultery was winked at more frequently than other inappropriate conduct is not clear. This Mason's punishment of a ninety-nine-year suspension indicates that the order took adultery very seriously even if it required the intervention of a state official for the subordinate lodge to act. There is other evidence that Masons looked upon marital infractions with some gravity. In December 1927, Carthaginian appointed a committee to investigate when the wife of one of its members "charg[ed] her husband with misconduct."[63] The lodge minutes were not specific about the nature of the misconduct; it could have ranged from obnoxious drunkenness to adultery to domestic violence. The conclusion of the investigation is also not available from the evidence. It is significant that the woman felt confident that the lodge would hear her grievance and, indeed, the lodge at least initially did.

The concept of un-Masonic conduct was extremely important not only in preserving the fraternity's image, but in mapping out respectable and unrespectable behavior for the black middle class. By defining certain activity as un-Masonic—either as it correlated to criminal behavior as defined by the state or inappropriate behavior as defined by social convention—Masons indicated what was, by inference, Masonic, and respectable, conduct. Un-Masonic conduct, and particularly the ways that Prince Hall Freemasons dealt with it, operated on other levels as well. It embodied the investment that black Masons held in their capacity for self-governance. Additionally, the responses of men who were charged with un-Masonic conduct reflected the social and emotional import of belonging to such a venerable organization. One particular case illustrates how charges of un-Masonic conduct functioned on these two levels.

In New York City in 1909, Hiram Lodge No. 4 undertook an action that would embroil it and the Grand Lodge of New York in legal wrangling for the next four years. The lodge charged Thomas S. F. Miller, M.D. and Charles Taylor with insubordination, found them guilty, and sentenced each to a twenty-five-year suspension. Utilizing the order's judicial system, Miller appealed his suspension to the Grand Lodge. The lodge's Commission on Appeals conducted its own investigation of the matter and, in June 1910, "made its report fully sustaining the action of Hiram Lodge in its conviction of Dr. Miller and the sentence imposed." Miller persisted, however, and filed a civil suit against the Lodge two years later in New York State Supreme Court, seeking "reinstatement and one hundred thousand dollars damages to his character and business." The lodge's chief commissioner of appeals, Major R. Poole, and Benjamin Bulmer, a lawyer who was not, interestingly, a Mason, handled the lodge's defense. The case did not make it to trial. A judge denied hearing the case on the grounds that Miller had "been tried as required by the law of the order" and had "not yet exhausted his remedies under that law." At the next Grand Lodge session in 1913, Grand Master Spencer made the lodge's victory the highlight of his speech. "Too much importance can not be attached to this victory nor too much credit given to those who are responsible for its outcome," he declared. "To have lost this case would not only have humiliated us in the eyes of our enemies, not only have saddled upon this grand body a debt impossible to meet, not only subjected us to all sorts of petty annoyances but made us the object of untold attacks and legal actions."[64] Spencer may well have been correct in his assessment. If Miller had succeeded in his suit, a precedent of using outside institutions to challenge Masonic law would have been established and probably would have led to more challenges by disgruntled ex-Masons.

To have their autonomy effectively stripped away by the state would have weakened the organization's tradition of self-government. Indeed, Prince Hall Masonic law, as the embodiment of black men's ability to govern themselves and to ensure the well-ordered functioning of the organization, was critical to the actual performance of the fraternity and the psychological benefits of membership. William Muraskin argues that the order's judicial system was a laboratory in which Prince Hall Freemasons learned how to participate in the political and civic processes of mainstream American society. "The Order," he writes, "is based upon an extensive body of laws and regulations; and in the interpretation of these laws, members of the fraternity learn to play the role of judge, juryman, advocate, prosecutor, and witness."[65] But the judicial process was less an opportunity for black Masons to "play" parts in the replication of a system that discriminated against them (this conjures up an image of minstrel or vaudeville performers in a satirical courtroom skit) than it was an opportunity for black men to express their collective autonomy. Even as they were denied the full complement of rights that accompanied American citizenship, black Masons collectively exercised sovereignty by participating in the legislative and judicial processes of the order. They were claiming a status of citizenship in an organization that transcended the boundaries and institutions of the nation-state. When black Masons observed the ancient landmarks that, for instance, guaranteed representational democracy or the right to appeal a lodge's decision, they claimed an inheritance to a centuries-old tradition more than they expressed a compensatory desire to belong to the American political and judicial system or sought to "practice" the civic roles that would accompany membership in the body politic.[66]

Thomas Miller's case against the Grand Lodge of New York was important evidence that Prince Hall Freemasonry, as an autonomous organization, was capable of exercising sovereign authority based on the democratic principles of suffrage and due process of law.[67] The case also reflected the vested interests that black Masons held in their membership in the order. Although the way in which Miller responded to having been suspended from the lodge may have been more extreme than most, the investment that he placed in being a Mason was not unusual. Miller sued the New York Grand Lodge for damages resulting from his suspension. This suggests that being suspended or expelled had the potential to undermine one's reputation within the larger community. Moreover, as a black doctor, Miller's practice probably profited from, if not relicd on, his image as a respectable and trustworthy individual. Whether or not he actually lost patients is somewhat immaterial to the fact that he perceived that he *would* lose patients if his reputation were not vindicated. As far as Miller was concerned, his character was being questioned by his lodge and that could reverberate throughout his entire community, to his detriment. For Miller, as well as most other Masons, the reputation that Freemasonry conferred on them was as important a testament to the prestige of the Craft as the fact that the fraternity operated according to democratic legislative and judicial procedures.

When Masons leveled charges of "un-Masonic" conduct at each other or rhetorically invoked their role as producers, they constructed their gender identity on a discursive level that then became concrete through the various relationships that they had with one another and with the larger community. But if manliness for Masons became manifest through their engagement in the marketplace, their adherence to producer values and respectability, and their self-positioning as providers and patriarchs, it was also brought into being through the order's ritualistic trappings. In this sense, manliness was a performative project.

Members of Prince Hall enacted their gender identity through performance as much as they did through rhetoric. For Masons, a collective middle-class black male subjectivity was the product of intimate, esoteric rites as well as calculated, public self-representation. From the very beginning of one's initiation into the Craft, his status as a middle-class man was affirmed and his body became the representation of that status. But this status was a contingent one. It relied, on the one hand, on juxtaposition against those black men who existed outside of the sanctum of Freemasonry. But it was also contingent, in that black Masons' gender identities were shaped by the hierarchical nature of the fraternity itself.

Notions of hierarchy suffused Freemasonry and were most palpable in the relationship between the first three Blue Lodge degrees: Entered Apprentice,

Fellow Craftsman, and Master Mason. These three degrees carried significant symbolic value. It was a particularly gendered symbolism, with each degree signifying a stage of the male life cycle. While "the first degree is a representation of youth, the time to learn, and the second of manhood or time to work, the third is symbolic of old age, with its trials, its sufferings, and its final termination in death."[68] Status based on symbolic age—as well as meritocracy—structured the meanings that Prince Hall Freemasons attached to these degrees and the rituals through which they enacted them. Even though Masons proclaimed adherence to an egalitarian philosophy, they also placed a premium on the recognition of station. The emphasis upon station could be seen in not only the initiation rituals members had to go through but the very positioning of Masons of various degrees within the lodge. When the lodge was opened in the third degree—signified by the presence of only master masons—all lodge members positioned themselves equidistantly from an "imaginary point" in the center of the room. This reflected the equality of those present as well as the geometrical principles upon which Freemasonry was based. No such egalitarian arrangement obtained when the lodge was opened in either the first or second degree. Because, according to Grimshaw, "the Lodge of an Entered Apprentice may contain all the three classes, and that of a Fellow Craft may include some Master Masons . . . the doctrine of perfect equality is not carried out in either."[69] In the presence of one another, then, Masons of different degrees or stations were constantly reminded of their place in the hierarchy of the Craft.

Perhaps the most revered reminder of the hierarchy among men within the Masonic universe was the rite of initiation. Advancement through the ranks of Freemasonry was marked by rituals that continually highlighted the differences between men while simultaneously creating a bond based upon the order's ultimate egalitarian philosophy. Initiation rituals were by no means uniformly practiced among Freemasons and, given the racial, ethnic, regional, and national diversity within the world of Masonry, these rituals undoubtedly contained disparate meanings for those who underwent them. The underlying core themes of Masonry's foundation in the Judeo-Christian belief system, the rational organization of the natural world, the brotherhood of man, and the dignity and indispensability of artisanal labor, provided an overarching framework for what were otherwise lodge-specific ceremonies. Moreover, the secrecy of the rituals—both in their symbolic nature as well as in their private performance—reified the difference between the sacred world of Freemasonry and the profane world of non-Masons.[70]

The formation of these bonds began with the initiation of an individual into the degree of Entered Apprentice. A candidate for initiation, barely clothed to symbolize his nakedness and sometimes blindfolded, was led around the lodge room in order to be lectured to or interrogated by other members. Circumambulation variously symbolized the journey of the sun from east to west and the passage "of the soul through the underworld after death." Lectures included lessons in the moral foundation of Masonry, the importance of charity and brotherhood, and the indispensability of secrecy. Moreover, initiates were most likely interviewed by the lodge's worshipful master. "Not only should they [Worshipful Masters] be satisfied with the moral standing of the candidate, but the intelligence as well," wrote one Mason.[71] Masons being raised to the second and third degree also traveled around the room listening to lectures on the principles of the Craft and being questioned by their fellow Masons. The initiation rite of the fellow craftsman incorporated more of the naturalistic symbolism of Freemasonry, although the allusions to geometry and architecture were twinned with the supernatural references to the "Great Artificer of the Universe" and the "Divine Artist." The most prominent aspect of the initiation rite of the third degree included the symbolic death of the fellow craftsman and his figurative reincarnation as a master mason. This ritual was modeled after the legend of Hiram Abiff, the master builder of King Solomon's temple. In the legend, Hiram was assassinated by jealous apprentices who were upset by his refusal to disclose the secrets of the Craft. In the ritual, Masons playing the role of Hiram's apprentices, or "ruffians," harassingly questioned the fellow craftsman. After his persistent refusal to share the secrets, the ruffians symbolically murdered and buried him. The fellow craftsman would later be "discovered" by the worshipful master who, exalting his steadfastness, would then raise him from the grave. The fellow craftsman would figuratively be reborn as a master mason.[72]

The commitment to hierarchical relationships persisted beyond mere initiation rites. In addition to having to pass trials set up by one's "superiors," which might include hazing, the paraphernalia one received upon initiation indicated one's position in a particular strata of the fraternity. Every Mason who was made and raised within the Blue Lodge, for instance, received a lambskin or leather apron that established a linkage between the modern "speculative" Masonry and the artisanal labor tradition that characterized ancient and early modern Masonry. Entered apprentice's aprons, however, were "entirely without ornament." As Masons advanced to the second and third degrees they were allowed to adorn their aprons with various insignia, including colored trimming, lining, and rosettes. Status was further displayed on the apron through the embroidery of specific emblems indicating one's office.[73] Moreover, as Masons were raised to different degrees, they received different passwords that were commensurate with their level within the fraternity.

These passwords were not only intended to reify the distinction between the sacred world of Freemasonry and the profane world. They were also intended to reinforce the hierarchy within the order. "In all of the ancient mysteries as is the case in our own Craft," one Mason wrote, "a word was demanded not only for the purpose of distinguishing an initiate from a non-initiate but to distinguish the members of the various grades or degrees."[74] Finally, Masons were expected to display their reverence and respect for lodge officials and members of higher degrees through the "sign of fidelity." This physical gesture was "to be given by an inferior to his superior in rank and may be dropped after a minute or two of duration."[75]

Despite the various mechanisms that were utilized to produce and reproduce status difference within Prince Hall Freemasonry, the fraternity ultimately provided a homosocial space in which a collective identity of bourgeois manliness was constructed and nurtured.[76] The lodge room itself was a crucial site for the formation of these gender identities. Local lodges generally held semimonthly meetings in a duly consecrated room or suite and it was the material culture within the room and the ceremonious style of the meetings that held its greatest meaning. In short, the lodge room was sacred space.[77] Everything within the lodge was governed by a symbolic precision. Each lodge had an altar upon which sat the Book of the Law. During meetings, the Book of the Law was opened to passages that were particularly symbolic of the degree in which the lodge was opened. The lodge's warrant and constitution as well as a square and compass, symbols of Masonry, were also clearly visible. The position of officials and the rank and file was extremely important in the lodge meetings. Officers, including visiting grand officers and past masters, occupied physical positions within the lodge that were reflective of their status and were required to stay there throughout the duration of the meeting. Perhaps the most important presence in the lodge, outside of the most worshipful master, was the "tiler." Positioned at the outer door of the lodge room, the tiler guarded the sacred proceedings from outsiders. In essence, he maintained the inviolable nature of the Masonic sanctum.[78]

Although it was an inalienable right of Masons to visit lodges other than their own, they could not secure entry into a lodge until they sufficiently demonstrated their authentic Masonic status. When a visitor "alarmed" the door of a lodge, the tiler notified the brothers in attendance, who then elected an ad hoc committee to "investigate" the stranger. Most likely, the investigative committee interrogated the visitor on Masonic doctrine, his personal history in the Craft, and his current lodge affiliation. If the committee was satisfied with the answers, the stranger was allowed inside for the meeting.[79] The gatekeeping function of the tiler and the investigative committee was crucial

Lodge Room of Carthaginian Lodge No. 47, ca. 1912. (Courtesy of Harry A. Williamson Photograph Collection, Photographs and Prints Division, Schomburg Center for Research in Black Culture, New York Public Library, Astor, Lenox and Tilden Foundations)

to safeguarding the sanctity of Masonic proceedings. As the *Masonic Handbook* of Arkansas's Grand Lodge stated: "You are cautiously to examine him [a visiting brother], in such a method as prudence shall direct you, that you may not be imposed upon by an ignorant false Pretender, whom you are to reject with Contempt and Derision, and beware of giving him any Hints of Knowledge."[80]

Once it was determined that everyone present was a duly initiated Mason, the lodge was opened, generally with a pounding of the gavel and a prayer. After a reading of the minutes and assorted correspondence from the Grand Lodge and other subordinate lodges, members heard the petitions of prospective inductees and conducted initiation rituals within the three degrees. The rest of the meeting consisted of "labor" in the various degrees, which included lectures on the fundamental principles of Masonry, general announcements concerning the lodge in particular or the Craft in general, and a public accounting of the lodge's finances. There was ample time for socializing as well, with periods of "refreshment" between the more informational sessions.[81]

Strict behavioral guidelines governed Freemasons' conduct within the lodge and without. All Masons were expected to pay due deference to the most worshipful master, further indicating the hierarchical nature of the fraternity. Lodge members were to comport themselves respectably, which included refraining from acting "ludicrously or jestingly while the Lodge is engaged in what is serious and solemn," avoiding the use of profanity, and treating each other in a courteous fashion. Even debates were to be conducted with a tone of civility for, as Grimshaw noted, "the object of debates in a Masonic Lodge is to elicit truth and not to secure victory."[82] Perhaps the strictest regulation of behavior was the prohibition of alcohol within the lodge. The proscription against the consumption of spirits characterized American Freemasonry in general and was a tradition dating back to the 1840s, when Freemasons sought to combat anti-Masonic charges that the Craft was a facilitator of "drinking and debauchery."[83] The outlawing of liquor was such a cornerstone of Freemasonry's attempt to convey a respectable image that it was occasionally written into the Grand Lodge's constitution and subordinate lodge's bylaws.

The behavior expected of Masons was in keeping with the prescriptive norms of bourgeois manliness, prescriptive norms that placed more emphasis on production than consumption as the organizing principle of identity. These ideals were clearly articulated by the Grand Lodge of Arkansas. Regarding what was appropriate behavior at the conclusion of a meeting, the Grand Lodge's handbook stated: "You may enjoy yourselves with innocent Mirth, treating one another according to Ability, but avoiding all Excess, or forcing any Brother to eat or drink beyond his Inclination, or hindering him from going when his Occasions call him. . . . You must also consult your health, by not continuing together too late, or too long from home, after Lodge Hours, are past and by avoiding of Gluttony or Drunkenness, that your families be not neglected or injured, nor you disabled from working."[84] Moderation, not dissipation, was the key to living a Masonic lifestyle. Combined with the symbolic linkage between speculative Masonry and the artisanal laborer, the behavioral guidelines worked to produce a collective identity among Prince Hall Freemasons that was governed by notions of production and respectability.

While the bourgeois ideals that structured Masonic behavior were actuated within the homosocial space of the lodge, Freemasons also "performed" their bourgeois identities in public space. Indeed, the "stylization of the body" for public consumption was central to the Masons' project of constituting themselves as middle-class male subjects. To be sure, there was a specific choreography of performance that was intended to maintain the cryptic essence of the Craft. In a section entitled "Behavior in Presence of Strangers Not Masons," the *Masonic Handbook* of the Grand Lodge of Arkansas warned: "You shall be cautious in your Words and Carriage, that the most penetrating Stranger shall not be able to discover or find out what is not proper to be intimated; and sometimes you shall divert a discourse, and manage it prudently for the Honor of the Worshipful Fraternity." [85] Nevertheless, the public rituals of performance engaged in by Freemasons were integral to their collective gender identity formation for they marked the members of the fraternity as different from the rest of the community.

Dress, or paraphernalia, was perhaps the most important signifier of difference between Masons and non-Masons. Through the donning of particular types of clothing and accessories, black Masons literally fashioned an identity that was organized around the principles of production and respectability.[86] What Prince Hall Freemasons wore to signal their particular status depended on the occasion. For everyday activities, individuals would only wear a square and compass pin or ring. This was intended more to allow Masons to identify one another than it was to alert the non-Masonic public of their presence, although it could certainly have that effect. The easy availability of square and compass accessories through Masonic distributors, however, facilitated the practice of non-Masons passing themselves off as members of Prince Hall. The pervasiveness of this practice led some Masons to advocate the purchasing of special "Prince Hall" emblems through Grand Lodges so that they might "be able to distinguish a genuine brother from an imposter." [87]

For more ceremonious occasions and public representations, the standard sartorial ensemble consisted of formal or semiformal dark suits, white leather or lambskin aprons, medallions, white gloves, and, for the most worshipful master, a black top hat. Masons were particularly proud of their dignified attire. The members of Carthaginian, for example, consistently claimed that they were pioneers in " 'requir[ing]' that whenever the Degree of Master Mason was conferred, each member and visitor must appear clothed in full evening dress. Also, it [the Lodge] was the first to make the use of white gloves compulsory, going to the extent of providing them for the use of visitors." In November 1904, before Carthaginian had even received its official charter, the lodge "raised" its first candidates to the degree of Master Mason in a service in which the collective cost of the ceremonial robes exceeded nine hundred dollars. According to Carthaginian's official history, a local Masonic newsletter observed that the ceremony was the first time that Brooklyn

Members of Carthaginian Lodge No. 47, 1905. Harry A. Williamson is seated second from the left. (Courtesy of Harry A. Williamson Photograph Collection, Photographs and Prints Division, Schomburg Center for Research in Black Culture, New York Public Library, Astor, Lenox and Tilden Foundations)

Prince Hall Freemasons had been raised to that degree in "full ceremonial costume," replete with "robes . . . of velveteen appropriately trimmed to indicate royalty." A month earlier, the lodge celebrated its institution under dispensation in an equally elaborate affair. The ceremony was covered by the *Colored American* magazine, which reported that "the new Lodge is composed entirely of young men, its membership comprising a number of the representative and progressive citizens of both Brooklyn and Manhattan Boroughs. From all indications the organization bids fair to become an active and important factor in the fraternity in this district. New societies usually commence operations with their paraphernalia incomplete in some respect, but Carthaginian enters the field with a very handsome outfit, complete in every particular." [88] This representation of the lodge's investiture conflated the respectable character of Carthaginian and the sartorial style of its ceremony. Indeed, the article suggested that the ceremonial clothing of the lodge's members was a reflection of their respectability and a harbinger of future success.

The *Colored American* article cursorily described a private lodge ritual for a public, non-Masonic audience. In many cases, Masons engaged in public rituals that allowed the larger community to directly observe the ritualistic and respectable trappings of the sacred world of the Craft. These public ceremonies included the dedication of Masonic lodges, the laying of temple cornerstones, parades, official dinners, drill team competitions, and funerals. There was a certain utility to these public rituals beyond the collective gender identity formation that they facilitated. Dignified performances of Masonic ritual, some argued, had the potential of attracting potential candidates. "I might suggest that a public dedication," Harry Williamson wrote to a fellow Mason, "might be the means of drawing interested men into wishing to join your Lodge."[89]

Some public rituals, such as parades, were intended to exhibit—not necessarily reveal—the nature of Freemasonry to the largest possible number of people. The opening parade of the centennial celebration of Massachusetts's Grand Lodge in 1908 through downtown Boston, for instance, was not only witnessed by much of Boston's black community; it was also attended by the governor, mayor, and "prominent officers of the State and city." The ceremony to celebrate the laying of the cornerstone of the Masonic temple in Harlem in the spring of 1926 was initiated by a parade whose circuitous route covered from 155th to 126th Streets and from Bradhurst to Lenox Avenues.[90] Parades were conspicuous displays of the Masonic presence within the black community. They provided black Masons with high visibility, yet they also must have produced a distance between the fraternity and the larger, non-Masonic community. It was probably this distance, rooted in the exclusivity of the order, that piqued the interest of many men. One can only speculate how the orderly marching and stately dress of the members of the local Prince Hall lodge might have attracted men who were not Masons. To be sure, the parades probably alienated many men given the undoubtedly pretentious nature of some of the displays. However, the parades contained a particularly magnetic quality.

Perhaps the most conspicuous public "performers" within the Masonic universe were the Knights Templar. Officially the Chivalric Rite in the Commandery of Knights Templar, it was a more martial fraternity than either Blue Lodge or Royal Arch Masonry. Whereas the prevailing symbolism of the latter groups linked speculative Masonry to a tradition of artisanal labor, Knights Templar symbolism contained militaristic iconography and ritual. Individual chapters were called encampments or commanderies. Commandery leadership was made up of a commander, senior and junior wardens, captain gen-

James Robert Spurgeon, junior warden and past master by affiliation of Carthaginian Lodge No. 47, 1907. (Courtesy of Harry A. Williamson Photograph Collection, Photographs and Prints Division, Schomburg Center for Research in Black Culture, New York Public Library, Astor, Lenox and Tilden Foundations)

eral, and generalissimo.[91] The Knights Templar uniform was more evocative of a European field marshal than it was a nineteenth-century craftsman, replete with sash, epaulets, insignia, and sword. Knights Templar held Grand Military Balls and drill competitions. The *New York Age* covered one drill performance that was held in conjunction with a picnic in Harlem in 1906. The drill corps of the Ivanhoe Commandery, made up of "gentlemen of standing and integrity" and "some of the most prominent Masons" of New York City, provided an exhibition during the intermission of a performance by the New Amsterdam Orchestra. The drill, according to the newspaper, was "extremely pretty," and the "intricate manoeuvres were gone through quickly, accurately and in perfect time."[92] Occasionally, Knights Templar turned Masonic events into statelike affairs. When the president-elect of Liberia, C. D. B. King, his wife, and other government officials were honored in New York in 1919, Knights Templar stationed themselves outside of the hall, giving the event an air of regality. "A very striking feature of this occasion," one history noted, "was that the guests walked under 'an arch of steel' formed by the swords of Knights Templar of the Grand Commandery from the entrance of the building to the door of the banquet room."[93]

The martial exhibitions of the Knights Templar, in addition to the more civil performances by members of Blue Lodge Masonry, enabled Prince Hall Freemasons to construct a collective gender identity in the presence of, and in opposition to, African Americans and African Caribbean immigrants who were not Masons. Of course, these performances were not unique to the black community. People within the African diaspora have a long history of participating in and witnessing a variety of public, community-building rituals, including Negro Election Day in northern American colonies, Jonkunnu in Jamaica and the Carolinas, and black militia parades in the postbellum urban American South.[94] What is significant about the public performances of Prince Hall Freemasons was the way in which they were framed within a context of respectability. From the specific dress to the orderly movement to the black press's coupling of the performative acts with the respectable character of the participants, Prince Hall Freemasons actively engaged in a gender identity formation that was both reflective of their class position and distinctive from the mass of black folk. Combined with the private rituals that marked the internal dynamics of the fraternity, black Masons constantly formed their identities as middle-class black men in opposition to a public that they defined as decidedly not bourgeois.

Private and public rituals of performance, then, augmented Masonic discourses of production and respectability in the project of maintaining an exclusive sense of brotherhood. Through these discourses and performances, Freemasons were engaging in a class-bound gender identity formation that relied on, and reinforced, qualities of manhood that were intrinsic to the self. That is, members of Prince Hall articulated an individual and collective manhood that was determined by how they decided to live their lives, the everyday choices they made, the ways in which they interacted with one another and their communities. Manhood, in this sense, was an aspect of their identity that was formed in the self and exhibited outward. But gender identity is also configured in relationships. In constructing a gendered sense of self, men and women utilize negative referents against which to position themselves as gendered subjects. This can be seen, in part, through the public rituals of performance themselves. Another way that black Masons articulated a gendered subjectivity through the deployment of an oppositional manhood can be seen in the discourse surrounding "spurious" Masonry.

Using charges of spurious Masonry (other terms included "bogus" and "clandestine"), black Masons authenticated themselves as descendants of ancient—and, subsequently, modern European—Freemasonry. Prince Hall Freemasons leveled charges of spurious Masonry against black fraternal orders that claimed to be Masons but that did not trace their history back to African Lodge No. 459. By accusing spurious black Masons of practicing a false version of the Craft, Prince Hall Freemasons reinforced their own status as legitimate heirs to the tradition of Freemasonry. They often framed the language of these charges in terms of class. That is, the repudiation of these other fraternal orders involved casting their adherents as either uneducated men who were too lazy to practice "real" Masonry or charlatans who wanted to benefit from the advantages of Freemasonry without living up to its ideals, or both. Race also operated in the discourse of spurious Masonry. In claiming descent from European Freemasonry, Prince Hall Freemasons maintained that they were as authentic as white American Masons. The general white Masonic policy of nonrecognition of Prince Hall, however, forced them to constantly defend their status as legitimate Freemasons. One of the ways that they did this was to pursue blacks practicing spurious Masonry even more vigorously.

Although white Masonic attitudes were by no means monolithic, the governing bodies of white American Masonry tended to either not recognize Prince Hall Freemasonry as a regularly constituted Masonic tradition or, if they did recognize it, to follow a "separate but equal" policy. New York's white Grand Lodge, for instance, unofficially recognized Prince Hall's New York Grand Lodge as being a regularly constituted lodge but did not extend official recognition, which would have, among other things, allowed visitation rights between the two bodies. The white Masons of Washington State officially recognized Prince Hall Freemasonry in an 1898 resolution; but, since the state's Grand Lodge was "'not unmindful of the fact that the white and colored races in the United States have in many ways shown a preference to remain in purely social matters, separate and apart,'" it did not endorse visitation.[95]

For the most part, the different positions that white Masons held regarding the legitimacy of Prince Hall were shaped by regional differences. Progressive white Masons found their liberal ideas about race overshadowed by the hard-line stance of southern lodges. "I believe," wrote G. A. Kenderdine, a white Mason from Iowa, to a prominent black Mason, in 1930, "many northern G[rand]. Lodges would recognize Prince Hall Lodges but for the fact that they know it would create ill will and sever connections with many southern Grand Lodges." Indeed, three decades earlier, Washington State's Grand Lodge was castigated by southern white lodges when it issued its "separate but equal" proclamation.[96]

White Masons rarely rejected the legitimacy of Prince Hall Freemasonry purely on the basis of race. Most often, they relied on Masonic law and the "historical record" to challenge black Masons' right to claim descent from modern European Freemasonry. Many white Masonic authorities argued that the chartering of African Lodge No. 459 by the Grand Lodge of England was unconstitutional since it contravened the Provincial Grand Lodge of Massachusetts's authority to decide whether or not to grant Prince Hall and his fellow brethren a warrant. Others claimed that African Lodge had failed to obtain a new charter after English Freemasonry was reorganized in the early nineteenth century. Still others argued that, around the time of Prince Hall's death in 1808, the African Lodge became inactive and its reconstitution did not conform to Masonic law and procedure.[97] The belief that Prince Hall Freemasonry was "irregular" was subscribed to such an extent that several white Grand Lodges sued black Grand Lodges and Imperial Councils of the Nobles of the Mystic Shrine over their use of similar names.[98]

Black Masons responded to the white policy of nonrecognition in a number of ways. Prince Hall Freemasons in the nineteenth century, for instance, held out the hope that the Masonic doctrine of the equality of man would eventually lead to the integration of white and black lodges. White racial attitudes, particularly around the turn of the century, however, made recognition a more realistic goal than complete integration.[99] In seeking recognition, black Masons presented a variety of different arguments. One invoked the universality of Freemasonry. The Craft, this argument went, offered truth and wisdom and knew no boundaries of race, religion, or status.[100] Another argument was culturally nationalist in nature and, as such, was in contradistinction to the universality argument. In this response to the nonrecognition policy of white Masons, blacks pointed to what they perceived to be the African roots of Freemasonry. The racist white denial of the legitimacy of blacks practicing a form of fraternalism that was grounded in African culture and history allowed black Masons to point out the absurdity of the white Masonic position. This specific argument was made by John E. Bruce, a prominent New York journalist and Prince Hall Freemason, in response to the suits that were brought against black Shriners by whites. Bruce suggested that the fraternalism on which the Order of the Nobles of the Mystic Shrine was based originated in the Middle East and Africa. This fraternalism was evidence of the presence of "civilized" black and brown men "centuries before white men had a civilization" of their own. "The white Southern Shriners," Bruce wrote in 1922, "have deliberately appropriated to their own uses the signs, grips, passwords, symbols and insignia of an ancient Negro fraternal order, founded in Arabia and Egypt, and now have the audacity to question the right of Negroes to take and enjoy what is their own."[101] Bruce and others who made this argument were exhibiting a racial chauvinism that would mark the Garveyites' thought and rhetoric about white people. The most prevalent black Masonic response to nonrecognition was a capitulation to the "separate but equal" policies of white lodges. For those who took this position, recognition of their legitimacy was enough. As such, they sought to assuage white Masons' fears that they were seeking visitation rights or the integration of Prince Hall and white lodges. Suggesting that these fears were as unfounded as the "social equality" argument expressed by white southerners in debates over the integration of schools and public space, the author of an unidentified editorial wrote that "our [Prince Hall] ambition for social equality in Freemasonry in America is just as much a fallacy, as is our reputed ambition for social equality otherwise."[102] In general, over the course of the early twentieth century, black Masons went from maintaining a faith in the universalist tenets of Masonry—and, for that matter, American liberalism—to adopting a realist position in the face of white intransigence concerning interracial commingling in not only the public sphere, but also the Masonic universe.[103]

Throughout this period, however, black Masons persevered in their attempts to achieve recognition. On the one hand, they did this by bypassing white American Masonic governing bodies and stressing the international recognition that Prince Hall received. "It is not our purpose to call in question the right to recognition of the colored Masons in the United States by their white fellow Masons," one Mason wrote. "That should give him no concern, especially when he knows he is recognized in all other countries, and the only barrier in some of the States of the Union is the color of his skin, not Masonry."[104] On the other, they laid claim to a "regular" status by rooting out what they perceived to be spurious Masons within their own racial ranks. This included Grand Lodges alerting each other to the presence of spurious Masons within their jurisdictions and assisting one another in legal suits brought against bogus bodies, usually by sharing materials from their respective archives.[105] What is striking about the discourse surrounding spurious Masonry was the articulation of class and status. In emphasizing the need to eliminate bogus lodges, Prince Hall Freemasons engaged in the construction of a collective identity that was oppositional to the lower-class, "unrespectable" black men who they felt predominated in clandestine Masonry.

Spurious Masonry, according to various Prince Hall authorities, emerged from many different sources. In some instances, bogus lodges were the offspring of factionalism within Grand Lodges. The "rebellion" against the First Independent African Grand Lodge of Pennsylvania by two local lodges in the early nineteenth century, and their subsequent formation of the Hiram Grand Lodge of Pennsylvania in 1837 under an apparently fabricated warrant from the white Grand Lodge of Ohio, was one origin of spurious Masonry.[106] Another source was the National Compact, which existed between 1847 and 1877. After the experiment at establishing a national governing body of Prince Hall began to unravel in the late 1860s, existing National Compact Grand Lodges merged into the original Grand Lodges. Those local lodges that had been chartered under the National Compact—and the Masons who were made in them—and which continued to practice Freemasonry outside of the jurisdiction of Prince Hall became designated as bogus.[107] Individual Masons were also responsible for spreading spurious Masonry. In these cases, it was usually brothers who had been disciplined by their lodge and who subsequently started their own lodges without the sanction of any Prince Hall governing body. "There are a number of individuals calling themselves Masons," the black Puerto Rican bibliophile and Mason Arthur Schomburg wrote, "who have been expelled, suspended for cause and have without right or authority in dark places and in devious and questionable ways, enticed and suggested and requested innocent men to join their clubs."[108]

In his denunciation of spurious Masonry, Schomburg deployed a specific language that questioned the character of the men who practiced it and, by extension, their class status. For Schomburg, spurious Masons approached the Craft in a "mercenary" fashion, looking for "personal gain," and, as such, the lodges that they constituted were "masquerading in the community as lodges with no cloud whatever to protect it of right to exist or respectability or honesty of purpose."[109] Others engaged in a similar discourse when characterizing the men they described as spurious. The Grand Lodge of Illinois's Committee of Investigation of Spurious Organization criticized one self-ascribed Grand Master for conferring "kitchen degrees"—so called because they were awarded in private homes as opposed to duly constituted Prince Hall lodges. This spurious Mason and others, according to an open letter from the committee, were guilty of "deceiving and fleecing money out of the pockets of all who have believed their unmitigated lies." The committee not only characterized this individual as a swindler; it went on to label his entire lodge as one that was lacking members of any social rank:

> It was observed in the parade of your body to attend divine service St. John Day, among the eighty-one (81) men in line there was not one man from among the Old Citizens of Chicago, not a single professional man, business man, active church man, indeed not any man connected with any of the various activities in this the greatest progressive metropolis of America. We ask the question why? The answer is simply this, Negroes of the said class could not be fooled or induced to follow any man representing any thing without first knowing that such a man possessed a reasonable degree of intelligence, self-respect, honesty, respect for the citizens and the race to which he belong[s].

The committee's criteria for judging social rank and respectability included, among other things, economic status and civic participation. Additionally, they defined social rank in terms of how long an individual had been in the city. In this sense, they distinguished between "respectable" Old Settlers and "outlandish" southern migrants.[110] Others expressed the similar idea that spurious Masonry maintained a healthy existence because less educated African Americans from the South were moving into urban areas and joining bogus organizations. A Mason from St. Paul, Minnesota, reflected that the "influx of newcomers" was responsible for Compact Masons "gaining a solid foothold" in his state.[111] In other words, Prince Hall Freemasons cast spurious Masons as men of ill-repute who roamed the countryside and urban streets looking for uneducated and uninformed men to join their fraternities. Rhetorically, it was similar to the way in which Old Settlers and middle-class reformers admonished migrants to refrain from fraternizing with street-savvy bootleggers, gamblers, pimps, and other disreputable individuals.

The way in which Prince Hall Freemasons framed spurious Masonry, then, drew on class and regional distinctions. In depicting spurious Masons as either unscrupulous confidence men or naive and provincial hayseeds, members of Prince Hall engaged in an oppositional gender identity formation that allowed them to arrogate for themselves the status of "respectable" citizens. This relational process of identity formation and self-representation can clearly be seen in Harry Williamson's undated lecture on the history and state of the Craft:

Those unrecognized pseudo Masonic bodies which we generally characterize as "bogus," are to be found in operation throughout the country.
Judging from some of the literature being circulated by them, the unsus-
pecting individual would imagine that those organizations were representative institutions in their supposed localities. While it is true they do have
some very estimable citizens in their membership, careful observation will
convince one that the most prominent men of our race in the past or at the
present time, local or national, if Masons at all, have been found enrolled
under the banner of the descendants of Prince Hall. The chief stock in trade
of the bogus elements appears to be high sounding titles and multifarious
degrees.[112]

The belief that Prince Hall Freemasons were the exemplars of respectability
and manliness is perhaps best captured in the metaphor of the lighthouse,
used by W. Devoe Joiner, a member of the Research Committee of New York's
Lewis Hayden Lodge No. 69. "As a lighthouse sends its beams into the tempestuous darkness of the dreadful night to warn the striving, struggling mari-
ner of the lurking rocks latent in the black storm-swept sea," he wrote, "so
Masons of African genealogy display to the world their beacon which is the
name of Prince Hall to warn all to shun the bogus mason and bid all follow the
path of ancient and lawfully constituted authority, Prince Hall Masonry."[113]
Joiner did not merely differentiate between the "respectable" men who in-
habited Prince Hall and the "uncultivated" individuals who practiced clandestine Masonry. In invoking the idea of the lighthouse or beacon, he suggested
that the Craft was the one true avenue through which other black men could
become refined and manly. Indeed, to the question, "Does Masonry make
us better men?" members of Prince Hall emphatically answered in the affirmative. In order to sustain this claim, however, Joiner and others needed to
construct a negative referent against which they could position themselves.
Prince Hall Freemasons, already respectable members of their community,
could only participate in an uplift ideology if there were people who needed
to be raised up, improved. By defining bogus Masons to be precisely that,
members of Prince Hall constituted themselves as paragons of respectability
and manliness.

Freemasonry, William Grimshaw wrote in 1903, "teaches reverence for the
Master Builder of the Universe and for His revealed will; loyalty to the government under whose protection it exists." He continued that Freemasonry
"nourishes no bigotry, harbors no schisms, asks no man at the threshold
of the order what is his creed, color or politics, whether he be prince or

peasant; but rather if he be a true man, moral in action, loyal in purpose, one who seeks the good of others, and will ever be ready to do his part to honor the order into which he seeks to enter."[114] Grimshaw captured the psychological investment that many black men held in the order's ideals. Religious faith, civic responsibility, and a commitment to the equality of man were constitutive elements of the Masonic tradition. Since class and gender were deeply implicated in the development and maintenance of this tradition, these elements were also constitutive of bourgeois manliness as constructed by black Masons. In this sense, class distinction served, to paraphrase historian Glenda Gilmore, as a marker of black manhood.[115]

The male subjectivity that was produced, and reproduced, within the Prince Hall lodges contained multiple ethnicities. Blacks from the United States and the Caribbean came together under the Masonic banner to practice an exclusive brotherhood that was grounded in production and respectability. The objective and subjective determinants of class, then, trumped ethnicity and national identity in the gender identity formation of black Masons. In other words, class formation eroded what might have otherwise been ethnically inflected variations of black manhood. In articulating a collective gender and class identity that was different from a normative white bourgeois manliness only in degree, not in kind, African American and African Caribbean men were unable to transcend dominant Anglo-American configurations of gender, class, and power. Given the hegemonic nature of masculinity, this is not altogether surprising. But those who became Prince Hall Freemasons were adherents to a tradition that rejected—theoretically and ideologically at least—racial difference. The universal egalitarianism of Freemasonry encouraged them to think about gender identity in the same terms as their white, middle-class counterparts. Black men who joined the Garvey movement expressed similar commitments to production and respectability as constitutive elements of manliness even as an essentialist belief in racial difference, manifest in ideas of racial chauvinism and race purity, produced a slightly different norm for achieving and maintaining the status of manhood.

A Spirit of Manliness

On 27 August 1914, shortly after his twenty-seventh birthday, Marcus Garvey, an African Jamaican, wrote to Travers Buxton, the secretary of the British anticolonial organization, Anti-Slavery and Aborigines' Protection Society. Garvey was writing to thank Buxton for his efforts in providing him with money to return to Jamaica. He had recently returned to his native island after having spent four years traveling in Central and South America and Great Britain. In England, where he had been since 1912, Garvey had attended law courses at Birkbeck College. He also worked on London's waterfront where, through his contact with African and African Caribbean seamen, he was drawn into the circle of pan-Africanist activists who were loosely formed around Duse Mohamed Ali and his journal, *African Times and Orient Review*. Garvey's sojourn to the metropole of the British empire solidified his radicalization that had begun several years earlier when he began using his journalism and printing skills to highlight the labor exploitation of workers in countries such as Panama, Ecuador, Colombia, and Venezuela. The result of this movement across the "New World" and the "Old" was his founding of the organization about which he was writing to Buxton—the Universal Negro Improvement and Conservation Association and the African Communities League.[1]

Garvey's letter to Buxton was one of the first announcements of the establishment of the Universal Negro Improvement Association (UNIA). Within a decade of his letter, Garvey and others had transformed the organization from a small collection of Jamaican men and women who advocated self-help as a remedy for the race's problems to a global fellowship of people of African descent who shared an ideology of anti-European colonialism, national self-determination, and racial purity. Although the ideology of the UNIA was nationalist at its core, regional, local, ethnic, and sociopolitical variations contributed to different articulations of Garveyism according to time and space.[2] The complexity of the UNIA was reflected not only in the various local chapters but in the thought of the organization's intellectuals. According to historians Robert A. Hill and Barbara Bair, Garvey was a "man who embodied the contradictions of his age." Growing up in a colonial environment and emerging as a leader in a modernizing United States, Garvey drew on various nineteenth-century Western intellectual trends, ranging from the ideas of the "self-made man" to New Thought and social Darwinism. Garvey's thought, however, was not merely a replication of Western, and specifically Anglo-American, values. In articulating the position of the New Negro, Garvey and his supporters started with a "strong foundation in the mainstream intellectual tradition, borrowing from that tradition while creating new racial imperatives."[3]

During the association's early years, Garvey and his compatriots were avid supporters of the Tuskegee model of progress and its chief architect, Booker T. Washington. Along with an accommodationist stance in southern politics and race relations, advocates of the Tuskegee model propounded the idea that African Americans should elevate themselves through learning industrial trades, building economically self-sufficient communities, and internalizing bourgeois values such as thrift, sobriety, industry, and Victorian standards of morality. By taking this position, Washington and his circle placed the onus of advancement on blacks themselves, often blaming them for their subordinate position in a racist, exploitative southern political economy. Garvey, while still in Jamaica, made similar claims about the peasant population, calling them at times "contemptible" and "outside the pale of cultured appreciation." He lamented, for example, that the rural areas of Jamaica were full of "villainy and vice of the worse kind, immorality, obeah, and all kinds of dirty things."[4] Garvey encouraged a path to progress that was similar to the Tuskegee idea being preached to blacks in the American South, sans an explicit endorsement of political accommodation. A report for the Kingston *Gleaner* discussed the efforts of the UNIA to build an industrial school in Jamaica. "The need for industrial training for intelligent productive labour, for increased usefulness in agriculture and the trades, for self-respect and for the purification of home life" required the development of such an institution. It was this proposed school that took Garvey to the United States on a fund-raising tour in 1916 and opened another stage of his career as an influential figure in black diasporic culture and politics.[5]

Paradoxically, Garvey's early thought also contained elements of the Talented Tenth model of progress. Articulated by several intellectuals and activists, particularly W. E. B. Du Bois, this model held that the path to advancement lay not in industrial education and political accommodation; rather, liberal education and political agitation against disfranchisement and segregation provided the best route to civil and economic equality. Furthermore, it was the responsibility of the educated elite to act as the advance guard for racial progress. Garvey did not engage directly in the debate between Du Bois and Washington (although he would later criticize Du Bois's liberal education agenda), nor did he share Du Bois's determination for civil equality. He and the UNIA leadership, however, did direct an intellectual paternalism toward the Jamaican working class. Part of the UNIA's early agenda was that the "intelligent must lead and assist the unfortunate of the people to rise," a reverberation of the Talented Tenth philosophy.[6]

The same eclecticism and contradictions that shaped Garveyite thought characterized the definitions of manhood espoused by the UNIA leadership and its fellow travelers. Several discourses of manhood intersected in the philosophy and practice of Garveyism—discourses that included, among others, the producer ideal of the nineteenth-century artisan, the self-made man doctrine of the late-nineteenth-century bourgeoisie, and the frontier ideology associated with Theodore Roosevelt and American imperialism. Encompassing this constellation of disparate ideas was a prescriptive discourse that was structured by late-Victorian emphases on producer values and respectability.

In this sense, Garveyite constructions of manhood were similar to the gender identity formation of mainstream middle-class black men, including Prince Hall Freemasons. Like the traditional black elite and the emerging black bourgeoisie, Garveyites exhibited a positive identification with western European and Anglo-American traditions of manliness. Both Garveyites and Prince Hall Freemasons also used gender and age as central categories through which to construct a manly sense of self; that is, they defined themselves against black women and black boys. Similarly, they both used race as a negative referent in the construction of black manhood, although their nationalist predisposition ensured that Garveyites engaged in this oppositional construction on a more sustained basis. The formation of a collective gender identity among Masons and Garveyites was different in one crucial way. Whereas Masons situated themselves *as men* against the "unrespectable" working class, Garveyites positioned themselves as manly men against black men who adopted liberal, antinationalist politics. That is to say, political ideology, more than class and status, became a primary negative referent for those who espoused Garveyism although they, too, occasionally articulated an anti-working-class bias. Still, manliness for Garveyites was a concept that was determined by ideology as much as by class.

It is important to point out that no single, unifying idea of manhood was held by members and supporters of the UNIA; rather, appropriate gender conventions in Garveyite thought were fragmented, ambiguous, often inconsistent, and constantly being redefined, as they were in the thought and lived experience of most American men. Although Garvey and other intellectuals associated with the movement adhered to white, middle-class standards of manhood, this adherence was not a mere replication. Nor was it identical to the ways in which the traditional black elite and politically mainstream black bourgeoisie experienced their gender identity formation. The racial chauvinism and nationalist agenda of the UNIA influenced its members' constructions of manliness in different ways. Part of the purpose of this chapter is to explore how the UNIA refashioned, sometimes imperceptibly, late-Victorian definitions of manhood. In inventing a manly self, Garveyites drew on western European and Anglo-American models of manhood and, in the process, subtly reshaped them.

In the spring of 1920, J. R. Ralph Casimir, a resident of Dominica, wrote to Marcus Garvey seeking advice on how to organize a local division of the UNIA. Garvey responded that Casimir must "have as officers men who are honest, straight-forward and interested in our movement[,] remembering that it is only men who possess these qualities [who] will be able to handle the situation with success."[7] Indeed, as a prerequisite for becoming a member of the UNIA, good character was probably only second to the ability to pay dues. The organization's constitution allowed for the chartering of local divisions only when "seven or more citizens . . . whose intelligence is such as to bring them within respectful recognition of the educated and cultured of such a community" applied for affiliation. Officers in particular were to be the models on which the rest of the membership would pattern their moral and social lives. The *Negro World* stressed as much, claiming that the "officials of the U.N.I.A., from the President-General down, are men and women of the highest integrity, men and women of education, culture and refinement . . . men and women of stainless reputation." The association placed much emphasis on forthright behavior in determining its national and local leadership. A potential officer was expected to "be free from criminal conviction" and "of reputable moral standing" and, indeed, was not approved "until his character and qualifications have satisfied the High Executive Council." Furthermore, once in office, they were "required to maintain a high order of respectability," and any instance of drunkenness, debauchery or disruptive public behavior could result in their impeachment. Showing up at a meeting intoxicated, for example, called for a three-month suspension and repeat offenses could result in expulsion.[8]

When Garvey wrote to Casimir, he was engaging in a transnational production of class identity. Here was a Jamaican who, after having recently moved his organization's headquarters to New York, was writing to a fellow African Caribbean and British subject to indicate the importance of respectability to the movement's success. Indeed, class, status, ethnicity, and nationality were salient concerns for Garveyites and their contemporaries; the complex nature of these categories, and their interrelatedness, remain ubiquitous obstacles in the historical interpretation of Garveyism. The UNIA was a mass movement and, although many of its members and leaders were of the professional middle class, some of its opponents criticized it for mobilizing the most "unrespectable" members of the working class. Occasionally, Garveyites traded on the image of doing battle against an elite, color-conscious black leadership on behalf of the downtrodden masses, but there is no doubt that the UNIA's economic and social agenda spoke directly to the needs and desires of the emerging black bourgeoisie and, furthermore, was critical of many aspects of black working-class culture. Additionally, the federal government and black opposition frequently focused on the Caribbean roots of Garveyism, although the UNIA was clearly an international movement.

This complex interplay of ethnicity and class prevents any facile interpretation of Garveyism, particularly given the different regional characters of individual local divisions. Given this, the UNIA remains a fruitful avenue for exploring the ways in which middle-class black men experienced their gender identity formation during this period.[9] This is not to say that the rank-and-file members were primarily of the professional or business classes. Indeed, working-class African Americans and African Caribbeans formed a significant part of the UNIA membership, partly drawn in by the organization's militant racial chauvinism and its economic nostrum of land and property ownership. Nor is it to suggest that Garveyite ideology can be made synonymous with black middle-class thought. What I do want to suggest, however, is that the rhetoric and prescriptive literature that emerged out of the movement's leadership corps was reflective of a specific set of bourgeois ideas about gender that circulated among middle-class African American and African Caribbean men.

The least debated conclusion about the Garvey movement is its transnational character. Unlike class makeup, the ethnic diversity of the UNIA was fairly apparent although it contributed to much controversy among Garvey and his opponents. Although the majority of UNIA divisions in the 1920s were located in the United States, according to Winston James, "a significant segment of its leadership, and a substantial proportion . . . of its rank and file members, were of Caribbean origin." African Caribbean Garveyites existed in New York, Boston, and Miami, as well as in other cities without large concentrations of African Caribbean immigrants, such as Philadelphia; Baltimore;

Detroit; Pittsburgh; Gary, Indiana; and Newport News, Virginia.[10] With such a visible presence of African Caribbean nationalists in major urban areas, mainstream African Americans and whites latched onto ethnicity as a category through which to interpret the UNIA's radicalism. Ethnicity, in other words, became central to the ways in which they described and, in many cases, criticized the movement. A reporter for the *Washington Eagle*, for example, calculated that at one particular convention, 90 percent of those in attendance were either African or African Caribbean. The *Norfolk Journal and Guide* put forward similar statistics—both in the actual number and in their lack of scientific measurement—in its coverage of the New York convention in 1920. This particular reporter utilized statistics to disparage the sincerity and efficacy of the organization's nationalist ideology. "Eighty per cent of those attending it are West Indians," the reporter assessed, "residing, for the most part, in the United States, and who would not return to the West Indies if they could, and who have no intention of going to Africa, as they find the United States, and especially New York's Black Harlem, plenty good enough for them and their purposes."[11] An informant for the Federal Bureau of Investigation (FBI) also described the UNIA as overwhelmingly Caribbean and attributed the radicalism of the movement to just that. In two consecutive reports, William A. Bailey pointed out that "the radical element consists almost entirely of the foreign element amongst the colored race." He further reported that he had never attended a meeting of the New York chapter where there were "more than one or two American negroes." Garveyites "expressing radical sympathies," he wrote to his handler, "are, with the few exceptions mentioned, all foreign negroes, mostly of West Indian Birth."[12] There was undoubtedly much exaggeration behind these assessments of the ethnic makeup of UNIA meetings and conventions. Although African Caribbeans may have had a relatively high profile in the large media market of New York, the backbone of the movement consisted of both Caribbean immigrants and African Americans. Moreover, many of the UNIA's national officers were native-born blacks. Still, the organization's ethnic composition remained a source of tension between the UNIA and its opponents.

Occasionally, differences of ethnicity and national identity contributed to contentious intraorganizational relationships, but the judgment by some of the movement's opponents that ethnic tension would result in widespread "bloodshed between the West Indian Negroes and American Negroes" was certainly hyperbole.[13] On the whole, African American and African Caribbean immigrants coexisted and cooperated with one another in UNIA locals across the United States. The notion that it was primarily a movement of Caribbean agitators did not correspond to reality. William Ferris, the Yale- and

Harvard-educated African American literary editor of the *Negro World*, wrote in response to this prevailing myth in 1923. "The Universal Negro Improvement Association is recruited," he wrote, "not from the island of Jamaica, but from the black peoples of the world. Two-thirds of the two-score divisions, whose membership runs into the four figures are located in the United States of America." To support his statement, Ferris pointed to the cosmopolitan character of the parades that began the 1920 annual convention. The parades were marked by the "bright, resplendent banners with Barbados, Jamaica, Grenada, St. Kitts, Antigua, Cuba, Haiti, Porto Rico, Santo Domingo, Trinidad, Demarara, New York, New Jersey, Pennsylvania, Washington, Virginia, North Carolina, Georgia, Florida etc., emblazoned upon them."[14] Ferris's observation, supported by most journalistic treatments of the annual conventions, reflects the international constituency of the movement. His observation also indicates, however, that ethnicity and nationality were not subsumed under the rubric of a monolithic blackness. Garveyites retained their ethnic, national, and regional identities even as they advocated a collective diasporic one. The creation of separate leadership positions over African, African Caribbean, and African American populations reified those ethnic, national, and regional differences.

Class was as knotty an issue as ethnicity and at times these operated as mutually constitutive categories in both the popular representations and internal politics of Garveyism. Opposition to the UNIA often framed its critiques of the movement in terms of class. Both African Americans and African Caribbeans who challenged Garveyism represented the movement, and particularly its leadership, as charlatans who took advantage of uneducated, "unrespectable," working people. In January 1923, eight prominent African Americans wrote to the U.S. Attorney General, Harry M. Daugherty, hoping to speed up the indictment of Garvey on charges of mail fraud. The Garvey movement, they wrote, "is composed chiefly of the most primitive and ignorant element of West Indian and American Negroes. The so-called respectable element of the movement are largely ministers without churches, physicians without patients, lawyers without clients and publishers without readers, who are usually in search of 'easy money.' In short, this organization is composed in the main of Negro sharks and ignorant Negro fanatics."[15] Cyril Edwards, an African Jamaican immigrant, expressed a similar sentiment. Presuming to speak "on behalf of thousands of hard-working intelligent West Indians," Edwards argued that "by no stretch of imagination must the utterances of the 'leaders' and empire builders" of the UNIA "be regarded as indicative of West Indian effort." Rather, one had to look at the upwardly mobile segment of the immigrant population. In a letter to the *Globe*, Edwards

drew class distinctions between a "respectable" African Caribbean community and the "unrespectable" UNIA. "Real West Indian effort in Harlem is
[illegible] by the scores of capable professional men and home builders," he
wrote. "The U.N.I.A. is popular in Harlem no one will deny, but its popularity
is largely confined to a certain element of American and West Indian Negroes
and is not representative of the best elements among both peoples. The movement has grown as a consequence of its publicity organ, the Negro World,
which gives out each week exaggerated and highly colored reports calculated
to inflame and excite the minds of the near-illiterate and the oppressed."[16]
Edwards's statement, like the letter to Daugherty, was inaccurate and disin-
genuously so. Like the ethnic diversity that characterized its locals within the
United States, the UNIA appealed across class lines.

To be sure, many UNIA local divisions consisted of predominantly
working-class blacks; and, from the perspective of middle-class blacks, these
memberships might have met all of the criteria of "unrespectability." Activity
in the Kinston, North Carolina, chapter, for instance, was sporadic due to
economic downturns and the fact that most of its members were migrant
farmers who worked in the strawberry fields during the spring and summer.
The majority of the members of the Woodlawn, Pennsylvania, chapter were
migrants who had left "the Turpentine Camps of the South" to go work at
the Jones and Laughlin Steel Plant. An FBI agent reported that the UNIA
had taken the place of the church in the lives of these migrants. "Formerly
most of these negroes belonged to the church, now, owing to the teachings
of MARCUS GARVEY, only about one hundred of them attend." In order to
combat this, a local black preacher requested that the agent look into en-
listing a missionary to work "among these ignorant colored people."[17] The
likelihood that very few of the Kinston or Woodlawn Garveyites either owned
homes or completed a high school education would have qualified them as
the "primitive" and "near-illiterate" audiences for Garvey about which many
middle-class blacks warned the government.

Many other chapters, however, were made up of members whose status
stretched across the spectrum of class. Although it is impossible to say with
any certainty, there were probably just as many chapters with cross-class
membership as there were chapters with exclusively working-class memberships. This is particularly true of the large- and medium-sized urban areas
in which the UNIA was active. The Negro World reported on a regional membership drive meeting in St. Louis which attracted the editor of the St. Louis
Argus, a state judge, an attorney, several high school teachers, and a representative from the African Methodist Episcopal General Conference.[18] When
Marcus Garvey spoke before a local in Buffalo, close to 750 people turned

out, many of whom, according to an FBI agent, "seemed to be of the better class of Buffalo's colored people."[19]

The Los Angeles division of the UNIA was another local that consisted of working- and middle-class blacks in both its leadership and rank and file. A robust division with an estimated membership of one thousand in 1921, it was organized in 1920 by John D. Gordon, a prominent local Baptist minister and a UNIA national officer, and his brother, Hugh; J. W. Coleman, an Old Settler, businessman, and member of several fraternal orders; W. H. "Pop" Sanders, a local activist; and Joseph and Charlotta Spear Bass, editors of the black newspaper, the *California Eagle*. The division's first president was Noah Thompson, a businessman, journalist, and political activist.[20] According to an FBI surveillance report, the class makeup of the Los Angeles division contributed to the economic success of several of the organization's businesses. "Most of the members are prosperous," A. A. Hopkins reported to his superiors, "and monetary contributions and the sale of bonds in the various GARVEY ventures have been very successful." According to Hopkins, the middle-class members of the chapter tended to be African American and government employees on the federal, state, and municipal level.[21] The success of the Los Angeles division was short-lived, however. Tension between the division and the parent body over control of local funds led to the splintering of the division into factions. In late 1921, Thompson, the Basses, and others who were suspicious of the parent body's handling of financial matters created the Pacific Coast Negro Improvement Association (PCNIA). The split that occurred is instructive in terms of exploring the ways in which class and ethnicity were implicated in the internal politics and external representations of Garveyism.

Almost from the beginning of its existence, the Los Angeles division had butted heads with the parent body over the failure of the latter to issue payments on death insurance claims for several members of the Los Angeles and Riverside chapters. In August 1921, Noah Thompson attended the annual convention as the Los Angeles delegate intent on receiving clarification on this matter as well as the more general fiscal methods of the organization. Thompson, a vociferous advocate of fiscal responsibility as well as greater cooperation between local and national offices, managed to get a proposal calling for the opening of the UNIA's books passed. The convention tabled his second proposal, which would have required referenda on major financial transactions of the body. Thompson returned to Los Angeles with a critical assessment of the fiduciary capacity of the parent body but suggested that members of the division remain loyal to Garvey. Several members who felt that Thompson's report was an act of disloyalty in and of itself called for his resignation. In October and November, Garvey dispatched national officers to Los Angeles in order to try to keep the division intact. When Captain E. L. Gaines, formerly of Pasadena, arrived in Los Angeles to investigate, Thompson and his supporters issued a letter of protest to the New York office. The letter accused Gaines of conducting secret sessions with the anti-Thompson faction. Shortly after the letter was made public, Gaines revoked the original Los Angeles charter and appointed new officers for the division. Thompson, the Basses, and others responded by creating the PCNIA.[22]

Although it is impossible to determine whether or not the split occurred completely along class lines, class was implicated in the ways that the participants perceived the controversy and in how those outside of the organization interpreted it. According to the editors of the *California Eagle* and the foremost historian on the incident, the majority of the members of the division sided with Thompson and left with him to join the PCNIA. The major propagandist for the PCNIA, Joseph Bass, described the anti-Thompson (or pro-Garvey) faction as suffering from "ignorance, superstition and bombast" — loaded terms that were evocative of working-class "unrespectability." When Gaines appointed an allegedly illiterate individual as the chairman of the division's Board of Trustees, those who had joined the PCNIA criticized the UNIA for "installing ignorance" in the leadership ranks of a once honorable organization.[23]

Individuals who ostensibly perceived the split with more objectivity also interpreted it through the lens of class. FBI agent Hopkins judged that it was primarily "the better element of the negro population, including church people, Federal, County and City employees, and those who are seeking to avoid any racial trouble or clashes" who left with Thompson. He also suggested that ethnicity and national identity figured into the splintering and reconfiguration of Los Angeleno Garveyism. The pro-Garvey faction that remained in support of Gaines's reorganization of the division, according to Hopkins, was "composed principally of West Indian negroes and the radical element." Hopkins's assessment about the ethnic dimension of the division's dissolution and reconstitution is somewhat dubious, particularly given the dearth of African Caribbean immigrants in Los Angeles and the fact that none of the principal actors in the split were of Caribbean origin.[24] But this point is less important if we consider how Hopkins was deploying ethnicity in this case. In determining which was the most subversive to national security, "the conservative and patriotic stand of THOMPSON" or the "radical element" of Gaines and Garvey, Hopkins conflated class, ethnicity, and political ideology. In other words, the federal government should be more concerned with the existence of what he inferred to be a working-class, radical, African Caribbean contingent than with, again what he inferred to be, a respectable, church-going, middle-class, and native-born black population.[25] The prominent opponents of Garveyism who wrote to Attorney General Daugherty also framed the split between the UNIA and PCNIA in terms of class, referring to Thompson as "a distinguished colored citizen" who "was attacked by members of Garvey's Los Angeles division, who, it is alleged, had been incited to violence by Garvey himself."[26] The implication of the letter was that the easily led masses posed a threat to Thompson and, by extension, other respectable citizens.

Certainly, these representations of the Garvey movement and its split in Los Angeles were not reflective of reality. Many solidly middle-class Los Angelenos stayed in the pro-Garvey camp after the division's fracture, including J. W. Coleman.[27] Garveyites had to continue to defend their organization, in Los Angeles and elsewhere, from charges that it was largely composed of poor, illiterate, ignorant, criminal-minded, and violent blacks. One way that Garvey did this was through the carefully cultivated self-representation as a respectable, in many ways, middle-class black man. Garvey crafted a very specific self-image for popular consumption that resembled, as historian Judith Stein has noted, the "heroic biographies of the Victorian age."[28] Amy Jacques Garvey, his second wife, and William Ferris also contributed to Garvey's representation as a respectable, middle-class African Jamaican. Their narratives highlighted his birth in 1887 to Marcus Garvey Sr., a sporadically employed mason, small landholder, and "a man of brilliant intellect and dashing courage," and Sarah Garvey, also a property owner, petit merchant, and "a sober and conscientious Christian, too soft and good for the time in which she lived"; his adolescent apprenticeship at a small press and, later, the Government Printing Office; and his sojourn through Central and South America and England. Written after he obtained a place in the American consciousness, the narratives of Garvey's life portrayed him as the prototypical self-made man, whose childhood in Jamaica prepared him for his newfound leadership position. Of his experience as a printer's apprentice, for instance, Garvey wrote: "At fourteen I had enough intelligence and experience to manage men. I was strong and manly, and I made them respect me. I developed a strong and forceful character, and have maintained it still." He provided his life as a model for other black men for their journey to success. Independence, strong character, aggressiveness and intelligence—all qualities needed to attain manliness—were integral to his process of self-making.[29]

These representations and counter-representations consistently marked the interactions between Garveyites, their opponents, and the federal government. Each had their own investment in constructing an image of the UNIA as being constituted of particular social classes and ethnic groups. Understand-

Marcus Garvey's wedding photograph, Christmas 1919. (Courtesy of Marcus Garvey
Portrait Collection, Photographs and Prints Division, Schomburg Center for Research
in Black Culture, New York Public Library, Astor, Lenox and Tilden Foundations)

ing this relationship between class and ethnicity is perhaps more important
than objectively determining the actual class and ethnic makeup of the organization itself. To be sure, the UNIA was a diverse organization with African
Americans and African Caribbeans, unskilled and skilled industrial workers,
agricultural laborers, service employees, professionals, entrepreneurs, and

civil servants. Trying to identify the exact class character of the movement, however, prevents us from understanding, to quote historian Daniel Walkowitz, "the middle class as a constructed category with multiple and changing historical meanings."[30] What is important here is that many Garveyites, particularly at the local and national levels of leadership, were middle-class either by objective material standards or from a specific ideological commitment to bourgeois values. Their adherence to bourgeois notions of manliness, like that of Prince Hall Freemasons, can be clearly seen in their rhetoric and prescriptive literature.

■ "As far as the Negro race is concerned," Garvey wrote in 1923, "we can find but few real men to measure up to the higher purpose of creation, and because of this lack of manhood in the race, we have stagnated for centuries and now find ourselves at the foot of the great human ladder." John E. Bruce, an influential member of the UNIA and regular contributor to the *Negro World*, felt that "the Negro in alien lands is a human chameleon, a mere automaton, a bump on a log; a spineless coward, and worshipper [sic] at the shrine of the white man." Bruce went on to rhetorically ask: "Why should the Negro now be a follower and imitator, with such a record behind him, and such a glorious future before him, if he only will wake up?"[31] Garvey's invective, immersed in the language of social Darwinism but with religious overtones, located the failure of the black race to evolve in the lack of male character among African Americans and African Caribbeans. Bruce placed the emphasis on the lack of initiative, a culturally coded male quality. To be sure, these were rhetorical devices used to stir up nationalist sentiment and, in other statements, Garvey, Bruce, and others stressed that black men did indeed possess qualities necessary to ensure the advancement of the race. However, by engaging the minds of black men with an initially negative assessment of their manhood, Garvey and Bruce positioned the UNIA as the path to "true" manliness and racial progress.

Gendered rhetoric around the issues of entrepreneurship, racial progress, race purity, and nation and empire building was commonplace within the Garvey movement. One could hardly open up the pages of the *Negro World* or attend an evening of speeches by Garveyite officials in a packed Liberty Hall without reading or hearing references to black manhood. Garveyites often deployed the concept of manhood in the universalist sense to connote the conditions of the race in general. We should not, however, underestimate the visceral and cerebral connections that black men made between their gender identity and nationalist rhetoric when, for instance, they read in the *Negro World* that the UNIA was "striving for freedom and manhood" or when they heard Garvey pronounce that "it is a spirit of manliness which we believe must first exert itself if this race is to be free."[32] But rhetoric was not the only means through which male Garveyites articulated a collective and individuated gendered self. Prescriptive literature, largely delivered through the *Negro World*, combined with rhetorical oratory to inculcate black men with bourgeois ideals of manliness. Through these methods, men within the UNIA constructed their own gender identities along the lines of the American bourgeoisie.

Several models of manhood were present within the rhetoric of Garveyism. One was frontier manliness, or the manhood that was embodied in the American icons of the Indian fighters and homesteaders, exemplars of nineteenth-century individualism. A. H. Maloney, a Trinidadian-born professor of psychology at Wilberforce University and a contributor to the *Negro World*, captured this theme when he wrote, in 1924, that the politics of Garveyism "represents the crystallization of the virile element within the race, the pioneering element, the element that is not afraid to stake its fortunes upon the proposition of striking out upon the adventures of national house-building."[33] This equation of pioneering and virility resonated for middle-class men in the late nineteenth and early twentieth centuries in the emergence of, what one historian describes, "passionate manhood."[34] Throughout the nineteenth century, bourgeois manliness had been defined through intellectual capacity, self-control of one's emotions and natural (but "uncivilized") urges, and participation in the public realm of politics and business. By the third quarter of the century, white middle-class men expressed anxiety over what they felt to be the overwhelming influence of female morality and its result, "overcivilization." The fear that men were becoming effete, either through the stifling moralizing of women or their own excessive intellectual pursuit, contributed to the growth of physical culture following the Civil War. Emphasis on building the body rather than the intellect gained much currency during this period.[35] Moreover, white middle-class men began to witness various assaults on their previously exclusive domains: women were entering the public sphere of politics—through various reform movements and suffrage activism—and the professions; immigrant men were challenging the political control of the urban bourgeoisie; and working-class men and women were disrupting the stable world of industrial capitalism through labor agitation.[36] Finally, the individualism that had sustained middle-class ideas of manhood through most of the nineteenth century was disintegrating under the pressure of corporatization. Men who had traditionally looked to independent entrepreneurship for their economic livelihood and social identity were increasingly becoming bureaucrats in the civil service and midlevel managers in the corporate capitalist economy. This produced a longing for the individualism of the frontier which, despite its "closing" in 1890, still held a significant place in the American imagination.[37]

The advocacy of physical development and rigorous engagement with the frontier was embodied in Theodore Roosevelt and his "cult of strenuosity." The male body, and particularly physical strength, became the prime indicator of male character. A strenuous life was the manifestation of self-control, still a necessity for the attainment of manhood for the middle class. The frontier also remained a significant place and process in which middle-class manliness could be forged. The mastery of not only one's self but one's environment was essential to this rationale, evident in the flourishing of organized athletics and hunting clubs. Furthermore, the discipline and aggressiveness associated with the military and, indeed, war itself, signified middle-class manliness. Imperialism thus became rationalized, in part, as an expression of Anglo-American manhood.[38]

Garveyite rhetoric clearly reflected the importance of the frontier and the mastery of self and environment. Along with Maloney, Garvey and others discussed the need for black men to master their surroundings. "God placed man on earth as the lord of Creation," Garvey wrote in 1923. "The elements —all nature are at his command—it is for him to harness them[,] subdue them[,] and use them."[39] One editorial in the *Negro World* drew the connections between self-mastery, the control of one's environment, and athleticism: "Just as the powerful swimmer uses the resistance of the water and the eagle the resistance of the air to propel themselves forward, so does the masterful man bend circumstances to his will." The editorial judged that "if the black man will be resourceful, capable, efficient, if he will be strong, brave and true, he will come into his own and find his place in the sun." Garvey, though not directly referring to athleticism, linked bodily development with racial advancement by advocating the strengthening of "physical muscles" as an imperative rather than the strengthening of "spiritual muscles."[40]

The importance of frontier manliness occurred repeatedly in UNIA members' references to Garvey. Indeed, it is significant that Uzziah Minor, the presiding officer at a Washington, D.C., meeting in 1920, introduced Garvey as "the Theodore Roosevelt of the Negro race" to a wildly applauding crowd. Garveyites also equated Garvey with that other great trailblazer, Moses. Moses did not enjoy as much prestige among the middle class as Roosevelt, to be sure; however, the legend of Moses leading the tribe of Israel out of the wilderness certainly lent credence to the image of Garvey as a pioneer for the black race. Dr. John D. Gordon, assistant president-general, spoke at the organization's 1920 convention and prophesied that "this Moses of our race . . . is going to inspire us with true manhood through his entire exertion and help this race go on to success." His allusions to the Old Testament did not stop there. He went on to concretely link Israel's, and by implication the black race's, liberation with manhood. "God gave Canaan to the children of Israel," he reminded the audience, "but they had to be men enough to fight for it."[41]

In Garveyite thought, Africa became the frontier—the primary site where black manhood could be realized and asserted. As white middle-class men were transferring the psychological import of the American West onto growing cities, rapidly expanding national markets, and the Caribbean, Latin America, and Asia, intellectuals in the UNIA looked to other areas as well.[42] Ferris located the frontier in Africa when he told an audience at Madison Square Garden in 1920 that "the new Negro believes in blazing a path for himself, in Africa, if necessary." African redemption, however, was more than a mere rhetorical exercise. Although it was undoubtedly used to arouse UNIA audiences, African redemption consisted of concrete agendas and policies. Starting in 1920, the UNIA attempted to make inroads into the continent through Liberia. Europeans and white Americans had discovered the wealth of Africa, Garveyites argued, but they should not be left alone to reap its benefits. The exploitation of Africa's natural resources was the birthright of its descendants and provided the opportunity for the reaffirmation of their manhood. "Negroes everywhere must get that courage of manhood," Garvey argued, "that will enable them to strike out, irrespective of who the enemy is, and demand those things that are ours by right—moral, legal and divine."[43] Manhood, capital development, and political independence were inextricably linked in Garveyite thought and found their potential fulfillment in Liberia.

The first practical step toward African redemption was to develop an economic relationship with the Americo-Liberian elite. In May 1920, the UNIA sent to Liberia the first of several delegations. It initially consisted of J. W. H. Eason, the socialist Hubert Harrison (both of whom backed out), and Elie Garcia. John E. Bruce, who did not go at the insistence of his doctor, wrote letters of introduction to President C. D. B. King and Supreme Court Justice J. J. Dossen. Describing the members of the delegation as "gentlemen of culture and refinement, character and ability," Bruce assured King that they represented blacks in the diaspora "who have sent them to the Mother Country to . . . open wider the door of opportunity in Africa, commercially, industrially and intellectually for the sons of Africa throughout the world." He wrote to Dossen that the delegation "will inform you fully of what the organization is accomplishing in a practical way towards Negro Manhood and Independence."[44]

The UNIA planned to repatriate between twenty and thirty thousand families who would, they hoped, increase the agricultural production of the small country. Economic development would also include the establishment of trade between Liberia and the black diaspora through the Black Star Line; the repatriation of small business owners, financiers, and industrialists; and the introduction of professionals who would improve the infrastructure, education, and health care systems of the country. The second delegation that visited Liberia in 1921, for instance, consisted of a surveyor, an agriculturalist, a pharmacist, and a UNIA member employed in the building trades.[45] Plans for the "colonization" of several areas in Liberia accelerated in the winter and spring of 1924 when the UNIA dispatched a delegation that included Lady Henrietta Vinton Davis, the fourth assistant president-general. In February, the delegation met with several Liberian officials and developed a logistical and operational outline for constructing a UNIA settlement along the Cavalla River in Maryland County. In June and July, the association sent goods, material, and a team of experts to prepare the sites for a larger repatriation in October. The team, which Garvey described as "pioneers [who] were all responsible men, of families, with one exception," included three engineers, a shipwright, and a carpenter.[46]

The relationship between the UNIA and the Liberian elite collapsed that summer, however. On the orders of President King, according to Garvey, the advance team was forcibly deported almost immediately upon their arrival. Moreover, in late June, the Liberian consul in the United States—a man who Garvey referred to as "another Negro of miscegenationistic [sic] tendencies, being himself a hybrid, originally of British Honduras"—issued a directive that his office not grant visas to UNIA members.[47] Several factors contributed to the aborted attempt by the UNIA to establish an economic and political foothold in Liberia, including an entrenched elite eager to play various sources of revenue (whether it be the British and American governments or the UNIA) against one another; foreign interest in keeping Garveyite influence to a minimum; ties between the Liberian government and American industrialists; and factionalism within the Liberian elite over immigration policy and political ideology. Certainly, the well-known agenda to "colonize" Liberia did not endear the UNIA to the country's ruling class. The "civilizing mission" ideology of redemption did not hold weight among Americo-Liberians, an already Westernized group in terms of culture and religion. Likewise, the economic potential of the UNIA could not compete with the resourceful governments of the United States and Great Britain or wealthy corporations such as Firestone Rubber Company, which ended up leasing the same land that was initially earmarked for UNIA settlement.[48]

Although the UNIA's fall from its already precarious grace in the eyes of the Liberian elite was the result of complex personal, economic, and political relationships, in Garvey's view, the failure of colonization was largely due to the fallibility of King and the machinations of mainstream African American leaders. As opposed to the pioneers of the UNIA, Garvey portrayed Liberian officials as untrustworthy, selfish, "degenerated and weak morally," and easily susceptible to "harmful letters or communications" from organizations such as the NAACP (National Association for the Advancement of Colored People).[49] The UNIA constructed images of its agents of colonization as manly pioneers who were going to bring industrial capitalism, race consciousness, and "civilization" to a relatively backward continent. In this sense, the frontier model of manhood coexisted with another model prevalent in Garveyite thought: that of the self-made man.

In the rhetoric of nationalism and African redemption, Garveyites combined the realms of the material and the ideal. Pioneers, they argued, were the avatars of economic progress and the destruction of the psychological barriers of racial inferiority. The concept of self-culture, or the idea that success was dependent upon physical, mental, and spiritual self-development, figured heavily in the ways in which the UNIA conceived of racial progress and manhood.[50] Ferris explained the nature of man in these terms at a UNIA meeting in 1920. Acknowledging the influence of Ralph Waldo Emerson, the nineteenth-century philosophical doyen of self-culture, Ferris illustrated the difference between men and lower animals: "In proportion as a man has brain power, in proportion as a man has thought power, in proportion as a man has will power, in proportion as a man has self-possession and self-control, in that proportion will he be the master of his own fate and the architect of his own destiny." Ferris associated intellect, morality, aesthetics, and spirituality with manhood. Of course, his statement could be interpreted to mean humanity in general, rather than men in particular. However, in the same speech, he praised the UNIA and the Black Star Line with teaching "the Negro to feel that he is a man." Furthermore, it was not merely the "pecuniary prospect" that Ferris associated with manhood; rather, it was the alternating aspects of struggle and mastery associated with the marketplace that allowed blacks involved with the UNIA to achieve their manhood.[51]

Ferris's definition of manhood utilized the watchwords of Victorian manliness: "self-possession" and "self-control." Armed with intelligence, moral fiber, and an indomitable will, black men could become the masters of their own fate and, quite literally, the captains of their own ships. In effect, Ferris claimed, African Americans and African Caribbeans had the potential to become self-made men if they followed the moral and ideological dictates of the UNIA, which stressed individual and group "self-reliance."[52] The doctrine of the self-made man, as several historians have astutely argued, is a false credo that has animated the mythology of American masculinity and social mobility from the colonial era of Benjamin Franklin to the Gilded Age of Andrew Carnegie. Myth or not, the idea of the self-made man informed much of Garveyite thought on black manhood, evident in one of Garvey's lessons: "Man is the individual who is able to shape his own character, master his own will, direct his own life and shape his own ends."[53]

Several UNIA members operated from a negative position when discussing the ideal of the self-made man and its necessary components—strong character, an enterprising mentality, and an independent will—as they related to African Americans and African Caribbeans. Bruce, for example, castigated a UNIA chapter in Boston in 1923 when he argued that "the history of civilization shows that whenever the Negro has been under the domination of European races he has lacked the spirit of Independence." Reverend J. D. Brooks, the UNIA's secretary-general in 1920, criticized the lack of an entrepreneurial spirit among African Americans. "God gave us a man of power and of vision," he told his Washington audience, "and of prophecy—and the Negroes lack vision. They had praying, singing, and shouting. They had splendid things that led up to one thing, but we had no vision that would make us see ships sailing from Boston, New York, and Baltimore, manned and controlled by Negroes, because our spirits had been broken."[54] Brooks equated entrepreneurship with manliness when he suggested that it was Garvey's economic program that would "rekindle the spirit of manhood in the American Negro." UNIA intellectuals consistently defined this "spirit of manhood" by successful engagement in the marketplace. Moreover, by juxtaposing a pre-Garveyite religious "vision" and a Garveyite capitalist "vision," Brooks implicitly derided emotional spirituality by separating it from, and suggesting it impeded, the entrepreneurial spirit needed to achieve a collective black manliness. In doing so, he feminized the domain of religion, a tactic that Garveyites would employ when criticizing anti-Garveyite members of the black clergy.

Although occasionally Garveyites deployed the same idyllic self-images of the republican producer as Prince Hall Freemasons, they mostly engaged in a rhetorical fashioning of the self-made man that was based on the turn-of-the-century captain of industry rather than the nineteenth-century figures of the yeoman and artisan. Like others committed to corporate and industrial capitalism, Garveyites connected progress and manhood to economic modernization. One flyer advertising stocks in the Negro Factories Corporation, a UNIA subsidiary, overtly used masculinist language to attract potential investors:

Mr. Black Man
What are you Master of? Can you not see that
the White man has full control of every living thing?
Now what are you going to do about it?
MY ADVICE TO YOU IS TO
Get busy and prove yourself a man and not a monkey
A true man always finds and makes a way
for himself, and it is now up to every Negro
to make a place for himself in the great
FIELD OF COMMERCE[55]

The flyer deployed several gendered images. Independence and commercial initiative were certainly explicit, as was the differentiation between man and monkey. The imagery of slavery was also used, with the flyer suggesting that blacks were not, on the whole, masters of themselves but still slaves. In order to become masterless, black men had to become involved in the marketplace as captains of industry and commerce, not merely as industrial workers and rural peasants. Progress, then, was linked to capitalist initiative, which, in the minds of Garveyites, was a manly endeavor.

An entrepreneurial outlook alone, however, was neither sufficient for the progress of the race nor the achievement of manliness. Character was also necessary. A statement by Bruce, although made in 1914, reflected the Garveyite position on the importance of character in terms of black leadership. Speaking to a group of alumni from Virginia Theological Seminary, Bruce argued that "character and culture in the Negro will constitute the saving qualities of the race. . . . Character and culture, then money[.] These constitute the greatest need for the present." Character and financial success, of course, were not mutually exclusive; indeed, in the world of self-made men, one flowed directly from the other. A strong character led to material prosperity. Garveyite discussions of wealth reflected this intimate connection between the two. Without rejecting materialism, Garvey distinguished between the person with character and the one without: "One lives, in an age like this, nearer perfection by being wealthy than by being poor. To the contended [*sic*] soul, wealth is the stepping stone to perfection; to the miser it is the nearest avenue to hell."[56]

The issue of character emerged consistently when disputes among association officials erupted. Clashes between UNIA leaders occurred regularly over financial matters, policy direction, and personality conflicts. Impeachment was one tool for unilaterally resolving such conflicts. The summer of 1922 was a particularly bloody one as far as the dismissal of top UNIA officials was concerned. At the organization's annual convention in 1922, several officers were impeached, including Dr. Joseph D. Gibson, the UNIA's surgeon general, and J. W. H. Eason, the "Leader of American Negroes." Although abuse of power and dereliction of duty were usually cited as the reasons for impeachment, it was as much a political tool as a constitutional one. Official charges included specific infractions as well as the more implicit impugning of the impeached individual's character. For instance, Garvey's accusations against Gibson ranged from drunkenness, embezzlement, professional misrepresentation, and character assassination to, in general, "conduct unbecoming a gentleman."[57] Eason's alleged impeachable offenses included the misuse of organizational funds, the inappropriate sale of organizational memorabilia for personal gain, and dereliction of duty, but these were folded into the general charge of "conduct unbecoming an officer and disloyalty." Both Gibson and Eason were found guilty and expelled from the organization.[58]

The impeachment process, and the internecine feuding that triggered it, were not merely petty politics. Substantive issues such as ideological direction and organizational strategy lay behind the quarrels among the UNIA's leadership, as did personal animosity. As in the black Masonic tradition, the presence of a procedure for disciplining its members was evidence of the organizational autonomy and the institutions of self-government that were deemed necessary for the survival of the nationalist movement. Given their lack of involvement in and protection by the American legislative and judicial processes, we should not underestimate the psychological importance that many Garveyites placed in the convention's capacity to make rules and adjudicate disputes in a parliamentary manner. The investment in self-determination that characterized the impeachment process foreshadowed, for many Garveyites, the role that a black-male-led government would play once the UNIA founded its black nation. Equally important is the centrality of character in these impeachment proceedings. Along with concrete indictments ranging from embezzlement and insubordination to fraud and treason, indirect and direct assaults on one's character tended to accompany the charges and countercharges that characterized UNIA infighting.

The connections that Garveyites made between racial progress, a capitalist "vision," character, and manhood repeatedly surfaced in the discourse of UNIA intellectuals, who sought to instill the ideas of bourgeois manliness into African American and African Caribbean men through discussions of the organization's objectives. But Garveyites' commitment to Victorian gender conventions was more than rhetorical. UNIA leaders exhorted the rank and file—and blacks who had not yet signed on to its nationalist agenda—to live by the standards of bourgeois manliness. In doing so, they invoked the imperative of leading lives of respectability.

▨ Periodically, the pages of the *Negro World* contained a behavioral guide for Garveyites transparently titled "Instructions for Members of the Universal Negro Improvement Association." In addition to stressing that members be loyal and financially supportive, the circular urged the importance of being fiscally responsible. Several of the thirty directives also concerned other conduct considered by the UNIA to be appropriate, including regular attendance at meetings and prudent political participation (which included voting along the lines of the UNIA's endorsements and refusing to sell one's votes). Three of the charges were succinct, but rather trite, prescriptions for behavior: "Always respect authority and obey the law," "Be a good citizen," and "Behave decently, always and everywhere."[59] At first sight, these recommended actions seem contradictory to the nationalist rhetoric of Garveyism. How could those who argued that the only way that the race could advance was through the existence of a sovereign black nation simultaneously direct their fellow members to practice citizenship under what they perceived to be an indifferent, often oppressive, government? One answer lies in the importance Garveyites placed on respectability. In this sense, they encouraged their members to act properly within the confines of American legal and moral conventions while, at the same time, they advocated an eventual, though limited, repatriation to Africa.

The UNIA's emphasis on respectability in the prescriptive literature directed toward black men reflected more an affinity with bourgeois gender conventions than a working-class resistance to middle-class hegemony. To be sure, *respect* was important in constructions of working-class masculinity, particularly when it concerned one's skill and competence in the process of production. *Respectability*, as a sociohistorical concept, however, has structured the ways in which upper- and middle-class men and women have interacted with each other. Respectability has encompassed the values with which the bourgeoisie has distinguished itself from the working class and, as George Mosse argues in the European context, the traditional aristocracy.[60] Unlike Prince Hall Freemasons, and other mainstream middle-class blacks, who used respectability as a way of creating a collective class and gender identity based on exclusion, Garveyites' adherence to respectability was not the product of a desire to socially and politically integrate into the dominant society. It was in keeping with a bourgeois mentality—and therefore signaling their inability to transcend the hegemonic conventions of late-Victorian society—but one that would eventually flourish in Africa.

Despite the broad constituency of the UNIA in terms of class, Garveyites still used respectability as an important cornerstone of a collective identity. Although the migratory movements and urbanization of African Americans and African Caribbeans from roughly 1910 to 1930 contributed significantly to the power base of the organization, UNIA intellectuals and leaders criticized both as potentially hazardous obstacles to racial advancement. Whereas the old black elite and middle-class reformers viewed the influx of largely unskilled and semiskilled black workers and their families as a possible menace to their own political inclusion and integration into social institutions, UNIA commentators remarked on the threat it posed to the rejuvenation of the race.[61] William Ware, the president of Cincinnati's local, felt that the results of migration were anything but positive, especially given the crowded and unsanitary housing provided by industrial firms and the minimal efforts by municipal government to control the vice located in black sections. He attributed the immoral conditions in black neighborhoods to the over-concentration of workers. "I have dozens of cases on file where poor Negro laborers must pay $10 a month for one room," he declared, "which, were they able to see it who censure the Negro's impulse to live a better life, would explain much of the vice that exists in Negro districts." Along with dirty streets and foul air, black residents had to live with "blind tigers, gambling dens, [and] disreputable houses of all kinds," which "certainly do not tend to make for good citizenship." Ware was concerned about the impact of the urban environment on the lives of children, who, he argued, were "forced through circumstances to witness the vilest scenes and to hear indecent and shameful language every day in the year."[62]

Ware was not alone in his apprehension over the effects of city life on the children of the race. Carrie Mero Leadett, an occasional contributor to the *Negro World*, felt that negligent childrearing on the part of some urban parents prevented blacks from successfully competing with other races. "In a busy congested metropolis like New York, with its crowded streets and its over-crowded apartments," she wrote, "much of the real home atmosphere is lost and it is very hard to guide and direct the young life in the way we would wish it to go." Discussing a neighboring household, she lamented that "father went to the poolroom, mother went to the movies and baby played in the streets until 11 or 12 o'clock at night." Leadett was more concerned with the duty of refined motherhood and suggested that if black women read to their children more, consistently instilled ethics in their children, and generally presented themselves as paragons of respectability, the race would become stronger.[63] What is important here is that both Leadett and Ware criticized certain elements of urban conditions and working-class culture but, unlike mainstream reformers, they did so with an overarching nationalist objective. That is, their adherence to, and espousal of, respectability was geared toward building a physically and mentally superior black population.[64] Still, we should not overlook the irony in the fact that, by espousing respectability among the black, particularly urban, masses, the organization for the "common Negro" assaulted the cultural institutions and practices of the "common Negro."

In addition to criticizing the child rearing, homemaking, and leisure practices of segments of the black working class, Garveyites were censorious of African Americans and African Caribbeans—particularly black youth—who were absorbed in consumer culture. Thrift and conscientious consumption, along with a solid work ethic, were cornerstones of the respectability preached by the UNIA. In a decade of increasing prosperity for the nation's middle classes, Garveyite intellectuals evinced a concern that the growing black bourgeoisie was marching relentlessly into the den of materialism. Younger blacks, they argued, "think more of today than of tomorrow, more of the dance hall and a good time than of their own future or the possibility of the race." Speaking of the generation coming of age in the 1920s that was "absorbed in conventionalism and nothingness," one author lamented that "most of our New York young college men think at present only of sport and a good time, women!" Moral self-restraint and economic common sense were needed to combat the decadence of this "age of material advancement," another writer counseled. "The senses and their impulse must be held in check" for "the over-valued pleasures indulged in too often destroy the capacity for enjoyment." The writer offered a remedial suggestion: "The immediate speculations that look more timely than the real investments of the future must be shunned." Similarly, a regular contributor urged UNIA members to lead ascetic lifestyles by reducing the money they spent on food, fashion, and social activities. "While you are strong, healthy, and young," the author wrote, "you will be tempted to neglect [the need to save], forgetting that every day you are getting nearer and nearer to that point in life when you will not be able to earn as much as you earn now." The author combined this plea to individual conscience with a racial consciousness: "You owe it not only to yourself, but to the race, to begin saving."[65] Given the writers' nationalist dispositions, their critique of consumerism in mostly white markets was entirely consistent; but their criticism was also shaped by a commitment to respectability and production as markers of black manhood.

Garveyite critiques of consumerism were directed toward aspects of modern urban culture as well as the sexual revolution that characterized postwar American youth culture. Alcohol and jazz, in particular, were targets of Garveyite invective. The abuse of alcohol, in the midst of Prohibition, concerned UNIA intellectuals and commentators. One editorialist, who considered drinking to be "a suicidal habit of Harlemites," argued that part of the problem lay with the "un-Christian, law-breaking, mercenary white men" who imported the "vile hootch" into black neighborhoods. A less conspiratorially minded writer was not so much interested with the origins of alcohol importation; rather, his or her main concern was the successful enforcement of the Volstead Act. Praising the New York City police department's decision to close down the speakeasies that "honeycombed" Harlem, the writer spoke at once to both the resourcefulness of those committed to drinking and the dangers posed by alcohol: "Delicatessen shops, cigar shops, tailor shops, drug stores, even private apartments are manipulated for dispensing the poison that cannot cheer and does not fail to stupefy." The writer concluded that "the selling of this poisonous concoction is most damaging to the race." [66]

Garveyites ascribed to jazz the same properties and inherent dangers that they did to alcohol. The effects of jazz were psychological and potentially physiological. Citing the overstimulating nature of this modern form of music (embodied in its "quick and staccato tempo"), one article suggested that the various rhythms and melodies generated "sights and imaginations which overpower the will, and thus reason and reflection are lost, and the actions of the person are directed by the stronger animal passions." Ultimately, it affected its audience in the same way as a narcotic or a stimulant, leaving them in a drugged or intoxicated state. Black youth, in particular, were susceptible to the dangers of jazz. "To overcome the effect of jazz music," the article stated, "one has to have the knowledge of its harmful results, and the reflective and sobering impressions of life's experience." [67] Garveyite attitudes toward jazz, however, were not monolithic. One article, appearing in the Negro World six months later, proposed that a concert and jazz band contest be held in Chicago. The article celebrated the bands of the Fifteenth Regiment of the New York National Guard and Eighth Regiment of the Illinois National Guard—largely responsible for importing jazz into Europe during World War I—and the musical accomplishments of Lieutenant James Reese Europe, bandmaster of the New York Fifteenth. Furthermore, a Jamaican local sponsored the Universal Jazz Hounds. Given Garvey's disparaging comments toward jazz in the late 1930s, it is difficult to reconcile the various attitudes exhibited by Garveyites. [68] One possible explanation is that jazz was strongly condemned by UNIA intellectuals only in its urban, working-class nightlife context. In this sense, the wild spontaneity of the jazz quartet, amidst the drunken, lewdly dancing crowd in the corner speakeasy undermined the respectability needed for racial progress. When it was performed within the orderly confines of an all-black regiment, a national contest, or a fund-raising event, however, the unique form of music seemed to warrant less vitriol. Garveyites' assessment of jazz seemed to be conditioned by whether its mode of performance was respectable or indecent.

In addition to castigating blacks for participating in cultural practices that were, in their minds, associated with the materialism of the postwar era, Garveyites also denounced the relaxed sexual mores that accompanied the Jazz Age and the emergence of the "New Woman." UNIA intellectuals admonished young women against using makeup, smoking cigarettes, and going to dance halls. Young men and women who engaged in sexual relationships outside of marriage also became targets of UNIA rebukes, as did gay men and lesbians. In espousing very traditional models of sex, marriage, and the family, Garveyites participated in the same discourse around the connections between sexuality and racial rejuvenation that Anglo-American and European nationalists did. For them, as well as the UNIA, strong races and nations were predicated upon a normative heterosexuality and procreative sexual relations between mentally and physically healthy individuals.[69] Garveyites sought to police the sexual behavior of blacks, particularly of black youth, as well as their leisure and consumption practices.

In their public objections to jazz, alcohol, and, in general, more modern forms of commercialized urban leisure, UNIA intellectuals opposed the consumer ethos that was gaining ground in the 1920s. The work ethic still primarily figured into UNIA nostrums: men, in particular, were admonished to toil industriously, conscientiously save their resources, and avoid the dangerous traps of pool halls, speakeasies, gambling dens, and brothels. UNIA commentators advised men to engage in sexual relations although they encouraged such activities to occur in a marital context and be geared toward racial reproduction.[70] This is not to say that modern ideas of leisure, consumption, and sexuality did not enter into the Garveyite worldview. The consumer ethos of the 1920s was so pervasive that it would have been impossible for Garveyites to maintain a hermetically sealed Victorian worldview. Norton G. G. Thomas, an associate editor for the *Negro World*, for instance, took issue with the puritanical efforts of the Harlem clergy to include all forms of leisure in their crusade against alcohol and jazz. "I am at one with the ministers of the Gospel when they seek to make Harlem cease from its wickedness . . ." he wrote, "but to proscribe those Secret Order shows, balm to Harlem men folk's souls, Sunday basket ball [sic] and dancing, if the latter savor not of the early Victorian era, is a bit too thick for me." Other evidence that consumer culture was infiltrating the UNIA's otherwise ascetic nationalism included the Negro World's coverage of a football game between Lincoln University and Hampton Institute, played in New York on an unusually warm November day in 1929. "The game as a whole was quite interesting, and the spectators enjoyed it immensely," the article reported. "New York could e[a]sily stand another game before the season closes, say 'Howard vs. Lincoln.' You know when you get the New York boys started, it's just too bad; and since they were disappointed and could not strut their racoons and great grizzleys [sic], another game here would just set it right."[71] The newspaper's tongue-in-cheek reference to black men in fur coats—a common sight among the well-to-do and college students in the 1920s—suggests that the UNIA's initial hard-line stance on consumer culture softened as the decade came to a close.

Still, the emphasis on respectability did not lose importance for Garveyites. Indeed, if the sexual liberalism and consumer ethos of the 1920s signaled the entrance, in part, of American society into a postwar, modern era, then Garveyites, regardless of their age and gender, might be considered more antimodern than Victorian. Respectability and its inherent critique of excessive consumption and non-normative sexuality characterized Garveyite thought and prescriptions for behavior. As respectability also embraced, and generated, a criticism of working-class culture and behavior, the social performances expected of blacks, and particularly black men, reinforced not only the nationalist rhetoric of the UNIA but its bourgeois underpinnings as well.

Along with the discursive construction of manhood within rhetoric and prescriptive literature, Garveyites engaged in a performative gender identity formation. In a similar vein to Prince Hall Freemasonry, the UNIA attempted to construct an ideal black manliness through rituals of performance. These rituals occurred in both private space (as in meetings and court receptions) and public space (as in parades). Unlike Prince Hall, the UNIA did not exist as a secret society. Its nationalist and overtly political agenda required a more expansive membership—including women and children—which prevented it from maintaining the same exclusivity as the Masons.[72] In many ways, the goals of the Garvey movement merely necessitated a militant, racially conscious membership eager to pool its resources and police its sexuality. The UNIA's membership was determined more by a nationalist pragmatism than by an arcane idealism. Given the relative inclusiveness of the UNIA and the more populist character of its congregations, it is difficult to draw analogies between the gendered performances of male Garveyites and those of black Masons. Still, there are parallels between the UNIA and Prince Hall Freemasonry in that the performances of manliness—particularly in public rituals—revolved around the ideas of production and respectability.

The most visible representation of Garveyite manhood was the Universal African Legion. The paramilitary arm of the UNIA, the African Legion consisted of active male members between the ages of eighteen and fifty-five. It was structured hierarchically like a national army, with commissioned and noncommissioned officers, and enlisted men ranked according to work status and skill level. The purpose of the Legion was to "prepare men for service by teaching them military skill and discipline and registering them according to the various trades in which they have been trained." The ultimate objective of the auxiliary was the preparation of black men for the redemption of Africa. On a more practical level, the Legion provided protection for UNIA officials and visiting dignitaries.[73]

On the surface, and most readily identifiable to UNIA members and external observers, the Universal African Legion represented the militaristic spirit of the New Negro nationalist. An anonymous letter enclosed in a 1920 British military intelligence report inquired as to whether officials knew of military training being provided to "hundreds of foolish colored men." Signed by "a Negro who dislikes the British but who has sense enough to foresee disaster," the letter suggested that the UNIA planned to use the Black Star Line "to smuggle these men with arms into Africa and the West Indies." The letter was summarized by a British agent and therefore its authorship is inconclusive; however, the agent expressed similar concern, suggesting that "steps be taken to suppress this Universal African Legion . . . as it will surely lead to bloodshed." J. W. Jones, an informant for the FBI, likewise expressed concern after he infiltrated the Newport News, Virginia, chapter. "In order to be prepared for this movement in Liberia," Jones reported, "he [Garvey] is going to organize a military branch in this country." He notified his superiors that companies consisting of sixty-four men were being "formed on strictly U.S. Army basis" and that at least two hundred men drilled "every Thursday night at the Elk's Hall."[74]

Government paranoia was not necessarily unfounded. The Legion did indeed have a militaristic agenda, as fantastical as that agenda may have been. Members of the UNIA discussed the military potential of the Legion and encouraged those chapters that did not have auxiliaries to organize immediately. James N. Nesbitt, for instance, reminded Negro World readers of the potential of military organizing. He recalled the support of black involvement in World War I because "the Negroes would get a chance to get good training . . . for we really do need it." Furthermore, he implored veterans to "come out from under cover; come out in the light and train and teach each other." This was the prevailing sentiment among Garveyites. The African Legion attached to the Detroit local was "made up of men who had military knowledge, and, as a result of that, were able to train others."[75]

The UNIA's constitution provided the proper guidelines for the organization of the paramilitary auxiliaries. Each local Legion consisted of an officer corps that followed a chain of command from the commander-president down to second lieutenant. The commander of the UNIA Boy Scouts was also attached to the Legion as a second lieutenant. Prospective officers were "selected by the men of the Legions"; examined on, among other things, "Geography of Africa," "Languages," and "Signalling"; and were finally commissioned by the national office of the minister of legions. Previous military experience played an important role in who was commissioned. As one Philadelphia Garveyite remembered, he was "made a lieutenant" because he had served in the army.[76] Each local auxiliary also maintained a staff of noncommissioned officers, enlisted men, and departments such as a quartermaster corps and commissary. There was indeed a focus on soldiering in the African Legion. Despite the fact that Legionnaires rarely had arms, much less live ammunition, the parent body expected local divisions to train this paramilitary wing in self-defense, survival methods, and military maneuvers.

Discipline, duty to the race, and cooperation with one's fellow blacks were important cornerstones of the African Legion's philosophy. "No body of men without discipline and strict obedience of lawful orders can accomplish much," warned the authors of the Book of Laws. Legionnaires were also admonished to be courteous to one another and to uphold their commitment to the UNIA. Without loyalty and cooperation, the building of a black nation would be next to impossible. Furthermore, Legionnaires were expected to maintain unsullied characters by avoiding drunkenness, immorality, and dishonesty. Perhaps the Legion's oath best captured the Garveyite ideology of manhood and its links to duty and character. An inductee committed his "whole life" to the UNIA, swore never to disgrace himself or his uniform "by insubordination or contemptuous behavior," and promised to "defend the cause of the U.N.I.A. and A.C.L. from all enemies within and without" in the "cause of the Redemption of Africa."[77]

The Universal African Legion most likely provided different meanings of manhood to individual members. The martial trappings of the auxiliary probably appealed to both middle- and working-class Garveyites through its invocation of racial heroism and militant self-defense. This was reinforced by the pride that most African Americans and African Caribbeans held in the black soldiers returning from service in Europe. For those Garveyites who adhered more to bourgeois values, however, the Legion reinforced the links between sacrifice and duty while emphasizing the necessity of self-restraint and an ascetic lifestyle in shaping strong character. For rural southern Garveyites or recent migrants to urban industrial centers, the Legion may have tapped into a feeling of manhood that was predicated upon an importance and visibility in the community that was associated with the Legionnaire uniform. Although the Legion may have appealed to different class-based sensibilities, we cannot overlook the male bonding that occurred in this corporatist but hierarchical auxiliary—male bonding that was circumscribed by notions of character, discipline, and sacrifice.[78]

The Legion, however, represented more than martial constructions of manliness. Along with a focus on soldiering, there was an emphasis on labor, evident in the fact that no members received salaries unless they were already employed by the UNIA. Ranks were also structured by skill level. Below the commissioned and noncommissioned officers, Legionnaires were grouped into First Class Master Workmen, Second Class Skilled Workmen, and Third Class Unskilled Workmen. Furthermore, a main responsibility of the auxiliary was to ensure "that every man . . . be put to useful work at his trade or profession for the rehabilitation of the ancient glories of our Motherland Africa."[79] The Legion functioned not only as the UNIA's proto-national army; it operated as an educational institution as well. Individual chapters provided "instruction in the several trades and professions," doubtlessly hoping to enhance the collective racial economy and to instill producer values in African American and African Caribbean men. The Universal African Royal Engineer Corps—an ancillary branch of the Legion—of Detroit, for example, offered lessons in bricklaying, carpentry, mechanical and civil engineering, "electricity," and "radioing." The New York Royal Engineering Corps provided instruction in similar trades, in addition to blacksmithing, masonry, and "general mathematics."[80] Classes not only offered the opportunity for advancement within the Legion; they reinforced the Garveyite ideology that manhood was defined, largely, by the capacity for production.

Examining the idea of production, as it was embodied in the Legion, requires consideration of the likelihood that manhood held different meanings for black men, meanings that were informed by their different class positions. On the one hand, the Legion, as it was discussed in the constitution and by the Legion's leadership, represented middle-class ideas of work ethic. The majority of Legionnaires, through an exposure to the disciplined nature of the auxiliary and the introduction to practical skills, would develop producer values of industry, sobriety, punctuality, and thrift. This was in keeping with the entrepreneurial, self-made man ethos of the movement.[81]

On the other hand, for the thousands of industrial and service workers, rural sharecroppers, and unemployed black men forming the enlisted backbone of the African Legion, the connections between production and manhood represented far more than a commitment to bourgeois gender conventions. Rather, for them, the ideas of manhood being articulated may have been more in tune with the dominant values of working-class masculinity: independence from the industrial specialization and regimentation being introduced around the turn of the century; competence and pride in highly skilled positions in the labor process; and an ethos of mutuality (a rejection of "acquisitive individualism") directed toward one's fellow workers.[82] This is necessarily speculative because neither the UNIA's constitution nor journalistic descriptions of the work carried out by the Legion offer us a comprehensive view of how rank-and-file Garveyites constructed a sense of male identity. They do not consist of the actual voices of these men nor did the Legion approximate the typical "shop floor" experience of working-class blacks, most of who were relegated to the unskilled and semiskilled sectors of the wage-labor force. Given that the UNIA was generally anti-union and the Legion did not expressly organize men according to craft or the industry in which they were employed, it would be an exaggeration to suggest that the auxiliary functioned in the same manner as a trade union. However, in an era where very few black workers were admitted into traditional craft and emerging industrial unions, the Legion may have contributed to the construction of manhood in the lives of black men, as the unions did for the native-born and immigrant white working class.[83] As opposed to the mystical trappings of craftsmanship that Prince Hall Freemasons provided, the Legion's focus on practical labor provided working-class black men with an avenue for constructing their gender identities. These identities were predicated on the organization of men around the concept of work and skill level, the exclusion of women and boys, and the fostering of male camaraderie based on mutual advancement.[84]

For both entrepreneurial-minded Garveyites who adhered to bourgeois values and those industrial workers and agricultural laborers who formed the majority of the auxiliary, the African Legion was significant in shaping constructions of black manhood. Garveyites used the organizational structure and the educative potential of the Legion to instill industriousness, pride in skill, and a mutualistic ethos in working-class blacks, as well as to offer them useful skills for the labor market. Although this emphasis on work ethic may have been imbibed differently by Garveyites of different class backgrounds, it still solidified definitions of manhood within the paradigms of production and racial collectivity. In addition to the martial constructions of manhood that the Legion invoked, the emphasis on labor and skill level reinforced both middle-class notions of manly work ethic and working-class definitions of masculinity.

The Legion was particularly prominent in UNIA meetings, fund-raising events and other functions, and parades. The visible presence of Legionnaires must have attracted many African Americans and African Caribbeans to the Garvey movement in much the same way that public rituals of performance by Knights Templar attracted blacks to Prince Hall Freemasonry. One individual who was "converted" to the UNIA after witnessing the martial performance of the Legion was Thomas Harvey. A veteran of World War I, Harvey joined the UNIA's Philadelphia local in 1920 after hearing people talk of the organization's program of economic nationalism and African redemption. Even though he had become an "active" member, he did not become an enthusiastic supporter of the UNIA until he witnessed a meeting at which Garvey spoke. Harvey's reminiscence of the meeting, which was held at the Olympia Theater, highlighted the presence of the Legion. "The place was packed to the rafters," he recalled, "people all in uniforms, parading up and down like they were somebody. After a while, someone got up and shouted, 'Attention!' and everybody stood up and this little short man was striding in with all these men following with Garvey was Chief Justice James Dorsey [Dossen] from Liberia and a fellow who was then Commissioner for Pennsylvania." After hearing Garvey discourse on global disarmament, Harvey began attending meetings regularly and joined the Legion. Because of his previous military experience, he rose through the ranks, becoming vice president of the Philadelphia local in 1930 and president in 1933.[85]

Another UNIA event at which Legionnaires were prominent was the court reception, or the "At Home." The reception was held during the annual conventions in the month of August, in the "official residence" of the potentate or "at some place of high moral and social repute." Respectability dictated who was included on the guest list, with "those distinguished ladies and gentlemen of the race and their male and female children whose character, morally and socially, stands above question" being among the suggested attendees. Age figured prominently in who was invited, as did one's record of public behavior. Prohibited were females younger than eighteen and males younger than twenty-one. Anyone "whose morality is not up to the standard of social ethics" or anyone with a felonious criminal record was similarly barred, unless the felony had been "committed in the interests" of the UNIA. The primary purpose of these receptions was to recognize and celebrate the race work done by members of the UNIA. The receptions also provided an opportunity for members to view the disciplined auxiliaries of the organization in full regalia. In addition to the political atmosphere of the receptions, there was ample time given to social interaction. Reminiscent of the debutante balls of the traditional black elite, the UNIA presented "young ladies," guests dined and heard speeches and, after supper, attendees participated in a ball "with all the courtliness of training, natural gift for dancing and love of music."[86]

The Court Reception of the 1924 annual convention catered to five hundred guests, but according to a report in the *Negro World*, it attracted five thousand spectators. Held in Liberty Hall in New York, the reception was a mixture of baroque decor and nationalist iconography, a blending of the protocol of a European state dinner and the atmosphere of a Pan-African Conference. The furniture, greenery, lighting, and ornamentation evoked "some Oriental court in which the rulers of ancient days disported themselves on festive occasions" while in the center of the back wall, "a huge satin banner with a black cross superimposed on the red, black and green colors" signaled the more serious missions of nation building and African redemption. Indeed, there was a profound articulation of the nationalist imperative of the UNIA, present in the configuration of the auxiliaries before and during the reception. Prior to the arrival of guests, "the full force of the legions in uniform was lined up in formation, giving a military aspect to the occasion, while Black Cross nurses in their immaculately white uniforms, and the juvenile boys and girls all in uniform added to the impressiveness of the scene," the *Negro World* reported. "The band meanwhile discoursed sweet music to the great delight of the crowd which increased in numbers as the hour approached for commencing the ceremonies." The Legion formed two parallel lines through which the guests, including organization officials and visiting dignitaries, passed on their way to the dais. Depending upon the national background of each guest of honor, the band played either the "Star-Spangled Banner," "Rule Britannia," or the "African National Anthem." After choral performances and the presentation of the "Ladies of the Royal Court of Ethiopia," the event turned into a tribute to individuals' service to the race. The title "Duke of Nayassa" was conferred upon Guatemalan George C. Reneau for, in part, being a "Successful Business man." E. Elliot Rawlins, a New York doctor, was inducted as a "Knight Commander of the Nile," and Isabella Lawrence of Belize was made "Lady of the Distinguished Service Order of Ethiopia" for her "Faithful and Distinguished Service to the Negro Race." Others present were similarly inducted into knighthood or lady-hood while some received gold or silver Crosses of African Redemption. After dinner, there was dancing and toasting, with the evening ending around 3 A.M. In addition to imperial aspirations and, as historian Robert A. Hill insightfully terms, "a keen appreciation of the exigencies of statecraft," gender was heavily coded in these particular functions. The Legion reaffirmed for the guests the links between militarism and the masculinist politics of the UNIA in much the same way that it had for Thomas Harvey and undoubtedly many present at Philadelphia's Olympia Theater.[87]

Perhaps the most spectacular public ritual of the Garvey movement was the parade. Although local divisions had occasional parades or participated in municipally sponsored ones, the most elaborate ones were held in connection with the organization's annual convention in New York City.[88] The parades consisted of marching auxiliaries, bands, choirs, and organization officials riding in convertible automobiles. Press reports described a charged atmosphere along the "gayly bedecked" blocks of Lenox and Seventh Avenues between 125th and 145th Streets, the normal parade route. "All Harlem is on the thoroughfare, in festive mood," reported the *Negro World*. "Housewives cease from their daily round and sit at the window." The paper went on to describe numbers of spectators climbing onto "theatre, house portico and roof" in order to get a better view. The *New York Times* estimated that thirty-five hundred members participated in the parade to launch the 1924 convention, a parade led by "mounted police" as well as division marshals on horseback. Floats with such titles as "Pleading Africa's cause at the League of Nations" and "Ethiopia builds the flag of Africa" were also part of the parade. Black Cross nurses and "negro Boy and Girl Scouts" marched, as did African Legionnaires, who were "uniformed in black with red trimmings and much gold lace."[89]

Outside of Garvey and the leadership cadre, the Legionnaires were the most prominent participants in the parade. Either on horseback or foot, they displayed the military preparedness of the UNIA and its nation-building agenda. They also operated in a more functional way, regulating other marchers who carried banners expressing either solidarity with the nationalist movements in Ireland and India or protest against the conditions of blacks within the diaspora. Most banners signified the militancy of the New Negro, reading for instance: "Down with lynching," "Uncle Tom['] dead and buried," "Join the fight for freedom," and "Africa must be free."[90] As protectors of this political sentiment, the Legion represented the masculinist nationalism of the UNIA. Wilmer J. Roberson, a Legionnaire, articulated this role to his comrades during the 1924 convention. Explaining the necessity of the auxiliary, he rationalized that the UNIA "needed soldiers to wear the principles of this great organization, not only at heart, but as a garment also." Through "his uprightness, his determined expression, and his nobility," the Legionnaire's performance would alert observers to the respectability and militancy of the UNIA's nationalist program.[91]

Other UNIA members discussed the need for able-bodied men to participate in the nationalist agenda. Irene Gaskin, writing to the *Negro World* prior to the 1924 convention, exhorted male Garveyites to show loyalty to the cause of the UNIA, and to do so publicly in the presence of the organizational-cum-national flag. Explaining the flag's color, she wrote: "Red, for the blood, which must be spilled if needs [sic] be; black for our race, which will be purified a hundred per cent in the next age; green for the grass which besprinkles the land of our forefathers, Africa. Our flag, boys," she concluded, "means loyalty to our country and the protection of our women in our motherland, Africa." Her letter called for nationhood and its defense in a militant manner. Furthermore, she placed men at the forefront of the defense of nation and black womanhood. She did not refer directly to enlistment in the UNIA's paramilitary arm although she did discuss the flag in a military context, suggesting that men remove their hats and salute the "tricolor." Ida E. Ash, however, expressly connected the Legion with the flag and nation building. Ash implored men to protect the flag of the Black Star Line, reminding them that it "must never touch the ground, but must wave from the heights of Liberia, our native land, forever, as a symbol of the black man's capacity for self government." She continued, "So men, prepare by joining the Universal African Legion."[92] Roberson, Ash, and Gaskin's exhortations contributed to Garveyite constructions of manhood. Embodied in the Legion, black men, as responsible protectors, would ultimately be the foundation of the new black nation. The public performances reinforced this idea for Garveyites and alerted the broader community to the character, discipline and, if necessary, militarism, of the organization's men.

Describing one parade, Amy Jacques Garvey wrote, "The onlookers could not help but catch the spirit of the occasion; they clapped, waved flags and cheered themselves hoarse as thousands of coloured men, women, and children, smartly uniformed, with heads erect, stepped to the martial strain of good music. Here indeed were New Negroes on the march."[93] Although Jacques Garvey referred to the important representations of both men and women, her description points to the uses of public performances in the rehabilitation of the cultural images of black men. Popular culture throughout the late nineteenth and early twentieth centuries represented blacks as dull-witted, fun loving "darkies," unsuccessful imitators of genteel whites, and, by the release of D. W. Griffith's *The Birth of a Nation* in 1915, as sexually rapacious savages. These representations, moreover, were antithetical to those of white and, by definition, normative manhood: rational, industrious, civilized, and virtuous—in a word, manly.[94] Within this context of popular culture, particularly early film, Garveyites sought to project their own images. Indeed, the "smartly uniformed" African Legion, with its military re-galia and orderly marching, was the antithesis of the tattered clothing and Jim Crow dance step of the Plantation Follies. The UNIA donned European-style uniforms and attempted to refashion gender identities along European and Anglo-American lines of bourgeois respectability. The nationalist displays served notice that African American and African Caribbean men, primarily, were capable of mastering technology and their environment, being indus-trious, protecting women and children, and above all, governing themselves. By marching in uniforms and military formation, the African Legion turned popular images of black men on their head and, in the process, attempted to construct a black manhood tied to labor and "civilization." The Legion counter-appropriated the rituals of high imperialism, thereby disrupting the dominant cultural stereotypes of black men.[95]

The modes of self-representation within the Garvey movement were more complex than a mere aping of European nationalist and imperialist ritual. Historian Robert A. Hill argues that there was an aspect of parody involved in the public performances of Garveyites and, moreover, that this was a function of the African Caribbean constituency of the movement. "In the Caribbean," he writes, "all popular, public entertainments entail a strong element of mas-querade and burlesque of aristocratic and monarchical forms that hark back to the folk celebrations during slavery." He goes on to admit, however, that in addition to the travestying of European culture, Garveyite performance con-tained aspirations of "colonial middle-class . . . piety and respectability."[96] It was this emphasis on respectability—and, I would add, production—that dominated Garveyite rituals of performance. And it is this emphasis that illustrates the hegemonic power of white, middle-class culture and gender conventions in the lives of middle-class African American and African Carib-bean men who joined the UNIA. Of course, these performances were critical in allowing black men to lay claim to a bourgeois manliness, an identity that was denied them through economic marginalization, political and social in-equality, and either demonization or infantilization through popular cultural representations. But the very project of constituting themselves as bourgeois subjects, in many ways, demonstrated an inability to transcend the gender conventions of the dominant culture.[97]

■ As the prescriptive literature and public performances of Garveyites sug-gest, the UNIA's commitment to a respectable manliness turned on a re-lational process in which "unrespectable" working-class culture was posi-tioned as a negative referent in the construction of black manhood. Migrant laborers, unemployed city dwellers, bootleggers, and others employed in the underground economy, however, were not the only referential points for Garveyites. In constituting an individual and collective gender identity, male Garveyites positioned themselves against white men as well as black men who opposed the nationalist politics of the UNIA. In other words, race and ideology served as important categories through which Garveyites engaged in the process of gender identity formation.

In employing race, and particularly blackness, as a marker of manliness, Garveyites negotiated the discourses that underpinned hegemonic notions of white, bourgeois manhood. This negotiation involved subscribing to the core logic of these discourses while contesting the racially chauvinist and racist images that these logics depended upon and circulated. As such, the relational process of gender identity formation for Garveyites maneuvered delicately between the antithetical categories of "civilization" and "the primitive," mind and body, and the material and the spiritual.

In many ways, black men in the UNIA constructed their gender identities against a white manhood that they claimed was less "civilized." This was at a time when there was an increasing identification on the part of middle-class white males with "primitive" cultures, particularly those of American Indians and Africans. For instance, fraternal associations began to incorporate Indian iconography and imagined native cultural practices into their initiation rituals. Minstrelsy also became an increasingly present fixture in the theatrical performances of middle-class men's clubs. As historian Gail Bederman argues, by 1890, the "natural man," as opposed to the cultivated Victorian patriarch, gained much currency among middle-class whites. As middle-class white men, however, were beginning to construct their gender identities in more physical and emotional terms—terms that appropriated the perceived "natural-ness" of blacks and American Indians—those men involved in the Garvey movement were still very much framing manliness in terms of civilization and the intellectual. To be sure, reason and self-control were still important determinants in becoming a man by white, bourgeois standards although manhood was increasingly being linked to the body. For many Garveyite men, however, the assertion of manhood still depended heavily on the mind.[98]

The rhetoric of several of the leading UNIA intellectuals evinced ambivalence over balancing "civilized manliness" and "natural masculinity." On the one hand, Garveyites rejected the assumed "primitive-ness" of African American and African Caribbean cultures and de-emphasized the location of black manhood in the body. Garvey, for instance, repudiated the label of primitive when he spoke to a cheering Philadelphia crowd six months after he escaped an assassination attempt: "I am alive today and you are alive also; and because we are alive—not as savages—not as pagans—not as barbarians, but as civilized Christian men, we say what is good in this present age for other civilized Christian men is also good for us."[99] Garvey's elevation of civilization and Christianity over barbarism and paganism, however, did not neatly translate into the dismissal of black male physicality. In a speech two months later, he again stressed the civilized nature of blacks while simultaneously praising their "great physical and military prowess." In discussing the role of people of African descent in World War I, Garvey reminded the audience that "it does not take savage men, barbarians and pagans to win a war fighting against civilized men." He continued that "it takes civilized men to win a bloody conflict fighting against civilized men, and two million of us proved our higher civilization when we, by our prowess, won the war for the white man, when he was unable to win it for himself."[100] In positing that their civilized state contributed to black men's physical and military superiority, Garvey not only illustrated how "civilized manliness" and "natural masculinity" could be reconciled. His statements also exemplify, to borrow from Bederman, the "protean" nature of the "civilization" discourse itself.[101]

Additionally, when Garveyites invoked the doctrine of the self-made man, they played on the connections between capitalism and manliness but they did not merely replicate middle-class white constructs of manhood. Indeed, Garveyites criticized certain aspects of white manhood even as they positively identified with its core elements. The relationship between morality and industrial progress, for example, provided Garveyites an avenue to assert a superior manliness. In March 1924, Garvey delivered a critique of the "economically and scientifically . . . progressive" races by pointing to the destruction of World War I. "For the Anglo-Saxon to say that he is superior because he introduced submarines to destroy life," he intoned, "or the Teuton because he compounded liquid gas to outdo in the art of killing, and that the Negro is inferior because he is backward in that direction is to leave one's self open to the retort, 'Thou shalt not kill,' as being the divine law that sets the moral standard of the real man." Invoking love for one's fellow human, rather than the impulse to make war, as "our highest purpose," Garvey stressed that Africans and, by extension, people of African descent, were "unsurpassed" in this regard. Furthermore, he questioned the supremacy of Europeans by stating, that "from the white man's standard, he is far superior to the rest of us, but that kind of superiority is too inhuman and dangerous to be permanently helpful."[102]

Despite his invocation of the Sixth Commandment, Garvey's diatribe was not so much a sermon as it was an example of black messianism: the idea, developed during the nineteenth century, that black people were morally superior to whites and had a specific mission to spiritually redeem the world.[103] Black messianism, and the religious imagery that accompanied it, pervaded the rhetoric of Garveyism. What became crucial to UNIA intellectuals, however, was the negotiation between the "natural" moral superiority and religiosity of blacks and the assertion of a black manhood that was tied to the secular world of business, politics, and empire. As they balanced reason and physicality in their rhetorical constructions of manliness, Garveyites also balanced the sacred and the secular; that is, they claimed a spiritual superiority to white men while praising them for their material progress.[104]

If UNIA intellectuals stressed their Christian and civilized natures, however, they did so within a temporal context rather than an otherworldly one. They advocated a balance between religiosity and materialism in the lives and worldviews of blacks. The UNIA leadership rejected excessive spirituality, evident in Reverend J. D. Brooks's bifurcation of the religious "vision" that characterized African American culture and the capitalist "vision" that characterized the nationalist politics of Garveyism. Robert L. Poston, a Kentucky-born journalist who held various offices in the UNIA, urged members not to sacrifice material progress to spiritual complacency. "The great trouble with us as a race of people," the Negro World paraphrased one of his speeches, "is that we are too weak and too child-like. We need power in money and power in intellect, and then we need spiritual power." In Poston's thought, the former would lead to the latter: "Firmly plant yourselves in the earth, extract therefrom its wealth; provide for your families, study science and arts and in that way you are connecting yourselves with God." Poston's neo-Calvinist position on economic development and salvation reflected dominant Garveyite thought.[105] Some UNIA intellectuals used religion and religious imagery to reinforce the necessity of industrial progress. James Robert Lincoln Diggs, a sociologist and a Baptist minister, used messianic rhetoric to promote the Black Star Line. "We must have ships," he argued, "if the vision of a philosopher called to our service and appointed by Jehovah and his son, the Messiah, will lead us on to victory."[106] Clearly referring to Garvey when he used the term "philosopher," Diggs's statement represented the capitalist "vision" of the UNIA while cloaking it in religious rhetoric.

While Garvey consistently used religious references in his rhetoric, he did not do so at the expense of addressing the worldly needs of blacks. He often cast his social Darwinian arguments in theological language. God approved of human competition and respected men who controlled their surroundings and "exercis[ed] authority over the world." Apparently, the Almighty was an admirer of manly men. Garvey rejected blind faith as a tool of liberation. He disregarded the notion that African Americans and African Caribbeans could merely "live religion" in the modern industrial societies without going "food-less and shelterless." Invoking a completely material argument for racial progress, he implicitly pointed to the impotence of the mainstream black church as an economic and political institution. "Let John D. Rockefeller with all his billions try to live religion," Garvey speculated, "and in twenty-four hours he will be begging bread around New York."[107] Like Brooks's distinction between religion and economic endeavor, Garvey's statement evoked the model of the self-made man while positing excessive spirituality as the potential obstacle to that realization among black men.

In suggesting that an engagement in the marketplace was an avenue to achieving, and maintaining, manliness, Garvey and other UNIA intellectuals implicitly feminized religion or, more specifically, strict adherence to Christian doctrine. "I am not one of those Christians who believe that the Bible can solve all the problems of humanity," Garvey wrote. "The Bible is good in its place, but we are men."[108] It is significant that he used "humanity" rather than "mankind"; by framing the "problems of humanity" in gender-neutral language, his use of "men" becomes gender-specific. While Garvey did not specifically claim that adherence to the Bible was unmanly and therefore feminine, William Yancey Bell expressed concern that many people did make this equation. Bell, pastor of the Williams Institutional Colored Methodist Episcopal Church in New York City, supported Garveyism but was not a member of the UNIA. At a speech given before the UNIA in 1923, he addressed the role of Christianity in racial liberation. Arguing that it was the "fundamental need of the world" and the most powerful tool in unifying the race, Bell also reinforced the idea that Christianity was "socially militant" and manly. "You hear all too much about turning the other cheek . . . [a]nd so you say Christianity is the religion for women, and old women at that." He responded to this interpretation by pointing out that "Jesus is all the time trying to call out the best, the noblest and the manliest in men and society." Similar to the masculinization of Christ in social gospel doctrine between 1880 and 1920, Bell portrayed the Redeemer as worldly, manly, and militant. Blacks, in redeeming Africa and the diaspora, should use the weapons of the "ballot" and "economic force" rather than a pacifist mentality.[109] Bell distinguished particular forms of religious practice and did so in gendered terms. Pacifism was effeminate and would get blacks nowhere while the "militant" social consciousness of Jesus provided the moral framework for political and economic activism and was, therefore, manly.

The feminization of pacifist Christianity was not deployed solely in the theological musings of Garveyites; it was also a tactic used to discredit black clergy that opposed the UNIA. During the UNIA convention in 1920, several delegates reported on the progress of the movement in their particular regions. James Young of Pittsburgh, for instance, stated "that the preachers . . . are our biggest hold-back." Two years before his impeachment as surgeon general, Dr. Gibson, a delegate from Boston, reported that the "preachers were our biggest enemies . . . [b]ecause they are weak-kneed." Gibson's biggest criticism was that they charged exorbitant fees for the use of their churches as meeting places and then criticized the movement. Of course, not all ministers were tarred with such a broad brush. Several of the leading UNIA officials and supporters were ordained members of the clergy, including Bishop George Alexander McGuire of the nationalist-oriented African Orthodox Church, who was chaplain-general of the organization in the early 1920s.[110] Still, Garveyites charged ministers with being dependent upon others — mainly whites and politically mainstream blacks — and pawns of the organization's enemies. Although an ardent supporter of the church and a religious man himself, John E. Bruce leveled a harsh criticism against black clergy in July 1920, suggesting that they were obstacles to the program "to lift the Negro from a state of dependence to one of independence and manhood." Articulating opposition to the prevalence of white philanthropy as a tool for progress, Bruce included black preachers in his list of culprits. "It is too bad that so many Negro clergymen elect to pose as mendicants," he lamented. "No wonder that some of them have so little backbone." Bruce's critique sought to distinguish between Garveyites who adhered to self-help as the route to "independence and manhood" and other leaders who, relying upon aid from well-meaning whites, perpetuated their status of dependency and were, therefore, barriers to the realization of a collective racial manliness.[111]

Garveyites utilized the same gendered language when they maligned black secular oppositional leadership. "Old school" politicians, largely beneficiaries of Republican patronage, and prointegrationists were attacked most frequently in this vein. The "Old Negro," invariably represented as a male but not a man, was being swept away by the determination, vigor, and manliness of the "New Negro," Garveyites argued. A. H. Maloney characterized this "changing order" as the "entrance of our race upon its manhood state." Although Maloney never explicitly referred to the UNIA, his discussion of the new style of black leadership was a thinly veiled tribute to the organization. Maloney claimed that this new group of leaders enjoyed widespread support "from the masses," and only experienced "opposition . . . from the effete leadership."[112] His assessment of mainstream leaders who relied on political plums and philanthropy to maintain their positions not only cast them as dependents but also constructed the UNIA as the opposite—an organization of manly producers of wealth, ideas, and, eventually, nations and empires.

Perhaps the biggest critic of mainstream leaders and liberal reformers was Garvey himself. He attacked this group as a generic class, but he never hesitated to single out specific individuals for criticism. "I have come across so many weaklings who profess to be leaders," he wrote in *Philosophy and Opinions*, "and in the test I have found them but the slaves of a nobler class." Here, he disparaged them as being dependent, a condition antithetical to being manly. In another section, he directly questioned their manhood and even went so far as to equate them with animals. "Nearly everyone who essays to lead the race at this time does so by first establishing himself as the pet of some philanthropist of another race," he wrote. In the process, he "humiliate[s] his own manhood, and thereby win[s] the sympathy of the 'great benefactor', who will dictate to him what he should do in the leadership of the Negro race." [113] Garvey's rhetorical use of the terms "slave" and "pet" dehumanized black leaders while it simultaneously de-masculinized them. Of course, the foremost leader who relied on philanthropy, Booker T. Washington, was among the heroes in Garvey's pantheon. Although the UNIA began to criticize the philosophy of Washington—years after his death and largely in response to his political accommodationism, not his use of patronage— the criticism never approached the level of ferocity that was directed toward other leaders, particularly W. E. B. Du Bois and the NAACP.

The debate between the UNIA and the NAACP and, more specifically, Garvey and Du Bois, became particularly acrimonious in the early 1920s. Because of his political coming-of-age in a three-tiered color system in Jamaica, Garvey was hostile to what he perceived to be the color consciousness and "internal race prejudice" of Du Bois and other light-complected blacks. Du Bois, like other established African American leaders, viewed Garvey as an unsophisticated rabble-rouser who erroneously used the racial dynamics of a society like Jamaica to discredit progressive black leadership in the United States. The incendiary rhetoric of both merely contributed to the perpetuation of hostility.[114] Responding to an article in *Century* magazine in 1923, in which Du Bois referred to him as fat, black, and ugly, Garvey took Du Bois to task on several different levels. Calling him a "lazy, dependent mulatto," Garvey suggested that Du Bois hated his black ancestry and held an unnatural devotion to white culture. He criticized Du Bois's adherence to the potential of liberal education and coalition politics and argued that the civil rights leader "and those who think like him can see and regard honor conferred only by their white masters." This implicit denunciation of Du Bois as a slave, coupled with the direct use of the description "lackey," worked to map Du Bois (and the NAACP) and Garvey (and the UNIA) onto the dual positions of unmanly dependence and manly independence, respectively. Positioning his own Victorian-like struggle to become a self-made man against what he characterized to be the effete and aristocratic background of Du Bois, Garvey asked: "Now which of the two is poorer in character and in manhood? The older man, who had all these opportunities and still elects to be a parasite, living off the good will of another race, or the younger man, who had sufficient self-respect to make an effort to do for himself, even though in his effort he constructs a 'dirty brick building' from which he can send out his propaganda on race self-reliance and self-respect."[115] Of course, it was a rhetorical question. There was clearly no doubt in Garvey's mind that he, the younger man, was manlier and thus better fit for leadership.

Other individuals would make similar claims about the more manly nature of Garveyites in relation to integrationists and liberal reformers like Du Bois. Wheeler Sheppard, "a Voluntary Field Speaker of the UNIA," for instance, published a treatise in 1921 in which he attacked the liberal educational philosophies of Du Bois. Sheppard's critique of Du Bois degenerated into an ad hominem attack, at one point lambasting him as "an intellectual deformity and a moral leper; a mere shadow occupying a man's place; yes, an erratic pest better off dead and buried." Sheppard's hyperbolic criticism of the "groveling and non-productive doctrines" of Du Bois relied on a gendered idiom: Du Bois and like-minded people lacked reason, morality, productive capacity and, as a result, were merely shells of men. In contrast, Garvey, in the eyes of Sheppard, was "a self-reliable adventurer seeking new worlds to conquer."[116] By placing themselves against advocates for integration and liberal education, UNIA intellectuals grabbed the torch of "true" manhood for themselves.

Garveyites operated in a relational process of gender identity formation that relied on positing liberal reformers, anti-nationalists, mainstream clergy, and white men as the opposite of manly men. These juxtapositions worked themselves out more in the rhetoric of Garveyites than in anything else. Still, African Caribbean and African American men who read the periodic screeds in the *Negro World* that castigated mainstream blacks for not having manhood or who heard the bellicose jeremiads in Liberty Halls that questioned the "civilized manliness" of the white bourgeoisie certainly must have identified with the intent of the authors and speakers. That is, they probably understood it as propaganda geared toward increasing the membership rolls of the UNIA; but they probably also bought into the idea that their manhood was indeed superior to that of black liberals and the white middle class. In other words, their own gender identity may very well have been shored up when the gender identity of mainstream black men and white men was disparaged.

▨ In June 1923, Garvey gave his last speech before being incarcerated to await trial for mail fraud. In the speech, he reaffirmed the idea that the UNIA provided deliverance from the dependence that characterized blacks' historical relationship to dominant Western societies. "Men, we want you to understand that this is the age of men, not of p[y]gmies, not of serfs and peons and dogs, but men," he reminded the audience, "and we who make up the membership" of the UNIA "reflect the new manhood of the Negro."[117] Much of the Garveyite rhetoric employed during the 1920s used masculinist language to discuss the UNIA's agenda, including its ideas of leadership, its program of capitalist development, and its philosophy of African redemption. This gendered rhetoric was part of a discursive practice geared toward constructing definitions of black manhood. In part, UNIA intellectuals drew on the same discourses of manhood prevalent among the white bourgeoisie between 1880 and 1920. In the process, however, they reshaped the meanings of early-twentieth-century manliness so that they had greater relevance for their own lived experience.

Like Prince Hall Freemasons, Garveyites constructed manliness within the idiom of production. John E. Bruce, discussing the promise of organization among blacks, directly invoked the producer idiom: "We are a race of consumers. We can be if we will a race of producers, but in order to attain to this position in the social progression we must organize!" Although he did not set up a rigid dualism of production/consumption as a gendered opposition, Bruce clearly suggested that production was a masculine endeavor. He offered character sketches of four different types of black men in modern society, one of which was "the earnest loyal manly Black who realizes the fact it is to families, nations, races to whom Almighty God gives missions." It was this "manly Black" who realized "that the Black race has a mission no other race can perform for it—that its mission is the concentration of energy along lines which make for progress and development."[118] Bruce's analysis did not directly mention the UNIA, and his invocation of organization, cooperative economics, and discipline could have referred to the Freemasons. However, Bruce's allusions to a messianic mission predicated on the development of the black race and, by extension, the black nation, spoke directly to the Garveyite agenda.

Unlike black Masonic conceptions, then, Garveyite notions of producerist manhood were embodied in the development of nation and empire. Still, there were core commonalties between the constructions of manliness articulated by Masons and Garveyites. Both rooted the achievement and maintenance of manhood within the public sphere of the marketplace. Moreover, respectability figured prominently in the gender identity formation of men in Prince Hall and the UNIA. That there were differences is perhaps overshadowed by the fact that both Freemasons and Garveyites adhered to the underlying core values of bourgeois manliness as constructed, and lived, by the white middle class.

3

Our Noble Women and
the Coming Generations

Through the rhetoric and prescriptive literature of their respective organizations, and the rituals of performance in their daily lives, African American and African Caribbean men who belonged to Prince Hall Freemasonry and the UNIA (Universal Negro Improvement Association) constructed a gendered sense of self that was shaped by race, ethnicity, class, status, and political ideology. At its root, their individual and collective gendered identity, as a "configuration of practice," drew upon conceptions of production, patriarchy, and respectability.[1] In the case of Prince Hall Freemasons, these conceptions were class- and status-bound. Those blacks who did not conform to bourgeois values and a middle-class work ethic (unemployed and uneducated men, recent migrants, industrial laborers, backwoods southerners) were incapable of achieving, let alone maintaining, the state of manhood. In the case of Garveyites, production, patriarchy, and respectability were structured more by political ideology. Blacks who did not agree with or, indeed, challenged the nationalist imperatives of the UNIA were, as it was often put, "mere shells of men." In both, however, black men used other black men against which to position themselves as authentically manly.

While Prince Hall Freemasons and male Garveyites constructed themselves as manly men in relation to those men they considered less than manly, they also formed their gender identity in opposition to other social groups—namely black women and black youth. Manliness, as these men articulated it, was organized around the categories of gender and age as much as it was organized around the categories of race, ethnicity, class, and ideology. The presence of women and, primarily, boys in the lives of these men, both as passive objects in the discursive realm and as active agents in larger, concrete social formations, reveals the relational nature of the process of gender identity formation.

It is also the presence of these groups, particularly women, that exposes the complexity and inconsistency in the constructions of manhood formed and experienced by these men. Production and patriarchy constituted the core elements of a black, middle-class male identity for these men even as they regularly witnessed black women working in the wage-labor force, engaging in racial uplift work in the public sphere, and resolutely pressing for the protection of their own and the race's civil rights. Similarly, respectability formed as vital a part of the racial and gender identity of black middle-class women as it did of men.[2] Production, respectability, and empowerment vis-à-vis one's family and larger community, then, were not the aspirations solely of black men. They were, however, still crucial in the ways in which men thought about, and performed, their gendered subjectivity.

Black women and black youth operated within the gender identity formation of black middle-class men in primarily two ways. In the discursive sense, Prince Hall Freemasons and male Garveyites utilized black women and boys as negative referents in the rhetoric, organizational framework, and rituals of their respective movements. Through their relationships with the women's auxiliaries of local lodges, the national independent Order of the Eastern Star, and various youth departments within the fraternal organization, black Masons articulated a gender identity that was grounded in notions of providing for, and protecting, black families, black communities, and the race in general. Moreover, manliness was something that was to be achieved and asserted in the public spheres of commercial and community development. Male Garveyites constructed a similar gender identity in relation to the female leadership of the UNIA, auxiliaries such as the Black Cross Nurses, and the juvenile regiments of the organization. The nexus between manliness and the public sphere obtained more in the UNIA than in Prince Hall Freemasonry, however, given the latter's nature as a secret society and the former's commitment to the trinity of capital, nation, and empire. Middle-class ideals of domesticity and the public-private organization of gender roles played an important part in the *conceptions* of manliness for men in these movements. Equally important for these men was the distinction between manhood and boyhood. By allowing them to distinguish between the "preexisting social categories" of men, women, and boys, biological difference and the life cycle were crucial in these men's self-definition as gendered subjects.[3]

Women also participated in the gender identity formation of men within the Masonic and Garvey movements in more active ways. As Prince Hall Freemasons and male Garveyites discursively deployed the image of domestic femininity against which to construct an individual and collective gender identity that was rooted in ideas of production and patriarchy (and nation building and empire in the case of Garveyites), women within and around the movements asserted their own roles as political activists, community leaders, and institution-builders. To be sure, many women asserted their presence within the confines of hegemonic gender conventions, which dictated the public-private dichotomy of men's versus women's roles. Many, however, challenged those same masculinist assumptions that relegated black women to the subordinate status of helpmate in a gendered framework of racial progress.

Black men's responses to these challenges varied. Some men used the women's arguments that they were equally suited for leadership positions— and their actions to that effect—as an opportunity to motivate themselves, and others, to be more active members of their respective movements. Others, particularly within Prince Hall Freemasonry, responded to women's assertions of organizational autonomy by attempting to quash whatever independent actions they undertook. Finally, some men recognized women's authority even as they sought to contain that authority within a traditional women's sphere that was still ancillary to the "real" work of men. The ways that men handled the assaults on the legitimacy and effectiveness of their leadership—whether leading to acrimonious relationships with women or not—reveal an important aspect of their attempts to construct a gender identity in accordance with a black bourgeois subjectivity. This chapter, then, is concerned with how black Masons and male Garveyites positioned themselves as "manly" men against black women and black boys and how women, either through affirming or challenging their patriarchal posture, contributed to the gender identity formation of these men.

In his 1924 treatise on black leadership, Trinidadian-born psychology professor A. H. Maloney mapped out the importance of women to racial progress. "No race, no nation can rise higher than the honor and the dignity and the majesty of the womanhood of that race or nation," he wrote. "Let us keep our womanhood pure; let us respect the womanhood of our race and we shall be secure when we begin to build up empires and establish ourselves as a great and mighty people."[4] Although tinged with the imperial aspirations of Garveyism, Maloney's assessment of the place of women within racial progress was not unlike the assessments made by black women in the early twentieth century. Since at least the 1890s, black women reformers, intellectuals, and activists such as Anna Julia Cooper, Mary Church Terrell, and other members of the National Association of Colored Women (NACW), articulated a similar position. Black clubwomen attempted to introduce domestic efficiency, temperance, and middle-class standards of morality into the lives of working-class and poor blacks; pressured municipal and state governments to provide better social services and cleaner environments in black communities; created educational institutions and support networks for the elderly and disadvantaged youth; and engaged in political struggles around suffrage and lynching. The idea "that a nation can rise in the scale no higher than its womanhood," informed much of this reform and political activism. Whereas the correlation between the status of women and racial advancement was interpreted by black men to strengthen their assumptions that they were responsible for the protection of "their" women, it was used by black women to support their claim that they themselves were the best-equipped to lead the race into the twentieth century.[5] These divergent internalizations — generated by the larger social structures of racism in which very few black men or black women had sufficient opportunities and resources to realize their fullest potential — characterized much of the interaction between men and women within the Garvey and the Masonic movements.

Prince Hall Freemasons interacted with women in a number of different capacities. On the local level, lodges tended to have attached to them women's auxiliaries that included the members' wives. Black women also traveled in fraternal circles through their involvement with the national organization, the Order of the Eastern Star (OES). Ladies' auxiliaries did primarily private work that was associated with the private and public function of the lodge to which they were attached. The OES, a sororal and fraternal association whose membership was restricted to Freemasons and their female relatives, took on more public responsibilities, although its members, like Prince Hall Freemasons, were ambivalent regarding overt political activism.

Ladies' auxiliaries provided support for Masonic lodges through their fund-raising activities, hosting of various entertainments, and more "domestic" tasks. The Plumb and Level Club was the ladies' auxiliary that was attached to Carthaginian Lodge No. 47. It was established in September 1922, seventeen years after the lodge received its official charter. Membership in the auxiliary was limited to the "female relatives" of the Masons. Founded by Mary Helps and Minerva Williams, the club most likely evolved out of the semiannual "Ladies' Nights" that were held at Carthaginian. On these occasions, the lodge was opened "for the enjoyment of the families of members and friends." Ladies' Nights were purely social affairs where, according to a lodge program, "the Cream of Society vied with one another to make our entertainments joyful and long to be remembered."[6] The Plumb and Level Club, however, was organized as a network of the wives and daughters of Carthaginian members; meeting on a monthly basis enabled them to more effectively pool their resources and talents to assist the lodge in a variety of ways. Fund-raising was one of the main responsibilities of the auxiliary.

Women paid dues, sponsored vaudeville performances and dances, and organized fairs. Monies raised through these means were put to various uses, including increasing the amount of the lodge's Charity Fund and purchasing ornaments for the local Masonic temple.[7]

Ladies' auxiliaries also fulfilled particular responsibilities at meetings of the Grand Lodges. Women of local auxiliaries entertained the female relatives of Masons who traveled to the Grand Lodge conventions. These entertainments included receptions and day trips through the specific city and its surroundings. The Diamond Jubilee of the Most Worshipful Grand Lodge of the State of New York in 1920 included a "Ladies Session." There are no records of what transpired at this afternoon meeting but one might suppose that the session was included within the official program in order to give Masons' wives and daughters throughout the state an opportunity to communicate to each other the various activities they were conducting and possibly coordinate these activities on an interauxiliary level.[8]

In addition to this public capacity, ladies' auxiliaries performed more private tasks. In this sense, a specific sexual division of labor characterized the ladies' auxiliaries' relationship to the Masonic lodges. Members of the Plumb and Level Club, for instance, performed tasks such as making banners, sewing the aprons and other elements of Masonic "costumes," and cooking and serving meals at "special occasions on Lodge nights."[9] For African Americans and African Caribbeans who continued to find it difficult to realize the public-private organization of gender roles that should have accompanied their claims of being middle-class, the work engaged in by ladies' auxiliaries allowed these men, and probably many of the women, to maintain that they did, indeed, represent the social and economic "cream of society." Masons encouraged one another to support the efforts of the auxiliary in its public and private work. The women "are doing a work of help and uplift for the craft primarily," one Mason reminded his brethren at a meeting, "and it should be our duty and pleasure to render of [sic] support and appreciation."[10]

While most, if not all, of the work carried out by the ladies' auxiliaries was directed toward maintaining the smooth functioning of their particular lodges, the OES existed as an adjunct to Prince Hall Freemasonry but operated independently of it. Founded in the mid-nineteenth century, the OES emerged out of the confluence of several interrelated trends in thought concerning Masonry, women, and reform. Even though anti-Masonry, as a coherent movement, had ceased to be a major political force or a threat to the Freemason tradition by the 1830s, Masons continued to be the target of suspicion of many Americans. One reason was its continued secrecy as an institution. Another was the repeated claim by Masons that the Craft instilled men with virtue, thereby obviating the need for them to obtain morality through the home and the church. From the viewpoint of women and evangelical clergymen, this last claim usurped their moral authority vis-à-vis middle-class men. In response, they attacked Masonry as an exclusive, secular association of men more concerned with the sociable qualities of alcohol than the moral security of the home, community, and church. Masons answered these charges by arguing that they were as concerned with temperance as ministers and women reformers. They also reminded their critics that religious themes were incorporated into their secular rituals and that moral instruction was integral to the functioning of the lodge. Since Masonry had moved from the tavern to the lodge, they argued, the movement posed no threat to the family or the moral precepts of society. Indeed, the charity work and mutual assistance engaged in by Masons reflected a commitment to the family as the foundation of a healthy, prosperous, and virtuous nation. Finally, they attempted to assuage the concerns over the exclusion of women by suggesting that, as inherently moral beings, women were not in need of the spiritual and ethical instruction that Masonry provided to men.

Masons also responded to the resurrection of anti-Masonic feelings by re-affirming the separate sphere ideology of Victorian America. They pointed out that the lodge was no place for the delicate and virtuous constitutions of elite and middle-class women. The lodge, and its gendered exclusivity, was necessary to instill morality in men who were daily immersed in the corrupting public world of business and politics. The lodge, then, was not the competitor of the home, but its ally. These arguments, however, were not completely convincing to women who countered that, without their presence, lodges ran the risk of reinforcing men's basest qualities rather than reforming them. In order to combat this continued suspicion, Masons began including women into the periphery of the fraternity, largely through introducing women's columns in their monthlies, creating ladies' auxiliaries, and opening up the lodge to women for specific events such as lectures. By the early 1850s, however, Robert Morris went further by creating honorary degrees of the Eastern Star for female relatives of Masons.[11]

Although there is no strong evidence that black women held these same attitudes, or mounted similar criticisms, toward Prince Hall Freemasonry, the desire for inclusion into the Masonic universe must have been present. For, in 1874, Thornton A. Jackson, a black Mason in Washington, D.C., received "several degrees" of the Eastern Star from a deputy of Robert Macoy, who was the publisher of Morris's Eastern Star rituals, a prominent Masonic ritualist, and, according to Jackson, "the Supreme Patron of the Rite of Adoption of the World."[12] In addition to the degrees, Jackson received "a letter of authority empowering me to establish this Order among our people" thereby allowing him to state unequivocally that the origins of black chapters of the OES were "pure and undisputed." By 1876, he had established nine chapters in Virginia, Maryland, Washington, and Pennsylvania. After being organized, these chapters were "adopted by some regular constituted Masonic lodge, thereby more closely uniting our Masonic family."[13]

In 1880, the first black Grand Chapter of the OES was founded in Washington, D.C., by the prominent African Methodist Episcopal bishop J. W. Hood.[14] The creation of Grand Chapters and subordinate chapters proceeded apace over the next quarter century. In 1907, delegates of Grand Chapters met in Boston, at the initiative of Letitia L. Foy, in order to strengthen the OES by establishing ties of cooperation and standardizing the ritual work. Another rationale for the development of this Supreme Grand Chapter, according to one historian of the OES, was "to encourage the organization of Chapters, that they might cooperate in the great labors of Masonry, by assisting in and in some respects directing the charities and other work in the cause of human progress." In 1910, the Supreme Grand Chapter changed its name to the Interstate Conference of Grand Chapters and its constituencies agreed to meet regularly on a biannual basis.[15] Like Prince Hall Freemasonry, the OES grew at a tremendous rate during the first twenty-five years of the century. By the ninth biannual meeting of the Inter-state Conference, held in 1924, Sue M. Wilson Brown, the grand matron, was able to boast that the OES had thirty-five Grand Chapters, thirty-five hundred subordinate chapters, and over one hundred thousand members. The OES also claimed adherents in Canada and Liberia as well.[16]

The OES emerged during this period as a prominent social institution with the financial resources and personnel to match its claim that it was participating in the "great labors" of Freemasonry. Brown, for instance, pointed out to the attendees of the 1924 conference that its combined treasury was roughly $500,000. She also reminded them of the many subordinate chapters that owned property, ran printing presses, supported homes for the elderly and orphanages, and assisted lodges in the maintenance of Masonic temples. Like their fraternal counterparts, members of the OES also provided money to chapters' Burial Funds and Endowment Departments from which the families of deceased members could withdraw. In terms of the human resources of the organization, the OES's membership lists included many women who were involved in the black women's club movement, including the sixth president of the NACW, Mary Talbert. In addition, Mrs. C. D. B. King, the first lady of Liberia, was the "Royal Matron" of Liberia's Grand Chapter.[17] The financial and human capital of the OES allowed the organization to become more than a sororal and fraternal association or a mutual aid society; it also became a venue through which black women and men sought to affect social change.

Unlike Prince Hall Freemasonry, the OES was not gender-exclusive; both women and men belonged to subordinate and grand chapters. By the 1920s, the coexistence of men and women within the organizational framework and governing structure of the OES would lead to intense conflict between it and Masonic Grand Lodges in some jurisdictions. Initially, however, the presence of both sexes was considered desirable and, indeed, indispensable to the functioning of the OES. Membership in both the subordinate and grand chapters was restricted to men who attained the level of Master Mason and their female relatives. Only those who had reached the majority age of eighteen were considered eligible for admission. The application process of the OES was similar to that of the Masons, with one exception. Interested applicants submitted a petition for membership, as opposed to having to wait for nomination by an existing member. After submitting a petition, prospective initiates still had to endure the rigorous selection process by having their application evaluated by an investigatory committee. Even master masons who were "in good standing" in a particular lodge had to revisit the background checks that marked their initial effort to join Freemasonry.[18]

Although the leadership and rank and file consisted of both men and women, the OES was clearly geared toward providing social networks for women. In the words of New York's grand master Edward Eato at the turn of the century, "the need of a systematic organization, where female members of our relative families can find a sphere [for] usefulness, where its permanency can be established and where, to a certain degree, the symbolisms and ritual of the fraternity can enhance the knowledge in the minds of its advocates, are some of the reasons given for the establishment of the adopted rite or Order of the Eastern Star."[19] The sororal meaning of the organization was reflected in the symbolism of the Eastern Star itself. The five points of the star represented female biblical figures. According to one of the historians of Prince Hall Freemasonry, the five women symbolized a purported female attribute: "Jephtha's daughter represents the force of a vow; Ruth represents devotion, Esther represents fidelity, Martha represents faith, Electa represents patience."[20] They also, however, exemplified women at different stages in the life cycle — as daughter, wife, widow, sister, and mother. Significantly, the symbolism of OES doctrine and ritualism reduced the identity of woman to her relationship to men and the family.[21]

The ways in which black women were motivated by the prospects of joining the OES, or understood their participation within the organization — an organization that represented women's activism as an adjunct to the "real" work of men—were complex and most likely varied. For many women, the acceptance of this confining system of "controlling images" reflected a particular class position.[22] Even as black women who joined the OES had access to women's associations that operated completely independent of male control or involvement, there was a particular desirability about belonging to an organization in which they were identified largely in terms of their relationship to an industrious, sober, and dependable man and a family that was arranged, ideally at least, around the bourgeois principle of separate spheres. Laying claim to domesticity reinforced these women and men's assertions of their middle-class status. It also reaffirmed their arguments that they were social and economic citizens whose civil rights and social opportunities must be guaranteed precisely because of their class status.[23]

Other women, particularly younger ones and daughters of Masons, may have understood the auxiliary symbolism as nothing more than archaic rhetoric that had no bearing on their participation within the private and civic affairs of Masons and the black community at large. In fact, their involvement in the OES may have conformed to what historian Ula Taylor describes as "community feminism." Discussing black female activism in the early twentieth century and the way in which black women activists were cast as helpmates, Taylor writes that community feminists are women whose "activism is focused on assisting *both* the men and women in their lives . . . along with initiating and participating in activities to 'uplift' the community. Despite this 'helpmate' focus," she continues, "community feminists are undeniably *feminists* in that their activism discerns the configuration of oppressive power relations, shatters masculinist claims of women as intellectually inferior, and seeks to empower women by expanding their roles and options."[24] This characterization applies to women who joined the OES; but it is also important to recognize the social currency that came with being able to identify, and represent, oneself as a member of a bourgeois family that was organized around a nuclear household, separate spheres, and, for some, even patriarchy.

Acceptance of being cast as helpmates in the "great labors" of Masonry reflected the longing to achieve and maintain respectability more than it did an acquiescence to patriarchal authority. This is evident in the way that the OES's governing structure was organized. The order's leadership consisted of elected and appointed officers. Elected offices within grand and subordinate chapters were reserved for both men and women, ensuring a gender-balanced leadership. Yet power within the OES was vested primarily in the position of grand matron. She was, in a sense, the chief executive and judicial officer of the order. Matrons had the power to appoint officers and committee members, grant dispensations and charters to new chapters, adjudicate on all legal matters, and suspend chapters' warrants and individuals. Matrons also held the power to "arrest the jewel," which meant temporarily removing elected and appointed officers for "violating the oath of office, openly and grossly neglecting the duties thereof, failing to show proper respect to the authority of the Grand Matron or Grand Patron, [and] speaking disparagingly of the Order." Suspensions of this sort, in addition to revocations of chapter warrants, were subject to review at the annual meetings of the grand chapters.[25]

Within this framework of governance, men occupied an accessorial position. Grand patrons and associate grand patrons held leadership positions for primarily two purposes. One was strictly supplemental in that they were expected to "assist and advise" the grand matron and to act in her stead when she was unable to. Actions by patrons, however, were to be undertaken in consultation with the matrons. The other function they fulfilled was to provide an official Masonic presence within the OES. According to the United Grand Chapter of Missouri, the grand patron "shall keep [the chapter] well informed on custom, usage and procedure as used in Masonic Institutions. He shall aid the Grand Matron in adapting such customs, usage and procedure to the administration of the affairs of the Order of Eastern Star of this Jurisdiction as shall be beneficial and becoming to the Order as the Adoptive Rite of Masonry." The grand patron also acted as the official liaison between the grand bodies of the OES and Prince Hall.[26]

Significantly, the gendered division of authority was different in the OES's early years. From the 1850s to the mid-1870s, grand matrons functioned as assistants to grand patrons in white OES chapters. It was not until there were "demands throughout the nation" in the 1870s that, despite resistance by Robert Morris and Robert Macoy, the governing structure was reversed in favor of the female members.[27] Whether or not black OES members participated in this national call for the elevation of women within the hierarchy is not clear. As discussed earlier, it was primarily men who established subordinate and grand chapters until at least 1880. Nonetheless, it was a woman, Letitia L. Foy, who convened the first national gathering of black OES chapters, suggesting that at some point between 1880 and 1907, women asserted their power within the leadership ranks of the order. By the 1920s, women were clearly ensconced in the administrative hierarchy—a reality that ultimately led to conflict between the OES and Prince Hall Freemasonry. Black women's involvement in the leadership ensured that they would influence the direction of the OES in its institutional workings and its public activism. In this sense, female members of the Eastern Star enjoyed more power and independence than women in the UNIA.

Women were an important part of the UNIA from its inception—in its organizational structure as well as in the work that the association conducted. In its earliest days in Jamaica, the organization incorporated into its agenda work similar to that being done by the black women's club movement in the United States. One of the early objectives of the UNIA, as listed in the Kingston *Gleaner*, was "to rescue the fallen women of the island from the pit of infamy and vice." A purpose of the industrial school being advocated by Garveyites in 1915 was the "training [of] our young women to be good and efficient domestics."[28] Much of this discourse surrounding women and girls of the race was generated by the nationalist ideology that held that the health and progress of the race, and ultimately of the black nation, rested on efficient, virtuous mothers and stable homes. For instance, at an early UNIA meeting in St. Ann's Bay, Jamaica, Marcus Garvey provided a simplistic and forthright strategy for racial progress: "If we want to rear a country of good and healthy men we must care [for] our women." Black women, he continued, are "the mothers of the nation and if they are weak and puny we cannot but produce a generation of weaklings." At the same meeting, Amy Ashwood, the UNIA's cofounder, secretary of the Ladies' Division, and Garvey's future first wife, reminded the women present that it was upon them that "the making of our men" depended. Jamaica needed "good women, women whose influence in the home can be influence felt for good, that influence that will inspire our men to do good and noble things."[29] The mixed-sex composition of the organization was influenced by the nationalist imperatives of instilling in African Caribbeans, and later African Americans, the necessity of healthy home environments and, by the early 1920s, racially pure ones as well.[30]

This sentiment persisted throughout the heyday of the UNIA and manifested itself in the prescriptive literature of the *Negro World*, the work of the association's various auxiliaries, and the UNIA's organizational structure. As early as two months after its founding in August 1914, the association had a Ladies' Division with a president, vice president, and associate secretary. Women were also a part of the overall leadership of the UNIA although not in any executive capacity until 1919. Amy Ashwood was the associate secretary for early 1915. Several women, including Ashwood and Marcus Garvey's sister, Indiana Garvey Peart, were among the UNIA's Board of Management in 1915 and its Board of Directors in 1918. In 1919, Julia E. Rumford was the organization's acting secretary-general and in that same year, Henrietta Vinton Davis was appointed international organizer.[31]

Despite the presence of these women within various administrative positions, Garveyites expected men and women to fulfill clearly defined gender roles that approximated those of the nuclear, patriarchal family. As historian

Barbara Bair points out, "the organizational pattern of men's and women's leadership roles was not separate and equal but separate and hierarchical." Both the parent, or national, body and local divisions maintained separate leadership systems based on gender, with men in the organization preserving ultimate decision-making control. On the national level, UNIA officers were generally male. At the local level, chapters staffed various positions such as associate secretary and assistant treasurer with women, but the UNIA's constitution suggested that each chapter should also have a Board of Trustees, consisting of "five *male persons*," which would supervise the finances. Chapters were set up with separate women's departments with lady presidents; however, their reports were submitted to the male presidents "for presentation to the general membership." Furthermore, ultimate disciplinary and personnel matters were subject to the discretion of the male presidents. It was "the prerogative of the Male President only to declare an office vacant on the breach of the Constitution by any officer, or discharge a committee or its chairman." [32] Unlike the OES, in which women held executive power, the UNIA's constitution allowed for the male presidents to operate in the manner of Victorian patriarchs and, indeed, encouraged them to do so.

Of course, the familial character of the local chapters and the paternal role of the male presidents were more metaphorical than literal. The words "family" and "father" do not appear in the constitution—at least not in connection with the structuring of the organization or the role of its officers. What was literal, however, were the requirements the UNIA placed on its local and national leadership in terms of marital relationships. The framers of the constitution stressed the importance of racial purity when they required that all "officers and high officers . . . shall be Negroes and their consorts or wives shall be Negroes." Anyone "whose life companion is of an alien race" could not expect upward mobility within the organization's ranks. Interestingly, the obligation of "high officers" to marry within the race extended to both men and women as the terms "consort" and "life companion" are gender-neutral. However, in discussing the duty of the "Potentate and Supreme Commissioner," the titular head of the UNIA, the constitution dictated that "he shall marry only a lady of Negro blood and parentage, and his consort shall herself by virtue of her position be head of the female division of all organizations, societies and orders." [33] By using gender-specific language to codify the marital status of the potentate, the UNIA effectively precluded the possibility of a woman becoming the supreme commissioner, symbolic leader of blacks worldwide. The language was intended to do more than ensure male control of the UNIA, however; it was also the strategic application of the Garveyite rhetoric that admonished black men to respect black womanhood.

The hierarchical organization of gender within the UNIA, and particularly the emphasis placed on the black woman as wife, mother, and helpmate, extended to the main female auxiliary of the association, the Universal African Black Cross Nurses. Whereas the Universal African Legion symbolized the productive capacity of New Negro manhood, the Black Cross Nurses represented the black woman as nurturer and caregiver, presumably outside of the process of production. The auxiliary's membership consisted of "women of Negro Blood and African Descent between the ages of sixteen and forty-five." The nurses provided healthcare information—such as sanitation methods, personal hygiene, and safety instructions—and medical relief to UNIA members and the larger black community. Auxiliary members were also expected to be trained in the relief of victims of more catastrophic events such as "pestilence, famine, fire, floods, and other great calamities." One historian of the Garvey movement also suggests that they were being "groomed for liberation wars in Africa," in which case they would function as the medical units of the Legion.[34] The nurses disseminated medical information through classes, the distribution of literature, and weekly columns in the *Negro World*. They also directly intervened in the lives of UNIA members and residents of their communities, providing home care for the sick and shut in, and collecting and redistributing clothing, food, and other supplies. In reaching communities that were not beneficiaries of public programs or private charities, they were "heirs to decades of black women's charitable work" and acted as role models for young black girls.[35]

The auxiliary, similar to the Legion, was structured hierarchically with national and local boards of governance. On the national level, a central committee consisting of the president-general, a universal directress with at least three years of experience as a graduate nurse, the secretary-general, and a surgeon general ("who shall be a Bacteriologist"), possessed ultimate decision-making power. On the local level, the chapter presidents exercised control over policy but the auxiliary leadership consisted of a matron (the lady president of the local), a head nurse, secretary, and treasurer. Most members of the auxiliary did not have nursing backgrounds but, in certain communities, Garveyite women did receive training and formal certification at area hospitals.[36]

Garveyites applied the same principles of organizing gender roles to the younger members of the UNIA. Male and female juvenile regiments occupied important positions in local chapter activity. UNIA scouts, particularly boys, assumed the same function as scouts in the larger society: to instill character, discipline, and a sense of moral and national duty in young adults. The governing structure of the juvenile departments was heterogeneously gendered.

The constitution dictated that the superintendent of the local chapter be a lady vice president and the first assistant be a "loyal member" without specific reference to gender. The secretary was "one of the best learned Juveniles (male or female)," and the only requirement expected of the teachers was that they be "loyal members" as well.[37]

Pedagogy in these youth auxiliaries was explicitly gendered, particularly once the children entered the preadolescent stage. From ages one to seven, considered the infant class, there was no distinction between the instruction of boys and girls. By Class 2, ages seven to thirteen, boys and girls received different training. Both learned black history and "Etiquette" and received "disciplinary training by the Legions"; they were also instructed in the production of souvenirs to be sold by the UNIA, with girls using "cloth, needle and thread" and boys making "souvenirs with wood and carved with tools instead of with needle." By adolescence, young males and females were loosely attached to the adult auxiliaries. Boys entered the Cadet corps where they learned military discipline and strategy, flag signaling, and black history; girls entered a "prepatory nursing class" in which they were prepared for more private roles, taking classes in uniform making, etiquette, "Elementary principles of Economy," and "Domestic Science." Juveniles of all ages were expected to carry themselves in a respectable manner—recognizing their deferential relationship to adult authority and refraining from using profanity and engaging in disorderly conduct. The UNIA took great pride in the work being done among its young members. In an article subtitled "Training the Future Men and Women of the Race," a reporter for the *Negro World* extolled the Philadelphia local. "Sons and daughters of the future African government are being trained in a manner befitting new Negro thought," the article boldly stated. Along with instruction in religious matters and public behavior, these nascent nationalists were learning to be proud of their black heritage. The reporter concluded that the "young are growing in the atmosphere of ideas and ideals, born of a revolutionary thought."[38]

The UNIA carried out this instruction of black youth in the midst of a changing economy and society, which, by the mid-1920s, experienced the emergence of the New Woman and decidedly post-Victorian gender conventions. In addition to increasing their political power through achieving suffrage, many women were also improving their economic status. In the 1920s, women constituted roughly half of the American population enrolled in colleges and universities. These women were looking past employment as teachers and increasingly becoming white-collar workers in government agencies, professional and business offices, public departments, and retail stores.

Moreover, married women remained in the wage-labor force at a greater rate than wives of an earlier generation. As labor historian Alice Kessler-Harris remarks: "To significant numbers of women, marriage and work no longer seemed like mutually exclusive alternatives." Although the economic fortunes of women fluctuated during the decade (in terms of the types of opportunities and the gender gap in wages and salaries), the 1920s heralded new possibilities.[39] Of course, these new possibilities were largely limited to middle-class white women. Despite the fact that urban black women coming of age in the 1920s were, in the aggregate, as educated as second-generation immigrant and native-born white women, they were still largely excluded from white-collar employment. In 1920, three-quarters of black working women were either agricultural laborers, domestics, or laundresses and this changed little during the decade. In northern cities, Jacqueline Jones reminds us, "black women's work . . . was synonymous with domestic service." Black women performed professional work within the community as teachers, librarians, nurses, and social workers, although they were either excluded from, or segregated within, the larger national professional organizations. The overwhelming majority, however, continued to labor in the agricultural and service sectors of the economy.[40]

Within this context, then, outside of the celebration of their blackness, there was nothing particularly revolutionary about the UNIA's training of juveniles. When we consider the ideology of gender as it was reflected in the instruction of or duties expected of the Black Cross Nurses, courses in uniform making and domestic science did not substantially challenge the social reality of black women's economic opportunities. To be sure, Garveyites were looking toward a future in which black women no longer needed to engage in work outside of the home—potentially a progressive move given the history of slavery, sharecropping, and, in general, the economic marginalization of black women, men, and families.[41] Given the challenges to patriarchy that were occurring in the larger society, however, the Garveyite attitudes concerning gender were decidedly orthodox. As the organizational framework of the Black Cross Nurses and the juvenile regiments suggests, Garveyites adhered closely to late-Victorian, bourgeois ideals of femininity and manliness. While manhood, as reflected in the structure and performance of the African Legion, was informed by militarism and production, feminine identity was largely tied to domesticity and the family. A shared nationalism and an emphasis on collective duty influenced both, but ultimately Garveyite men were put into the position of protector while Garveyite women were relegated to the position of supporter. Conformity to these gender conventions and their reproduction through youth involvement in the UNIA continued to allow men within the Garvey movement to construct their gender identity within the paradigms of production and patriarchy.

Prince Hall Freemasons also sought to shape the development of black youth. Through the establishment of boys' organizations, Masons hoped to instill a commitment to producer values and respectability into what they often referred to as the "coming generations" of black men. These efforts were intended not only to reproduce bourgeois notions of manliness within black boys; by identifying themselves as the shepherds who would guide boys into adulthood, Masons invoked the relational axis between boyhood and manhood. In other words, like Garveyites, black Masons used age as a central category through which to define manhood and reinforced their own gender identities by defining themselves in opposition to boys.

In a crucial sense, the way that Masons discussed the need to mold black boys signified a major difference in the ways in which black men and white middle-class men incorporated the presence of boys into their gender identity formation. As historians of masculinity have argued, around the turn of the century, white middle-class men began to express concern that the rambunctious, aggressive, and impetuous nature of boys was being suppressed by excessive contact with mothers and female teachers. This "overcivilization," they argued, posed the threat of physically and mentally enervating boys and, as they reached adulthood, producing a generation of weak-willed and weak-spirited men. The United States was emerging as an industrial and imperial power, and the prospects of inheriting a generation of young men plagued by neurasthenia concerned many middle-class men. To counteract the effects of "overcivilization," men began to celebrate, and nurture, the same qualities in boys that, since the colonial era, had been denounced as harmful vices that needed to be reformed. Competition, mischievousness, combativeness, and an ersatz savagery were now being tolerated, if not encouraged, in various quarters. Boarding schools, athletic associations, and organizations such as the Young Men's Christian Association (YMCA) and the Boy Scouts were developed as interventions to "provide 'boyish' experiences so that boys would not lose touch with the sources of manhood." At the same time, men recognized that these same qualities were important in their own gender identity formation as adults. Through the hero worship of the cowboy—and his personification in Theodore Roosevelt—and the transformation of father-son relationships into that of friends rather than stern parent-submissive child, adult men sought to blur the lines between boyhood and manhood. The Victorian archetype of the self-controlled, excessively rational, manly man gave way to the post-Victorian model of the energetic, impulsive, "passionate" man that was closer in sentiment to his younger male counterpart. As E. Anthony Rotundo argues, "the notions of boyhood and manhood were converging."[42] If, for middle-class white men, "manhood was no longer defined by its opposition to boyhood,"[43] age remained an important differentiating marker in the gender identity formation of black men. The fundamental need of maintaining a distinction between stages in the male life cycle persisted among black men, many of whom were only a generation, or in some cases, only years, removed from the rural South—an environment in which socioeconomic conditions and racial "etiquette" all but eradicated the boundaries between black adults and children.

Prior to the Great Migration, the majority of African Americans who lived in rural southern areas endured a racist political economy in which boyhood and manhood intersected at several levels. On the one hand, black youth had limited access to the same public education system that provided white children the environment in which they could interact with one another in age-based grades and thereby develop a peer-group consciousness. Even in areas that had public schools for black children, the political power of planters ensured that these schools would be closed during the planting and harvesting seasons. As a result, black boys and girls were often forced to enter the wage-labor market and interact with adults at an earlier age than white youth. One historian has found that in the South in 1900, almost 50 percent of black boys between the ages of ten and fifteen, and 30 percent of black girls in the same age category, worked for wages. This significantly outstripped the percentage of white boys (22.5 percent) and girls (7 percent) who were engaged in wage labor. Enrollment numbers were also exceedingly low for black teenagers. In 1890, less than 0.5 percent of southern black children old enough to attend secondary school actually did so. By 1910, the numbers had risen to a measly 2.8 percent of the entire population of black teenagers in the South. These figures did not change significantly until large numbers of blacks began migrating to northern and midwestern urban areas between 1910 and 1920.[44]

On the other hand, black male adults were often confronted with being infantilized by southern racial "etiquette." The patterns of deference that characterized black-white interaction precluded black men from enjoying the title "Mr." while, at the same time, making it dangerous to object to being referred to as "boy."[45] With black boys being forced to enter an adult's world—even as adolescence was increasingly being identified by educators and psychologists as an essential phase of the life cycle—and black men consistently being treated as anything but social adults, the distinction between manhood and boyhood became all the more important. Certainly, in southern urban areas and in the North, the blurring of the lines between black manhood and boyhood did not exist to the same degree that it did in the rural South. Still, the collective memory of their own experiences, or that of their parents and grandparents, plus the intellectual and cultural representations of blacks as a childish race, must have spurred many black men to clearly demarcate the developmental boundaries of manhood.[46] One of the ways that they accomplished this was through the establishment of juvenile departments that were attached to the fraternal and sororal societies.

Both Prince Hall Freemasons and Eastern Stars discussed the imperative of bringing up boys and girls in the Masonic tradition and implemented these strategies through the development of youth organizations. Like the adult orders, no overarching national youth organization with uniform doctrine and ritual work existed. Rather, auxiliaries were organized on a statewide basis. Subordinate chapters of the OES established juvenile departments in which "the youth of our fraternity are given burial benefits as well as valuable training in the conduct of business and social affairs." In her speech at the 1924 Inter-state Conference meeting, Brown called on her fellow Eastern Stars to create even more juvenile departments. She also suggested cooperating with the National Association for the Advancement of Colored People (NAACP) in the development of Junior Divisions "in which Race History is taught and black ideals instilled into our young people thus fitting them for the leadership of the next generation."[47]

One of the coeducational youth organizations that was run jointly by Prince Hall and OES was the Order of Bees for Boys and Girls, founded in 1921 in a Chicago YMCA.[48] Its purpose was "to train and prepare the minds of the child and youth so that when they become of age, if able to qualify, they will be inclined to fill the ranks of our Grand old Order, and not be so easily susceptible to evil or wrong persuasion." Although the Order of Bees was officially independent of Prince Hall and OES, it functioned as a training ground for future Freemasons and Eastern Stars. In order for a hive, or a subordinate chapter, to be organized, the initial petition had to be signed by three master masons and three sisters of the OES. Membership, however, was not limited to relatives of Masons or Eastern Stars. Rather, it was open to anyone under the age of eighteen or twenty-one who believed "in the existence of a Supreme God" and who managed to survive the recommendation and investigative process. Meetings of the hive were as ritual-laden as those of Masonic lodges and OES chapters. In addition, members of the Order of Bees received "scriptural, social, fraternal, [and] military" instruction. Those who oversaw these meetings, however, were careful not to present the children with a deluge of doctrinal and ritualistic information so as not to interfere with their familial obligations or scare them away from Masonry with excessive technical discussion of fraternal tradition. Thomas H. Samuel, the author of the ritual, reminded the sponsors of the Order of Bees that "the ceremonies should be clean and concised [sic] in its [sic] meaning and no attempt should be made to confuse the child's mind with too strong or binding obligations, and his or her parental duties, but the necessity of inculcating the minor principles of Masonry in the life of the boy or girl that the desire to become a Master Mason, Heroine Crusader or an O.E.S. may grow upon them is quite obvious." Ultimately, Freemasons and Eastern Stars expected the Order of Bees to whet the appetite of black youth for further involvement in fraternal and sororal work. It was, in effect, a recruitment tool even as it purported to instill black children with morality, industry, and "the highest ideals of life."[49]

While the Order of Bees was organized along the lines of the OES—that is, a mixed-sex order with boys and girls sharing power—other youth divisions were confined to black boys.[50] Knights Templar in western Pennsylvania, for instance, organized the Circle of Constantine in February 1926. The Circle was open to young males from the ages of sixteen to twenty-one. Membership was open to both relatives of the fraternal members as well as individuals who were recommended by a knight. The impetus to the Circle's organization, according to its founder, was his "realizing the necessity of throwing around our youths the fartherly [sic] arm of protection and the importance of properly instructing them into right mode of clean living and maner [sic] of conducting meetings and the endeavor of building good character[.]"[51]

In the early 1920s, several Prince Hall grand masters also attempted to establish an organization for black boys modeled along the lines of the white youth fraternity, the Order of the Builders for Boys. Although Harry Williamson, one of the initiators, accommodated white Masons' concerns regarding the sharing of rituals between blacks and whites, he was optimistic about the possibilities that a black Order of the Builders for Boys represented. "I feel that only through such organizations," he wrote to the president of the Central Council of the order, "supplemented with the Craft itself, will many of the knotty problems of the differences due to complexion be brought to any system of 'understanding.' It is through the citizen of the coming generations that such adjustments will be promulgated and effected, therefore it lies within the province of the Craft of both races to direct the youth toward liberty, equality, fraternity, and tolerance."[52] Whether or not Williamson and other members of Prince Hall successfully organized a black counterpart to the Builders is unclear. The fact that Williamson was still trying to form a youth organization in the late 1930s suggests that the first attempt failed.[53]

Other Masonic lodges and OES chapters, however, managed to create these auxiliaries. Although some may have been more inspired by race consciousness and community development than others—such as the OES chapters that Brown hoped would double as NAACP Juvenile Divisions—the overall hope of the adults who organized them was that they would funnel the "best" of the race's youth into their organizations. These juvenile auxiliaries functioned in another manner, one that was intimately connected to the construction of collective and individual gender identities of black men and women. By reinforcing the distinction between boys and men, and girls and women, Freemasons and Eastern Stars reaffirmed their own status as social adults. For black men involved in Masonry, cultivating environments in which they could impart the principles of manhood to black boys through instruction in the doctrinal, ritualistic, and moral aspects of the Craft allowed them to articulate a manly identity in the process. Their role as educators in the virtues of manliness attested to the presence of manhood within Prince Hall Freemasons. In this sense, black boys were important as negative referents in the gender identity formation of these men. The presence of women within the OES, as well as female Garveyites, functioned in similar ways. By framing the work that these women did within the paradigm of domesticity and the private sphere, black Masons and Garveyites continued to lay claim to a gender identity that relied on bourgeois, Victorian notions of production.

In 1903, the grand master of New York and past grand patron of the Eureka Grand Chapter, Edward V. C. Eato, reflected on the existence and indispensability of the OES. He pointed out that the Eastern Stars' work had been "productive of good results" and that, in large part, this was due to the fact that it had been "so ably presided over by the Worthy Grand Matron." He concluded his address with a sentiment that revealed how many Masons felt about the work that was being done by women in the Masonic universe. "With honorable and exalted purposes in view for the dissemination of light, charity and benevolence," he declared, "I fully recognize the worth of the institution as one that will prove of great value in its sphere of labor, owing to the fact that it co-operates in the great benif[i]cent [sic] work of Masonry."[54] Eato's characterization of the work of the OES and particularly its dependence on the very existence of Masonry reflected a predisposition to think about, and represent, women's work as ancillary to men's. Indeed, the OES toiled, according to Eato, in its own "sphere of labor," which presumably differed from the sphere that Masons occupied. Eato's praise of the OES revealed an adherence to the ideology of separate spheres. Eato was not alone in this; nor were the Masons. In talking about women within, and around, their respective movements, Prince Hall Freemasons and male Garveyites discursively constructed and represented women's activism within the framework of domesticity, despite the fact that the social reality of women's organizational work was very different. By continuing to frame it as such, however, black men sought to reaffirm their gender identity as respectable producers and patriarchs.

Much of the Masonic praise for the OES centered on the latter's work in the homes for the elderly and orphanages that were scattered throughout the country. Masons and Eastern Stars jointly ran homes in several states, including Illinois, Indiana, Tennessee, and Georgia. In Nashville, the Home for Widows and Orphans sat on thirty-seven acres of land and was valued, in the mid-1920s, at $100,000. The Masonic Orphanage of Americus, Georgia, was built in 1898. It began with a campus of less than thirty acres and only a boys' dormitory, but by 1933, the orphanage occupied one hundred acres of land and consisted of three buildings, one of which accommodated girls. The "inmates" were taught domestic science, agricultural methods, and were required to attend Sunday school. Masons and Eastern Stars were proud of the work that was done in Americus as well as Nashville. The homes, according to various reports, were practically self-sufficient and free of debt. Sue Brown boasted of the Nashville home's campus "upon which they raise much of the provisions consumed by the inmates of the Home." John Wesley Dobbs, grand master of Georgia, described in his annual address the agricultural education delivered to disadvantaged youth at the Americus orphanage and suggested that, combined with religious instruction, it offered them unbounded opportunities. "We have seen them come out and take their places in society," he pointed out, "better prepared to be good citizens and lead useful lives because of the training received at our Home." [55] The OES was also indispensable in the construction and maintenance of several Masonic temples, including one in Birmingham, Alabama, and another in Boley, Oklahoma. [56]

Although Eastern Stars engaged in some political activism, Masons tended to focus on their sisters' work in the private sphere. [57] In their public writings and addresses, Masonic officials employed a particular selectivity in discussing the civic activities of the OES, narrowly defining their work as supplementary to that of Prince Hall lodges. In commending the OES's financial contribution to the Americus orphanage, for instance, Dobbs acceded that "too much praise cannot be given the noble women who belong to the Order of the Eastern Star." Ultimately, however, Dobbs claimed that the home was "a monumental credit to our Masonic brotherhood in Georgia." [58] In the same vein, Dr. A. Baxter Whitby, the grand master of Oklahoma, celebrated the work of the Oklahoma Grand Chapter of OES while descriptively rendering it as the travails of self-sacrificing wives and mothers. "Strikingly so," Whitby declared, "do we find recorded here and there in Masonic history the silent yet glowing achievements of our Noble Women of the Order of the Eastern Star."

Whitby's praise for the "silent" efforts of the OES was motivated by their financial contributions to the construction of the Masonic temple in Boley. Although the decision to build the temple was due to the "sound judgement and good common sense" of Masons, Whitby suggested, it was the support of the OES that brought about its completion. After the fund-raising drive stalled, according to Whitby, the OES stepped up and provided succor to the Masons in their darkest hour. "Then it was that the Noble Order of the Eastern Star of Oklahoma," he proudly recalled, "with 3000 women led by that brilliant[,] enthusiastic and Christian woman, Mrs. Lillie Talliaferro, our present Grand Worthy Matron, came to the front, laid down upon the altar all of their many years' hoarding and said to Grand Master, G. I. Currin, 'We bring you our all and pledge ourselves to help you to complete the work so worthy begun.'"[59] Even as Masons and Eastern Stars joined efforts in community activism—activism that, albeit centered on the exclusivity of fraternalism, was still civic-minded—men regarded the work done by women as crucial to group progress yet supplementary in nature.

The ways in which Masons situated the efforts of the OES only within the context of their own proactive initiatives had the effect of framing Eastern Stars as passive participants in the "great labors" of Masonry. In this sense, Masons utilized a trope of heroic womanhood: female activism that was indispensable to the efforts of men but that, at the end of the day, was generated by a desire to sacrifice oneself to the greater cause of men's activism. To be sure, black women themselves occasionally contributed to this narrative. Sue Brown, for instance, employed a gender essentialist argument to highlight the activities of the order when she declared: "Woman has always been known as a homebuilder, although the great world knows little of her deeds of heroism, her self-denial and her real devotion to suffering humanity. By experience she knows what it is to be widowed and homeless, therefore she has gladly contributed her part in furnishing and supporting Homes for widows and orphans."[60] Brown's invocation of the black woman as "homebuilder" was not a complete acquiescence to the public-private organization of gender. Elsewhere she advocated responsible practice of the recently acquired vote.[61] Similar to black clubwomen, Brown envisioned women's work in the home and in other private institutions as the avenue through which they would best be equipped to affect political change and race progress. Endorsing the idea that women were more moral and selfless than men did not necessarily translate into an acceptance that women were not as capable of occupying leadership positions.[62] This ambiguous juxtaposition of private and public work, moral sentimentalism and practical politics, gender essentialism and sexual equality, however, did not characterize the way that Masons interpreted the activities of the OES. For them, woman as mother, wife, and helpmate informed the ways in which they discussed the OES and their own efforts within a masculinist fraternal tradition.

Men and women of the UNIA engaged in a similar contestation over the meanings of manhood and womanhood as they were articulated in the organization's activism. To be sure, the ways in which UNIA intellectuals discussed black femininity were not monolithic. Black women were often rhetorically depicted as self-sufficient, fearless foot soldiers in the quest for liberation and nationhood. Marcus Garvey, for instance, introduced Henrietta Vinton Davis to a UNIA audience in 1920 as the right honorable international organizer, referring to her as "our modern Joan of Arc." In 1919, a Professor Buck told a crowd at Madison Square Garden in New York that whites "will find we mean business to such an extent that if our men are not enough, by the living God, our women are ready to[o]." Referring to the Ethiopian defeat of the Italians at Aduwa in 1896, Buck affirmed the collective power of black women. "If you never had a fight with a woman," he told the applauding audience, "you ask the Italians what the Abyssinian King did to him [sic] with women, and they will tell you how black women can fight when their honor is at stake."[63] Even though male UNIA intellectuals occasionally talked about women as active members on the "front" of racial liberation and nation building, the overwhelming representation of woman was that of wife and mother, caretaker of the Garveyite home, and producer of good UNIA men. This ideology of gender posited men as the economic providers and physical protectors of women and was heavily influenced by the Victorian ideologies of domesticity and separate spheres. Of course, the domestic ideal for blacks, as well as an increasing number of whites, was largely prescriptive rather than representative of social reality.[64] However, examining how male Garveyites discursively deployed the images of the black woman as wife and mother reveals how such ideas continued to contribute to their gender identity formation.

Adhering to the nuclear family model of progress, most UNIA intellectuals elevated the role of wives and mothers in sustaining stable homes and families. One of the most emphatic and prolific advocates in this area was John E. Bruce. "The starting point in the making of the Race, is the home," he wrote in 1922. "The master work . . . of the Negro is the establishment of good homes, where the rising generation, under a healthy and helpful environment, may imbibe correct principles of living."[65] In an address to a congregation, as part of a celebration of the pastor's wedding anniversary, Bruce reinforced the importance of healthy unions between men and women. "The Home influence is the mightiest and most potent force in the development of a race, and

the better the wives and husbands we have the better this race is going to be."
He specifically highlighted the role of women. Suggesting that they were the
"architects and builders of the race," Bruce defined the "good" woman as the
one who "sustains by her thrift and industry in the home by precept and example the dignity of her position as wife and mother."[66] He placed enormous
responsibility on black women when he argued that, along with the clergy,
a "virtuous[,] educated Christian Womanhood" would form the vanguard of
racial progress. Bruce linked these ideas to the development of black men by
claiming that the "home and the church must be the MAN-factories" in which
generations "must be equipped and prepared to take up the work of their
fathers."[67] The home, then, as well as the family, were viewed by Bruce as the
fundamental units of liberation. Other Garveyites, including many women,
shared his view.[68] This did not, however, conflict with Garveyites' assertion
that racial advancement would best be achieved through the development of
capital. If women were the central figures of their model of progress, men
were to be the end results. Racial advancement depended on both as black
wives and mothers produced, through safe, clean, and moral homes, honest
and industrious sons who would grow up to be "true" men by successfully
performing in the marketplace and respecting, providing for, and protecting
black women.

One of the reasons the race was in a marginalized position, many Garveyites argued, was due to black men's failure to complete this process. This
inability, according to UNIA secretary-general J. D. Brooks, "served to break
the spirit of the American Negro." Brooks praised the "protectionless Negro
women" for simultaneously being able to maneuver between the "bad Negro
. . . on one side and the bad white man . . . on the other side." Referring
to the common dynamic in the South, in which a black woman avoided telling a male relative or friend of an insult or assault by a white male, for fear
of what might happen if he tried to defend or avenge her, Brooks rebuked
black men for allowing it to continue. "We need a little bit of backbone," he
intoned.[69] Bruce equally chastised black men, reminding African Americans
and African Caribbeans of the duty of the "head of a family to safeguard the
honor and protect the virtue of its womenfolk" for the "moment the men of
any Race permit the cheapening of their women, the polution [sic] of their
women, their Race is doomed."[70]

Bruce's sentiment, although exaggerated from the perspective of the early
twenty-first century, held much currency among black nationalists and white
supremacists in the 1920s. Present in white America's consciousness since
the early seventeenth century, the fear of miscegenation and racial amalgamation became extremely pervasive between the 1890s and 1920s when it

received scientific sanction. Everyone from scientists, academics, and journalists to populist politicians and vigilante groups shared an acute anxiety over racial intermixture. These were expressed in diverse ways, ranging from racial degeneracy and race conservation theories to arguments for segregation, immigration restriction, eugenics, and extralegal racial violence.[71]

The UNIA voiced a similar concern over interracial sex and its disingenuous euphemism, "social equality." In a pamphlet stating the objectives of the organization, Marcus Garvey compared the UNIA's virile agenda to the "race destroying doctrine" of the integrationist reformers in the NAACP. The UNIA "believes in, and teaches the pride and purity of race." All those who had not yet accepted this doctrine of racial purity, Garvey urged, "should be encouraged to get together and form themselves into a healthy whole, rather than seeking to loose their identities through miscegenation and social intercourse with the white race."[72] Garvey cloaked the agenda of racial purity in moralistic terms. Slavery in the New World had, on the one hand, encouraged whites and blacks to break the "laws of nature" through interracial sexual relations and, on the other, provided the descendants of Africa with Christianity and "civilization," tools they could use for the salvation of the "benighted" continent. It was now up to the "moral-standard-man," he argued, to accept the latter values and reject the immoral desire to interact sexually with whites. Furthermore, the UNIA was the logical alternative for these "men of the highest morals, highest character and noblest pride . . . among the masses of the Negro race who love their women with as much devotion as white men love theirs."[73] Garvey confronted the myth of the "black rapist," the image of the marauding black male, loosed from the paternalism of slavery and now a dangerous threat to white womanhood everywhere. He rejected this myth, prevalent in American popular and political culture, by emphasizing that black men had acquired morality, civilization, and a "normal" desire for black women.

The need for physical protection of black women from sexual exploitation at the hands of white men formed a key underpinning of the racial purity discourse. As Bruce unequivocally stated, the violation of respectable womanhood signaled the rapid decline of any race. The UNIA thus positioned itself as the defender of black women and did so in masculinist language. At a meeting in Philadelphia, Garvey warned whites of the New Negro mentality. "Let a white man take care of his women and hang any one who bothers them, but he . . . must take the consequence if he is caught fooling with negro women," he told the crowd.[74] Garvey's statement, although clearly defining the boundaries of interaction between white men and black women, tacitly endorsed the practice of lynching. His acceptance of the rationale behind southern segregationist thought led to his meeting with the second most powerful member of the Ku Klux Klan, Edward Clarke, in Atlanta in 1922. The meeting engendered severe criticism from both mainstream and radical black leaders who perceived the entente as Garvey's approval of white supremacy.[75] Whether or not the meeting represented Garvey's accommodation to the virulent racism of the Klan, it reflected two ideas that the two groups held in common: racial purity and the integrity of the women of their respective races. These ideas became official policy of the UNIA in 1920 when it drafted the Declaration of Rights of the Negro Peoples of the World at its convention in New York. One of the resolutions of this "manly Declaration" was the assuming by black men of the role of "sworn protectors of the honor and virtue of our women and children."[76]

In the same Declaration, another resolution revealed the importance of economic provision. Garveyites articulated grievances over the inability of a large segment of the black population to secure an equitable family wage. Moreover, this complaint was male-centered. Black men, the resolution went, "are discriminated against and denied an equal chance to earn wages for the support of our families, and in many instances are refused admission into labor unions, and nearly everywhere are paid smaller wages than white men." Protection, in the eyes of male Garveyites, extended to economic support. One article in the *Negro World* suggested as much and did so in resoundingly Victorian language. The article encouraged men to "again place our women upon the pedestal from whence they have been forced into the vortex of the seething world of business." Further, it placed responsibility on men by suggesting that there would be "more mothers, more virtuous wives, and more amiable and lovable daughters" if men fulfilled their role as protectors.[77] The number of women in the UNIA who embraced this argument — or the number who equated black men's acquisition of a family wage with their own departure from the wage-labor force — is uncertain. Some clearly envisioned higher wages for men as an opportunity for them to escape lives of drudgery within an exploitative labor market; others may have viewed the patriarchal argument for family wages as an implicit indictment of their work, either waged or community, in the public sphere.[78] What should be kept in mind, however, is that the economic support of women was integral to male Garveyites' formulation and assertion of manhood rights.

The discursive constructions of bourgeois manhood and womanhood were not limited to the rhetoric of the movement. Through public and semipublic performances, Garveyites juxtaposed the representation of man as the public, productive citizen and woman as the private, nurturing wife and mother. These idealized images were articulated in the semipublic atmosphere of the court reception, or the "At Home." Just as the Legion reaffirmed for the guests, as well as the readers of the *Negro World*, the links between militarism and the masculinist politics of the UNIA, the visual and textual representations of black women emphasized their femininity. Press coverage of the receptions provided specific descriptions of the evening gowns worn by female guests. Other semipublic affairs took on the characteristics of the social events of high society. The Ladies of the Royal Court of Ethiopia, for instance, regularly held fashion shows, balls, and banquets.[79] While these events raised funds for the organization, they also reinforced the hierarchical nature of the organization itself. It is not difficult to imagine the social distinctions that were produced through the juxtaposing of the Black Cross Nurses, in uniforms that signaled private and public *work*, and the female attendees of various receptions and balls, in satin and crepe de chine evening gowns that evinced *leisure*. The presentation of women as queens, baronesses, and countesses symbolized the self-empowerment of the movement even as it recognized difference based on class and status.[80]

Nationalist iconography of black women as wives and mothers was also present within the public rituals of performance. Women were present in the UNIA's parades, although, as several historians have pointed out, the roles they performed were often cast as supplementary and subordinate.[81] Indicative of this were the Black Cross Nurses units. In the 1920 convention parade, the nurses accepted the position of helpmates to the Legion by following the Philadelphia local of the UAL with a banner that read, "We are ready to support our boys." The *Negro World* endorsed the nurse's role, suggesting that they would encourage the men "to make the supreme sacrifice on the battle plains of our beloved Africa, where their banner inscription, 'We Mean to Aid Our Boys,' will be realized in faithful and loving ministrations." If the Black Cross Nurses represented nurturing support in the context of war, they also signified the black woman as mother. A description of a float in the 1924 convention parade read, "twelve nurses, in their white uniforms, sit sewing, in cradles recline Negro babies, a huge black papier mache cross towering at the rear of the float."[82] By stressing the maternal nature of the nurses, the UNIA sought to represent the black woman as the ideal of private domesticity and the corollary to the public, productive man. These representations reached their ideological and performative climax when, in 1924, the UNIA deified Jesus as the "black Man of Sorrows" and canonized "the Virgin Mary as a Negress." The canonization of the Black Christ and the Black Madonna, according to the *New York Times*, "was achieved by elaborate ceremonies conducted before oil paintings of the sacred subjects, which were covered with veils and wreathed with heavy fumes from censers swung to and fro by acolytes."[83] The "Africanization" of Jesus and the Virgin was clearly an example of race pride and racial chauvinism and has been part of a longer black nationalist tradition extending until at least the 1970s. In this case, the canonizations reinforced the importance Garveyites placed on equating womanhood with motherhood.[84] Given the fact that Jesus was an artisan, it is not inconceivable that they wanted to reinforce the role of men as producers.

For Garveyites, the representations of manhood within the frameworks of militarism and production and womanhood within the paradigm of domesticity and motherhood were motivated by the imperatives of nation and empire building. Of course, women in the UNIA were not completely reduced to the role of healers and nurturers, evident in the militarized Universal African Motor Corps, which was commanded and staffed mainly by women.[85] Nor did the public performances of women as wives, mothers, and helpmates necessarily hold the same meanings for female and male Garveyites. The Black Cross Nurses represented a tradition of black women's community work and provided Garveyite women the space in which to assert their capacity as coequals in community and national development. From male Garveyites' perspective, however, the dichotomous positioning of the Legion and Black Cross Nurses reaffirmed their own gender identities as economic providers for, and physical protectors of, women, race, and nation. Although the nurses' role reflected real and symbolic agency, as Darlene Clark Hine notes concerning the image of black nurses in general, it did not undermine the commitment that Garveyite men held in the ideology of separate spheres.[86] The public celebration of motherhood—like the discursive representations of domesticity deployed by black Masons—solidified, rather than challenged, male Garveyites' gendered sense of self. Various other activities by women within both movements, however, would contest the patriarchal posture of Masonry and Garveyism and would, as a result, force black men to defend their manhood.

▆ While rhetorical and performative representations of women as wives and mothers were critical to the formulations of manliness for Prince Hall Freemasons and Garveyites, women within and around these movements carved out spheres of authority that were not limited to their roles as supporter, reproducer, and nurturer. To be sure, Eastern Stars and, especially, female Garveyites did not eschew the importance of motherhood. In many ways, motherhood became a central organizing principle for their political activism. It did not, however, translate into acceptance of a subordinate or helpmate status in all cases. Women in the UNIA, for instance, often invoked motherhood but did so within the larger context of black women's potential leadership. In this sense, female Garveyites' reliance on their status as women (and mothers) of the race often challenged male authority. These challenges manifested in articles in the *Negro World*, debates and speeches at UNIA meetings, and their very presence in the organization's public rituals. Women in the Eastern Star did not invoke motherhood as frequently and vehemently as female Garveyites, largely because they did not adhere to nationalist theories of race conservation. Some did, however, challenge male authority by asserting an organizational autonomy from their Masonic brethren. Men within the UNIA and Prince Hall Freemasonry responded to these challenges in various ways; the reactions to these encroachments on their sphere of authority illustrate the way in which power and leadership were central to the gender identity formation of middle-class black men.

In 1925, Amy Jacques Garvey, Marcus's second wife and de facto leader of the UNIA during his incarceration, wrote an editorial that appeared on the women's page of the *Negro World*. Jacques Garvey, the associate editor of the newspaper, was extremely critical of the male leadership of the organization and, by extension, the black race. "We are tired of hearing Negro men say, 'There is a better day coming', while they do nothing to usher in the day," she exclaimed. "We are becoming so impatient that we are getting in the front ranks, and serve notice on the world that we will brush aside the halting, cowardly Negro men, and with prayer on our lips and arms prepared for any fray, we will press on and on until victory is ours." Jacques Garvey's editorial simultaneously reflected, on the one hand, the deep symbiotic relationship between motherhood and activism and, on the other, the tension between domesticity and the independent New Woman. For Jacques Garvey, motherhood remained a central category through which black women could impact, and further, the nationalist agenda of the UNIA. Arguing that women were "the backbone of the home," she reminded her audience that "by their economic experience and their aptitude for details [women can] participate effectively in guiding the destiny of nation and race." Even as Jacques Garvey elevated the primacy of maternalism, however, she did not reduce the importance of woman to her capacity for producing and raising children. Indeed, the "modern woman" was capable of contributing to the development of race, nation, and empire precisely because she was expanding her role beyond that of mother. "She prefers to be a bread-winner than a half-starved wife at home," Jacques Garvey wrote of the New Woman. "She is not afraid of hard work, and by being independent she gets more out of the present-day husband than her grandmother did in the good old days."[87] In merging the domestic space of motherhood and the public sphere of the marketplace as compatible sites for the production of modern black female identity, Jacques Garvey mounted a feminist challenge to the organization's male leadership.

Her challenge was not directed at disabling effective leadership where she saw it; rather, it was directed at opening up the channels of power to women. As Ula Taylor argues, Jacques Garvey "instructed black women to be competent mothers and to affirm men in the movement for self-determination. At the same time," she continues, "she went beyond a relational view of self by anchoring her discourse within the refashioning of gender roles so that women could do their part as political leaders in building the black nation."[88]

Jacques Garvey's challenge in this particular editorial relied on both a politicization of motherhood and an elevation of women's nonmaternal role in racial progress. At other points, Jacques Garvey and other women questioned men's leadership capabilities more directly. In a 1927 editorial, "Listen Women!" Jacques Garvey revisited the centrality of motherhood and coupled it with a more direct attack on the inadequacies of black men. "Negro women," she wrote, "are the acknowledged burden bearers of their race. Whether this is due to the innate laziness of Negro men, or to their lack of appreciation for their noble women, we are not quite sure."[89] Female Garveyites expressed similar sentiment in other venues. At a "ladies' night" or "mothers' union" sponsored by the Kingston, Jamaica, local, Ada Hyatt, the first lady vice president, castigated black men and encouraged women in the audience to do the same. "If by so doing, ladies, we help to remove from them that dominant 'wishbone' and substitute real 'backbone,'" she declared, ". . . then, ladies, the fruit of our labor in so having them with us tonight shall have been realized." Lizan Clarke, the second lady vice president, also rebuked the male members at the meeting, suggesting that "unless they throw aside slovenly mode of living . . . the women, with their determination, will put the men in the rear and go forward as so many Joans of Arc" in the cause of African redemption.[90] In the opening parade of one of the UNIA's international conventions, a female contingent was preceded by two women carrying a banner which read: "God give us real men."[91]

Jacques Garvey's editorial, Hyatt and Clarke's speeches, and the women's auxiliary's banner employed shame as a rhetorical tool through which to criticize black male leadership. In doing so, they directly and indirectly challenged male authority. In other instances, women in the Garvey movement made more concerted and concrete efforts to not only raise questions about men's capacity for leadership but to elevate themselves within the organization's power structure. One such occasion was the 1922 international convention. On August 31st, the last day of the convention, Victoria W. Turner, a delegate from St. Louis, submitted a list of resolutions upon which a majority of the women delegates were signatories. According to the *Negro World*, the submission of the resolutions by the women delegates was prompted by the "feeling that they had not been given proper recognition during all the former sessions and" they were "determined that they would be heard before the convention closed." The resolutions, which were prefaced by the dictum that "no race can rise higher than its women," included reserving the top leadership position in the Black Cross Nurses and Women's Motor Corps for a woman; giving more committee work and executive positions to women; and providing more opportunities for women to become field organizers and to initiate and implement plans "to elevate our women . . . without restriction from the men." After submitting the petition, several delegates took to the floor to reiterate the point that women in the association, in general, felt "curbed to a great extent in the exercise of their initiative powers in formulating plans which would make for the good of the organization." When Garvey, who had been absent for most of the session, returned to chair the meeting, the resolutions were amended and adopted, but not before he informed the delegates that the UNIA was an organization that already recognized the value of women's leadership and that "women already had the power they were asking for under the constitution." Unfortunately for the petitioners, the amendment process removed most of the resolutions' "teeth" concerning the expansion of women's roles at the executive and field organizing level.[92]

As Garvey's rejoinder to the women delegates' concerns suggests, men within the movement were somewhat attentive to issues of gender. Black men within the organization responded in a variety of ways when women challenged their authority. In many cases, their reactions expressed support for the women taking more active roles in nation-building efforts; these encouraging responses, however, were often coupled with a similar self-criticism and a plea for black men to reclaim their supposedly "lost" authority. At the above-mentioned "Ladies' Night" in Kingston, for instance, the treasurer, U. A. Leo Grant, praised Clarke's speech. He pleaded with the men in the audience, however, to "not sit back and permit the women to form the vanguard of the army . . . without a struggle for supremacy."[93] At other points, male Garveyites were unequivocally critical of what they perceived to be women's incursion into men's domain. In a June 1924 article in the Negro World, Reverend George E. Carter inveighed against women's political activism. His criticism was couched in nationalist ideas about race conservation rather than an overtly antifeminist position, although they were clearly mutually reinforcing. Carter felt that women's involvement in "public life" would detract from their role as reproducers of the race. "The love for adventure," he wrote, "the idealism of politics and desire to reform the evils of society will fascinate some women so much that this love will supercede the love for home and children; therefore, the race reproduction will be greatly jeopardized."[94]

Immanent in these patriarchal responses to the charges set forth by female Garveyites was an invocation of Victorian ideologies of separate spheres and "true womanhood." Men in the UNIA who were averse to women taking on more politically active roles employed a language that cast women as frail individuals who needed to be protected. Black women had a role in nation building but, many male Garveyites argued, their greatest assistance would be through the reproduction of the race and the transmission of morality and cultural values to children. In response to an article by one of the UNIA's leading critics, Cyril Briggs, who inaccurately reported that Jacques Garvey was in control of the UNIA during Garvey's incarceration and that the organization was divided over it, the *Negro World* deployed an image of Jacques Garvey as the domestic ideal. "It is beneath the dignity of common decency to attempt to drag the name of an innocent and helpless woman into an arena where she cannot properly defend herself."[95] Marcus Garvey utilized the same rhetoric concerning the responsibility of men to remain firmly in control of the organization's leadership. In a message from the federal penitentiary in Atlanta shortly after his conviction, he dispensed a charge to his organization concerning Jacques Garvey: "You, I feel sure, have done your duty by her and will continue to shield and protect her, while, because of my imprisonment for you, I find it impossible to do my duty." Ironically, the book in which this message appeared was edited, published, initially distributed by, and even ghost written in some parts, by Jacques Garvey herself, in an attempt to protect the name and honor of her husband.[96]

Garveyite women's challenges to male authority amounted to brush fires of discontent that men sought to contain through the deployment of the rhetoric of domesticity. Women in the OES confronted male authority in the Masonic movement in a more direct, often adversarial manner. Where the former resembled sporadic guerrilla infighting, the latter was analogous to full-scale military campaigns. Female Eastern Stars engaged in constitutional and legal wrangling over the meaning and practice of leadership within the organization. In the early 1920s, the confrontation between the OES and Prince Hall Freemasonry reached particularly bellicose levels. These confrontations led to a rethinking, among Masons, of the legitimacy of the system of adoption as a relationship between men and women in the Masonic universe.

The level of discord that existed between the OES and Freemasons was a topic of discussion at the OES's Ninth Biennial Conference in 1924. Sue Brown identified two specific problems—one internal to the organization and the other external. On the one hand, in many Grand Chapters there was some confusion over the division of authority within the chapter's leadership. There was a tendency on the part of many a grand patron, according to

Brown, to forget that it was his role to be the grand matron's "legal adviser or assistant, not her superior dictator." On the other hand, there was an external threat to the OES's sovereignty. This came from the Masonic Grand Lodges in various jurisdictions. Brown pointed out to her audience that in many instances, the grand worshipful master falsely arrogated to himself a position of authority within the OES, "thus proving to the members of the other race either that our men have no confidence in their women or that we are not yet ready for our own leadership." [97] Although tension between the OES and Prince Hall existed in Washington State, Louisiana, and West Virginia, Brown and others were especially concerned with the antagonistic relationship that existed among the fraternal and sororal circles in the Missouri jurisdiction. This controversy led to court battles and the ultimate splintering of the Missouri Grand Chapter of the OES. At its root, the conflict was over women's autonomy and men's assumption of leadership of the race.

Problems in Missouri began in the summer of 1920, nearly three decades after the United Grand Chapter had been organized by five subordinate chapters of the OES. [98] During its annual meeting in Hannibal, the Grand Chapter adopted a revised constitution, which, among other things, prohibited prospective grand officers from holding positions of leadership in other grand bodies. Although the constitution did not explicitly refer to Prince Hall's Grand Lodge of Missouri, the grand master, Crittenden E. Clark, asserted that the OES's new regulations amounted to "direct discrimination" against Masons. Moreover, he decried, this "flagrant effrontery" was being practiced by "a subsidiary body." As a result, in January 1921, Clark issued an open letter that prohibited Masons from affiliating with the OES in any manner whatsoever. [99]

In order to alleviate this inter-organizational tension, the OES appointed a committee, which consisted of grand matron Lottie Gamble, grand patron William Jacobs, and grand secretary Marie A. Hedgeman, to meet with Grand Lodge members. Eastern Stars and Freemasons interpreted the intention behind the formation of such a committee differently. Clark framed the formation of the committee as an act of contrition on the part of the OES. He suggested that the committee, in meeting with officers of the Grand Lodge, "conceded that the United Grand Chapter was wrong, that it had violated Masonic usages, customs and laws and that they were doing things that the Most Worshipful Grand Lodge could not tolerate, and prayed that the Grand Lodge would take charge of the Grand Chapter, and purge it of its many wrongs." Members of the OES Grand Chapter, however, hoped to present their side to the entire Grand Lodge, thereby prompting its officers to overturn Clark's decision. Although there is no consensus on the rationale behind the appointment of the committee or the June meeting, the representatives of the Grand Chapter and the Grand Lodge agreed to hold a joint special session in October to draft a new constitution. In the meantime, a supervisory committee of five Masons was established in August to oversee the daily functioning of the OES.[100]

Initially, Gamble backed the Clark plan for the reorganization of the Grand Chapter, although she would later argue that her public support was a strategic holding pattern aimed at mitigating the tensions between the two orders. After Gamble issued an open letter in support of the Clark plan, Clark rescinded his earlier prohibition against Masonic affiliation with the OES.[101] In late September, however, one week before the special joint meeting, several members of the United Grand Chapter served injunction notices against Gamble and Clark. Led by Mary F. Woods, they sought to prevent Gamble, Clark, and others from taking records from Grand Chapter offices for use in the special joint session. According to Woods, the revised constitution did not violate Masonic principles. She also argued that the constitution of the Grand Chapter could not be abrogated by any organization other than the OES and, as such, the Freemason's attempt to reorganize the OES was a clear violation of its constitution.[102] Wood's efforts led to a breakdown of the Clark-Gamble agreement: Gamble encouraged her fellow Eastern Stars not to attend the special joint session while litigation over the injunction was pending, and Clark issued a letter nullifying Gamble's declaration and reminding Freemasons to attend. Although the court awarded Woods the injunction on 6 October, the special session began in Mexico, Missouri, the day after—right on schedule according to Clark's original plan.[103]

On the morning of 7 October, Masonic and OES officers from throughout the state met in the Second Baptist Church in Mexico. With Grand Matron Gamble absent, the attendees of the special session—most likely at the initiation of Clark—voted to establish a new Grand Chapter. A constitution was written and adopted and new officers for Harmony Grand Chapter were elected the next day. In a proclamation issued to Missouri Freemasons three weeks later, Clark specified the hierarchical relationship that existed between the Grand Lodge and Harmony Grand Chapter: "After the Grand Chapter was duly dedicated, Grand Master Crittenden E. Clark by authority given him at the last Grand Lodge session, declared the Harmony Grand Chapter, Order of the Eastern Star, duly adopted by the Most Worshipful Grand Lodge of the State of Missouri and its jurisdiction." Furthermore, Clark decreed that Masons could not affiliate with any OES grand body other than Harmony. Clark's proclamation deployed familial language to reinforce the relationship of power between the orders. Harmony Grand Chapter was the Grand

Lodge's "newly adopted child," Clark affirmed. He further implicitly likened those Eastern Stars who supported the initial rewriting of the constitution in the summer of 1920 and those who remained loyal to Gamble to wayward children. "It is to be hoped," he concluded, "that from now on all strife in our happy family will be forever banished, and that all branches of the Order will work together for the uplift of the race and the betterment of mankind."[104]

Despite Clark's paternalistic posturing—or, perhaps, because of it—Gamble immediately declared Harmony to be an illegitimate organization. Using the terms "clandestine" and "spurious" to delegitimize the new grand chapter, Gamble and the United Chapter's leadership engaged in a Masonic discourse to criticize Clark's obvious effort to control the Missouri OES.[105] This conflict manifested itself outside of mere rhetorical sparring. The establishment of Harmony led to several splits within existing subordinate chapters, which ultimately ended in court battles over who held the legal rights to retain the extant records, property, and other assets of the organization.[106] The fall and winter of 1921 witnessed Gamble and other Eastern Stars attempting to hold together a faction-ridden order.

Members who stayed loyal to United Chapter mounted various criticisms of Clark's actions. On the one hand, they personalized the schism by suggesting that it was a power play by Clark in response to his losing an election for the post of grand patron several years earlier. On the other hand, some who were critical of Clark's authoritarian maneuver employed a gendered critique. Marie A. Hedgeman and Robert P. Jackson, United's grand matron and grand patron in 1924, suggested that Clark's actions represented a potentially intrinsic element of men's nature. "It is most unfortunate but true," they wrote, "that these crimes are promulgated among certain types of men who are inducted into a Masonic Lodge, become elevated after a few years to the position of Grand Master, which sudden elevation and the exercise of such high prerogatives causes these peculiar types of men to become drunk with authority and mad with power."[107] As Hedgeman and Jackson's criticism suggests, men within the OES fell on both sides of the split. Still, the primary manner in which both camps framed the schism was that of a conflict between the sexes. Even Kansas City's major black newspaper, in an editorial critical of both sides, depicted the controversy as "growing out of the strained relations between men and women who are under solemn obligation to be exemplars of friendship."[108]

Prince Hall Freemasons certainly viewed the conflict, and particularly its origins, as stemming from the ambiguous position of women within the Masonic universe. As the OES, a predominantly female organization, began to assert some form of autonomy, many black Masons attempted a historical revisionism of the relationship between the two orders. In 1930, New York's grand master, Daniel T. Teagle, argued that the OES had "no connection whatever with Ancient Craft Masonry" and that "neither a Grand Lodge nor a Grand Master possesses any more authority or jurisdiction over the Eastern Star than they do over the Knights of Columbus." He supported his conclusion by invoking the separate spheres argument made by Edward V. C. Eato three decades earlier: "The Eastern Star is an excellent organization in so far as its principles and sphere of activity are concerned and this reviewer wishes them well but takes the position of 'hands off' because of the following reasons: The Star is not a Masonic group nor an allied body in any sense of the word; it does not predicate its membership upon the Masonic standing of its aggregate membership; that it is a sovereign body in itself, with its own code of laws and procedure." [109] On its face, there were several errors in Teagle's argument. One did have to be either a Mason or a female relative of a Mason to become an Eastern Star. Moreover, the two orders were intimately connected in their community service and entrepreneurial endeavors. The organizational framework, symbolic rituals, indeed, the very history of American Masonry and the OES were so inseparable that Sue Brown lamented the fact that in the major chronicles of Prince Hall Freemasonry there was "no mention whatever of the O.E.S. or any other department of *female Masonry* among our women." [110] Brown clearly situated the sororal-fraternal tradition of the OES within the official archive of black Masonry.

Several years later, Harry A. Williamson echoed Grand Master Teagle's separate sphere argument but incorporated a specific gendered mythology in contesting the legitimacy of the relationship between Masonry and the OES. Williamson's mythology utilized Biblical scripture and evinced a certain biological essentialism. Citing the origins of Masonic ritual in the construction of King Solomon's Temple in Jerusalem, Williamson quoted the second book of Chronicles: "And Solomon told out threescore and ten thousand *men* to bear burdens, and fourscore thousand to hew in the mountain, and three thousand and six hundred to oversee them." According to Williamson, the fact that all Masonic ritual flowed out of this monumental feat of labor "prove[d] conclusively that the institution of Freemasonry must operate similarly amongst men alone as only these could have been bearers of burdens and hewers in the mountains because the element of physical strength as a requirement was necessary for the work, therefore, those of the female sex were eliminated from work upon the Temple." Combined with the proliferation of the institution of Masonry through the "building trades" throughout modern history, Solomon's charge provided enough evidence to Williamson that "Freemasonry in its every aspect has been confined exclusively to persons of the male sex and at no time during its known history has there ever been the least indication that an auxiliary of any character has been attached to it[,] particularly one comprising persons of the female sex."[111] Williamson's blatant, and not very persuasive, eliding of Prince Hall Freemasonry's connection to the OES—or even Carthaginian's sponsorship of the Plumb and Level Club—is not so much curious as it is astonishing. The attempt to rewrite a narrative of Prince Hall Freemasonry that ignored the intimate relationship and, indeed, interdependency of black Masons and Eastern Stars was deeply disingenuous.

When set aside Clark's earlier disavowal of the OES's autonomous behavior as an unauthorized act of a "subsidiary body," Williamson and Teagle's distortion of the history between the two orders reveals one of the ways in which manhood, as a social construct, is malleable and continuously being remade. During the early decades of its existence, the OES represented, for Freemasons, the relationship between men and women as one of public producers and private nurturers, as one of patriarch and helpmate. As women began to assert an autonomous identity within a perceived masculinist fraternal tradition, however, black Masons sought to erase a history of cooperative gender relations that had marked Prince Hall Freemasonry. By doing so, they reified the links between manliness, an exclusive fraternal heritage, and racial leadership. Freemasons' efforts to recast the relationship of women to Masonry in this way were akin to male Garveyites' attempts to frame their own roles in the movement as primary nation-builders in relation to female Garveyites' roles as secondary supporters and women in need of male protection.

■ Within their respective movements, Prince Hall Freemasons and male Garveyites drew certain connections between production, patriarchy, respectability, and manliness. In doing so, they laid claim to being "race men," or individuals capable of leading the race to economic, social, and political progress. During a period in which access to full economic and political citizenship—or, in the case of Garveyites, economic independence and national self-determination—was often framed as "manhood rights," women within these movements were subordinated in a masculinist model of racial advancement. But, like black women in the Baptist Church, as Evelyn Brooks Higginbotham has argued, female Garveyites and Eastern Stars did not idly sit by and accept their relegation to an inferior status. Indeed, they challenged the idea that there was an immutable connection between manhood and leadership through their own activism around their roles *as* women, mothers, and political actors.[112]

Black men within Prince Hall Freemasonry and the UNIA, however, were not merely engaged in a power grab. Their perceptions of women within their respective movements and the ways that they responded to women's assertion of power and leadership were not simply attempts to jealously protect their positions. Rather, they were fundamental aspects of the gender identity formation of black Masons and male Garveyites. In articulating a manly sense of self that was shaped by the ideas of production and patriarchy, they positioned themselves against women who, they consistently argued, were better equipped to inhabit the domestic space of the home and the private sphere of community development. In this sense, women functioned as negative referents in the social construction of middle-class black manhood.

As in their relationship to female auxiliaries, Prince Hall Freemasons and male Garveyites articulated a gendered sense of self through their links to juvenile organizations. Whether it was the Circle of Constantine or the UNIA Cadet Corps, black youth also served as negative referents in the gender identity formation of black Masons and Garveyites. In their assuming the role of shepherding black boys into adulthood, these men reaffirmed the boundaries between boyhood and manhood—boundaries that were all the more critical given the tendency to infantilize black men in scientific discourse and popular culture. Yet the young men that they purported to guide toward a manly life were, by the early 1920s, increasingly rebelling against bourgeois ideals of manhood. Through the cultural production of the Harlem Renaissance and the youth culture of the Jazz Age, black males coming of age during and after World War I resisted the Victorian social conventions upon which manliness was based and began to usher in more modern notions of masculinity.

Discontents

The Life and Death of Wallace Thurman

Wallace Thurman, a twenty-three-year-old black writer, arrived in New York in the late summer of 1925. Born nearly half a century after John E. Bruce, Thurman was a native of Utah and spent the first two decades of his life in the western United States. Little is known about Thurman's early life. His relationship with his parents—or what can be gleaned from his vague accounts—was relatively nonexistent. He considered himself the "neurotic son of neurotic parents" but he spent most of his youth in the care of his grandparents. After graduating high school he initially studied medicine at the University of Utah before attending the University of Southern California where he majored in literature. He remained in Los Angeles for a few years after college, working for the post office and attempting to edit and publish a magazine, the *Outlet*. After the magazine failed, Thurman, who had been reading about the burgeoning arts movement in Harlem, moved to New York and began editing for several magazines, including the *Messenger*, published by the black socialists A. Philip Randolph and Chandler Owen.[1]

Thurman's life in New York and his participation in the arts movement known as the Harlem Renaissance, was marked by cynicism, iconoclasm, and a certain nihilism. He wrote several articles for major journals, including pieces that were critical of the "Negro literary renaissance" and the "Negro bourgeoisie" for the *New Republic* and the *Independent*. It was Thurman who, in 1926, spearheaded the publication of *Fire!!*, the literary magazine that irreverently broke with the older Harlem literati and their emphasis on the propagandistic potential of cultural production. In addition to his attacks on polite black middle-class society, Thurman's iconoclasm manifested itself in a flouting of the standards of bourgeois respectability. In a letter introducing himself to Claude McKay, an African Jamaican poet and novelist, for instance, Thurman downplayed his literary achievement and his professional history. "Outside of that," he wrote, referring to his articles, "I have done very little

Wallace Thurman, Langston Hughes, and friend. (Courtesy of The Yale Collection of American Literature, Beinecke Rare Book and Manuscript Library)

since coming to Harlem . . . except learn many variations on old vices, increase my capacity for holding synthetic gin and become more and more a pariah among my own people." One of his good friends, the author Dorothy West, remembered that "he earned the enmity of many hostesses by . . . his own inability not to pass out and be carried bodily from a party."[2]

At the young age of twenty-eight, Thurman felt he was entering "the vale of middleage." His five years in Harlem, occasionally broken up by visits to Los Angeles and Salt Lake City, had been an extremely intense period. By 1930, he had written one novel, *The Blacker the Berry*, collaborated on one Broadway play, *Harlem*, and attempted to publish two of his own literary magazines. Thurman's intensity at work was accompanied by a reckless lifestyle that was exacerbated by his alcoholism. The author Langston Hughes—also a close friend—suggested that Thurman's nihilism was the result of his perfectionist tendencies. He "wanted to be a great writer, but none of his own work ever made him happy." As a result, Hughes recalled, Thurman "contented himself by writing a great deal for money, laughing bitterly at his fabulously concocted 'true stories,' creating two bad motion pictures of the 'Adults Only' type for Hollywood, drinking more and more gin, and then threatening to jump out of windows at people's parties and kill himself." His last attempt to write a great novel came in 1932 with the publication of *Infants of the Spring*, a bitter satire of the Renaissance itself. Within two years, Thurman died of tuberculosis. Prior to his death, he provided some insight into the source of his nihilism. "I have always gone in for things until I exhausted myself then dropped them," he wrote to a friend. "And this may be true of the erotic bohemian life I have been leading in Harlem." [3]

Even though most of Thurman's literary work was aimed at tweaking the respectable sensibilities of the black middle class, the fact that he was financially able to matriculate at an out-of-state, private university and, for a short period, worked as a federal employee, suggests that he was a member of the same black bourgeoisie that he so fervently criticized.[4] He was a younger member of the black middle class, however; as such, his rebellion against the dictates of respectability conformed to a broader pattern of middle-class youth culture during the Jazz Age.

The modern zeitgeist known as the Jazz Age embodied a myriad of cultural changes in American society. The revived stream of European immigrants through the mid-1920s, coupled with the migration of blacks from the American South and the Caribbean and of, to a lesser extent, Mexicans and Japanese, furthered the nation's urbanization. The populations of these vibrant, heterogenous, polyglot metropolises were increasingly connected through new forms of mass culture such as popular magazines that catered to a national audience, radio, advertising, and motion pictures. Mass consumption, which was facilitated by and mutually dependent on mass production, increased the importance of material goods and leisure in the lives of individuals and contributed to a primacy of pleasure. In terms of the nation's cultural production, a backlash against the Victorian trinity of absolute values, cultural hierarchy, and the truism of progress—already brewing before the Great War—coalesced with a generation of European intellectuals and artists recoiling from the carnage of four years of war to give birth to modernism. Significantly, the modernists' preoccupation with the "primitive" as a panacea for Western civilization's ills influenced, and coincided with, the increasing fascination that ordinary white Americans were having with the vernacular art forms of African Americans and Native Americans. The Jazz Age also witnessed the maturation of the New Woman—in her political, professional, and cultural guises—and with her maturation, the erosion of the restrictive gender conventions that characterized Victorian society.[5]

During this period, a generation of African American and African Caribbean men whose ideas of manhood diverged from those of the traditional black elite and the older members of the "new" middle class came of age. These men were, in a sense, rebels against the ideals of manliness that were articulated by Prince Hall Freemasons and male Garveyites. Where adherents to manliness talked of character, reason, production, self-denial, and respectability as being constitutive values of manhood, these iconoclasts constructed and performed their gender subjectivity through the elevation of the physical and sexual potency of the body, consumption and self-gratification, and an individual self-expression that was not confined by the black bourgeoisie's standards of propriety. Where proponents of manliness predicated their claims to manhood on the public-private organization of gender roles and hetero-normativity, many of these rebels resisted procreative heterosexuality and—in practical terms if not in principle—patriarchy as the norm. Their discontent with the restrictive nature of manliness gained expression through the culture associated with the emergent vernacular art forms of jazz and the blues; the cultural production of the Harlem Renaissance; and the concerted efforts to overthrow the repressive disciplinary regimes that characterized most black, and many white, college campuses. Indeed, if the funeral of John E. Bruce represents the figurative "death" of bourgeois manliness among the black middle class, then the immersion of Thurman and his ilk in the culture of the Jazz Age represents the "birth" of a more modern black masculinity.

As we will see in the next three chapters, younger middle-class African American and African Caribbean men challenged the canon of manliness in a number of ways. They challenged it through the career choices that they made (often in the face of parental and societal pressure to pursue a respectable occupation), their enjoyment of new, "unrespectable" modes of leisure, and the intimate relationships that they formed with both women and other men. They challenged it through the art that they produced, which celebrated the superiority of the potent primitivism of African and black folk culture over the spiritually enervated, less virile culture of Europe and Anglo-America. And they challenged it through the student strikes that racked college campuses throughout the 1920s, strikes by students who were as much concerned with gaining legitimate access to mass consumer culture—or at least having the right to that access—as they were concerned with participating in the decision-making processes on campuses or ensuring themselves a liberal arts education. As we will also see, however, these young men did not construct a more modern masculinity without some ambivalence. Even as they rejected the supremacy of bourgeois manliness in favor of a male subjectivity that was grounded in consumption and the body, they continued to subscribe to some of the same values that constituted the producerist model of manhood. Like Prince Hall Freemasons and male Garveyites, middle-class African American and African Caribbean men coming of age during and immediately after the war were incapable of completely moving beyond the social meanings of manhood as they were defined by the dominant culture.

Flaming Youth

Sometime around World War I, the writer Jean Toomer recalled, American culture changed. The shift in attitudes and mores, chiefly among middle-class American youth, did not occur rapidly; rather, it had occurred over the space of at least a decade. During his young adulthood in Washington, D.C., prior to the war, Toomer remembered, "there occurred something similar to what swept the youth of the entire country after the World War—a breaking away from old codes and conduct, the release of a 'free wild spirit,' flaming youth, not a little drinking and sexing." This gradual loosening of the moorings of respectability among young middle-class Americans was accelerated and, in some ways, legitimized by the nation's war experience. As opposed to the earlier "flaming youth," who, Toomer implicitly suggested, had to live their scandalous lives covertly, "the post-war youth lived his or her post-war way openly, as he had support of a national trend, a rebellion which soon became a popular fashion."[1]

In many ways, Toomer was referring to the transition from Victorian culture to a more modern ethos that roughly occurred between the 1890s and the 1920s. This shift, largely experienced by the middle class but present in society as a whole, influenced all facets of life, from attitudes toward work and leisure to social conventions concerning gender and sexuality. The much mythologized closing of the frontier and the increasing corporatization of the American economy, in addition to the entrance of increasing numbers of white women into the wage-labor market and pink-collar professions, undermined the earlier emphasis placed on the rugged individualism of the marketplace associated with Victorian manhood. The evolution of entertainment industries, particularly the theater and cabaret, blurred the lines between private and public social activity as well as encouraged more intimate interaction between men and women. Along with the emergence of motion pictures, these forms of entertainment legitimized leisure and public consumption—of food, alcohol, and, indirectly, sex—among the middle class.

Patterns of courtship changed as well. As women began to assert themselves within the public arenas of work and politics, sex and marriage became the means to personal happiness rather than the ends of obligation and duty. As such, middle-class youth participated in "new" rituals, such as dating, parties, and premarital sex, in order to achieve the goals of both personal fulfillment and self-gratification. In terms of sexuality, gay men and lesbians were beginning to identify themselves as homosexual; that is, rather than construct their sexual identities in terms of the gender role they assumed in the sex act—or allow themselves to be identified as gender inverts—gay men and lesbians began to identify themselves in relation to their object of desire. In doing so, they began to construct "queer" identities and cultures.[2]

Overarching, and contributing to, all of these changes was the United States's emergence as a consumer culture. Ushered in by an expanded system of mass production and distribution, and more sophisticated forms of marketing and retailing, the mass consumption of commodities fundamentally altered American society in terms of identity formation and social relations. Through the acquisition and use of material goods and the participation in certain forms of commercialized leisure, Americans constructed new individual and collective identities that were no longer bound by work, family, and local community. To be sure, mass consumption did not obliterate consciousness of class or ethnic difference. Neither did it create a culturally homogenous mass market. Working- and middle-class Americans of all ethnic backgrounds bent the new ethos of consumption to conform to the economic realities of their class position and the cultural customs of their own particular ethnic communities. Despite the fact that variants of class, ethnicity, race, and region prevented uniform patterns of consumption, American society as a whole experienced a transformation in which an ethos of consumption —the devotion to the idea that the acquisition, display, and use of commodities could provide personal self-fulfillment as well as signal one's social position—became the central organizing principle for how individuals experienced their own identity and interacted with one another.[3]

In terms of the gender conventions of the American middle class, the cultural transformation that accompanied the ascendancy of consumer capitalism precipitated a transition from a producerist model of manhood to a consumerist one. The self-made entrepreneur of the Victorian era gave way to the salaried professionals, suburban Babbitts, and male sex symbols of the Jazz Age. In the postwar period, achieving manhood became less dependent on imbibing the producer values of industry, thrift, sobriety, self-control, and character; rather, individuals constructed a masculine sense of self that was tied to the consumer goods they owned, the leisure practices they engaged in, and their physical and sexual virility. If manhood was defined by "self-sacrifice" until the first decade or so of the twentieth century, it had clearly become bound up in the pursuit of "self-fulfillment, self-expression, [and] self-gratification" by the 1920s.[4]

Toomer's recollection points out that the changing norms that influenced identity formation and governed social interaction did not affect the white middle class exclusively.[5] Indeed, the arrival of "modernity" in American culture as a whole shaped the evolution of the black middle class as well. This chapter explores how these changes manifested a different model of manhood to which younger African Americans and African Caribbean immigrants conformed. Black men and women who came of age in the years surrounding World War I began to reject the stultifying ideals and values that structured their parents' claims to respectable, middle-class status. This attitude included a repudiation of bourgeois ideals of manliness. Many younger blacks opposed the association of manhood with the marketplace and consequently spurned the idea that they had to pursue a traditional, middle-class career. They became ensconced in consumer culture through rent parties, cabarets, and, in general, the jazz scene. Moreover, they were comfortable challenging traditional Victorian notions of sexuality in their refusal to accept the conventionality and inevitability of marriage and in their open acceptance of (and for some, participation in) a growing gay subculture. To be sure, there was no monolithic performance of an alternative masculinity among younger blacks. Some unabashedly defied the expectations and prescriptions that accompanied middle-class male status while others tentatively tested the boundaries of what it meant to be a middle-class man in the early twentieth century. On balance, however, these young men rebelled against the dictates of manliness through their career choices, their participation in the youth culture of the 1920s, and their approaches to love and sex.

▨ Middle-class African American and African Caribbean men who came of age during the war and postwar period actively reshaped the meanings of manhood in the 1920s. Born in the last decade of the nineteenth century and the first decade of the twentieth, these men rejected manliness as the organizing principle of their gender identity. One of the areas in which they did this was work. Even as the maturation of consumer capitalism was contributing to an expansion of the black middle class, younger black men were making critical choices about their place in that expansion and, equally as important, their relation to the gender conventions of the bourgeoisie. These choices—as well as the ambivalence surrounding them and the anxiety that they produced—are best revealed in the lives of several individuals who eventually became involved in the Harlem Renaissance. Although the life stories of Claude McKay, Jean Toomer, Langston Hughes, Richard Bruce Nugent, Aaron Douglas, Rudolph Fisher, Eric Walrond, and Countee Cullen might, at first glance, seem anecdotal and not emblematic of the general experience of middle-class blacks, I would argue that in fact they were. As educated young men, they were confronted with the same questions regarding career paths and lifestyles as other middle-class youth. The only thing atypical about them was that their creative talent provided them more options (and, as we will see, occasionally more angst). But they still had to come to grips with fundamental issues such as how they were going to make a living, how they were going to be contributing members of society, and how their families and communities would receive their decisions.

Claude McKay, born in August 1890, was at the cusp of this younger generation. One of eleven children, Claude was born in Clarendon parish in the hill country of Jamaica. His father, Thomas Francis McKay, was a farmer with enough property to qualify him for suffrage. Influenced by British missionaries, Thomas Francis was devoutly religious and a deacon in the local Baptist church. Hannah Edwards McKay was a diligent farm wife and mother, taking care of the home and children, tending the gardens, and managing the family's livestock. Claude's memories of his mother as "sweet-natured" and his father as "honest [and] stern even to harshness" resonated with Marcus Garvey's depiction of his own upbringing. The ownership of property, a hard work ethic, and a pious demeanor—accompanied by a critical attitude toward the moral condition and syncretic religious practices of the poorer peasantry—solidified the family's position within the free black peasantry. Despite their dark skin and "pure" African origins, the McKays were "aspiring members of the middle-class," a position normally accessible only to white and mixed-race Jamaicans. Claude's relationship with his father was strained throughout most of his youth. Thomas McKay's authoritarian godliness and stern discipline alienated his son. Their relationship represented the classic Victorian father-son bond, one based on fearful respect rather than loving admiration. In contrast, Claude developed an affectionate and loving relationship with his mother.[6]

During much of his youth and early adolescence, Claude lived with his older brother U'Theo, a teacher, and his wife, in the environs of Montego Bay. While with U'Theo, he was exposed to free thought and began to write poetry. During his teenage years, Claude apprenticed with a woodworker and began an intellectual relationship with Walter Jekyll, "an English gentleman" who would become his "literary mentor." In 1909, after his mother's death, McKay moved to the Kingston area, where he worked in the constabulary and continued his education with Jekyll. He remembered, at the time, that he was "a zealot for the truth as something absolute." After returning home and "farm[ing] rather halfheartedly," Claude decided to go abroad and study agronomy in order to return and "teach the peasantry modern ways of farming."[7] His logical destination was the leading industrial and agricultural black college in the United States, Tuskegee Institute. Arriving in 1912, the "semi-military, machinelike" environment alienated McKay, who did not find it intellectually stimulating. He transferred in October of the same year to Kansas State College but, like Tuskegee, his new school could not keep his interests for very long. The aspiring artist moved to New York City in the spring of 1914, and in the summer he married his Jamaican sweetheart, Eulalie Lewars, who had followed him to the states. After a short-lived venture as a restaurateur, during which his marriage fell apart and a pregnant Eulalie returned to Jamaica, Claude worked in a series of unskilled and service jobs, including porter, fireman, houseman, and dining-car waiter on the Pennsylvania Railroad.[8]

Between 1914 and 1919, McKay began his career as a writer in earnest. He met and corresponded with many important literary and journalistic figures, including Crystal and Max Eastman, socialist activist siblings who published *Masses*, which later became *Liberator*. Claude moved to Harlem in 1917 and continued to write poetry that relied less on dialect verse and was much more militant in terms of content. In addition to his relationship with white leftists, he socialized with several black Marxists, including Hubert Harrison, Richard B. Moore, and W. A. Domingo. Moreover, he joined Cyril Briggs's African Blood Brotherhood, an organization that attempted to reconcile black nationalism with the international communism of Lenin. In the fall of 1919, he went to England where he expanded his intellectual circle. He joined the radical suffragette Sylvia Pankhurst's Worker's Socialist Federation and contributed to the organization's weekly, *Worker's Dreadnought*. He also spent time with black veterans who had remained in Europe. Loosely formed into a club, the ex-soldiers hailed mostly from Africa and the Caribbean, although there were a few Americans. McKay supplied them with issues from the African American radical press and, in turn, wrote about the club for the UNIA's *Negro World*. He also participated in the International Socialist Club, a group of politically radical theorists and activists dating from 1849, and continued writing poetry.[9]

McKay matured in many ways during his brief time in England. His major concerns as an individual and a writer, racial justice and class struggle, were intellectually sharpened through his association with black veterans and radical Marxists. Claude also experienced the growing movement of disillusion that was at the heart of European artistic and intellectual circles immediately following the war. Although by no means did he consider himself a modernist (at least in terms of technique), McKay's belief that "the world was passing gradually from the cutthroat competitive to a co-operative stage," weakened by the war, passed into oblivion as a result of his experience in England. McKay returned to New York in the spring of 1921 and became associate editor for *Liberator*. But New York could not hold his attention for long. After resigning from the staff because of editorial differences (and Max Eastman's resignation ten months earlier) in August 1922, McKay jumped at the chance to travel to the Soviet Union that fall. This would begin a twelve-year absence from the United States.[10]

Jean Toomer, born into an elite black family in Washington, D.C., in 1894, had a markedly different childhood than McKay, but their entrance into adulthood was strikingly similar. The prominent male figure in Toomer's early life was his grandfather, P. B. S. Pinchback. Pinchback was a beneficiary of the politics of Reconstruction, riding on the back of the Republican Party into the state senate and governor's house of Louisiana, and nearly into the United States Senate. Following Redemption, he continued to receive positions through Republican patronage until 1892, when he moved his family to Washington and opened a law firm.[11] According to several of Toomer's biographers, Pinchback was the epitome of the Victorian patriarch. "In his home," writes one, "the genteel conventions and traditional moralities were religiously observed." He was an authoritarian presence within his family, a stern disciplinarian who expected his three sons to pursue lucrative careers—and eventually enter public service—and his daughter to marry a successful member of the black elite. Pinchback's wife, Nina Hethorn, was the exemplary Victorian woman: a dutiful wife, nurturing mother, and hostess extraordinaire.[12] Indeed, Toomer's recollection of his grandparents were replete with Victorian platitudes: "Above all I was impressed by his man-strength—not so much his dash or his heartiness, or his domineering temper—but a thing in him that made you know he was solid and vital in life, as a man should be." Toomer described his grandmother as a "woman of her home, a wife-type finding in this home of hers fulfilling occupation."[13]

Because Toomer's father, Nathan, left his mother, Nina, within a year of his birth, Pinchback, the embodiment of Victorian manliness, was very influential in his life. As he later recalled, he learned from his grandfather "inportant [sic] life-factors," which included "a style of life—preference for a type of life in which a strong man is the head of the family and a sort of patriarch of his world." As two of his biographers suggest, however, Toomer may have been more influenced by his Uncle Bismark, the antithesis of P. B. S.

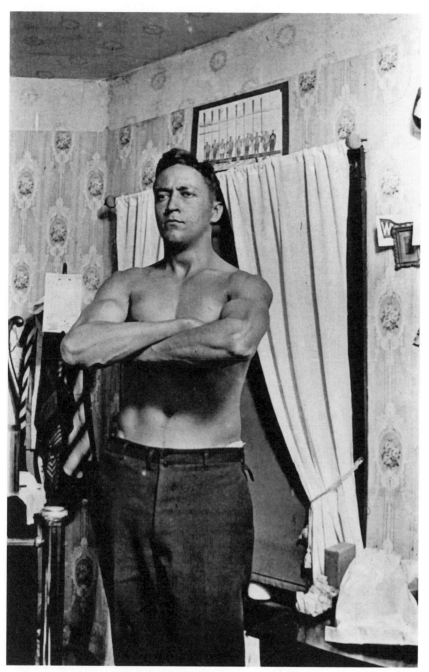

Jean Toomer. (Courtesy of The Yale Collection of American Literature, Beinecke Rare Book and Manuscript Library)

and, for Jean, "a kindred soul." Bismark, a Yale dropout, eventually received a medical degree from Howard University but failed to maintain a successful private practice. By the time he was in his thirties, he was residing in the Pinchback household with his parents, sister Nina, and Jean. Bismark's real interests did not lay in medicine or even the idea of a professional life; rather, his life was governed by the ethos of aestheticism. "In contrast to the public, group-oriented, dominating political man, often an irritant to those around him, focused on wealth and influence," Cynthia Earl Kerman and Richard Eldridge write, "Bismark showed the solitary, inner-oriented, intellectual reconciler, vitally interested in art and literature."[14] While in Washington, under the shadow of his grandfather, Jean was presented with two distinct models of manhood—models between which he would vacillate for most of his early life. As he matured, he fluctuated between an obligatory sense of pursuing a typical bourgeois career and an eccentric rejection of the sterility and market-oriented mentality that characterized Victorian culture.

Toomer's physical and sexual maturation was a source of continual stress as a teenager. Still a virgin, Jean's indulgence in masturbation created enormous feelings of guilt and depression. "So day after day, night after night, the fire burned me in short circuit," he recalled. "Moreover, having followed some strange inner thinking, I had come to the conclusion that the sex-act was mysteriously linked with [and would result in] an access to manliness. In other words, I explained my weakened physical condition as due to the fact that I had never touched a girl." Six feet and 135 pounds, Toomer began an intense regimen of dieting, exercise, and weight lifting. His immersion in physical culture, replete with cold baths and photograph collections of Adonis-like men, was geared toward combating masturbation, "that practice which more than any other bleeds away the body and soul of growing beings on earth." His training at the predominantly black Dunbar High School also helped him to direct his preoccupation with sex away from his ideal of manhood. "Two afternoons a week we drilled, the rookies learning the manual of arms, squad movements, and all that had to do with this aspect of soldiering," he recalled. The training "was masculine, as much or more of a man's world than handling a boat upon the open waters."[15] The Victorian dogma of self-control and the more modern sensibility attaching sexual experience to the achievement of manhood were at war in Toomer's psyche; during his high school years, the bourgeois ideal of manliness, embodied in his grandfather, emerged the victor.

The struggle between self-control and sexual gratification was not the only inner conflict Jean experienced while he was a young man. During the final years of high school, he began to grapple with the question of his future vocation. P. B. S. and Uncle Bismark implicitly figured in his thought process although, by most accounts, he did not find poetry and literature particularly engaging as academic courses. Even though he could not see himself following in Bismark's footsteps, Jean knew that neither could he replicate his grandfather's experiences as a lawyer, politician, and bureaucrat. "Of course, like any other young man in America of 1914," he later wrote, "I felt I had to do something; I wanted money, enough; I wanted sex and love and perhaps marriage, though marriage seemed more distance off . . . I wanted a certain health of body and spirit and a certain productiveness which I felt I could obtain in none of the usual ways." Toomer decided to enroll in the agriculture program at the University of Wisconsin. "I wanted something new, even raw, with the tang of a seawind in it, with the touch of the earth," he remembered, "and men struggling against the elements to produce what men need, to build what had not yet been built, to adventure and discover what had not yet been discovered." As with his ambivalence concerning self-control and self-gratification, Toomer opted to adhere to Victorian constructions of manliness, represented not only by the producer values he extolled, but also by a frontier individualist mentality.[16]

During the summer before his freshman year, two events occurred to which Toomer credited his maturation as a man. Interestingly, these events represent signal moments in the attainment of Victorian manliness and modern masculinity. After attending Wisconsin for a summer session, Toomer traveled with the Pinchbacks to a summer resort on the Chesapeake Bay. While there, he finally had a sexual experience. He "returned to Washington a full-fledged man, with intimate inside knowledge of the mystery that had plagued, intrigued and eluded me for years." Back in Washington, shortly before he was to return to Wisconsin, he finally convinced his skeptical grandfather of the utility of his major. As a result, Toomer recalled, P. B. S. "outdid himself to make me feel a man-member of the family" and he returned to the Midwest "with a revived and vivified sense of my duty to my family."[17] Regarding these diverse articulations of manhood, Toomer's "coming of age" can be explained, in part, by the fact that this autobiographical version was written in the mid-1930s, when sexual experience had become more integral in attaining masculinity. Nevertheless, it points to the historical transition in definitions of American middle-class masculinity and the inner conflicts that accompanied the changing nature of manhood. It reflects the complexity of masculinity in American culture and reinforces the idea that any such transition was not neat but rather occurred over the space of decades and created tremendous ambivalence within those who experienced it.

Toomer's ambivalence intensified during his first semester at Wisconsin.

Initially, he threw himself into campus life and was also active in athletics to the detriment of his other courses. But he remained conflicted about his future. Before the semester was over, he decided to withdraw from Wisconsin. Although he claimed that it was, in part, to be nearer to a young Washingtonian woman with whom he had fallen in love, Jean's vacillation between a productive and aesthetic lifestyle undoubtedly contributed. Concerning his decision to pursue a career in agriculture, he later assessed that "some of it was not pleasant to contemplate, but, on the whole, I felt I actually would like it. A lean hard life, sure enough, but a man's life of hardship and production," he continued. "But liking aside, could I do it? Was I cut out for a life of physical labor only . . . committed to the earth and the animals in their seasons, with no dances, no parties, no time or energy or hope to talk and think and follow some other craze?" His fascination with the hardy individual on the frontier and his obligatory notion of choosing a traditional career began to give way to an interest in an intellectual and aesthetic lifestyle. "To be at the soil-source of things meant less than to be at the heart-source of them," he wrote. "I was a man of feeling and I wanted to live from my heart."[18]

Over the next four years, between 1916 and 1919, Toomer moved around much of the country. He enrolled in both the American College of Physical Education and the University of Chicago, studying anatomy and pre-med. While there, he began reading socialist and naturalist literature. His stay in Chicago was short-lived, however. Toomer moved to New York where he took various courses in sociology and history at New York University and City College. After being rejected for military service, he spent time in Chicago, Milwaukee, and Washington, but ended up back in the Northeast, where he worked at a New Jersey shipyard and attended the Rand School of Social Science in New York.[19]

Jean had certainly cast a wide net; but in doing so, he alienated many people in his life—particularly his grandfather. Nellie McKay, Toomer's literary biographer, argues that by 1919, he was concerned that "his family and friends . . . were confused by his vacillating behavior. He had spent his money and that of others; he had spent his energies; and he was spending his life but not producing anything that was of value in the marketplace."[20] Within a year, however, Jean's inner conflict began to abate as he seriously entertained the idea of becoming a writer. In August of 1920, he expanded his literary and social circles when he was invited to a party given by Lola Ridge, an editor of the literary magazine *Broom*. At the party, he met Waldo Frank, a writer for the magazine *Seven Arts*.[21] Toomer had begun writing poems and short stories in 1919 and Frank encouraged his literary aspirations. It was not until a trip to the Deep South in 1921, however, that his artistic development became full-blown. He accepted a temporary position as the principal of a black industrial school in Sparta, Georgia. He only stayed two months but that brief period shaped his early career as a modernist writer. As several of his biographers point out, Toomer's immersion in black folk culture represented a critical moment in his growth as an artist.[22] Out of this experience, he wrote two plays and several poems and short stories. He returned to Washington with an intensified commitment to writing. By the summer of 1922, he was organizing a manuscript entitled *Cane*, publishing his poetry in *Liberator* and *Crisis*, and circulating among a black literary coterie based in Washington, D.C.[23]

The presence of Pinchback, both physically and mentally, in Toomer's life faded as Jean committed himself to becoming a writer. His grandfather died in late 1921. In 1922, at the age of twenty-seven, Jean finally felt comfortable in rejecting the traditional bourgeois gender ideals of his grandfather. It had not been an easy process. As late as that spring, he evidently felt uneasy solely pursuing an artist's life—uneasy enough for Frank to write him a letter assuring him that his decision was the right one. "Today, every rhythm, every will sent through the weave of America is fatal to creation," Frank counseled, ". . . and so often not alone economic pressure but the subly [sic] insidious Myth of 'the duties of manhood, the need of making ones [sic] own way' plunges the delicate artist tissues into a corrodent [sic] poisonous bath of American 'reality' which eats them up. Don[']t think that you will be helping yourself or America in a newspaper office or an advertising agency." Jean may not have opposed the "rottenness" of the "marketplace" as vehemently as Frank did, but he rejected it just the same.[24] In doing so, he repudiated its attendant gender connotations. This did not translate into an abjuration of the idea of manhood, only its Victorian manifestation. When he wrote to the mother of a teenage girl with whom he had fallen in love, Jean stressed his aesthetic nature. "When my own life shall have been summed up, I think it will be evident that one of my main concerns has been to stimulate and nourish Creative Values," he wrote. He stressed that he was an "artist," a "thinker," in touch with the "World Consciousness." Rather than assuring her of his ability to materially provide for the young woman, Toomer dwelled upon the nurturing aspects of his being. He felt that there were "three things I have no doubt: my ability to create (with words, and directly with life), my capacity to give and receive love, and my unfailing sincerity as regards both of them."[25] Toomer asserted his masculinity, in effect, through a reaffirmation of both his creative and procreative power. He laid claim to manhood not through the precepts of Victorianism and its reliance on engaging the public sphere but through a more affective model that stressed his ability to be an artist and a nurturing husband and father.

As Jean Toomer was resolving his own ambivalence, Langston Hughes was embarking upon a similar journey of self-discovery, although one less fraught with uncertainty. Hughes was born in Joplin, Missouri, in February 1902 to Carrie Langston, a schoolteacher, and James Nathaniel Hughes, an upstart businessman and lawyer. Carrie and James's marriage did not last long, however; by the time Langston was born, they were separated—James in Cuba then Mexico, and Langston and Carrie in Lawrence, Kansas, with her mother. It was in Lawrence that Langston spent his preadolescence with his grandmother. His mother often traveled through the Midwest seeking better-paying jobs. Langston remembered his grandmother as an extremely proud and pious woman, never one to seek a handout despite the fact that she often had trouble paying the mortgage and keeping food on the table. Hughes found solace in his books. The majority of his reading included stories of overcoming adversity, the chivalric and self-made man stories of the Victorian age, books "where almost always the mortgage got paid off, the good knights won, and the Alger boy triumphed."[26]

Hughes's grandmother died when he was twelve and he went to live with his mother, who was remarried and had another son. Hughes liked his stepfather, Homer Clark, a hard-working man who held down a number of menial and semiskilled jobs. Carrie contributed to the family income, usually doing domestic work. The family ended up in Cleveland, where Langston enrolled in high school. Comprised mainly of recent black migrants from the South and the children of eastern and southern European immigrants, Central High School exposed Hughes to ethnic diversity and political radicalism. While there, he began to read such literature as *Liberator* and *Socialist Call*. Still, Langston was the typical high school student. He participated in several clubs, ran track, became a lieutenant in the school's military corps and, during his senior year, edited the yearbook. He also began to write poetry. If his scholastic life approximated those of his fellow students, however, his personal life did not. Throughout his youth, his mother's marriage went through a cycle of dissolution and reconciliation. Langston's stepfather, frustrated at his inability to provide for the family, would often move to another city in search of work. Carrie would try to get along with Langston and his younger brother, Gwyn, but would eventually follow Homer. Langston decided to finish his education at Central. During the school year, he rented an attic apartment, survived on a meager diet supplemented by the families of friends, and immersed himself in literature. He also worked part-time for the Playground House, a community center, where he taught art to children.[27]

Following his junior year, Hughes's father re-entered his life as abruptly as he had left it. James Hughes was a lawyer and the general manager of an

American electric light company in Toluca, Mexico; he also owned a ranch in Temexcaltepic, a house in Toluca, in addition to property in Mexico City. The elder Hughes sent word that he wanted Langston to spend the summer with him in Mexico. Against his mother's wishes, but with the support of his stepfather, Langston eagerly looked forward to meeting James Hughes and accompanying him south.[28]

Almost immediately, James Hughes's intolerance of slackers and, on some level, his own racial self-hatred, became clear to Langston. "My father had a great contempt for all poor people," he recalled. "He thought it was their own fault that they were poor." His father used the term "nigger" liberally to castigate blacks and lower-class Mexicans for what he considered to be their lack of initiative and industriousness. In this sense, the word interchangeably referred to race, ethnicity, and economic status. The elder Hughes's antipathy toward blacks, Mexicans, Indians, and poor people was accompanied by an intense devotion to making money and climbing the social ladder. Indeed, he represented the classic version of the self-made man, the epitome of bourgeois manliness. Langston recalled that he "was too frugal with money"; this anti-consumption mentality was implicitly gendered. James Hughes would rail against Langston when he and the cook occasionally splurged on the weekly shopping. "My father stormed and said I was just like my mother, always wasting money," he remembered. His denunciation of excessive consumption, accompanied by a rejection of excessive spirituality ("He said greasers and niggers would never get anywhere because they were too religious, always praying.") and a social Darwinist perspective on success, reflected James Hughes's Victorian ethos of manhood—an ethos to which he expected Langston to conform.[29]

Although he soon realized that he had little in common with his father, Langston spent that summer and the next one in Mexico. These were not vacations, however. During the first summer, Langston's father began to teach him bookkeeping skills. Not very good at math, Langston chafed under his father's Taylorist methods. "It seemed that my father couldn't resist saying, 'Hurry up,' more and more," he recalled, ". . . and giving me harder and harder bookkeeping problems to have worked out by the time he got home from the office. Besides, he was teaching me to typewrite, and gave me several exercises to master each evening. 'Hurry up and type that a hundred times before you go to bed. Hurry up and get that page of figures done so I can check on it. Hurry up and learn the verb, *estar*.'"[30] The first summer was extremely draining on Langston. At one point, he considered suicide, going so far as to place a loaded revolver to his temple. His depression was caused in part by his alienation from his father and his mother's failure to respond to his letters.

At another point during his stay, Langston's hatred for his father precipitated a psychosomatic illness that left him in the hospital for several weeks. Although he recovered from his emotionally induced malady, Langston never fully purged his animosity toward his father. Some years later, writing to console a friend on his father's death, he wrote, "I am sorry because you liked him. The dying of mine wouldn't matter in the least to me."[31]

After his senior year back in Cleveland, Langston returned to Mexico. He realized that the only possibility of continuing his education rested with his father. James Hughes wanted Langston to go to college in Europe and study mining engineering. Langston, however, wanted to become a writer, which prompted his father to question the financial potential of such a career. As a compromise, Langston suggested Columbia University, mainly because he wanted to experience Harlem. James Hughes refused to spend any money to educate his son in the United States. During the next year, Langston taught English at a business college and a girl's school in order to pay for his first year at Columbia. He also wrote poetry and fiction, publishing several pieces in *Literary Digest*, *Crisis*, and its children's supplement, *Brownies' Book*. In the late summer of 1921, after a year in Mexico, Langston, with his father's half-hearted blessing, departed for Columbia, New York City, and, more importantly, Harlem.[32]

Langston's first semester at Columbia was dismal. He felt alienated from the larger white student body and spent most of his time with a fellow student from China. He struggled through his science and math curriculum; indeed, the only course he enjoyed was literature. Carrie, separated from her husband once again, had moved to New York. While she looked for work, Langston helped her financially with the money he received from his father. Consequently, he remained broke for most of the semester and answered his father's requests for itemized accounts of his expenditures with a simple "All gone." Langston managed to finish the year at Columbia but he was far from turning in a stellar academic performance. He decided to quit college, informed his father not to send any more money, and struck out on his own. He moved to Harlem and immersed himself in the bourgeoning arts movement by attending lectures and readings at the 135th Street library and publishing more poetry. In the fall of 1922, he decided to sign onto a ship's crew and travel.

Langston's initial assignment was as a mess boy on a mother ship that performed minimal maintenance on empty ships docked along the Hudson River. He enjoyed being away from Columbia, the Harlem literati, and the expectations these and others placed on his intellectual development. He wrote to a new friend that "after so many years in a book-world and so much striving to be a 'bright boy' and an 'intelligent young man,' it is rather nice to come here and be simple and stupid and to touch a life that is at least a living thing with no touch of books." Indeed, Langston's decision to take to the sea was as much a rejection of haughty intellectualism as it was a rejection of his father's bourgeois expectations. When he finally obtained a position on a ship heading for Africa, he threw all of his books into the sea. This was a tremendously liberating moment for Langston and a signal moment in the maturation of his masculine identity:

> It was like throwing a million bricks out of my heart—for it wasn't only the books that I wanted to throw away, but everything unpleasant and miserable out of my past: the memory of my father, the poverty and uncertainties of my mother's life, the stupidities of color-prejudice, black in a white world, the fear of not finding a job, the bewilderment of no one to talk to about things that trouble you, the feeling of always being controlled by others—by parents, by employers, by some outer necessity not your own. All those things I wanted to throw away. To be free of. To escape from. I wanted to be a man on my own, control my own life, and go my own way. I was twenty-one.[33]

He was a worldly twenty-one-year-old. Between 1922 and 1926 he visited or lived in western Africa, Paris, Italy, Harlem, and Washington, D.C. In 1926, with the aid of liberal philanthropist Amy Spingarn, Hughes enrolled in Lincoln University, a predominantly black school in Pennsylvania, and graduated with a liberal arts degree in 1930. Significantly, by this time he had completely rejected his father's goal for him to become a mining engineer and, instead, cast his lot as a professional writer.

Another passionate rebel against bourgeois manliness was the writer and artist Richard Bruce Nugent. Born in 1906 to a Washingtonian upper-class family, Nugent moved to New York while still a teenager. In New York, he performed menial, unskilled labor and, in the words of one historian, became a "professional Bohemian." Overwhelmingly eccentric and openly gay at a young age, Nugent became friends with Hughes and another writer in Washington, Waring Cuney. The three of them, along with other younger writers and older figures of the Washington cultural scene, spent many evenings in the literary salon of the black poet Georgia Douglas Johnson. Nugent became a secondary figure in the Renaissance, contributing drawings and short stories to many of the literary magazines. His unconventional public behavior, including his fashion taste, caused minor scandals in both Washington and Harlem. Jessie Fauset, the novelist, editor, and leading promoter of respectability among members of the Renaissance, felt that she "could forgive

Nugent's rather too deliberate eccentricities but" was "not prepared to pardon his untidiness." Carl Van Vechten, the white writer and socialite, found Nugent's flamboyance amusing. He related to Hughes an experience at an awards dinner sponsored by the National Urban League's Opportunity magazine where Nugent was "with his usual open chest and uncovered ankles." Van Vechten speculated that he would soon "be going without trousers."[34]

Nugent later looked back upon this period as an irresponsible and capricious phase of his life. Writing to Van Vechten some years after the end of the Renaissance, he declared that he had "no intentions of really becoming all over again, the vagabond I once was." He was somewhat critical of the Renaissance, reminding Van Vechten: "Remember I was of that spoiled crop—that NEW NEGRO bunch—the Niggeratti—and not the strongetst [sic] character in that somewhat far-fetched group." He reinforced what he believed to be the fantastical nature of the Renaissance, informing Van Vechten that "it is really an event each day as I discover and re-discover that life is real—life is earnest."[35] His penitence notwithstanding, Nugent's young adulthood, particularly his unorthodox fashion style and his open homosexuality, represented the New Negro in its boldest manifestation. His flight from middle-class standards of manliness, however, paralleled those of Toomer, McKay, and Hughes. In eschewing a traditional career for the arts, Nugent rebelled against the bourgeois nexus of manhood and the market.

All of these individuals—Nugent probably less than others—struggled with decisions to pursue a traditional education, which would presumably give them access to, or solidify their positions within, the black middle class. All of them ultimately repudiated careers that measured one's manhood by one's contribution to the marketplace. Their particular career choices represented not only a rejection of the black bourgeoisie but a resistance to conform to late-Victorian notions of manhood. Other younger middle-class blacks, however, were not so brash in their revolt against manliness. Some entered the arts and the bohemian world that accompanied it only after pursuing a traditional education and making traditional career choices. Aaron Douglas, for example, struggled between the legal profession and art as potential careers. After graduating from high school, Douglas worked several unskilled service and semiskilled industrial jobs in the Midwest. He admired the "mad hustle and two-fisted pioneer spirit" of cities like Kansas City, St. Louis, and Detroit. "The parts of these areas that I was privileged to see were smelly, harried, and uncouth, but honest," he wrote. "This was America," he continued, "the land of the free which promised a place for all who were willing to chip in and earn their way." Douglas later attended the University of Nebraska and received a B.F.A. in 1922. After teaching art in a

Kansas City high school for two years, he decided to become a professional artist. He moved to New York where he illustrated for several magazines and books, including *Vanity Fair, Opportunity,* and *Crisis.* Douglas supplemented his income by relying on individual and organizational patronage as well as doing unskilled service work.[36] Prior to moving to New York, Douglas's admiration for the "two-fisted pioneer spirit" represented his bourgeois aspirations, his investment in individualism and capitalist progress. By the time he immersed himself in the Renaissance, he had rejected the primacy of the marketplace, as is clear from his criticism of the "bottomless pit [of] commercial art where slaves [swarm?] and sweat . . . grinding away their souls for a penny and the worthless rubbish of this bourgeoisie civilization."[37]

Rudolph "Bud" Fisher did not share Douglas's disdain for "bourgeoisie civilization," but he did experience some of the ambivalence that character-ized the transition from Victorian manliness to modern masculinity. The son of a clergyman, Fisher was born in Washington, D.C., in 1897 and spent his childhood in Providence, Rhode Island. He attended Brown University, where he majored in both English and biology, was elected to Phi Beta Kappa, and received his B.A. and M.A. in 1919 and 1920. From all indications, Fisher was a diligent and ambitious student who took success quite seriously. He de-tested "the act of quitting," "mental cowardice," and cynicism toward life by those who had not yet endured any great hardships. Becoming a profes-sional success within the bounds of the black middle class was important to Fisher. While a graduate student at Brown, he justified his preoccupation with his studies to his friend and love interest, Dorothy Peterson, who evidently considered him to be too "cold." He responded that he felt caught between two worlds—those of reason and emotion—and, although neither by itself provided complete sustenance, he felt committed to the former. "And surely nothing lasting can be built on a mere, momentary emotion, a surge of feel-ing that holds for a moment," he wrote to Peterson. "And so I swing to the other extreme and check it all. Of course that's bad, too. Someday I'll grow up, and then I'll allow myself a proper mixture, a golden mean, of emotion and rationality—I'll feel as well as think—but for the present I guess I'd better just—think." Fisher's academic rigor paid off. After graduating from Brown, he received his M.D. from Howard University's medical school in 1924, in-terned at Freedman's Hospital in Washington, and held a National Research Council fellowship at the College of Physicians and Surgeons of Columbia University. He opened a private practice in Harlem in 1927, specializing in roentgenology. In addition to practicing medicine, Fisher became involved in the Renaissance, publishing several short stories and essays, as well as two major novels.[38]

Fisher was one of the few younger literati who became a primary figure of the Harlem Renaissance while pursuing a traditional middle-class profession. Other writers, such as Countee Cullen and Eric Walrond, became integrally involved in the Renaissance while simultaneously anchoring themselves in middle-class occupations. Walrond, born in 1898, was a native of British Guiana but was raised in Barbados and Panama. He ventured into journalism at an early age, writing for a Panamanian newspaper before, at the age of twenty, moving to New York and enrolling in City College and Columbia, where he took literature and writing courses. In addition to his pursuit of a career in journalism, Walrond performed stenographic duties for a British diplomatic office and, perhaps, worked in the same capacity for the black-owned Standard Life Insurance Company in Atlanta. He did not care for the New South, writing to a friend that Atlanta was "alright for anybody who want[s] to be a Babbitt; but for a poet or one who is sensitive to the finer things in life[,] it is a pig sty." Walrond's reference to Babbitt, the harried yet success-driven real estate agent and title character of Sinclair Lewis's 1922 novel, was a criticism of middle-class manhood. Although Walrond cast his professional lot in a traditional black middle-class occupation—he worked as an editor for several newspapers, including the *Negro World*, and, in 1925, became the business manager for *Opportunity*—he separated himself from mainstream middle-class manhood and its articulation through the marketplace.[39]

Cullen was another member of the literati who straddled the worlds of bourgeois respectability and urban bohemianism. This was reflected in both his class background and his professional life. Cullen's adoptive father, Reverend Doctor Frederick A. Cullen, was a Methodist Episcopalian minister, president of the Harlem branch of the National Association for the Advancement of Colored People (NAACP), and an entrenched member of the black middle class. His adoptive mother, Carolyn Cullen, was a classically trained musician and singer. Cullen received a prestigious education, attending the predominantly white De Witt Clinton High School on Manhattan's Upper West Side. He received his B.A. from New York University, graduating Phi Beta Kappa, and an M.A. from Harvard. By 1926, at the age of twenty-three, he was writing a literary column for *Opportunity* and had published poetry in leading magazines as well as his own volume of work, *Color*.[40]

Unlike some of the other literati who struggled between pursuing art and a career that would guarantee their entrance to, or preserve their place in, the middle class, Cullen entered the more traditional, bourgeois profession of journalism. His investment in his class status made itself clear while he was an undergraduate. In 1923, Cullen held a summer job as a hotel busboy in Atlantic City. He had no doubt, however, that, instead of a career, this was "just a job." He wrote to his close friend, Harold Jackman, "but it gives me time to study some of the vermins [sic] of the race, and since three fourths of every race is vermin, I am in with the masses." He continued that "my bourgois [sic] soul receives it [his mingling with working-class blacks] as one takes an ermetic [sic]—with disgust." Although the working class provided useful material for his poetry, Cullen had no desire to interact personally with them. "You see I am not at all a democratic person," he wrote, "I believe in an aristocracy of the soul."[41] Among younger blacks, Cullen is perhaps an example of one who was most committed to black middle-class standards of work and respectability, although his conformity was filtered through his romantic disposition.

Born between 1890 and 1906, and essentially coming of age between 1910 and 1920, the younger African Americans and African Caribbeans examined here were fortunate, by early-twentieth-century standards, in that they were in a position to pursue a post-secondary education and enter a profession that either ensured social mobility or stabilized their middle-class status. Some initially decided to pursue their artistic careers at the expense of securing a professional livelihood and, in turn, relied on odd jobs, philanthropy, royalties, and the help of friends, in order to supplement their incomes. Others chose the bohemian world of arts and letters only after they pursued a traditional career, and still others successfully straddled the two. Even as some brashly challenged—and others only timidly tested—the boundaries of middle-class manhood in relation to the marketplace and work experience, most of them rebelled against the respectability of bourgeois manliness when it came to leisure. The age of jazz was not limited to any one space or class. It exerted its cultural iconoclasm in urban areas throughout the country and incorporated middle- and working-class blacks and whites alike. Indeed, even though the sample of younger blacks here is skewed in the direction of those who participated in the Harlem Renaissance, their experiences as middle-class youth were shaped by a jazz culture that, while influenced by the cultural production of the Renaissance, was much larger than it and, in fact, brought its own influence to bear upon the arts movement.

■ Harlem, and perhaps Chicago, can generally be considered ground zero for the Jazz Age, but the cultural movement certainly was not limited to these major urban areas. New Orleans, Memphis, Kansas City, and St. Louis provided the cultural milieu in which jazz and the blues were created, and cities such as Washington and Los Angeles had their music scenes; but it was Harlem and Chicago that introduced jazz as a lifestyle into American popular culture.⁴² "It is farthest known as being exotic, colorful, and sensuous," James Weldon Johnson wrote of Harlem, "a place of laughing, singing, and dancing; a place where life wakes up at night." At the center of this burgeoning movement was the confluence of black working-class migrants from the South, the effects of Prohibition on the general nightlife culture of the United States, and the growing love affair middle-class whites were having with primitivism and the presumed innocent sensuality of blacks. Although he felt that blacks were "by nature a pleasure-loving people," Johnson argued that any assumption that residents of Harlem merely "jazz through existence" was patently false. The "vast majority of them are ordinary, hard-working people." In addition, there was a "solid, respectable, bourgeois class" in Harlem, "a large element of educated, well-to-do metropolitans . . . who view with indulgence, often with something less, the responses of the masses to these artless amusements."⁴³ Across the spectrum of the black community, the younger members of the established and aspiring middle class were doing more than observing the new jazz culture "with indulgence"; rather, they were eager participants. Leisure, once constrained by Victorian standards of respectability and morality, was becoming more pleasure oriented.

Indeed, jazz culture was far removed from the producer values of Victorianism. Much more than a particular musical form, jazz was a "spirit," according to the black journalist J. A. Rogers, "a balm for modern ennui, and . . . a safety valve for modern machine-ridden and convention-bound society." It was a singularly American phenomenon, largely created by the more "primitive," rhythm-oriented black cultural forms but characterizing the postwar lifestyle of the entire nation. "Jazz has absorbed the national spirit, that tremendous spirit of go, the nervousness, lack of conventionality and boisterous good-nature characteristic of the American, white or black," Rogers reasoned, "as compared with the more rigid formal natures of the Englishman or German." Rogers's essentialism was not solely one of race. For instance, he argued that although blacks were closer to nature and therefore more open to rhythm, class was a major variable in determining one's ability to experience the jazz "spirit." It was largely the "lower classes" of blacks that were instinctually capable of being rhythmic, whereas a "lack of spontaneity is evident to a degree in the cultivated and inhibited Negro." Ultimately, however, Rogers's assessment of the benefits of jazz was ambiguous. He felt that even as the new jazz culture opened up the possibilities of freer, more honest social relations, it also created opportunities for increased social vice. "And so this new spirit of joy and spontaneity may itself play the rôle of reformer," he speculated. "Where at present it vulgarizes, with more wholesome growth in the future, it may on the contrary truly democratize. At all events, jazz is rejuvenation, a recharging of the batteries of civilization with primitive new vigor. It has come to stay, and they are wise, who instead of protesting against it, try to lift and divert it into nobler channels."[44]

Jazz culture became an integral part of the leisure world of younger middle-class blacks, but not everyone was able to embrace it without ambivalence or a larger concern for their respectable social positions. Cullen, for example, expressed a certain pleasure in his participation in the new form of leisure but insisted that it was done within the confines of propriety. Concerning one of his first dates with his eventual wife, Yolande Du Bois, Cullen confided to Jackman, "I am afraid you would have been pained at our unconcealed and absolutely depraved delight in the jazz." He continued that "you have not lived unless you have felt as I did; I was wild, primeval, uncivilized (although I danced decorously)—and careless of it all."[45] Cullen's letter is revealing in terms of how class filtered some individuals' responses to the emerging jazz culture. The fact that Cullen, at the age of twenty, was both captivated by the sensuality of the music and concerned that he exhibit a certain amount of self-control speaks to the investment that he held in his class status. It also reveals the investment he held in the gender conventions of his social position. Cullen's mild anxiety that he perform within the bounds of middle-class respectability, even as he enjoyed the "primitive" nature of jazz, suggests that American society in the 1920s was concerned with more than just the New Woman—and her offspring, the flapper—challenging the gender and sexual conventions of a rapidly deteriorating Victorian culture. Jazz, as both a music and a lifestyle, threatened to undermine bourgeois manliness.

As Rogers declared in his essay, the jazz "spirit" was a potential reformer of human relations, a possible "leveler" through its "mocking disregard for formality." It not only brought middle-class whites to black neighborhoods in search of an authentic "primitive" experience; it also collapsed the class distinctions between blacks in the confined spaces of an urban world of leisure. To be sure, the black middle class attempted to fortify the boundaries of class and status by patronizing "decorous" and "respectable" cabarets. The proximity of working-class and affluent African Americans and African Caribbeans in urban areas, however, mitigated the chances that the latter could altogether avoid the former. Despite the fact that the black middle class juxtaposed the genteel performance within "respectable" cabarets and the vernacular dance within "jook joints" as markers of class difference, younger blacks increasingly engaged in leisure that bridged the social divide.[46] Through both private parties and more commercial leisure spaces, the youth of the black middle class mingled with working-class African Americans and African Caribbean immigrants.

Private apartment and house parties were the staples of middle-class and working-class black leisure. Johnson spoke of the "strictly social sets [of Harlem] that go in for bridge parties, breakfast parties, cocktail parties, for high-powered cars, week-ends, and exclusive dances." Many gatherings of the Harlem artistic set took the form of socials or afternoon teas. Hughes recalled that Jessie Fauset threw "literary soirées with much poetry and but little to drink" in her apartment on Seventh Avenue, where often the guests carried on conversations in French. Walter White, novelist and NAACP officer, and his wife, Gladys, often entertained at their apartment at 409 Edgecombe Avenue, one of the most prestigious addresses in Harlem. The apartment of Regina Anderson, a young librarian at the 135th Street branch of the New York Public Library, and Ethel Ray Nance, a secretary for *Opportunity*'s editor, Charles S. Johnson, was also a location known for its afternoon parties.[47]

Other participants and fellow travelers of the Renaissance were known for giving more decadent, or at least unrestrained, parties. Aaron Douglas and his wife, Alta, also residents of 409 Edgecombe, threw parties where revelers would contribute money "to the nearest bootlegger for a bottle of whatever it was that was drunk in those days, when labels made no difference at all in the liquid content." Singers Taylor Gordon and Jules Bledsoe were famous for their less than respectable gatherings. Perhaps the two most famous party-givers were Carl Van Vechten and A'lelia Walker. Van Vechten, who lived on the Upper West Side, held extravagant gatherings with his wife, the actress Fania Marinoff. At any Van Vechten affair, one could hobnob with a mélange of writers, actors, musicians, intellectuals, artists, and socialites of various ethnic groups, including the blues diva Bessie Smith and the opera diva Margarita D'Alverez; the writers Somerset Maugham and Nella Larsen; actors Paul Robeson and Rudolph Valentino; and artists Richmond Barthé, a black sculptor, and the surrealist Salvador Dali. Music, dancing, intellectual conversation, and gossip were the routine at "Carlo" and Fania's parties. A'lelia Walker threw even more elaborate galas. The daughter of Madame C. J. Walker, the black cosmetics magnate, A'lelia held soirées at both her Harlem townhouse and her rambling estate on the Hudson River. Hughes referred to her as "the joy-goddess of Harlem's 1920's" whose parties were so popular that they resembled a "New York subway at the rush hour—entrance, lobby, steps, hallway, and apartment a milling crush of guests, with everybody seeming to enjoy the crowding." Nor were they attended exclusively by the economic and artistic elite of black Harlem and white downtown. Walker's parties were a melting pot of ethnic groups and social classes. "At her 'at homes,'" Hughes recalled, "Negro poets and Negro number bankers mingled with downtown poets and seat-on-the-stock-exchange racketeers."[48]

As famous, heterogeneous, and well-attended as the parties and socials of Walker, Fauset, Van Vechten, and the Whites were, however, younger middle-class blacks enjoyed another version of the private party that predominated Harlem and other urban areas—the rent party. In part, these parties gained more popularity among members of the Renaissance who chafed at the exclusionary policies of white-owned clubs and who viewed "slumming," or the weekly incursions into Harlem by white intellectuals, artists, and socialites, as faddish voyeurism.[49] Rent parties occurred in spaces where working-class leisure reigned. Held in private homes where few white middle-class slummers dared venture, the parties allowed young working-class and middle-class African Americans and African Caribbeans to mingle and "let loose." With relatively high rents in Harlem (and other black neighborhoods in Chicago, St. Louis, Philadelphia, and Kansas City), the rent party started out as "more an institution of necessity than one of pleasure." In a neighborhood where close to half of the renters spent more than half of their yearly income on rent, these parties, like the practice of boarding, helped urban residents defray some of their living costs. Tenants would offer their rooms and apartments as venues for after-hours socializing and provide food and alcohol in exchange for a small cover charge that would hopefully, once totaled, pay their weekly or monthly rents. The party served not only the interests of the tenant; it also provided leisure space to "footloose, restless and unattached" urban-ites who had "little money to spend for pleasure and few inexpensive places to go." If the rent party started out as an "institution of necessity," however, it quickly became professionalized as even the low charge of twenty-five cents per person was enough in many cases to clear a sizable profit. The potential of profit consequently encouraged some people to throw parties on a regular basis regardless of their ability to make rent. Indeed, the ambitious entrepreneur might even throw a "rent party" in a rented dance hall, replete with a band and wait staff.[50]

Music, dancing, food, and alcohol were free flowing at these events. A visitor to a particular party could expect to enter a dimly lit room full of black bodies dancing to a lone piano. He or she might be offered a glass of corn liquor or synthetic gin (often at a low price), as well as a plate full of fried fish, chitterlings and pigs' feet, black-eyed peas, and cole slaw. If interested, the visitor could participate in a game of craps in the corner. The partygoer could also expect to mingle with a diverse group of African Americans and African Caribbeans. Hughes recalled regularly meeting "ladies' maids and truck drivers, laundry workers and shoe shine boys, seamstresses and porters" at rent parties. Although they attracted, and in many instances were given by, middle-class blacks, rent parties had a decidedly working-class character.

Wallace Thurman described a generic party: "The evening wears on. There is much noise and joy and drinking. Men who have worked on the docks or in the ditch all day perspire as freely during the night from a different sort of exertion. Women who have been cooking or washing or cleaning in some white woman's kitchen or house now lord it over their associates in their midnight rendevous [sic]. Prostitutes and pimps maintain a superior attitude. Here is low Harlem at its best, unspied on, unfettered and alive."[51] Rent parties, in effect, were the antitheses of middle-class respectability. The fact that porters and seamstresses, workers in the service sector that enjoyed a certain middle-class status, rubbed elbows with teamsters, day laborers, domestics, pimps, and prostitutes, suggests that modern urban leisure, along with generational change, was eroding the cultural grip of the social conventions of an earlier generation.

If the performances at rent parties reflected the younger generation's challenge to the dictates of polite society, they also represented challenges to the gender conventions of older middle-class blacks. Alternative models to Victorian manliness became apotheosized through the rent parties. One was the piano player, the centerpiece of any successful party. Usually the only musician at "rank and file" —as opposed to professional—parties, the piano player was responsible for creating a frenetic atmosphere for the revelers. Good piano players, Thurman wrote, "unconsciously become able to regulate the scale of people's emotions, and pick their music accordingly, becoming more and more primitive, more and more vulgar, as the evening advances." It was his responsibility to manipulate the crescendo until the wee hours of the morning when the "sound of the panting, passionate, hip-wiggling animals will merge with the blue harmonic orgy of the moaning piano strings, interspersed by inspired utterances from the gin-filled genie." At the end of the party, he usually found himself with "five dollars in his jeans, a woman on his arm, and a stomach full of gin."[52] Thurman's colorful rendering of the piano player, although intended as reportage, was written in a laudatory vein. Vulgar did not carry the same negative connotations for Thurman—a young, college-educated professional—that it did for the respectable middle class. His description reflects his own conception of masculinity more than it serves to accurately reflect how the piano player actually lived his gendered identity. For Thurman, the "gin-filled genie" was the literal embodiment of a masculinity that was defined by bodily virtuoso and sexual virility rather than character and producer values.

Another alternative model of masculinity that was rapidly gaining currency among urban African American and African Caribbean youth was the sweetback. Alternately called sweethearts or professional lovers, sweetbacks were men of the "lower middle class" who found employment, even in the service industry, difficult to obtain or hold. This chronic underemployment, combined with higher employment among women of the same economic class (albeit largely in the area of domestic service) and "the large preponderance of women over men is speedily bringing about a relationship of the sexes akin to that among the Indians," wrote Thurman. "The men dress up, strut, talk, loaf, smoke, gamble and fight, while the women do all the work." The sweetback was becoming a common presence in Harlem. "He can be seen at all hours of the day and night, dressed in flashy clothes, loafing in pool rooms, dance halls, speak easies [sic], or on street corners," Thurman declared. "He never works, but always has plenty of money for liquor and gambling, for isn't he often the pride and love of as many as a dozen hard working ladies?"[53] It was a rhetorical, but pointed, question that addressed alternative notions of manhood and gender roles within urban African American and African Caribbean immigrant communities. The sweetback represented a sharp divergence from the bourgeois ideal of manliness; his manhood was defined through the presentation of his body and his immersion in consumer culture much more than his commitment to respectability, character, producer values, or traditional notions of patriarchy and separate spheres.

The Harlem literati celebrated the sweetback and the piano player in their literature as well as their personal depictions of Harlem social life. Claude McKay, in his autobiography, remembered that he felt "flattered" when he was mistaken for a "sweetman" at a Greenwich Village party.[54] Like the piano player, the sweetback allowed younger middle-class blacks the opportunity to imagine the possibility of incorporating qualities and behavior previously considered unmanly by bourgeois standards into their gender identity formation. Men who made money through the nonproductive use of their bodies and who were only tangentially involved in the marketplace, offered an alternative masculinity to young middle-class blacks.

In addition to rent parties, cabarets and speakeasies were choice spaces for urban residents in search of leisure. Middle-class and working-class African Americans and African Caribbeans enjoyed music, alcohol, and camaraderie offered by restaurants and nightclubs with such exotic names as the Oriental and the Garden of Joy. Cabarets were particularly favorite places of the black middle class. Despite the conventional wisdom that they were "den[s] of iniquity, where the Devil holds high revel," James Weldon Johnson wrote, ". . . the average night-club is as orderly as many a Sunday-school picnic has been. These clubs are patronized by many quite respectable citizens." J. A. Rogers had a different take on cabarets. He differentiated between cabarets based on whether they catered to the middle class or the working class. "The

cabaret of better type provides a certain Bohemianism for the Negro intellectual, the artist and the well-to-do," he surmised. The more common cabaret,
however, encouraged vice. "The tired longshoreman, the porter, the house-
maid and the poor elevator boy in search of recreation, seeking in jazz the
tonic for weary nerves and muscles," Rogers argued, "are only too apt to find
the bootlegger, the gambler and the demi-monde who have come there for
victims and to escape the eyes of the police."[55] Regardless of the relative exploitation factor of particular cabarets, middle-class black youth frequented
these urban spaces. Rudolph Fisher, for example, remembered that cabarets,
just becoming popular during and immediately after World War I, offered a
recent college graduate like himself the opportunity to enjoy good food, alcohol, and entertainment with his friends. By the late 1920s, historian Kevin
Mumford notes, "[m]embers of the black middle class had caught on to the
speakeasy club craze."[56]

Most cabarets started out as places where blacks could go to unwind and
where black talent was showcased for black patrons. One could catch talented upstarts such as Gladys Bentley, "a large dark, masculine lady" who
dressed in men's formal wear, or Ethel Waters, a club singer who later became a premier actress. One could also enjoy other blues singers and dancers.
Fisher remembered visiting the Oriental where there was "a slim, little lad,
unbelievably black beneath his high-brown powder, wearing a Mexican ban-
dit costume with a bright-colored head-dress and sash," who was known for
"shimmying for enraptured women, who marveled at the perfect control of
his voluntary abdominal tremors." He continued that the dancer "used to
let the women reach out and put their hands on his sash to palpate those
tremors—for a quarter."[57] Like in rent parties, then, young men and women
of the black middle class who attended cabarets and speakeasies were provided with alternative models of masculinity, models that resembled little of
the manliness prescribed by the older, traditional middle class.

Musicians, dancers, professional lovers, and members of the underground
economy such as bootleggers, pimps, and number runners represented an
alternative masculinity that was not defined through respectable performance
in the public sphere or constructive engagement in the marketplace. These
men worked and played through an unrespectable—by traditional bourgeois
standards—use of the body or a "deviant" engagement in the marketplace.
Employment and wage discrimination, the relegation of blacks to the service
sector of the economy, and the low rate of unionization and the possibilities of job security made these alternative forms of employment attractive for
many new migrants.[58] Jazz culture created leisure spaces in which younger
members of the "new" middle class associated with these men. They appro-

Langston Hughes, Harold Jackman, and friends. (Courtesy of The Yale Collection of American Literature, Beinecke Rare Book and Manuscript Library)

priated ideas of manhood that incorporated the body and the pleasures of consumption and thus diverged from the model of manliness upheld by the older black bourgeoisie.

Leisure spaces also encouraged an alternative articulation of masculinity in terms of sexuality. Everyone from white middle-class slummers to working-class African Americans and African Caribbeans could visit cabarets, speakeasies, and rent parties and expect to witness, or participate in, a small but vibrant homosexual subculture. Gay and lesbian socializing occurred primarily in speakeasies and rent parties. One investigator for New York's anti-vice task force, the Committee of Fourteen, visited a speakeasy on 136th Street in Harlem where he found "several of the men . . . dancing among themselves" and "two of the women . . . dancing with one another going through the motions of copulation." The investigator "also observed two men who were dancing with one another kiss each other, and one sucked the other's tongue." Buffet flats, apartments where rooms could be rented on a nightly basis, also encouraged public heterosexual and homosexual sex. Initially developed in the late nineteenth century to provide travelers with rooming, some buffet flats took on particularly carnal characteristics in the 1920s, becoming more like rent parties with the added attractions of prostitution and live sex shows. One such buffet flat in Detroit provided a regular show of two men engaged in oral sex while another famous flat in New York, run by a black gay man, allegedly offered guests the opportunity to see a "'young black entertainer named Joey, who played the piano and sang but whose *specialité* was to remove his clothes and extinguish a lighted candle by sitting on it until it disappeared.'" Speakeasies, buffet flats, and rent parties were spaces through which black men and women of both the working and middle class could challenge the "social conventions of hetero-normativity" of the traditional black elite and the "new" black middle class.[59]

While men who participated in the gay subculture of speakeasies and buffet flats transgressed the boundaries of bourgeois manliness in private, others challenged them more openly. Black transvestites were not an uncommon sight in Harlem clubs as well as on the streets. Historian George Chauncey carefully argues that the "frequency" with which drag queens appeared "in Harlem's streets suggest a high degree of tolerance for them in the neighborhood as a whole."[60] The fact that transvestism was a regular phenomenon among both working- and middle-class residents of Harlem is significant in terms of how black masculinity was constructed and negotiated, particularly by black middle-class youth. Perhaps the most public transgression of gender conventions was the drag balls of the 1920s and 1930s. One of the most famous ones was the Hamilton Lodge Ball. Held annually, under the auspices of a local Odd Fellows lodge, the drag ball was heavily attended by both blacks and whites from various social positions. Hughes recalled that "it was fashionable for the intelligentsia and social leaders of both Harlem and the downtown area to occupy boxes at this ball and look down from above at the queerly assorted throng on the dancing floor, males in flowing gowns and feathered headdresses and females in tuxedoes [sic] and box-back suits." Drag balls were festive events, attracting thousands of spectators as well as hopeful contestants from up and down the East Coast. Referring to "a 'drag' at the Savoy," Jackman described the colorful costumes to Cullen: "The affair was very gay and the costumes were very elaborate—ostrich plumes, monkey fur, sequins, chiffon . . . silk, satin in all sorts of colors, shades and [prices?] of costumes."[61] That Hughes and Jackman attended these balls and participated in these public transgressions, if only as observers, does not necessarily point to a thorough acceptance of homosexuality among the broader black middle class. It does point, however, to a growing tolerance of, and general willingness to appreciate, the challenges to hetero-normative gender conventions that these "spectacles" represented. The drag balls, as well as the cabaret and rent party, encouraged performances of masculinity that deviated significantly from the producer values and respectability needed to achieve manhood by traditional middle-class standards.

Work and leisure were areas in which younger middle-class blacks defined and performed alternative forms of masculinity. These alternative constructions, however, were not free of ambivalence. In terms of the importance of work in the formation of male identity, many of the younger generation rejected the notion that the only way manhood could be achieved was through their involvement in the marketplace. Even as some younger middle-class blacks pursued conventional careers that allowed them to achieve bourgeois manliness through the marketplace, however, their participation in the jazz culture of the 1920s suggests that they were intent on challenging the same bourgeois manliness in the sphere of leisure. Marriage and sexual relations were other areas where traditional gender conventions were breaking down. Love and sexuality became primary modalities through which a modern masculine identity was negotiated.

In 1928 Wallace Thurman married Louise Thompson. Like her husband, Thompson grew up in the western United States, receiving an undergraduate degree in economics from the University of California, Berkeley, in 1923. She taught business administration at Hampton Institute in Virginia before moving to New York to pursue a graduate degree. Thompson and Thurman met when he hired her to type the manuscript of his novel, *The Blacker the Berry*. Their marriage was a surprise to most of their friends and acquaintances. "I have recovered from the shock sufficiently to be able to send my best wishes and congratulations," Howard University philosophy professor Alain Locke wrote to Thompson, "and to tell you how much I envy any man who has you for both a wife and a secretary." Thurman and Thompson, however, did not consider their union to be a conventional one. Indeed, Thurman found his sudden marriage to be "just one of those inexplaindable [sic] things that happens even to the best of us." He felt that both his and Louise's modern outlook would prevent them from replicating the stultifying institution of marriage. "My only point of extenuation," he wrote to McKay, "is that I happen to have married a very intelligent woman who has he[r] own career and who also does not believe in marriage and who is as anxious as I am to avoid the conventional pitfalls into which most marriages throw one. I assure you," he averred, "ours is a most modern expe[r]iment, a reflection of our own rather curious pe[r]sonalities." [62]

Although their marriage had started out as a "modern experiment," within six months it was in danger of failing. The beginning of 1929 boded well for Thurman's career, with the publication of his first novel and the Broadway staging of his and William Jourdan Rapp's play, *Harlem*. The play later traveled to Chicago and Los Angeles. By that summer, Thurman was in Hollywood overseeing the stage production and negotiating for a potential film deal. His marriage, however, was deteriorating quickly. Dorothy West, a friend of Thurman, placed equal blame on both parties for the marriage's failure. On the one hand, she felt that Thurman was not prepared for a stable life as someone's significant other. He "had long wanted to be a father," West wrote, "but he had not taken into consideration that he must first be a husband." Thurman, in other words, was not ready to give up his bohemian lifestyle. West also felt that Thompson shouldered some of the responsibility. She was not ready to be the supporting wife, especially when Thurman needed her the most. Thompson, according to West, left him on the night that his play opened on Broadway, an act that signaled her lack of devotion to him. "The fact that she could desert him at a crucial hour," West recalled, "did not make him see that she was as much a failure as a writer's wife as he was as a conventional husband."[63]

Thurman and Thompson's separation and the subsequent sniping through their respective lawyers were particularly acrimonious. The matter of separation alimony, what Thurman bitterly referred to as "a case of pure extortion," was the crux of the antagonism. Thompson had requested fifty dollars per week plus six hundred for transportation to Reno, Nevada, for the purpose of obtaining a quick divorce. Evidently, Thompson also threatened to use an event in Thurman's past in order to position herself more favorably in the eyes of the court. After arriving in Harlem in 1925, Thurman was arrested for having sex with another man in the bathroom of the 135th Street subway station. A "Fifth [A]venue hair dresser" had propositioned Thurman, who only accepted after the man offered him two dollars. At that point, "two plain clothes men, hidden in the porter's mop closet rushed out and took the two of us to jail." His wife had come across this information, Thurman lamented to Rapp, just as "she was fighting me for money settlement." Thurman denied, however, that sexual incompatibility was the problem in their marriage. He pointed out that they had sexual intercourse after she had found out about his indiscretion. "She has already admitted . . . that after her operation all was well sexually between us," Thurman wrote to Rapp, "and neither can she bring up that knowledge of that one incident in my life disgusted her so much so that she was unable to have further intercourse with me."[64] The issue of Thurman's sexuality did not become central in the ensuing settlement negotiations nor was there a final resolution of their divorce. The modern experiment at marriage, however, was dead within a year.

Thurman's brief attempt to conform to a superficially conventional lifestyle and his equivocal disavowal of his homosexual inclination reflect the ambivalence with which he negotiated his gender identity in the areas of love and sexuality. There were initial signs that Thurman was not committed to his marriage. He wrote to McKay, for instance, that he "[did] not believe in marriage for an artist of any type." The separation from Louise also left Thurman so embittered that he advised Hughes to never marry: "Had I remained single I would be financially secure for the next year." Thurman's concern that conventional marriage potentially threatened one's aesthetic core and financial stability suggests that he did not feel invested in the prescriptive gender conventions of an earlier middle-class generation. Rather than completely reject these conventions in favor of a gay lifestyle, however, Thurman resisted embracing a homosexual identity. Referring to his experience in the subway bathroom, he conceded that "the incident was true, but there was certainly noevidence [sic] therein that I was homosexual." He further complained that the rumor was enough to confirm him as gay in the eyes of his peers and the larger community. "And you can also imagine with what relish a certain group of Negroes in Harlem received and relayed the news that I was a homo," he wrote to Rapp in a note of resignation. "No evidence is needed of course beyond the initial rumor. Such is life."[65] Thurman, in other words, was an ambivalent rebel against manliness when it came to his sexuality. He could not conform to conventional manliness in terms of becoming a husband and a provider; nor could he completely reject the hetero-normative hegemony of bourgeois manliness. This ambivalence found its way into the lives of many younger middle-class blacks.

This ambivalence, and less than reverential attitude toward marriage, was not unique to young men of the black middle class. Younger black women, too, were rejecting the inevitability and conventionality of the traditional institution. Many professional black women did marry but were hardly willing to allow marriage to subsume their individual identity. Zora Neale Hurston, a folklorist, novelist, and playwright, was one of these women. A native Floridian, Hurston attended Howard University but graduated from Barnard College, where she studied anthropology under Franz Boas. In 1927, she married Herbert Sheen whom she had met at Howard. Sheen was a jazz pianist and, at the time of their marriage, a medical student in Chicago. By January of 1928, however, Hurston had "broken off relations" with Sheen, largely because she felt that he was a hindrance to her career. "I am just not going to let myself be annoyed," she wrote to Hughes. "I have too much to do and too much to live for to have some one nagging me and destroying my nervous energy." Although Hurston expressed a desire to divorce her husband, it was Sheen himself who initiated the process. By the summer of 1931, they were legally divorced. "Don[']t think I am upset," she wrote to her chief benefactor, Charlotte Osgood Mason, "for your lil Zora is playing on her harp like David. He was one of the obstacles that worried me."[66]

Another such woman was Eslanda Goode Robeson. A graduate of Columbia University and a "pathology technician" by the time she married Paul Robeson, Eslanda was heavily involved in his acting and singing career and shared his passion for progressive politics. During the mid-1920s, she expressed interest in acting herself but maintained that her first priority was Paul's career: "Of course I shall keep Paul's work first always," she wrote to the Van Vechtens. "I suppose I'll never get over that! We talked about that particular weakness—or was it strength—on my part one night—remember?" Paul and Eslanda's marriage, however, was not an exercise in stability. Paul's extramarital affairs created much strain between the two, resulting in repeated separations and reconciliations. Although her diary suggests that she was extremely bitter about Paul's flaunting of his affairs, Eslanda was much more sanguine in her personal correspondence. Initially, she had reconciled herself to Paul's infidelity, claiming that "now that I know that he has not only strayed, but gone on a hike, I've turned my mind over and given it an airing,—and I feel much better[.]" Four months later, she wrote another letter to the Van Vechtens, bubbling over the new life that the unofficial separation from Paul had afforded her. "I have no idea what Paul will do, but no matter what he does, we are fast friends, and understand each other better than ever before," she wrote. "And I am rid of a lot of silly young ideas I used to be boarded up with, and I am surprised at the great variety of ways in which I can have a good time. I am having a really good time for the first time in my life. And if I'm happy and he's happy, things are bound to come out right in the end." Part of this transformation in Eslanda was the shedding of her persona as wife, mother, and helpmate to her husband's career. In her words, she was "getting wild," which included socializing with attractive men, dining on rich food and expensive spirits, and dancing at cabarets. The following year, when divorce became a realistic possibility, Eslanda was less than enthusiastic. "I hemmed and hawed, and put off the evil day (divorce) as long as I could," she wrote to Carl Van Vechten, "hoping something would happen, but he insisted that he MUST have his freedom, and that I just HAD to give it to him, so I felt I must."[67] Despite Paul's pleas, the Robesons never officially divorced; rather, they led separate personal and professional lives and reconciled occasionally for emotional and financial stability. Theirs was a modern marriage taken to its logical extreme.

The relationships between Wallace Thurman and Louise Thompson, Zora Neale Hurston and Herbert Sheen, and the Robesons were indicative of a changing societal approach to marriage. Even as the marriage rate among young Americans was increasing from the latter half of the 1800s to the 1920s, the divorce rate was increasing exponentially, at a rate of 2000 percent. By the end of the decade, one in six marriages ended in divorce. In part, this was largely due to a shift in the cultural significance of matrimony. Marriage was no longer solely defined as a union between a man and a woman for the purpose of starting a family that would, in turn, fit into a larger social network. Rather, marriage was becoming more of a means through which to experience individual self-fulfillment. As such, divorces in the postwar United States were the result of interpersonal differences much more than they had been a generation earlier. Discontented spouses were more likely to get divorced without having to rely on older justifications—such as a breach of marital duty—that had characterized divorce in Victorian America. To be sure, women were still expected to enter marriage at the expense of their careers, and those women who did not conform to the conventional desire to become mothers were seen as aberrations.[68] These persistent cultural attitudes, however, did not preclude many women's resistance to marriage and motherhood.

Black women, even among the middle class, historically have not been financially dependent upon their male counterparts and, therefore, it is problematic to assume that the changing nature of marriage affected them in similar ways to native-born white women. Sporadic and anecdotal evidence, however, still suggests that black women of the "new" middle class were not immune to the same cultural trends. Gladys Wilson, a friend of Claude McKay, represented the "new" woman of modern black America. A nursing student in the Bronx, Wilson reflected on her personal life in one letter to McKay. She began by explaining the lack of a significant other in her life by suggesting that she was "reserved" when it came to being intimate with black men. She then offered a less personal reason that spoke to the larger cultural shifts that characterized gender relations in the 1920s, claiming that she was "like most modern women" in that she was "too independent and temperamental to hold an ordinary man looking for a wife[.]" The prospects of becoming a wife and mother did not thrill her either. "I am not at all inclined to be maternal or domestic," she wrote, "and my feminine qualities consist almost wholly of curiosity, indecision of mind and an almost fanatical love of beauty." [69] Wilson's assessment of herself as a modern woman who did not consider marriage and family as the ultimate self-actualization is indicative of a growing mentality among middle-class black women.

Another such woman was Ann Rucker, a friend of Arthur Schomburg. Rucker was married and had either gone through a divorce or was separated when she wrote a letter to Schomburg discussing the folly of marriage. She wished that she would never have to marry or enter a lasting, intimate relationship with a man again. Concerned that she might come across as a man-hater, she reassured Schomburg: "Don't conclude I despise your sex. On the contrary, life without them would be quite dull. But I just lack the trust and confidence necessary to look upon them as more than mere men." In another letter, she playfully criticized Schomburg for his male chauvinism by suggesting that he was "like the rest of your sex in one respect—too damned egotistical. You men just can't get it into your craniums that a woman can be happy and satisfied without a man." [70] Although Rucker and Schomburg's verbal "battle of the sexes" should not necessarily replace demographic evidence in determining a changing perception of marriage among the black middle class, it is indicative of a "new" black womanhood emerging in the postwar period. The attitudes of Gladys Wilson and Ann Rucker represented a modern articulation of womanhood in Jazz Age America.

Of course, marriage was not anathema to the middle-class youth of the 1920s but, by and large, these unions were based on the ideals of mutual respect, romantic love, and egalitarianism, as opposed to the "hierarchical and emotionally barren" relationships that characterized the typical Victorian marriage.[71] While the marriages of Wallace Thurman, Zora Neale Hurston, and Eslanda Robeson represented failed attempts at modern matrimony, the brief marriage of Countee Cullen and Yolande Du Bois more closely resembled Victorian wedlock. The union of the aristocratic boy poet and the genteel daughter of W. E. B. Du Bois is worth examining in detail because it sheds light on several issues of gender and sexuality that confronted young members of the black middle class in the 1920s: namely, marriage as an inevitable step in the process of becoming adult; the gender roles expected of spouses and the marital strain created by female economic independence; and the tension between individual sexual ambivalence and social obligations to wed.

Countee and Yolande met during the summer of 1923. She was pursuing a fine arts degree at Fisk University and Countee was enrolled at New York University, but they spent that summer in southern New Jersey. His family owned a summer home in Pleasantville and he worked at a resort hotel in Atlantic City. She and her family were most likely vacationing in the same area. Initially, Cullen was drawn to her not by her beauty but "by some indefinable magnetism of refinement and soulful honesty." He proceeded cautiously, however, for fear of coming across as ungentlemanly. "I would like to play the gallant cavalier," he confided to Jackman, "in order to talk to her alone, so as to verify my first impression of her." Indeed, Cullen was so cautious that he did not ask her to a dance for which he had no date because he had not known her for at least a week.[72]

In his early twenties, Cullen was less than enthusiastic at the prospects of becoming a husband. "I think Jehovah's slight-of-hand trick with Adam's rib was one of the greatest fiascos a god could have committed," he wrote to Jackman. "And yet some woman will probably make me eat an apple some day without any thought at all of the consequences." Although his observation may not have been more than the cynical musings of a young writer, Cullen did not hold heterosexual relationships—at least in the form of conventional wedlock—in high esteem. "True friendships, instead of marriages," he felt, "are made in Heaven. I fail to see any divine diplomacy behind most marriages; they are too easily disrupted."[73] Regardless of his philosophical feelings toward marriage, however, Cullen believed that a relationship with Yolande would serve a practical function. Shortly after meeting her, for instance, he confided to Alain Locke, "I believe I am near the solution of my problem." Although he was never clear about the "problem," a month later Countee assessed the possibilities of pursuing a relationship with Yolande, referring to potential "complications," which included the fact that she was two years his senior and "then that fear which is always at my heels."[74] What was the "problem" or the "fear" to which Cullen referred? He never clearly articulated what these might be but, taking his personal correspondence as context, it is reasonable to assume that his anxiety was rooted in an ambivalent sexuality. In other words, overshadowing Cullen's personal life during this period was his struggle between entering a conventional union with a woman and his desire to have intimate, sexual relationships with men.

There is general scholarly consensus that Cullen—along with several other members of the Renaissance—was gay, although one scholar of Cullen's life and work suggests that there is no conclusive proof. Gerald Early argues that "there is no evidence that Cullen engaged in any homosexual relations with any other figures of the Renaissance."[75] Despite the qualified nature of his statement—for, indeed, it does not claim that Cullen had *no* sexual relations with men—Early also seems to be focusing on activity as opposed to identity. In other words, he suggests that because there is no smoking gun to attest to Cullen's homosexuality then Cullen must have been heterosexual. This places a burden upon those looking for sexual diversity in the past—a burden that is not similarly shared by those studying "straight" historical actors. Given

Early's criterion, there is no evidence that Countee and Yolande had sexual relations and, thus, no conclusive proof that he was heterosexual. This is an important methodological point, but there is a larger substantive argument to be made. Given that homosexuality, as we have come to know it, is more of an identity than a specific set of acts, then Cullen clearly identified with a homosexual subculture even as he attempted to conform to the gender and sexual conventions of respectable society.

In his early twenties, Cullen confided in Locke, who, a bachelor his entire life, also identified with gay culture and most likely experienced sexual intimacy with other men. In a letter to Locke, Cullen praised Edward Carpenter's *Iölaus*, a literary and ethnographic anthology devoted to male friendship that was practically required reading in gay intellectual circles. *Iölaus* "threw a noble and evident light on what I had begun to believe, because of what the world believes, ignoble and unnatural," Cullen wrote. "I loved myself in it." After discussing his friendship with a man named Ralph Loeb, in which both had different views of what constituted friendship, Cullen pessimistically wondered about his future happiness as a homosexually identified man. "But I suppose some of us Erotics lads, vide myself, were placed here just to eat our hearts out with longing for unattainable things, especially for that friendship beyond understanding."[76] Despite his pessimism, Cullen developed romantic interests in a number of men. His off-and-on friendship with Loeb continued for at least two years. In addition, during the spring of 1924, Cullen was involved with a fellow student at New York University who he only referred to as Knapp. Their friendship probably never became fully intimate although Cullen clearly wished it would. "Knapp belongs to the order,—but his eyes are blue," he wrote to Locke. "However, I am afraid I must be content with spiritual sympathy from him as he has exalted ideas of constancy—but when one is hungry a few crumbs are a feast." One month later their friendship was over, causing Cullen to become depressed. Although he only referred to his breaking "all relations" with "K," it is clear he was referring to Knapp. "I have come quite definitely to the conclusion that I shall never again love anyone with all my heart and soul," he declared. "If I must be a libertine in order to preserve my health, my sanity, and my peace of mind, I shall do so; I shall make no further sacrifices."[77]

By the summer of 1924, Cullen evidently had become even more enamored of Yolande. He confided to Hughes that he was "somewhat enmeshed in the toils of the little naked God [Cupid], but the lady who is two years my senior only laughs and calls me an infant."[78] Cullen still expressed a sexual desire for men, however. That fall, a man who Cullen cryptically referred to as "L. R." entered his life. "L. R." was a mutual acquaintance of Locke and the possibility of a relationship with him intrigued Cullen. "The prospect of a mutually sincere adjustment is stimulating to me, as tenuous as it is," he wrote to Locke. "I am not in search of mere sympathy and a desire to be a martyr in the cause of a dubious bit of genius. But should the attachment be as sincere on the other part as on mine, there would be little, if any, problem for me to solve." Cullen requested that Locke intervene on his behalf. "Please pardon my urgency, but I *must* have an adjustment as soon as possible, or I shall be driven to recourse with E. W. and *that* I fear."[79] The "E. W." that Cullen referred to was most likely Eric Walrond. A month earlier Cullen had written to Locke describing a trip that he had made to Boston along with Jackman, Walrond, and another friend. Although the language was relatively veiled, there is reason to believe from one of the letter's passages, that Cullen and Walrond had a brief affair. "The trip was a revelation so far as Eric is concerned," Cullen intimated. "He was most surprisingly sympathetic and aggressive, but I am afraid he offers no lasting solution; he is too exacting (I almost said abandoned) and there are some concessions I shall never make. What a price to exact for a meagre [sic] mess of talent!"[80] Might Cullen have been referring to a night of sexual intimacy between the two? It is certainly possible, particularly given what appear to be the code words such as "sympathetic" and "lasting solution" that mark Cullen's description. In discussing his friendships with other men, Cullen deployed phrases to refer to, and romanticize, particular aspects of his sexuality, such as spiritual sympathy (a gay sensibility), adjustments (sexual relief), and permanent understandings (monogamy or perhaps a stable, reoccurring sexual relationship). This veiled language not only reflected his need to dissemble his sexual desire; it also reflected his genteel background. Cullen was a sexual bohemian trapped in Victorian conventions. His relationships with men and his obligatory sense to marry suggest that he was suspended between a Victorian sensibility and a more modern ethos when it came to his sexuality and gender identity.

Being a young middle-class man, a graduate of New York and Harvard Universities, and an accomplished poet by his mid-twenties, Cullen was obviously viewed by respectable society as a catch and he no doubt felt the pressure to commit himself to a woman of the same stature. It is not clear when, or why, Yolande began to return his earlier romantic entreaties but, by the fall of 1926, they had committed to a serious relationship. The topic of marriage was not far behind as Yolande felt that the Christmas holidays were a good time for Countee "to-er-do your asking." In that same letter, Cullen's attitude toward marriage and the investment he maintained in conventional gender roles is clear. "It[']s quite sweet of you to want to have so much money to take care of me," Yolande, a teacher in Baltimore, wrote, "[and?] I don't want you to think I'm going to be that kind of dead weight." Despite the potential conflict between Yolande and Countee's vision of what constituted marriage, Cullen did propose to her during Christmas and they began to plan their wedding for the following December.[81]

The engagement between the two was rocky to say the least. Perhaps there was pressure in being a high profile couple: the feeling of having committed to an arranged marriage based not only on love but on "blood, brains, culture, background, position and the handsomest of prospects."[82] The tensions were probably equally created by Yolande and Countee's divergent views of marriage. Countee held older, traditional attitudes concerning the gender roles within marriage, which Yolande, a college graduate and professional woman herself, did not share. "I cannot make myself over," she cautioned Cullen. "It seems as tho you want to put your wife upon a little pedestal [and] have her fold her hands and wait til you look that way again." Yolande evidently tested Countee's old-fashioned ideas about the husband-wife relationship by flirting with other men; she also made it unequivocally clear that she would not conform to his conventionality. "I'm afraid I must please myself in this matter—it's certainly my affair [and] mine only."[83] Cullen also had doubts about marriage, possibly caused by an overwhelming sense of manly duty to commit to a woman despite his sexual ambivalence. He evidently expressed some trepidation about making such a serious commitment to his friend, Guillaume Brown. Guillame's advice only reinforced the idea of marriage as a responsibility that accompanied social adulthood: "If, as you say, the days that [are] past seem happier than any you ever hope to experience in the future—wel[l], that is the inevitabl[e] result, I fear, of the increased awareness of life's realities that [comes] with manhood; but that awareness itself opens up new sources of happiness in compensation, and if we lose [some] of our enthusiasm we at least gain in spiritual equilibrium."[84] Guillaume appealed to Countee's sense of manly obligation and, given his genteel upbringing by solid, respectable citizens of middle-class Harlem, Countee was no doubt accustomed to the language of duty and sacrifice.

It is uncertain whether Guillaume's counsel assuaged Countee's doubts, but he maintained his commitment to Yolande despite her continuous balks. In October, Countee finally broke off the engagement even though Yolande felt that she "deserved" it. What actions may have precipitated such a response from Cullen are not altogether clear; again, it may have been Yolande's reluctance to replicate the conventional gender roles of a Victorian family. In one letter she wrote while they were still separated, Yolande recapped a dialogue that had been running through their engagement: "[J]ust last month you wrote to me these words[,] '—should you feel that you can subscribe to such old-fashioned ideas of matrimony, there is no woman I should so much care to devote the rest of my days to.'" In an ardent attempt to revive their relationship, Yolande affirmed that she was ready to "subscribe" to Cullen's vision of marriage. "It is natural for a man to expect his wife to find all her happiness in his company—You're right [and] all mine is in yours." Two weeks later the couple reconciled.[85]

The wedding, initially planned for the Christmas holidays, was postponed until the following spring. On April 9, 1928, Yolande and Countee were joined in wedlock by his father. The wedding was the society event of the year, with invited guests on the main floor, the public in the balcony, and crowds outside of Salem Methodist Episcopal Church in Harlem. Following the wedding, the couple honeymooned in Philadelphia.[86] Becoming husband and wife, however, did not alleviate the tensions. Within ten days, Yolande, back in Baltimore, wrote a letter apologizing for what was apparently a stressful honeymoon. This was significant enough to cause a brief separation. Three days later, an apparently jovial Yolande suggested that she could take their marriage or leave it. "In regards to . . . reconcili[a]t[ion]. Do as you like," she wrote to her newlywed. "I was perfectly willing to try again and still am. I believe that if both of us tried sincerely we could succeed but if you'd rather not—well s[ui]t yourself. In the meantime—good luck [and] a good time. Write when you can[.] Cheerio!!" Two months later, Countee, financed by a Guggenheim fellowship, left for Paris. Yolande joined him later that summer but their marriage was already beyond salvaging.[87]

W. E. B. Du Bois placed the blame for the marriage's failure on his daughter, although he felt culpable to some extent. The elder Du Bois concluded that sexual incompatibility was at the root of the disastrous marriage and, along with his wife, accepted some of the responsibility "because we are not frank on sex and do not teach the young." Yolande's sheltered life had not prepared her for marital intimacy and precipitated the troubles encountered by the young couple, Du Bois felt. "When a girl has been trained to continence [and] then suddenly loosed, the universe tumbles," he wrote to Cullen. Raised in a Victorian age, Du Bois was not an aberration in laying the culpability for the failed marriage at his daughter's feet. He thought it natural that a man inherently had a more mature, healthier sexual drive than a woman and that that was the crux of the problem. He suggested that Cullen take this into consideration when approaching "marital relations." "Arrange to be a friend[,] companion [and] co-worker with your wife and let love show itself chiefly there," Du Bois counseled his son-in-law. "Gradually [and] delicately the joy of sex will fit in place. But never over do it—for the sake of your brain work and your wife's more slowly developed desire, let your intimacies be at intervals—once in 3 or 4 days or once a week or even two weeks." [88] Du Bois's prescription resembled the companionate marriage, increasingly becoming the preferred model among the middle class in the 1920s, yet he still adhered to archaic ideas about how men and women responded to sexual activity. Excessive sex threatened to intellectually enervate the male partner while, for women, it could be "exquisite torture physically and mental humiliation." Du Bois's summation indicates that the classic Victorian denial of female sexual desire was still alive and well as late as 1928. [89]

It is doubtful that it was solely Yolande's sexual and emotional "immaturity" that caused the rift. Cullen may have been initially drawn to Yolande because she was safe. Though she was not overwhelmingly beautiful, he considered her his intellectual equal. Furthermore, being the genteel daughter of one of the central figures in black intellectual and political life, Cullen probably felt a relationship with her would benefit his career and maintain his class status and social position. That they were incompatible, both sexually and personally, was as much his fault as it was hers. His sexual ambivalence and conventional ideas about marriage undoubtedly contributed to the tensions between the two. True to middle-class form, however, respectability was paramount. Once the marriage became irreconcilable, W. E. B. Du Bois worked to maintain appearances. In September 1928, he suggested to Cullen that Yolande stay with him in Europe until Christmas, at which time she and her mother would find their own place. Then, in the summer, they could proceed with the divorce. This would, Du Bois felt, help to "keep down unkind gossip and enable the break to come after a decent interval." They eventually divorced in 1930. [90] Cullen would go on to marry again but his first attempt to conform to bourgeois manliness, by dissembling the homosexual core of his identity, did not succeed.

Cullen was only one of many men and women who were representatives of the growing "sexual perversion" that was criticized so heavily by respectable middle-class blacks and nationalists alike. Homosexuality, they argued, was only one of the ills of rapid urbanization but it was the most dangerous obstacle to the reconstitution and stabilization of the black family. One of the tireless crusaders against gay and lesbian subculture was Adam Clayton Powell, pastor of Abyssinian Baptist Church in Harlem. Powell attempted to root out homosexuality not only from urban leisure spaces but also from more respectable institutions such as the church. According to Powell and like-minded clergy, an increasing number of black pastors in Harlem were participants in this growing trend of moral "degeneracy." Although there is no substantial evidence that homosexuality was disproportionately present among black clergy, there is reason to believe that Powell's assessment was not completely a figment of his imagination. Thurman, after being arrested for having sex in the 135th Street subway bathroom, contacted an acquaintance who raised the bail money and sent it via a "minister friend." Once out of jail, Thurman found out that the minister's concern was motivated by more than mere altruism. "This minister took a great interest in men," he wrote a friend. "And to my surprise I discovered that he too belonged to the male sisterhood and was demanding his pound of flesh to keep silence." Thurman rejected the minister's offer and called his bluff, telling "him he could print it in the papers if he dared." The minister was less than discreet with his knowledge of Thurman and this may be how Louise Thompson came to find out about the incident.[91]

The younger generation of the black middle class, especially those involved in the Renaissance, were not nearly as dismayed by the growing homosexual subculture in urban areas. Indeed, as Eric Garber points out, many participants in the Renaissance were "homosexual, bisexual, or otherwise sexually unorthodox."[92] As such, even those who maintained heterosexual relationships were indifferent to the sexual unorthodoxy of their peers. Jean Toomer was one of the few members of the Renaissance who had negative, albeit ambivalent, feelings toward homosexuality. He argued that the gay man or lesbian was emotionally unfulfilled. They were always "craving" satisfaction and were ready to use violence to attain their goals of sexual fulfillment. Although his assessment of homosexuality was negative, Toomer saw some qualities worthy of praise. Gay men, he argued, possessed "a sense of art, a refinement of touch, subtlety of discernment, a goodness." Toomer further posed a false dichotomy, contrasting the male homosexual with the "he-man." The latter lacked the "psychological or spiritual dimension" that the former possessed. Despite this awkward praise, Toomer ended his discussion on another ambivalent note. He argued that society needed to treat homosexuals as individuals but cautioned that homosexuality was "one of the gravest problems of modern western civilization."[93] Others were more tolerant of, and less intellectually hostile toward, members of their circle who were gay. The Robesons reportedly loved to socialize with gay men and lesbians and never did so from a position of moral superiority. Aaron Douglas occasionally referred to gay men in derogatory terms—such as describing Alain Locke as "a bit too ladylike" or Richard Bruce Nugent as "a little fairy like"—but it did not preclude his socializing with them or recognizing their intelligence and talents.[94]

To be sure, the visible presence of Harlem literati and artists who were "sexually unorthodox"—either those who openly claimed a homosexual or bisexual identity or those who engaged in homosexual activity—encouraged a certain degree of open-mindedness among members of the Renaissance. The fact that people like Nugent, Thurman, McKay, and the sculptor Richmond Barthé did not go to great lengths to hide their relationships with other men, in addition to the fact that rumored homosexual relationships were often treated with a humorous nonchalance, suggests that there was a tacit acceptance of homosexuality by those who considered themselves heterosexual. Nonetheless, societal strictures still discouraged overt display of homosexuality, even among those who privately acknowledged romantic interest in the same sex, as in the case of Countee Cullen. Langston Hughes was another member of the Renaissance who dissembled his sexual identity. Even though most scholars agree that he possessed homosexual desires and occasionally acted upon them, whether or not he was gay-identified remains a contentious issue. Eric Garber argues that the "exact nature of [Hughes's] sexuality remains uncertain," while Arnold Rampersad suggests that his sexuality was much more complex, with a childlike, asexual innocence informing Hughes's identity more than anything else.[95] Hughes's dissemblance, however, points to a fluid sexuality. Trying to find its "exact nature" or relying on a psychosexual argument to explain it away does not adequately address the complex nature of that fluidity or the fact that it was part of his lifelong rebellion against middle-class standards of manliness.

Others who were more overt than Hughes with their "sexually unorthodox" natures were not as ardent in their resistance to hetero-normative standards of manhood. Claude McKay and Richard Bruce Nugent, for example, rebelled against the middle-class manliness associated with the marketplace as well as flaunted their sexual desires for other men. They both ultimately conformed, however, to certain conventional notions about what it meant to be a man: McKay in terms of his hypermasculinity and occasional homophobia and Nugent in terms of his eventual marriage. McKay, according to his biographer, probably considered himself bisexual but after his failed marriage, he had more relationships with men than women. He rarely discussed his sexual relationships with other men, which is surprising because he prided himself in being candid about sex. McKay was not shy, however, in inflating his own masculinity at the expense of others. He recalled, for instance, his first meeting with Locke in Paris. They had already established a correspondence that involved heated arguments over editorial judgments. McKay used the term "pussy-foot," a common derogatory phrase directed at effeminate men around the turn of the century, to describe Locke's editorial policies. McKay's depiction of their first meeting also generated distinctly different gendered images of both men: "Commenting upon my appearance, Dr. Locke said, 'Why, you are wearing the same kind of gloves as I am!' 'Yes,' I said, 'but my hand is heavier than yours.'"[96] Whether this comment was meant to highlight Locke's effeminate nature or the lack of radicalism in his writing is not necessarily important; McKay, I would argue, conflated the two. His own radicalism was a testament to his masculinity, so Locke's conservatism was evidence of his lack of masculinity and, by extension, his homosexual nature. Locke was not the only victim of this tactic. Charles Henri Ford, the author (along with Parker Tyler) of the gay novel *The Young and the Evil*, socialized with McKay in Europe, Morocco, and the United States and they were, from all indications, friends from the late 1920s to the mid-1930s. In 1938, the two had a falling out that was precipitated by McKay's criticism of Ford's poetry. His commentary on a poem about lynching was excessively caustic and homophobic:

> All your attempts of verse making stir up in me the same feeling of disgust. You try to hide your real self behind ellipses and a kind of radical formalism, precisely as the South tries to hide its hideous inhuman face behind vaporings of chivalry. But you cannot escape from that vitiating background. In addition there is the thick homosexual veil over your eyes, blinding you to everything else. It is something worse than homosexuality which is wrong with you. Edward Carpenter was homosexual, also was Oscar Wilde. But in your stuff I detect the quality of all that is ineffectual morbid and vile in Southern life. I would describe it as the excrement of homosexuality which exudes from your pores and stinks all through your essays of versification.[97]

McKay's responses to Locke and Ford were not mere homophobia; rather, they reflected his "queer" identity. He rejected the "cultural stance" of the fairy, the ultrafeminine homosexual, in favor of a more masculine "cultural stance" that rested on the presumption that his sexual desire for other men did not obviate his masculinity. In other words, McKay was an example of gay or bisexual men who separated their sexuality from their gender, a distinctly modern "bourgeois production" according to the historian George Chauncey.[98]

Nugent was a gay member of the Renaissance who McKay probably would have labeled a "fairy." Nugent was particularly flamboyant in his public behavior and one of the few literati who overtly wrote about gay subject matter. His contribution to *Fire!!*, for instance, was a short story called "Smoke, Lilies and Jade," which Hughes described as a "green and purple story . . . in the Oscar Wilde tradition." Like some of the other artists, Nugent went through occasional periods of depression and he linked them to his position as an artist and his sexual identity. Writing to Locke, for instance, Nugent explained his current state of depression as resulting "from the angle of a homo- or duosexual's juxtaposition to life or an artists'. Doubly hard and fascinating," he continued, "when regarded from the angle of both rolled into one." His equivocal stance on whether he was a homosexual or a duo-sexual (bisexual?) suggests that Nugent's sexuality, like that of Hughes and others, was more fluid than previously believed. Still, as he advanced into a more mature adulthood, Nugent began to conform to middle-class, hetero-normative standards of masculinity. Ironically, it was his relationship with another man that facilitated this transformation. Describing his relationship with a man named Flash, Nugent foreshadowed his eventual marriage to a woman. "He is good for me in that paradoxicall[y] enough, he brings out in me all of the so-called normal instincts that have been lying dormant in me," he wrote to Locke. "[In] all of us I guess. His constancy and ready and wiiling [sic] companionship make me more and more aware of some of the beau-ties of the possibility of more co[n]ventional marriage. And that despite the role I play in our imeddiate [sic] physical relationship."[99] Nugent had trav-eled a long journey, from being the emblematic rebel against manliness in his young adulthood during the 1920s to conforming to middle-class standards of manhood in the 1930s. Along the way, like other younger members of the Renaissance and the black middle class, his sexuality figured prominently in how he negotiated his masculine identity.

■ The bohemian lifestyle that typified the youthful jazz culture was antitheti-cal to bourgeois manliness in its rejection of the marketplace and producer values, and in its encouragement of excessive consumption. Many younger African Americans and African Caribbeans ridiculed the gender roles that ac-companied middle-class respectability, evident in their desire to form mod-ern marriages or pursue emotional and physical relationships with members of their own sex. Abstemiousness, in both leisure and sexuality, was not a slo-gan for this generation of the black middle class. Indeed, according to Locke, the younger generation was becoming less respectable, by the late 1920s, than even he and other mentors of the Renaissance had imagined. In 1930, he en-couraged McKay, who was working on a novel, to come back to the United States in order to "observe 'The Newest Negro,' who after all is quite a strange animal." The generation coming of age, Locke felt, "seems to be in a strange state of sexual transformation. Whether this conforms to the Renaissance formula as laid down by yours truly, I can't say. . . . But I do know that the Negro is shedding his puritanism."[100]

Locke was referring to younger, middle-class black students and profes-sionals because, as most intellectuals of the Renaissance concurred, black industrial workers, sharecroppers, and migrants were far removed from the "puritanism" that characterized Victorian America. Nevertheless, black middle-class youth, in their sexual indulgence and excessive consumption, were rebelling not against puritanism but against the standards of respectability and producerism that characterized the traditional black elite and the older generation of the "new" middle class. This rebellion included alternative models of manhood. Although there was much ambivalence surrounding these alternative models, by and large, younger blacks accepted them over the older Victorian constructions of manhood. Much of this rebellion against bourgeois manliness became manifest in the cultural production of the Harlem Renaissance.

5

A Man and Artist

In the spring of 1925, the sociological journal *Survey Graphic* published a special number entitled "Harlem: Mecca of the New Negro." The issue was inspired by a dinner sponsored, one year earlier, by the National Urban League's magazine, *Opportunity*, at which young black artists were recognized for creative output in the fields of poetry, fiction, essays, and playwriting. Paul Underwood Kellogg and Charles S. Johnson, editors of *Survey Graphic* and *Opportunity*, respectively, began planning the special edition and invited the master of ceremonies, Alain Leroy Locke, to act as editor. Johnson considered Locke "a sort of 'Dean' of this younger group" of black writers and suggested that others wanted him to "assume the leading role for the movement."[1] Locke, born in Philadelphia and educated at Harvard, Oxford, the University of Berlin, and the Collège de France, was an assistant professor of philosophy at Howard University in Washington, D.C. Although he considered himself too "leaden intellectually" to be an artist, Locke thought it his duty to be a "friend of poets." He assumed editorship of the special number of *Survey Graphic*, an issue that he felt "wont [sic] be as deadly sociological as most Survey issues."[2] Despite Locke's plan to highlight the younger black writers whose media were mainly poetry and prose, the *Survey Graphic* also included scholarly essays on race prejudice, the black church, and migration and urban culture by such older figures as black educator Kelly Miller, black social worker George E. Haynes, and white journalist Winthrop D. Lane. With other essays, including one by W. E. B. Du Bois and an introduction by Locke, as well as the creative works of younger blacks such as Langston Hughes, Claude McKay, Anne Spencer, and Jean Toomer, the *Survey Graphic* reached an audience of more than forty-two thousand, a number that doubled its circulation rate.[3]

By the end of 1925, Locke had expanded the *Survey Graphic* issue and Albert and Charles Boni, Inc., published it as a book titled *The New Negro*. In addition to a section entitled "Negro Youth Speaks," which included poetry, short stories, and a "folk play," the volume included numerous essays on the Negro's place in, and contributions to, American art, literature, and music. Similar to the *Survey Graphic*, it offered sociological articles, including essays on migration, the various centers of black intellectual and professional activity, the dynamics of racial prejudice and passing, and the "task of Negro womanhood." Du Bois concluded the volume with a pan-Africanist critique of the interrelatedness of imperialism, capitalism, and racism. The goal of the book, Locke boldly stated, was "to document the New Negro culturally and socially." The New Negro was emerging, according to Locke, largely as a result of the black population becoming "modern" through migration and urbanization. His advent (and here the editor's gender-specific usage is retained) accompanied the decline of the Old Negro, "a stock figure perpetuated as a historical fiction partly in innocent sentimentalism, partly in deliberate reactionism." Although the Old Negro was largely a literary construct, Locke reminded his readers that "the Negro himself has contributed his share to this through a sort of protective social mimicry forced upon him by the adverse circumstances of dependence." The collection of sociological and artistic evidence presented in the anthology, however, signaled both the literary and social death of the Old Negro. Both the demographic shifts and the artistic evolution within the black community had assured the changing order. "The mind of the Negro," Locke asserted, "seems suddenly to have slipped from under the tyranny of social intimidation and to be shaking off the psychology of imitation and implied inferiority."[4]

Locke articulated several interrelated ideas in his introduction. He suggested that in addition to contributing to the overthrow of the Old Negro by the New Negro, young African American and African Caribbean writers and artists were participants in the major cultural movement of the post–World War I era—modernism. As blacks were migrating from rural to urban areas and, hence, "from medieval America to modern," black intellectuals were rejecting sentimentalism in favor of a grittier realism in their social protest and literary pursuits. Locke spoke of a "new group psychology" that rejected the philanthropy, dependence, and debt that structured postbellum race relations and, instead, espoused self-determination, race consciousness and race pride, and the positive contributions of blacks to the development of American culture. Ultimately, it was the New Negro's artistic achievement and interaction with white intellectuals that would produce a change in blacks' status in societies with white majorities, specifically the United States. Believing that "mutual understanding" was "basic for any subsequent cooperation and adjustment," Locke rejected the separatist ideology of black nationalism. Rather, blacks' "more immediate hope rests in the revaluation by white and black alike of the Negro in terms of his artistic endowments and cultural contributions, past and prospective."[5] The coordinated outpouring of cultural self-expression known as the Harlem Renaissance, with its sophisticated network of artists, patrons, publishers, and social and political organizations, was encouraged, in part, by these hopes that literary and artistic achievement would solidify the position of blacks as citizens.

In response to the *Survey Graphic*, the southern white novelist Clement Wood claimed that there was "no more significant transition in America today than that of the Negro from the position of an awakening chattel to that of full manhood, economically, politically, socially and artistically."[6] The conscious gendering of the cultural movement continued in *The New Negro*. Indeed, in Locke's introduction, the abstract black intellectuals, artists, professionals, and peasants he discussed were all male. His final assessment of the potential of an arts movement invoked decidedly gendered images. The Negro, he felt, "now becomes a conscious contributor and lays aside the status of a beneficiary and ward for that of a collaborator and participant in American civilization."[7] Rather than accept Locke's assessment as embodying a universal male figure that represented the entire race, I want to argue that Locke was specifically referring to black men. In his imagery, the "Negro" emerges from a feminized and infantilized position of dependence and takes his place as an integral member of a male-dominated American culture.

Several tensions arose in the articulation of black manhood through artistic pursuit. One was the traditional equation of the arts with the feminine domain. As historian E. Anthony Rotundo points out, during the nineteenth century, Americans tended to associate particular careers with manhood or femininity. The law, for instance, was considered a manly occupation while the arts and the ministry were considered feminine pursuits. Although by the 1920s, younger Americans—particularly those who considered themselves modernists (such as Ernest Hemingway and F. Scott Fitzgerald)—no longer adhered to this rigid dualism, asserting one's masculinity through writing and painting did not necessarily mesh with earlier producerist models of manhood.[8] Another tension was the tendency to reinforce the "feminization" of blacks by celebrating the exotic "primitive" and the emotionality of black folk culture. Indeed, a cornerstone of the modernist thought of both black and white artists was that the spirituality and naturalness of the "primitive" folk would rescue the West from the grips of a calculating, materialistic, reason-bound "Nordic" civilization. The "primitive," furthermore, was consistently prefigured as a feminized being.[9] Thus, the paradox of celebrating "feminine" virtues within black culture while attempting to reject their own "feminization" contributed to the black male artists' ideas of masculinity.

Finally, the traditional relationship of patrons and artists formed a key tension. This dynamic suggested a state of dependence, still viewed as antithetical to achieving manhood by Victorian standards.

Although the role of art in society, the use of primitivism, and the inevitability of assuming a dependent position with a (usually white) patron may have presented problems for black male artists, these artists did not relinquish their claims to a "true" manhood to those more vociferous in defining it through capitalist endeavor, respectability, and notions of independence. In other words, although Garveyites and Prince Hall Freemasons were committed to bourgeois ideals of manliness, the male Harlem literati were equally invested in their gender identities, although in somewhat different and often more muted ways. Some invoked a modern sense of masculinity, elevating physicality above more abstract characteristics, such as reason and independence. They utilized the "primitive" in constituting new ideas of masculinity and, by locating the essence of manhood within the body as opposed to earlier nineteenth-century ideas of character, claimed that they were indeed men. Others circumvented the potential tensions by emphasizing their role as producers of art and literature and, consequently, invoked a masculine-coded "cult of production."[10] As the older poet and secretary of the National Association for the Advancement of Colored People (NAACP), James Weldon Johnson, wrote to a friend and supporter of the movement: "We are still on the job of getting over into the American consciousness the idea that in our cultural world the Negro is a creator as well as a creature—that he is a giver as well as a receiver—that he has aesthetic values as well as values physical, economic and otherwise."[11]

The actors in the Harlem Renaissance did not, by any means, subscribe to a monolithic masculine identity. As their ideas concerning the character of black art and literature—ideas that were influenced by age, class, and sexual orientation among other things—varied, so did their ideas concerning manhood. In general, however, the younger Harlem literati represented a more modern masculinity, a set of ideas about gender that were reflected in the new jazz culture of the 1920s. This chapter examines how those ideas were circulated through the cultural production of the Harlem Renaissance and the intellectual discussions surrounding it.[12]

▓ Beginning in March 1926 and lasting for the better part of the year, the *Crisis* conducted a symposium entitled, "The Negro in Art: How Shall He Be Portrayed." W. E. B. Du Bois and Jessie Redmon Fauset, editor-in-chief and literary editor, respectively, distributed questions concerning the artistic representation of the black working and middle class to various writers, editors, and publishers. Revealed in the questionnaire, among other things, was a concern that younger black writers, with the encouragement of white-owned publishing houses, might be limiting their portrayals to the "sordid, foolish and criminal among Negroes" at the expense of providing realistic depictions of the educated, professional strata of the black community. In general, those who responded, both black and white notables in the literary world, resisted the questionnaire's implicit argument that artists should conform to an obligatory balanced portrayal of the working and middle classes, or of folk and genteel culture. "True" art should transcend narrow cultural representations and speak to the universality of the black experience. Although some respondents, most prominently art critic Carl Van Vechten and novelist Julia Peterkin, suggested that the black folk possessed essential racial qualities of an "exotic" and "instinctive" nature which should be artistically celebrated, the majority of those whose answers were printed rejected the idea that any one black character, particularly one of a working-class milieu, should be thought of as representative of the race. Artists, in other words, should write what they were intimately familiar with but, simultaneously, they should not cater to the preconceived image of the "squalor" and "vice of Negro life" that Van Vechten advocated.[13] Benjamin Brawley, a black literary critic, succinctly articulated the complexities of the debate in his response to the survey: "An artist must be free: he can not be bound by any artificial restrictions. At the same time we heartily wish that so many artists would not prefer today to portray only what is vulgar. There is beauty in the world as well as ugliness, idealism as well as realism."[14]

To a certain extent, this debate was cast in terms of "propaganda versus art." Was the primary mission of the black artist one of representing an already culturally assimilated social group (the growing black professional class), a social group with a culture distinct from that of the white middle class (black urban, industrial laborers and rural sharecroppers), or some combination of the two? Or was the artist even bound by a duty to infuse his or her cultural production with the social concerns that characterized the "propaganda versus art" paradigm? Those who argued that it was incumbent upon black writers to provide literary representations of the "respectable" black middle class — a social group only excluded from the larger American middle class by dint of skin color — were often criticized as being propagandists and obstacles to "true" art. Conversely, those writers, usually younger ones, who focused upon the working-class folk opened themselves up to the charge that they indulged the literary tastes of a white public that wished to hold onto its stereotypes of blacks as an uncivilized people. The delicate negotiation of this dilemma was encapsulated in the response of Countee Cullen, whose ideas fell more into the former camp even though he was one of the younger participants in the movement. "Let the young Negro writer, like any artist, find his treasure where his heart lies," Cullen wrote, ". . . only let him not pander to the popular trend of seeing no cleanliness in their squalor, no nobleness in their meanness and no commonsense in their ignorance."[15] As Cullen's statement suggests, the representativeness of the folk was at the crux of the "propaganda versus art" debate. Were the sharecroppers and the newly arriving migrants that populated the literature of the day merely character types or were they emblematic of an essential black experience?

Many of the younger artists, caught up in the modernism of the postwar period, repudiated both the Victorian certitude of "progress" as well as the idea that art should be used only to portray the positive aspects of a particular social group. In this sense, their representations of black working-class culture were influenced by the intellectual currency of primitivism—the idea that the elemental nature of people who had been previously marginalized by the marketplace somehow offered the key to salvation for a Western culture preoccupied with the marketplace. The cultural milieu of the folk, particularly in the vernacular forms of the spirituals, jazz, and blues, offered a rich artistic source in addition to a worldview supposedly untainted by the materialistic values of industrial society.[16]

The celebration of the presumed spirituality, emotionality, and communalism of black folk culture—all qualities that worked to mark it as feminine—generated an intellectual discourse that sought to define cultural production in the language of the marketplace. Those employing this particular discourse tended to be older participants in the Renaissance, but that was not always the case. Locke's discussion of the cultural expression of the 1920s and the shift from sentimentalism to realism revealed his inclination to rely on a heavily gendered idiom of production. Despite his celebration of this transition, Locke felt compelled to not let the Old Negro whither away in a literary poorhouse, forgotten and unwanted. In his New Negro essay, "Negro Youth Speaks," he reminded the readers of the accomplishments of this older generation of writers. Some, such as novelist Charles W. Chestnutt, poet and critic William Stanley Braithwaite, and poet and novelist Paul Laurence Dunbar were firmly entrenched in the old literary style; others, such as Du Bois and James Weldon Johnson, Georgia Douglas Johnson, Angelina Grimké, and Anne Spencer, despite not incorporating modernism into their work, continued to produce important literature throughout the Harlem Renaissance. Regardless of the older generation's relationship to modernism or its literary production of the 1920s, Locke wanted its position in the development of the younger group made clear. "The generation now in the artistic vanguard," he wrote, "inherits the fine and dearly bought achievement of another generation of creative workmen who have been pioneers and path-breakers in the cultural development and recognition of the Negro in the arts."[17] Locke used language that evoked idealized images of nineteenth-century manhood—the artist as a skilled laborer and as a lone individual on the frontier. In part, he was in the process of constructing a predominantly male "tradition" of arts and letters in which to foreground the work of the younger artists. As such, his interpretation of black modernism and its predecessors contrived a hierarchy based on gender—a strategy also employed by white modernists.[18] In constructing this tradition, Locke employed masculinist language in order to claim a racialized manliness within the context of a hegemonic, white, middle-class manhood that was defined through, and performed in, the marketplace.

In addition to utilizing images of the artisan and pioneer, this assertion of manliness involved the very language of the marketplace. Locke again invoked the "cult of production" in an essay written three years after *The New Negro*, although in it he did not recapitulate the nineteenth-century producer ideal as much as he contradicted the stereotype of blacks as passive consumers. He suggested that a driving force behind the Renaissance was "a general desire . . . toward cultural expression and achievement," "a desire not to be merely imitative." He continued that the cultural production of the younger generation represented "a capitalization of the race's endowments and particular inheritances of temperament and experience."[19] I do not want to exaggerate Locke's use of the word "capitalization" to describe the literary output of the Renaissance, but we cannot overlook the importance of this language, particularly in the era of corporate capitalism. Locke compared the notion of black artists transforming their culture and experience into capital (and products which would, in turn, be consumed by the white middle class) to the conventional idea of blacks as merely tractable consumers.

Other members of the Renaissance used the masculinist language of the marketplace in discussing the role of the artist. In his history of Harlem, published during the twilight of the Renaissance, James Weldon Johnson praised the arts movement for imprinting on the American mind that the Negro "is the possessor of a wealth of natural endowments" and "a contributor to the nation's common cultural store." The Renaissance, in other words, offered substantial proof that blacks were not merely cultural consumers; they were producers as well.[20] Walter White, a novelist, NAACP officer, and one of the lead facilitators of the institutional objectives of the movement, also deployed a producerist discourse in discussing black cultural production. In his response to the *Crisis* symposium, he affirmed the need for artistic freedom and authenticity in regard to the representations of the black working class. He stripped the artist's role of its social implications (and responsibilities), stating that the "Negro writer, just like any other writer, should be allowed to write of whatever interests him . . . and should be judged not by the color of [his] skin but solely by the story he produces." At the same time, White rejected the inclination of some writers to restrict their literary representations of black culture to that of the working class merely because the market rewarded it. His discussion was implicitly gendered, as he referred to "true" artists as "honest craftsmen" and to those only interested in exploiting whites' stereotypes of blacks as "sycophants and weaklings." [21]

Locke, Johnson, and White all invoked the ideal of production in their framing of artistic expression as a manly activity. In part, this was a reflection of their commitment to bourgeois conceptions of manliness. Although considered New Negroes, all three were of the earlier generation that constructed its gender identity along the lines of Victorian convention. White, born in 1893, was the closest in age to the younger crop of New Negroes, but his discussion of art and his actual cultural production evinces an adherence to late-Victorian ideas of manhood.[22] This adherence to the ideals of manliness becomes clear when one reads the literary constructions of manhood present in Johnson's *The Autobiography of an Ex-Coloured Man* (1912) and White's *The Fire in the Flint* (1924).

Initially published anonymously in 1912, and later reissued in 1927, *Autobiography* is the fictionalized account of a biracial man's experience during the turn of the century.[23] Born in a small rural town in Georgia during Reconstruction, he is oblivious to race and the social dynamics it produces until he is rather abruptly made aware of his lineage—the child of a black woman and an estranged white man—as a preadolescent. After his mother's death, the protagonist travels throughout the South, first to Atlanta, then to Jacksonville, Florida. In Jacksonville, he works in a cigar factory and provides piano lessons to the "best class of coloured people" of the city (74). It is at this point in the novel that Johnson, through the protagonist, provides the reader with his evaluation of race and the politics of class. The narrator breaks down the African American population into approximately three classes. The first, which he labels "desperate," consists of "the men who work in the lumber and turpentine camps, the ex-convicts, [and] the bar-room loafers" (76). Although this class comprises only a small percentage of the race, he laments, it commands the largest amount of attention from the American public. He is careful to argue that the position of this "class" is not due to any natural moral deficiency; rather, it is structural forces, such as the economy, that create such "desperate" men.[24] The second class is made up of blacks engaged in the service sector and who, therefore, have the most interaction with whites. The third, which presumably the narrator and Johnson fit into, are the "independent workmen and tradesmen, and the well-to-do and educated coloured people" (78). The protagonist's murky delineation of class points to the indeterminacy of class boundaries in the African American population during the early twentieth century. It also allows Johnson to express his disillusionment with a system that prevents educated blacks from benefiting from social mobility. "There is to my mind," the protagonist states, "no more pathetic side of this many-sided question than the isolated position into which are forced the very coloured people who most need and who could best appreciate sympathetic co-operation, and their position grows tragic when the effort is made to couple them, whether or no, with the Negroes of the first class I mentioned" (80).

It is this tension between the protagonist's class sensibilities and racial heritage that dominates the novel's narrative structure. Throughout the book, the narrator expresses not only racial ambivalence; he also expresses anxiety about his ability to maintain the character traits that accompany, and ensure, his class position. Despite his exposure to working-class standards of behavior—through his employment at the cigar factory—the protagonist never loses his bourgeois bearings: "On the whole, though I was wild, I can't remember that I ever did anything disgraceful, or, as the usual standard for young men goes, anything to forfeit my claim to respectability" (83–84). Johnson's rendering of the plight of the black middle class is clearly presented in the protagonist's racial ambivalence, which culminates in his "passing" by "neither disclaim[ing] the black race nor claim[ing] the white race" (190). After traveling to Europe where he accompanies a millionaire as a personal musician and valet, he returns to the South to compose classical music based on Negro folk music. He eventually settles in New York, where he passes into white society and marries a white woman after revealing his true identity.

Johnson's portrayal of "passing" is a particularly gendered one and reveals how black middle-class men negotiated their masculine identities within a society and culture dominated by white middle-class males. Early in the narrative, Johnson expressed this negotiation of race and gender in the identity formation of black men as such: "And this is the dwarfing, warping, distorting influence which operates upon each and every coloured man in the United States. He is forced to take his outlook on all things, not from the view-point of a citizen, or a man, or even a human being, but from the view-point of a *coloured* man" (21, original emphasis). The literary expression of the construction of manhood as a relational process had its counterpart in the life experiences of Johnson and other members of the black middle class.[25] The classical singer Roland Hayes evinced this feeling of having one's manhood marginalized by one's race when, in 1923, he wrote to Johnson expressing his pleasure at the attention he was receiving in Paris and Vienna. "It is not [a] discomfortable feeling that one is a full man and that one is recognized as such," Hayes wrote. "I need not say more for you know only too well what I mean."[26]

This relational process of gender identity formation runs throughout *Autobiography* and shapes the protagonist's experience of "passing." As he struggles with his identity and his future in American society, he consistently measures himself against middle-class white men. First and foremost, this is governed by the logic of the marketplace and particularly one's position in it as either a producer or a consumer. "I had made up my mind that since I was not going to be a Negro," the protagonist admits, "I would avail myself of every possible opportunity to make a white man's success; and that, if it can be summed up in any one word, means 'money'" (193). As he becomes more and more wrapped up in "money fever," his obtaining work in financial trading, saving to the point of self-denial, and eventually owning property become essential to his appropriation of a white, middle-class male identity. Throughout the narrative, this money fever is juxtaposed against the "artistic" mentality and "natural" spirituality of blacks—as the scholar S. P. Fullinwinder argues, Johnson's implication that African Americans possessed a "unique racial genius."[27] The protagonist points out several times, for instance, that it is his "natural artistic temperament" that allows him to become musically proficient. Ultimately, it is his decision to relinquish this artistic and creative genius and, instead, to enter the marketplace, that signals his adoption of a white male identity. That gender, as well as race, composes the "ex-coloured man's" identity becomes all the more apparent when one considers that, of all the people who influence him, none, other than his mother, are women. His mother represents his first contact, as a child, with religion and music. By rejecting these cultural and "racial" characteristics of his African American heritage through his entrance into the rational, materialist world of business, the protagonist is also rejecting his biological and cultural connection to a "feminine" race.

The "ex-coloured man's" racial ambivalence is reflected in his vacillation between black culture, represented by the folk spirituals and ragtime, and the white-dominated realm of corporate capitalism. This vacillation emerges within the text as a tension between black manhood as a communally circumscribed construct and the individualism of the self-made man ideal. By the end of the narrative, the protagonist begins to regret his decision to pass into the identity of a white man. His compunction is shaped by his feeling, per-

Walter White and James Weldon Johnson. (Courtesy of The Yale Collection of American Literature, Beinecke Rare Book and Manuscript Library)

haps subconsciously, that black gender identity formation, as opposed to the construction of white manliness, is a collective experience. After attending an event at Carnegie Hall, at which several black political leaders have spoken, the protagonist reflects on his decision to forego casting his lot with educated blacks, "that small but gallant band of coloured men who are publicly fighting the cause of their race" (211). He ruefully continues: "Beside them I feel small and selfish. I am an ordinarily successful white man who has made a little money. They are men who are making history and a race. I, too, might have taken part in a work so glorious" (211). Despite his second-guessing, the "ex-coloured man" remains "ex-coloured," although he does not do so without wondering whether there is "an indefinable something which marked a difference" between him and his white male acquaintances (200). This "indefinable something," he suggests throughout his narrative, is the creative and artistic genius embodied in the black race. His passing into white society is essentially a rejection of that, the selling of his "birthright for a mess of pottage" (211).

The Fire in the Flint, Walter White's first novel, is more raw-edged than Autobiography. It is both less ambivalent and less subtle in its examination of the effects of race and racism in the lives of black men. Fire in the Flint depicts the lives of a middle-class black family in rural Georgia shortly after World War I. It specifically revolves around Kenneth Harper, a young doctor who has returned to his hometown. Central City is a cotton mill town full of "men, self-made, with all that that distinctly American term implies" (39). A graduate of Atlanta University and a northern medical school, and a veteran officer in the U.S. Army medical corps, Kenneth's initial plan in returning to Central City is to open a private practice that administers to the needs of black folk. He arrives determined to apply a pragmatic self-help philosophy to local race relations: "Booker Washington was right. And the others who were always howling about rights were wrong. Get a trade or a profession. Get a home. Get some property. Get a bank account. Do something! Be somebody!" (17) Kenneth's commitment to a conservative Tuskegeeism is counterpoised by his brother Bob's pessimistic assessment of race relations in the South and his more radical approach to racial politics. Bob "was the natural rebel, revolt was a part of his creed. Kenneth was the natural pacifist—he never bothered trouble until trouble bothered him" (24).

Kenneth is rudely awakened to the realities of the New South when he comes into contact with the poverty and squalor of Darktown, the enormously inequitable distribution of resources between blacks and whites, and the maltreatment of black women at the hands of white men. When he broaches the subject with one of the town's leading white citizens, Roy Ewing—who Kenneth has, significantly, treated for venereal disease—he is told not to disrupt the social and political order by protesting or complaining. The social order, according to Ewing, is preordained and kept in place by extralegal violence as well as blacks who know their place within it. "Lynching never bothers folks like you," he tells Kenneth. "Why, your daddy was one of the most respected folks in this town. But lynching does keep some of these young nigger bucks in check" (69–70). This conversation propels Kenneth toward a more radical position concerning race relations in the South. But what is key to Kenneth's disillusionment is his growing realization that white society's failure to differentiate between blacks precludes him from enjoying all of the perquisites that should accompany his education and class position. Kenneth realizes that the South is a society based on caste, not class. "One factor is fixed and immutable—the more intelligent and prosperous the Negro and the more ignorant and poor the white man, the graver the danger, for in the mind of the latter are jealousy and ignorance and stupidity and abject fear of the educated and successful Negro" (74).

Kenneth falls in love with a young woman, Jane Phillips, whom he has known since childhood and it is this relationship that facilitates his radicalization. When he becomes involved with helping sharecroppers organize, Jane proposes that they start a cooperative. "Kenneth began to be infected by her enthusiasm. He saw that her idea had possibilities. But, manlike, he didn't want to give in too soon or too readily" (143).[28] They are instrumental in organizing the National Negro Farmers' Co-operative and Protective League, which, along with becoming a way for sharecroppers to pool their resources, also functions as a self-defense group. At one of its first meetings, Kenneth gives a rousing speech that situates the organization's activities in a gendered framework. "No race in all history has ever had its liberties and rights handed to it on a silver platter—such rights can come only when men are willing to struggle and sacrifice and work and die, if need be, to obtain them!" he tells the group of men. "Only slaves and cowards whine and beg! Men and women stand true and firm and struggle onwards and upwards until they reach their goal!" He concludes with the question: "What do you choose to be—slaves or men?" (179).

As Kenneth becomes more radical, Bob channels his anger at Jim Crow into less militant objectives, namely to attend law school so that he can provide legal assistance to the black community. There is, in effect, a convergence of the brothers' mentalities and approaches to dealing with racism. But this fusion of philosophy and praxis is not fully realized, for both brothers die within days of each other. Bob avenges his sister Mamie's rape by fatally shooting two white men. A mob gathers and corners him in a dilapidated barn where a shootout ensues. The standoff allows Bob to assert his masculinity within a society in which black men are constantly told that they are not men: "Listen! The dogs sound like they're near! There they are! He wouldn't waste his precious bullets on dogs! Oh, no! He'd save them for the human dogs! God damn 'em! He'd show 'em a 'damned nigger' knew how to die! Like a man!" (234). With one bullet remaining after a prolonged siege, Bob shoots himself, whereupon his body is pumped full of bullets, dragged behind a car, burned in the public square, and dismembered by local children. Bob's death and Mamie's rape turn Kenneth further away from his already decreasingly conciliatory position and he decides to hunt down the ringleaders of the mob:

> What was the use of trying to avoid trouble in the South, he thought? Hell! Hadn't he tried? Hadn't he given up everything that might antagonize the whites? Hadn't he tried in every way he could to secure and retain their friendship? By God, he'd show them now! The white-livered curs! The damned filthy beasts! Damn trying to be a good Negro! He'd fight them to the death! . . . Denuded of all the superficial trappings of civilization, he stood there—the primal man—the wild beast, cornered, wounded, determined to fight—fight—fight! (268–69)

His mother succeeds in calming him down, which leads Kenneth to question his own manhood at failing to exact revenge for his brother. He finally gets the opportunity to "fight back" at the end of the narrative when he is accosted by a mob of fifteen after leaving the home of Roy Ewing, where he has been attending his ill daughter. Kenneth puts up a valiant effort but he is ultimately subdued and the novel ends with a newspaper account of his subsequent lynching.

Fire in the Flint was more tragic than *Autobiography*, but both were critiques of a social system that made it difficult, if not impossible, for African Americans to become successful. The tragedy in *Fire in the Flint* is that a "[black] man's ability or brain" are not recognized in the South or, indeed, in the United States in the 1920s. The tragedy in *Autobiography* is that the protagonist realizes this and, therefore, becomes "ex-coloured." In order to be successful, the "ex-coloured man" rejects his racial heritage. In Kenneth's case, his success leads to his death. But what is also interesting in these novels is that the authors' use of gender reveals their thoughts on the social construction of middle-class manhood. Johnson linked manhood concretely to a performance in the marketplace and the acceptance of bourgeois values and gender conventions. The "ex-coloured man's" gender identity formation involved an ambivalent, although ultimately complete, rejection of both the black folk and the idea that racial and cultural experience could contribute to any alternative definitions of manhood. White moved beyond defining manhood solely in terms of the marketplace, evident in the fact that Kenneth and Bob associate their manhood with their ability to stand up to white injustice and, in the case of Bob, defend black women from sexual assault. Ultimately, however, the point behind the novel is that the distorted logic of race prevents successful black men from enjoying the class status that should come with being self-made. In other words, White lamented the fact that race disrupted the natural relationship between manhood and the market; he did not challenge the very relationship itself. Other members of the Harlem Renaissance did challenge this relationship as they moved further away from Victorian standards of culture and its attendant prescriptions of manliness. Through their rejection of the centrality of the marketplace, they began to locate masculinity in the unreconstructed "primitive."

■ As Johnson and White adhered to bourgeois concepts of manliness, younger participants in the movement differed both in their vision of cultural production and the models of manhood to which they subscribed. Perhaps the most articulate rebel against the bourgeois ideals of manliness was Jean Toomer. Along with a modernist critique of industrialization (what he termed "the machine"), the scion of an elite Washingtonian family lambasted the tendency to equate manhood with business. "Why this insistence on Manliness, on the He-Man, on the Red-blooded Fellow?" he asked. He suggested that this preoccupation produced boorish American men: "He capitalizes his crudity and calls its [sic] Manliness. Whatever is not crude he calls effiminate [sic]. Charm, grace, tenderness, loveliness, refinement, culture—all are effiminate [sic] . . . Anything not crude action, not hard-boiled practically, that is, anything not business, is effeminate." [29] This was part of the dynamic that Toomer defined as "the Tyranny of the Anglo-Saxon Ideal." He felt that blacks were captives of the "Anglo-Saxon Ideal" and expressed concern that African American men were too devoted to pursuing the path to bourgeois manhood. He was pleased that a younger generation of Americans was beginning to reject materialism in favor of "the supreme position of the arts," but was simultaneously disappointed that it seemed to be mostly younger whites. "Can we say the same for yourselves [sic], we of the darker skins, of a somewhat different heritage?" Toomer asked Mae Wright, his main love interest. "We cannot. Paradoxical as it may seem, we who have Negro blood in our veins, who are culturally and emotionally the most removed from [the] Puritan tradition, are its most tenacious supporters. We still believe, in fact we believe it now more so than ever, that a man's worth should be gauged by material possessions." [30]

Toomer was generally referring to the expanding black middle class, not rural sharecroppers and urban industrial laborers. In discussing what he felt was the American tradition of repressive Puritanism, he argued that as blacks were achieving social mobility they were shedding their "natural," emotional selves and becoming sexual and cultural ascetics. "There are any number of Negroes who, psychologically, must be classed with the best of our 100% Americans," he complained. "It may turn out that the Puritan traditions will find its last stronghold among middle-class Negroes." Furthermore, "civilization," an alternative term for "the machine," was destroying the emotional and physical vitality of blacks as they entered the ranks of the bourgeoisie. This had already happened, he argued, to the Old Negro. Concerning these pre-Renaissance black literary figures—and perhaps older contemporary writers such as Du Bois, Braithwaite, and Chestnutt—Toomer felt that the "great majority of them are so entangled in 'progress' that when one does emerge, he invariably bears the ear marks of the emasculated social machine."[31]

For Toomer, the responsibility for this "emasculation" lay in the rapid industrialization and urbanization of the United States, in addition to class formation within the black community. Ultimately, he felt that it was the culture of the black folk, although it was in danger of being overwhelmed by "the machine," that held the most promise for blacks in their struggle against the enervating effects of modernity. The capturing of this premodern folk culture informed his participation in the early years of the Renaissance. He believed it to be his "privilege and duty" to help "crystallize" a "Negro" standard of beauty that would allow blacks to tap into their "natural," emotional selves.[32] "The mass of Negroes, the peasants," he wrote to fellow modernist author Sherwood Anderson, "like the mass of Russians or Jews or Irish or what not, are too instinctive to be anything but themselves. Here and there one finds a high type Negro who shares this virtue with his more primitive brothers." However, as blacks were increasingly moving to southern urban areas and the North, and developing a middle class, they were losing their "instinctive" culture. "The Negro of the folk-song has all but passed away: the Negro of the emotional church is fading," he intimated to his friend Waldo Frank. "A hundred years from now these Negroes, if they exist at all will live in art. And I believe that a vague sense of this fact is the driving force behind the art movements directed towards them today."[33]

Toomer did not remain a participant of the Renaissance for long. His multiracial background eventually led him to reject the circumscription of his art within racialized boundaries.[34] His early literary career, however, involved a celebration of the "primitive-ness" of the black folk and a rejection of "the Anglo-Saxon Ideal," the marketplace, and the conventions of manliness that accompanied them. His utopian view of black folk culture, a culture that was "feminine" by early-twentieth-century middle-class standards, did not correspond to a complete repudiation of manhood; rather, he merely uncoupled the concept of production and producer values, or the connection between the marketplace and manliness that constituted Victorian gender conventions, from his own definitions of manhood. This reconfiguration of masculinity was apparent in *Cane*.

Published in 1923, Cane was Toomer's major contribution to the literature of the Renaissance and, significantly, his last literary portrayal of black culture. A collection of thematically linked poems, character sketches, and short stories, Cane contains several themes: namely, the debilitating effects of industrialization and urbanization on southern black folk culture; the tension created within northern and urban black communities by class formation; the inability of black men and women to develop emotionally sustaining relationships; and African Americans' problematic dependence on Christianity. The book is divided into three parts, each representing a crucial stage in the evolution of the modern black experience. The first takes place completely within the rural South. The setting of the second part is the city (Washington, D.C., and Chicago). It is in this section that Toomer highlighted the centrifugal effects of modernity and the class tensions that it produces. The third section, which consists solely of "Kabnis," the longest character sketch of the book, deals with a northern, biracial, middle-class man's return to the South and his spiritual struggle that results in the rejection of his folk past. Generally considered the first modernist work of the Renaissance, Cane's form moves between poetry and prose. Toomer utilized natural imagery to evoke intense emotion in his characters and setting. Overall, Cane's mood is one of celebration of the "primitive" over "civilization." [35]

Women are the central figures in the southern part of the narrative and represent Toomer's identification of black folk culture with the "feminine" qualities of nature, sensuality, and emotionalism. There are "Karintha" and "Fern," "natural" black beauties who beguile every man with whom they come in contact. "Carma," a woman who is "strong as any man" (10), is held responsible for her husband's incarceration. He kills a man after being deceived twice by Carma: the first time over her alleged infidelity and the second time over her fake suicide. Then there is Louisa, the black woman caught in an interracial love triangle in "Blood-Burning Moon." In one of many instances, Toomer explicitly connected women and nature when he described the desire that Bob Stone—the white male of the triangle—has for Louisa: "She was worth it. Beautiful nigger gal. Why nigger? Why not, just gal? No, it was because she was nigger that he went to her. Sweet . . . The scent of boiling cane came to him" (32, original ellipses). Literary critic Nellie McKay suggests that Toomer used the fate of black women, as embodiment of nature, to represent the destructiveness that modernization wreaked upon black folk culture.[36] I want to suggest that Toomer also used the male figures in this first section of Cane to illustrate the effects of industrialization and urbanization on black masculinity. As he termed it in his intellectual discourse, "the machine" emasculated black men. This becomes a more prominent theme in the latter two sections of the book; however, there are hints in the rural sketches that he was developing a critique of "civilization" and its effects on a particularly virile, preindustrial masculinity.

In "Blood-Burning Moon," Toomer explored the problem of interracial sex in the rural South. The central characters form a love triangle: both Bob Stone, the son of a white planter family, and Tom Burwell, a black tenant farmer, love Louisa, the young black woman who works as a domestic in the Stone household. Tom wishes to marry Louisa but she demurs, partly because of her attraction to Bob. Stone, who desires Louisa mainly as an exotic "Other," overhears several blacks speculating on the potential clash between him and Tom. Enraged at the thought of Tom and Louisa together, he rushes into town and finds them at Louisa's home. A fight breaks out and Tom ends up slitting Bob's throat. Predictably, a mob of white townspeople gathers to lynch Tom, who is now resigned to his fate.

On the surface, "Blood-Burning Moon" addressed the prevalence of miscegenation in the rural South and, for the most part, the inability of black men to protect the honor and bodies of black women. It was much more ambiguous than that, particularly given Toomer's equivocal characterization of Louisa's feelings toward both Tom and Bob. The vignette represented a critique of industrialization and its effects on black masculinity. The setting, which alternates between the cane field and the small factory town, works as a metaphor for migration and economic modernization. The cane field is the site of rural black folk culture and, as opposed to *Cane*'s other short stories where women represent the "natural-ness" of the folk, it is a homosocial environment: "The scent of cane came from the copper pan and drenched the forest and the hill that sloped to factory town, beneath its fragrance. It drenched the men in circle seated around the stove" (29). In "Blood-Burning Moon," women do not inhabit this rural space. It is from here that Tom draws his strength. Tom's ability to protect the honor of Louisa is enhanced by his connection to the land, evident when he uses a knife to chase off other black men who have been spreading rumors about her relationship with Bob. The narrative moves into factory town where Louisa lives. Here, Tom awkwardly proposes to Louisa by stressing his economic future: "An next year if ole Stone'll trust me, I'll have a farm. My own. My bales will buy yo what y gets from white folks now" (30). Tom's hopes of protection and provision are dependent on production, which is further linked to the land, not industrial labor. Factory town, symbol of economic modernization, however, thwarts his realization of this goal. It is here where Tom kills Bob Stone; but it is also here where the lynch mob kills him: "White men like ants upon a forage rushed about. Except for the taut hum of their moving, all was silent. . . . The moving body of their silence preceded them over the crest of the hill into factory town. It flattened the Negroes beneath it. It rolled to the wall of the factory, where it stopped. Tom knew that they were coming. He couldn't move" (34). The mob hunts down Tom in "two high-powered cars with glaring searchlights" (34), further symbols of industrialism. "Blood-Burning Moon" is clearly a literary manifestation of Toomer's alienation from "the machine." Given Toomer's hostility toward the mechanistic culture of the early twentieth century, Tom's fate is inevitable. The virile masculinity of the black folk is redeemed through Tom's murder of Bob but, ultimately, it is destroyed in the factory, on the altar of modernization.

The theme of the "emasculated social machine" reappears in *Cane*'s second section, in the short story, "Theater." Class difference is explored more fully in this story about a brief encounter between a female dancer and a middle-class man in Washington, D.C. John is the brother of the stage manager of the jazz club at which Dorris dances. He has arrived prior to the dance rehearsal when his attention is immediately drawn to Dorris. John is a self-identified member of the black middle class and considers himself to be "dictie, educated, [and] stuck-up" (51). Toomer suggested that John is an outmoded Victorian, whose "body is separate from the thoughts that pack his mind" (50). It is not only the respectability and repressiveness that accompany his class position that prevents John from enjoying the primal atmosphere of the club; it is also his excessive rationality. He resists being caught up in the spontaneity of urban, working-class culture. Instead, "his mind, contained above desires of his body, singles the [chorus] girls out, and tries to trace origins and plot destinies" (50). In order to resist his attraction to Dorris, he objectifies her and the other dancers by reducing them to wild animals whom the "director will herd . . . and tame" (50). Once they begin dancing, "he wills thought to rid his mind of passion" (51). Both he and Dorris, however, are magnetically drawn to one another and Dorris diverges from the routine in an effort to break through his armor of respectability. While she dances, John falls into a daydream in which he and Dorris leave the club together. They end up in a room whose walls are "the flesh and blood of Dorris" (53). Instead of fantasizing about the transgression of class boundaries that being intimate with Dorris represents, John, in his dream sequence, "reaches for a manuscript of his, and reads" (53). The narrative returns to the club, where Dorris has stopped dancing: "The whole stage claps. Dorris, flushed, looks quick at John. His whole face is in shadow. She seeks for her dance in it. She finds it a dead thing in the shadow which is his dream" (53). Frustrated at her unsuccessful attempt to attract the attention and desire of a middle-class man, a crying Dorris runs to her dressing room where she is consoled by her friend. John represents the quintessential Victorian, incapable of integrating his mind and body into a total self and afraid of his passionate feelings. Instead of acknowledging his sexual desire, he mentally transforms the dancers into either characters in a novel or wild animals, and failing that, he forces all sexual feeling out of his body with mental exertion. Ultimately, it is his class position that prevents him from acknowledging Dorris; it is also, however, his class position that leads to his figurative impotency.

Toomer reinforced the themes of class difference, racial ambivalence, and the severing of the black bourgeoisie from its rural folk roots in the last section of *Cane*, titled "Kabnis." Ralph Kabnis is a northern, middle-class teacher who has taken a job at a school for blacks in rural Georgia.[37] His northern and urban upbringing has left him ill-prepared to cope with the crude reality of the South's natural and racial environment. The opening scene finds Kabnis in his cabin unable to fall asleep amidst the "night winds," "red dust," and nocturnal maneuvers of barnyard animals. As he walks out of the cabin into the night, "he totters as a man would who for the first time uses artificial limbs. As a completely artificial man would" (83). Toomer was revisiting the theme of urbanization, industrialization, and vitiated masculinity. Kabnis is alienated from his new rural world but when he thinks of Washington and New York, "[a]n impotent nostalgia grips him" (83–84). He is resigned to the decision he has made to come south; part of his resolution is to vicariously experience the perceived tranquility of the nearby black folk: "He forces himself to narrow to a cabin silhouetted on a knoll about a mile away. Peace. Negroes within it are content. They farm. They sing. They love. They sleep" (84). Here are people whose lives have not been contaminated by modernity.

Although Kabnis is middle class, he does not labor under repressive, bourgeois moral conventions. Indeed, he curses the excessive regulation of behavior that was characteristic of industrial and normal schools in the New South. Kabnis spends much of his free time with Fred Halsey, a biracial shop owner, and Professor Layman, a preacher. Halsey drinks and smokes and it is his association with Kabnis that eventually gets Kabnis fired when the school's principal finds them drinking in Kabnis's cabin. He fires Kabnis because he does not conform to the uplift ideology of black middle-class reformers. The dismissal frees him from the stifling atmosphere of this oasis of "civilization." Halsey offers him a job in his woodworking shop. "He's goin t work with me," Halsey informs the principal. "Shapin shafts and buildin wagons'll make a man of him what nobody, y get me? what nobody can take advantage of" (94).

Kabnis's new employment suggests that Toomer was linking artisanal labor, or production, with the attainment of manhood. It was more complex than this, however, as Kabnis is constantly infantilized—within the narrative and in Toomer's textual rendering—in his new environment. Kabnis, in his workmen's uniform, "is awkward and ludicrous, like a schoolboy in his big brother's new overalls" (98). It is clear that he does not belong in Halsey's world any more than he belongs in the overcivilized environment of the school. He becomes increasingly defensive of how others perceive him and begins to drink more. His defensiveness is exacerbated by his failure to reconcile himself to his racial and cultural past—namely, slavery and black folk spirituality; these are embodied in Father John, the blind old man who inhabits Halsey's cellar.

The final scene, which takes place in front of Father John, is Kabnis's baptism of fire, so to speak. Kabnis, Halsey, and two women, Cora and Stella, are spending Saturday evening drinking and playing cards. There is also Lewis, a young northerner like Kabnis, but a more militant believer in the liberatory potential of Christianity. Throughout the short story there are references to how virile Lewis is; but Toomer did not present him so much as an alternative model of manhood as a foil for Kabnis's racial ambivalence.[38] This racial ambivalence, or Kabnis's willful inability to realize the connection he has to the soil—represented by the cellar and Father John—works its way out through his class consciousness and his gender identity. When Lewis suggests, for instance, that Father John is the "spirit of the past," Kabnis responds that his "ancestors were Southern blue-bloods" (107). Throughout the scene, Kabnis rejects his historical linkage to the folk. This comes out in one particularly harsh tirade when he claims to have come from a long tradition of orators. At one point, he lashes out at Halsey: "An as f you, youre all right f choppin things from blocks of wood. I was good at that th day I ducked th cradle. An since then, I've been shapin words after a design that branded here. Know whats here? M soul. Ever heard o that? Th hell y have. Been shapin words t fit m soul" (109). Kabnis links his intellect to the act of production and, in doing so, tries to reclaim his manhood. Shortly thereafter, however, Cora forcefully nurtures him as if he were a child: "Halsey gives him a swig of shine. Cora glides up, seats him, and then plumps herself down on his lap, squeezing his head into her breasts. Kabnis mutters. Tries to break loose. Curses. Cora almost stifles him. He goes limp and gives up. Cora toys with him. Ruffles his hair. Braids it. Parts it in the middle" (110). For a brief moment, Cora's nurturing behavior prompts Stella, the other woman, to become jealous. The tension and potential confrontation between Cora and Stella is averted when Halsey grabs Stella, "pins her arms and kisses her" (110). The juxtaposition of Kabnis in Cora's lap and Halsey's forceful handling of Stella suggests that Toomer was contrasting the weakness of northern, "artificial" manhood to the virility of southern, rural masculinity. Kabnis's northern, middle-class background prevents him from achieving a singularly black masculinity precisely because he resists realizing the power that resides in the culture of the southern black folk. The story ends with Kabnis trudging up the stairs to start another day at work. Toomer's imagery leaves one with the feeling that this scenario will occur every weekend for the rest of Kabnis's life. He will continue to look awkward in "his big brother's new overalls"; he will continue to perform menial, meaningless labor; he will continue to get drunk and be coddled until he can somehow reconcile himself to the vitality of the black folk.

Toomer's major literary contribution was one of the first modernist attempts to reclaim the rural roots of African American culture. This reclamation project also involved delineating and endorsing a virile black masculinity not structured by the marketplace or the "finer" elements of respectable culture. Those characters who subscribed to the ideal of bourgeois manliness were typified by a symbolic impotency, while those who stayed rooted in black folk culture were represented as more virile and masculine. The latter's masculinity, however, was in danger of being undermined by the forces of modernization and class formation. In *Cane*, Toomer was presenting an alternative masculinity that was constructed against dominant, middle-class definitions of manhood. It involved a rejection of "civilization," producer values, and respectability while it celebrated physicality and sexuality as masculine qualities. This alternative model of manhood was also present in the novels of Claude McKay and his discussion of black cultural production.

Both in his intellectual discourse and his primitivist cultural production, McKay uncoupled masculinity and the market. He was even more adamant than Toomer in locating manhood in the body. Like his younger compatriots, he viewed "civilization," and particularly capitalism, with disdain and claimed that it was sapping the virility of African Americans and African Caribbeans, although he was not as critical of urbanization as Toomer. He expressed this sentiment in an acerbic theater review for the socialist magazine, *Liberator*. The fact that he had to view the Russian playwright Leonid Andreyev's play, *He, The One Who Gets Slapped*, from a segregated balcony of a New York theater provided the impetus for such an angry review: "He who got slapped was I. As always in the world-embracing Anglo-Saxon circus, the intelligence, the sensibilities of the black clown were slapped without mercy." McKay's review had more to do with the racial customs of Europe and the United States than with the play itself. "In the great prison yard of white civilization in which Negro clowns move and have their being," he caustically remarked, "your play is a baby babbling in the bedlam of the Christian market-place. And a baby has no chance under the cloven hoofs of the traders in the mart. It is marked for destruction even as I am marked; for, to the hard traders I am a mere pickaninny grown up, that has no claim to the privileges of a man." McKay used Christianity and capitalism to signify not only European and Anglo-American "civilization," but imperialism as well. His demonic depiction of the traders, accompanied by several allusions to "pale devils," spoke to the interrelatedness of the exploitation inherent in free market economies and the racist practices of post-emancipation societies. McKay's review served as a critique of the political economy of racism. Still his exhortations were directed more at black men than at white society to allow blacks to enter the "Christian market-place." Instead, he suggested that blacks get back to their "primitive" selves, which were increasingly being destroyed by the economic modernization of the West: "The prison is vast, there is plenty of space and a little time to sing and dance and laugh and love . . . to dream of the jungle, revel in rare scents and riotous colours, croon a plantation melody, and be a real original Negro." He suggested that this recognition and celebration of a black diasporic culture—one that was informed by both Africa and the experience of New World slavery—was more powerful, and life-affirming, than identifying with a staid, mechanical culture that he identified as white.[39]

McKay's critique of Western culture involved a negative evaluation of white, middle-class manhood and what he felt to be the unnatural constraints placed on sexuality and virile masculinity by bourgeois gender conventions. In a long letter to Harold Jackman that speculated on the interrelatedness of race, violence, and sexual desire in the United States and the West Indies, McKay essentially elevated a "primitive" blackness above an "overcivilized" whiteness and suggested that the former was both more healthy and masculine. "I know that a great body of white people, especially Nordic males, are neurotic about sex!" he wrote. He told Jackman that he felt "the primitive[,] carnal African rhythm in me very strongly." This rhythm, moreover, was an innately human, as opposed to racial, characteristic that whites (and an increasing number of blacks) were losing by their immersion in the culture of respectability. Whites, in particular, were "having so much of natural rhythm lifted out of them by highly civilized ways of living that they turn to Negroes, who they feel, quite rightly, have more of primitive rhythm than they."[40] McKay reveled in the perception and, he felt, actuality, that black men were more virile than middle-class white men. He stopped short of invoking a purely essentialist interpretation of the sexual sensibility and behavior of blacks, however, perhaps in order to mute the stereotypical conclusions of the sexual avariciousness of blacks held by many whites. He was not shy about claiming an enhanced sexual virility compared to Europeans

Claude McKay. (Courtesy of The Yale Collection of American Literature, Beinecke Rare Book and Manuscript Library)

and Anglo-Americans, although he rejected the notion that people of African descent were grossly libidinous. "To say that the black man is 'sexually unrestrainable' is palpably false," he wrote to the English newspaper *Daily Herald*. "I, a full-blooded negro, can control my sexual proclivities when I care to, and I am endowed with my full share of the primitive passion."[41] Moreover, he refused to make sweeping generalizations that set up a dichotomy of "primitive," sensual blacks and "civilized," repressed whites. "This, my dear boy, is the Freudian era of freedom in sex," he wrote to Jackman. "If the Negro is virile, it is all to his credit. He is no more so than the Italians! My characters are characters [and] not the whole Negro race."[42] These last two sentences speak to McKay's care not to tar all whites and blacks with the respective brushes of "civilization" and "the primitive." He felt that recent European immigrants were as instinctive, natural, and sensual as the majority of blacks; however, he also made clear that his working-class black characters did not represent the black experience in its totality. Rather, like Toomer, McKay felt that as African Americans and African Caribbeans were moving up the social ladder and accepting bourgeois standards of respectability, they were becoming less virile in the sense that they were adhering to a model of manhood that was devoid of physicality and sexual expressiveness.

Indeed, McKay felt that it was the "task of Negro artists" to prevent this devitalization of black culture, and specifically black manhood, in part, by celebrating the "primitive-ness" inherent in the increasingly urbanized black population. This primitivist race consciousness, more than a propagandistic portrayal of the middle class à la Johnson and White, motivated McKay's literary output. "The Negro artist can help the . . . race, corrupted by civilization, to see that it has something finer than the thing it hankers after in itself. That is one way of salvation, I believe, for the Negro race in the modern[,] civilized world."[43]

McKay's critique of middle-class respectability and black assimilationist desire contained an assault on the ideals of bourgeois manliness, not on manhood itself. He merely inverted the Victorian gendered hierarchies of technology and nature, self-control and sensuality, reason and emotion. Nature, sensuality, and emotion, qualities that were most clearly embodied in the black working-class, or "folk," became the markers for a modern masculinity. But, as we will see, McKay continued to lay claim to the idea of production as a central component of male gender identity. This ambivalence emerges in both his novels of the late- 1920s and the way in which he talked about the creative process of art.

McKay published his first novel, Home to Harlem, in 1928 and, within a year, he published Banjo: A Story without a Plot. In both novels, the protagonist is an unschooled yet street-smart young man from the southern United States. Both protagonists are veterans of World War I who are trying to acclimate to civilian life. The main character of Home to Harlem, Jake Brown, a "tall, brawny, and black" longshoreman, is returning to New York after serving with the U.S. Army in France (HTH, 3–4). Banjo, née Lincoln Agrippa Daily, is a "child of the Cotton Belt," "a type that was never sober, even when he was not drinking" (B, 11, 13). An unskilled laborer and a musician, he enlisted in the Canadian army during the war and is now living as a vagabond in the south of France. Both Jake and Banjo are ladies' men who surround themselves with fun-loving, indolent slackers; Jake hangs around other New Yorkers while Banjo belongs to a pan-African group of beachcombers. Both, however, develop strong relationships with Ray, the main crossover character between the novels. Ray is a college-educated Haitian writer whose breadth of knowledge ranges from Sapphic poetry to Tolstoy. In *Home to Harlem*, Jake meets Ray while both are working on the train, Jake as the third cook and Ray as a waiter. We are reintroduced to Ray in *Banjo* when he ends up in Marseilles as a starving artist.

In these two novels, Ray represents the modern black intellectual's struggle against a pervasive Western political and cultural imperialism while Jake and Banjo represent the innate "primitive-ness" of the premodern black folk. Jake and Banjo inhabit spaces that are untainted by the supervision of middle-class morality, both black and white. One of Jake's hangouts, the Congo, "was a real throbbing little Africa in New York" (HTH, 29). McKay described a Philadelphia buffet flat that Jake attends in strikingly primitivist terms:

> The piano-player had wandered off into some dim, far-away, ancestral source of music. Far, far away from music-hall syncopation and jazz, he was lost in some sensual dream of his own. . . . The notes were naked acute alert. Like black youth burning naked in the bush. Love in the deep heart of the jungle. . . . Like a primitive dance of war or of love . . . the marshaling of spears or the sacred frenzy of a phallic celebration. . . . Black lovers of life caught up in their own free native rhythm, threaded to a remote scarce-remembered past, celebrating the midnight hours in themselves, for themselves, of themselves. . . . (HTH, 196–97)

Similarly, Banjo and his crew spend their days conspiring to get drunk and their nights making music in the Senegalese-owned bars in the Ditch. Their world is governed by the need for collective survival and the desire for communal gratification. Banjo, with the instrument for which he is nicknamed, creates an atmosphere that is structured more by sensuality and emotion than by self-control and producer values: "Handsome, happy brutes. The music is on again. The Senegalese boys crowd the floor, dancing with one another. They dance better male with male or individually, than with the girls, putting more power in their feet, dancing more wildly, more natively, more savagely" (B, 48). Although this last description of the dancers speaks to the performance of masculinity in homosocial and homoerotic spaces, what is important for our purposes now is to recognize that McKay was describing an environment in which middle-class values held little currency. The jazz clubs and buffet flats functioned as physical havens from the tentacles of Western culture or, as he termed it elsewhere, "the white hound of Civilization."[44]

If these leisure spaces represent the absence of Western cultural hegemony, Ray is the intellectual expression of McKay's modernist perspective on the potentially destructive effects of Western political hegemony. Describing Ray's family history during the American marines' occupation of Haiti, McKay referred to the United States as the "monster of civilization" and the "steamroller of progress" (HTH, 155). In a conversation he has with a fellow beach bum from England, Ray berates the modern corporate capitalist culture of the United States. " 'I didn't sense any soul-destroying honesty there,' " he assesses. " 'What I felt was an awful big efficiency sweeping all over me. You felt that business in its mad race didn't have time to worry about honesty, and if you thought about honesty at all it was only as a technical thing, like advertising, to help efficiency forward' " (B, 145). Ray's search for a "soul-destroying honesty" epitomizes McKay's modernism, a cultural project that, similarly engaged in by other modernists, advocated the expression of "terrible honesty," as opposed to the idealism and repressiveness of Victorian cultural production.[45]

McKay transparently dealt with many issues of external conflict (the relationship of black workers to the labor movement) and internal conflict (color prejudice, class antagonism, and nationalist politics) confronting the black community.[46] I want to suggest that he was also writing through other complex issues in these novels, especially in what I believe were the new formulations of masculinity, gender relations, and sexual identity that he explored through his characters. Scholar Hazel Carby suggests that McKay, in *Home to Harlem*, attempted to work out urbanization and class formation of the post–World War I era through the "sexual politics" of his novel. In her analysis, it is his female characters that are essential to understanding "both the means by which male protagonists will achieve or will fail to achieve social mobility and as signs of various possible threats to the emergence of the wholesome black masculinity necessary for the establishment of an acceptable black male citizenship in the American social order."[47] I essentially agree with Carby on the importance of examining McKay's use of gender, but, in terms of the "politics" of masculinity, I would argue that rather than affirming a mainstream, middle-class definition of a "wholesome," "acceptable black male citizenship," McKay was attempting to redefine black masculinity in relation to the "American social order"—or, given the diasporic bent of *Banjo*, the modern, postwar world order. While this redefinition included gender relations, it also involved a homosocial (in some cases, homoerotic) environment of black working-class men. European and Anglo-American males, in addition to black women, served as crucial negative referents in McKay's literary constructions of masculinity.

McKay thoroughly rejected early-twentieth-century bourgeois ideals of manliness and, instead, elevated culturally defined qualities that were previously considered unmanly. The virile masculinity of Jake and Banjo is shaped by aggressive sexuality as opposed to self-control, commonsensical intuition rather than calculated reason, and an aversion to the corrupt environment of the marketplace. McKay was not overly romantic about a purely innocent and "primitive" black masculinity; indeed, he understood that people of African descent were, in general, denied access to power as it was defined and wielded by dominant social groups and nations. "There must be something mighty inspiriting in being the citizen of a great strong nation," Ray speculates. "To be the white citizen of a nation that can say bold, challenging things like a strong man. Something very different from the keen ecstatic joy a man feels in the romance of being black" (HTH, 154). Ray equated the status of being a black man to political impotence in the larger context of international and domestic power relations. Ultimately, however, distinct racial qualities allowed blacks to withstand the harsh forces of imperialism and industrial and corporate capitalism. Again, through the feelings of Ray, McKay articulated this idea: "That this primitive child, this kinky-headed, big-laughing black boy of the world, did not go down and disappear under the serried crush of trampling white feet; that he managed to remain on the scene, not worldly-wise, not 'getting there,' yet not machine-made, nor poor-in-spirit like the regimented creatures of civilization, was baffling to civilized understanding. Before the grim, pale rider-down of souls he went his careless way with a primitive hoofing and a grin" (B, 314). The power of black manhood was precisely the "primitive," nonbourgeois (or antibourgeois) nature of black men, the majority of whom were urban wage laborers or rural sharecroppers. In celebrating this "marginalized" or "subordinated" male subjectivity, McKay posited it in relation to a vapid, mechanical white middle-class manhood consumed with the marketplace and the bourgeois values of excessive rationality, industry, self-control, and respectability.

Some ambivalence is present in McKay's literary constructions of black masculinity. Despite his vitriolic censure of capitalism, McKay's male characters struggle with their own relationship to the marketplace. To be sure, none are involved in entrepreneurship but neither can they completely repudiate the connection between their manhood and the public sphere of production. Jake, for instance, works as hard as he plays and both are crucial to the formation of his gender identity. In New York, he becomes involved with Congo

Rose, a singer who is so enthralled with his sexuality that she wants him to become her own professional lover. " 'I've never been a sweetman yet,' " Jake responds to her request. " 'Never lived off no womens and never will. I always works' " (HTH, 40). Part of this rejection of Rose's offer is Jake's need for independence, the desire not to have "his lady riding him with a cruel bit," which is the rumor circulating around his friend, Zeddy, who has become a sweetman (HTH, 87). But an obligatory sense of being a producer is also essential to Jake's resistance to becoming a gigolo. While he is working on the docks in New York, a union organizer informs him that the regular workers are striking and he is, in effect, crossing the picket line. Jake quits the job, telling the organizer, " 'I've done worked through a tur'ble assortaments [*sic*] o'jobs in mah lifetime, but I ain't nevah scabbed it on any man.' " The man responds, " 'Fine, fellow-worker; that's a real man's talk,' " and requests that he join the union. This, however, is where Jake's class consciousness ends: " 'Nope, I won't scab, but I ain't a joiner kind of fellah . . . I ain't no white folks nigger and I ain't no poah white's fool' " (HTH, 45). Later, Zeddy, who has been organizing black scabs, and Jake argue over the politics of racial and class solidarity. Zeddy's status as a sweetman and a scab represents the antithesis of Jake's sense of manhood. Eventually, Zeddy's relationship with his female "sponsor" emasculates him.[48] Through the characters of Jake and Zeddy, McKay mapped out a fundamental relationship between masculinity and work in *Home to Harlem*. Production, carried out in a homosocial arena and subject to a working-class code of ethics, comprised part of McKay's definition of masculinity.

Production, as an active engagement in the marketplace, did not translate into the individualism of the self-made man; nor did it translate into the lock-step mentality of the Babbitt. Rather, there is a resistance by the male protagonists to the homogenizing effects of the market. Ray, for instance, rejects the marketplace of corporate capitalism when he worries that he and his girlfriend, Agatha, have become "slaves of the civilized tradition": "Once upon a time he used to wonder at that great body of people who worked in nice cages: bank clerks in steel-wire cages, others in wooden cages, salespeople behind counters, neat, dutiful, respectful, all of them. God! how could they carry it on from day to day and remain quietly obliging and sane?" (HTH, 264–65). For Ray, Jake and Banjo literally embody the antidote to this overly mechanical world that is generated by a materialistic European and Anglo-American bourgeois culture. Both define their masculinity, in part, through physicality, a voracious sexuality, and their ability to negotiate their way through life by common sense and wit. Banjo, more so than Jake, separates his masculine identity from the realm of production. Work is more a means of survival than a core value in his gender identity formation: " 'Ise a true-blue traveling-bohn nigger and I know life, and I knows how to take it nacheral. I fight when I got to and I works when I must and I lays off when I feel lazy, and I loves all the time becausen the honey-pot a life is mah middle name' " (B, 305). It is this attitude that attracts Ray to Banjo and his lifestyle. When Banjo asks Ray to leave Marseilles and travel with him, the possibilities initially intrigue him. "Stopping here and there," Ray whimsically speculates, "staying as long as the feeling held in the ports where black men assembled for the great trans-port lines, loafing after their labors long enough to laugh and love and jazz and fight" (B, 319). Although McKay ended the novel rather ambiguously, the implication is that Ray does indeed leave with Banjo for a vagabond lifestyle.

Ray's relationships with Jake and Banjo can be read as McKay's attempt to write through the complex dilemma of the black intellectual. Confronted with his own bourgeois education and the "nacheral" lives of his working-class companions, Ray feels torn between the cultured world of the West and the "primitive" world of the black folk. Although he recognizes that he shares a "common primitive birthright" (B, 321) with Jake and Banjo, he also real-izes that to return to this, after having lived so long in the "civilized" world, would be an inauthentic attempt to reclaim his cultural past.[49] This dilemma, moreover, is worked out through the framework of masculinity. It is Ray who has to negotiate his racial identity within the context of capitalism and im-perialism, and this negotiation is influenced by his gender identity and class position. The major female characters in both novels are working-class pros-titutes and entertainers, women who, by the very nature of their work, are outside of the realm of production and incapable of achieving bourgeois re-spectability.[50] In effect, the conflict between respectability and libertinism, "civilization" and "the primitive," reason and emotion, is resolved on the ter-rain of gender—specifically, Ray, Jake, and Banjo's masculine identity. This becomes particularly clear near the end of Banjo, when Ray, who has been mulling over Banjo's invitation, wonders whether "a black man, even though educated, was in closer biological kinship to the swell of primitive earth life. And maybe his apparent failing under the organization of the modern world was the real strength that preserved him from becoming the thing that was the common white creature of it" (B, 323). His thought is broken by Banjo's abrupt question, "You gwine with a man or you ain't?" (B, 325). Banjo's re-jection of the marketplace, respectability, and bourgeois manliness is a re-flection of his masculinity. Ray's presumed decision to accompany Banjo is the middle-class affirmation of that virile, "primitive," antibourgeois mascu-linity.

The homosocial environments in which the gender identities of McKay's characters are formed and maintained produce an ambiguous sexuality. *Banjo*, more than *Home to Harlem*, explores the homosocial nature of the construction of masculinity. Although Banjo is an inveterate womanizer, he develops an intimate relationship with Ray. Shortly after they meet, for instance, Banjo, who is captivated by Ray's educated worldliness, professes his new friendship in a rather awkward but gentle way: "Ef I had some real dough I'd put it on you so you could have time to make good on that theah writing business" (B, 149). In addition to his desire to financially support Ray, there is closeness between the two that surpasses brotherly love. This is expressed when a group of white bon vivants, fascinated with the "primitive" sexual nature of blacks, invite Banjo to travel with them to French resorts. Ray, who views this as the fetishizing of black male sexuality, expresses his opposition to Banjo, who perceives it instead as jealousy. In the ensuing exchange, we find out that Ray himself has hustled his way across Europe in a similar fashion and that Banjo has been "around Paree" with "a dandy hoojah" (B, 221–22). It is not clear what Banjo's role will be within this group of sexually ambiguous whites and we are never quite sure what transpires on his excursion. What is important, however, is that his decision to go causes a brief rift between him and Ray. Indeed, the chapter is titled "Breaking-Up."

McKay was relatively indeterminate about mapping out the sexual and personal boundaries between Banjo and Ray. With regard to the personal relationships of the main characters, there is a structural parallel between the two novels. In *Home to Harlem*, Jake is reunited with Felice, a prostitute who he has been searching for since they slept together on his first night back in New York. The end of the novel finds Felice, who has renounced her profession, and Jake presumably leaving Harlem in order to begin their new reformed lives together. Similarly, in the second novel, it is Ray and Banjo who are leaving Marseilles. When Ray regrets that Latnah, an Arab woman and the only major female character, cannot accompany them, Banjo expresses his desire to make this an exclusively male adventure. "'Don't get soft ovah any one wimmens, pardner,'" he warns Ray. "'Tha's you' big weakness. A woman is a conjunction. Gawd fixed her different from us in moh ways than one. And theah's things we can git away with all the time and she just kain't. Come on pardner. Wese got enough between us to beat it a long ways from here'" (B, 326). The symmetry between Felice/Jake and Ray/Banjo is not complete, in part because we find out in *Banjo* that Jake and Felice are married and have children. There is no similar conclusion to Ray and Banjo's relationship. More importantly, however, McKay was ambiguous enough to suggest that both of them could have either traveled around sleeping with numerous women or with each other. Also significant is McKay's suggestion that this ambiguous sexuality did not preclude the masculinity of either Ray or Banjo. The rejection of the marketplace and bourgeois respectability was more important in the formation of their gender identities than an indubitable commitment to heterosexuality.[51] This can be attributed to McKay's own bisexuality; equally as influential, I would argue, is his modern reconceptualization of masculinity, which was devoid of bourgeois, late-Victorian values. Sexuality in general, as opposed to a solely regimented and normative heterosexuality, was crucial in his construction of manhood.

In his novels as well as his intellectual discourse, McKay, like Toomer, sought to posit a more healthy, expressive masculinity against a mechanistic and overcivilized manliness. Langston Hughes also rejected this "Anglo-Saxon" ideal, although he did not as forcefully articulate his renunciation in terms of gender as McKay or Toomer did. In his classic essay, "The Negro Artist and the Racial Mountain," published in the *Nation* in 1926, he argued for the need to eschew the overwhelming constraints of respectability and considered the black folk as the potential wellspring for such efforts. Although he did not specifically refer to the "tyranny of the Anglo-Saxon" ideal, he objected to "this urge within the race toward whiteness, the desire to pour racial individuality into the mold of American standardization, and to be as little Negro and as much American as possible." The "racial mountain" to which Hughes referred was the acceptance by the "colored middle class" of European and Anglo-American standards of morality and aesthetics; the mountain served as an obstacle for any "would-be racial artist to climb in order to discover himself and his people." On the other side, however, lived the black folk who, Hughes claimed, "still hold their own individuality in the face of American standardizations." Black vernacular culture, particularly in the forms of the blues and jazz, contained the seeds for a truly black art and literature. It was in these cultural forms that Hughes found his creative fount and his refuge from bourgeois civilization. Jazz, he felt, was the most powerful idiom of folk culture, "the eternal tom-tom beating in the Negro soul— the tom-tom of revolt against weariness in a white world, a world of subway trains, and work, work, work."[52] His assessment of the cultural politics of the Harlem Renaissance was an unequivocal affirmation of the folk and, in effect, an elevation of "the primitive" over "civilization."

Hughes resisted, in retrospect, the idea that primitivism dominated his literary creativity. In his autobiography, he attributed the break with his major patron, the wealthy widow, Charlotte Osgood Mason, to his inability to live up to her aesthetic expectations. "She wanted me to be primitive and know and feel the intuitions of the primitive," he recalled. "But, unfortunately, I did not feel the rhythms of the primitive surging through me, and so I could not live and write as though I did." Hughes disassociated himself from the "primitive-ness" of Africa, however, not the rural and urban folk culture of black America. He celebrated the lifestyle of industrial workers and rural sharecroppers and, concomitantly, rejected the centrality of the marketplace of bourgeois culture and all of its attendant gender conventions. The "eternal tom-tom" offered him and others an alternative to the rat race of middle-class manliness: "Work maybe a little today, rest a little tomorrow. Play awhile. Sing awhile. O, let's dance!" [53] His identification with black folk culture was no less subtle than McKay's or Toomer's. Hughes only differed with the two in the extent to which he associated that culture with a more healthy masculinity. Still, his prescriptions on how to cope with a world that was being increasingly dominated by corporate and industrial capitalism anticipated, and reverberated through, Banjo and Jake.

Writers were not the only members of the generation of the "newest" Negro to embrace "the primitive" as an aesthetic inspiration *and* a model of manhood. Aaron Douglas, the premier graphic artist of the period, was a vociferous critic of traditional Western culture. Douglas was heavily influenced by the post-impressionist technique of Pablo Picasso and Henri Matisse, German expressionism, the less well-known British vorticism, in addition to the cubist and art deco style of his early mentor, the German Weinold Reiss.[54] Douglas was very protective of modernism and was critical of any intellectual assault on the art form. When asked by his fiancée, Alta Sawyer, if he had read a particular essay that attacked cubism, he responded in the negative but offered a critical assessment of antimodernism: "It is the conservative, reactionary, artistically impotent, the die-hard. It is the mind that wishes to force literalism, intellectualism, everything upon art, but *art* itself." Douglas suggested that antimodernists, in their enslavement to traditional approaches to art, were incapable of understanding modern art and, therefore, "artistically impotent." In a sense, he was reinscribing the Victorian dichotomy of mind and body with values that favored the latter. Modernism, with its component of primitivism, in effect, was the more virile art form in its catering to visceral experience as opposed to cerebral observation.[55]

Racial essentialism was also an important cornerstone of Douglas's modernist thought. Like McKay and Toomer, he revolted against the "Anglo-Saxon" ideal and the tenacious hold it exerted upon black artists. "Most of us feel that we have reached the heights when we have depicted their chalky faces and disgusting sentimentality," he wrote to Sawyer, "or filled yards of canvas with feeble imitations of their second rate 'little masters'." Concerned that his diatribe might be construed as anti-white, he continued: "Hate them? No, my dear. I don[']t hate them at all. I almost pity them. They are so impossible.

I am, however, beginning to realize how good it is to be black. Otherwise this awful grinding gristmill of mediocrity would long ago have devoured us. As it is we are free to think, to feel, to play with life, to enjoy life. Our white brother is sick. Spiritually sick. . . . He spoils everything he touches." [56] This essentialism in Douglas's artistic thought placed him squarely in the young vanguard that produced *Fire!!* In an open letter concerning the purpose of the magazine, Douglas wrote that the "Negro is fundamentally, essentially different from their Nordic neighbors." He continued that they were "proud of that difference," which included "greater spiritual endowment[,] greater sensitivity, greater power for artistic expression and appreciation." [57] In late 1925, nearly a year before the only issue of *Fire!!* was published, Douglas wrote to Hughes about the exciting prospects of infusing the nascent movement with a vibrant art and literature rooted in the African and black folk tradition. At a time when the " 'Nordic' overlords" were clinging to tradition—he pointed to the construction of St. John the Divine cathedral in upper Manhattan—and were "afraid to look into the face of real art," it fell upon the younger Harlem artists to break out of the constraints of the respectability of bourgeois culture. [58]

Douglas's essentialism, on the one hand, reinforced the stereotypical notion that blacks possessed a primitively "feminine" and infantile culture. Like Toomer, however, Douglas celebrated this difference as a positive aspect of the racial self-definition that characterized the Renaissance. Still, he could not escape using masculinist language—or earlier models of manhood—to discuss his artistic output. Douglas's rationale for his participation in the arts movement was circumscribed by the "cult of production." "Let's bare our arms and plunge them deep[,] deep through laughter, through pain, through sorrow, through hope, through disappointment, into the very depths of the souls of our people and drag forth material crude, rough[,] neglected," he charged. "Then let's sing it, dance it, write it, paint it. . . . Let's create something transcendentally material, mystically objective. Earthy. Spiritually earthy. Dynamic." [59] Douglas equated his artistic work with the craftsmanship of an artisanal laborer: taking a raw natural resource and shaping it into a consumable product. His reliance on production did not invoke the ideals of Victorian manliness, however. Rather, the idea of production—and the more abstract concept of "creation"—was a way of reconciling artistic pursuit, primitivism, and masculinity. This becomes clear in a letter he wrote to Sawyer, in which he argued "man must divide his strength between love and responsibility or rather ambition. If he is to maintain his position as king of his kind he must love to his fullest capacity. He must also create and produce to his fullest capacity." [60] Hale Woodruff, an art teacher at Atlanta University and a peripheral member of the Renaissance was even more adamant in locating his artistic output within the idiom of production. "Many think that the only way to prove you're working is to punch a clock," he wrote to Alain Locke. After detailing how much time he spent painting in France, he assured Locke that "the clock I punched then was the love and reverence for art and my employer was a burning desire to create and produce."[61]

Many of the younger Harlem literati felt that their role in the Renaissance was the reclamation of "the primitive," or the folk, in the midst of a modernizing, industrializing, and, they argued, desensitizing market culture. In their art and literature, and the ways in which they talked about their position as black artists, people like McKay, Toomer, and Douglas offered an alternative definition of masculinity. In part, this was a manifestation of a growing trend among middle-class American men to constitute their masculine identities through physicality and sexual virility as opposed to the earlier markers of reason, character, and producer values. While white men were using blacks and other "primitive" peoples through which to vicariously construct their masculinity, the younger New Negroes were using the "Anglo-Saxon" or "Nordic" bourgeois male as the model against which they constructed theirs.[62] Older notions of manhood, however, would not give way so quickly. Independence figured prominently in many of the Harlem literati's artistic discourses, as did the idea of production. Both of these concepts were asserted as central components of their masculinity, particularly when these writers and artists were confronted with the issues of patronage and propaganda.

■ Any successful artist — indeed, any successful artistic movement — needs financial backing. The Harlem Renaissance was no different. Much of the funding for the movement came from individual patrons, philanthropic foundations, and civil rights organizations. Individual artists obtained private funds, Guggenheim fellowships, or *Opportunity* prizes, to name but a few ways by which they could finance their creative work.[63] Although external support was necessary for their cultural production, some of the younger beneficiaries intellectually rebelled against it (even as they accepted specific funding), particularly when it threatened their independence as artists. At the same time, they tended to conflate the "Negro intelligentsia" and white philanthropists as forces that potentially undermined their artistic freedom. In other words, they resisted what they perceived to be the political agendas and propagandistic goals of the Renaissance establishment and the dependency-forming relationships with white patrons. This resistance often employed masculinist language through the concepts of independence and production, cornerstones of Victorian constructions of manhood.

One of the major private patrons of the Renaissance was Charlotte Osgood Mason, a matronly white benefactor also known as "Godmother." Mason exerted her maternal influence through Locke, who introduced her to most of the young talent and also informed her of their progress. Godmother was a disciple of primitivism and felt that the spiritual salvation of modern, European, and Anglo-American civilization could be found in the cultures of Native Americans and the African diaspora. Hughes recalled that she believed that blacks "were America's great link with the primitive, and that they had something very precious to give to the Western World." Mason was concerned that many blacks "had let the white world pollute and contaminate that mystery and harmony, and make of it something cheap and ugly, commercial and, as she said, 'white.'"[64] In contrast to McKay and Toomer, who also saw in primitivism and black folk culture an alternative to a devitalized manhood, Mason emphasized the infantile and feminine nature of "the primitive." In a letter to Locke relating her desire to secure a film from Africa in order to "enlighten and educate the American Negro" on the benefits of "primitive life," she asserted that "the film must make them thankful that they are the brown child[ren] of the world." Indeed, she consistently infantilized Locke, Hughes, and others by referring to them as "dear boy," "precious child," and "brown bug."[65]

Godmother's infantilization of her charges was encouraged, on some level, by the artists themselves. In particular, Hughes and Locke corresponded with Mason in occasionally obsequious missives. The forty-three-year-old professor, for instance, referred to himself once as "Your Alain" and called himself "a very busy, half-distracted boy." Zora Neale Hurston surpassed Locke in the art of sycophancy, assuring Mason in one letter, that she was a "bum and Godmother's pickaninny." Not all beneficiaries of Mason's philanthropy used the tactic of self-diminution. Hall Johnson, a musician, described his relationship with Godmother in decidedly masculinist terms, writing that, after his meetings with her, he always felt "like Antaeus, the powerful giant of Greek mythology, whom no wrestler could vanquish because the Earth was his mother and everytime he touched her in a fall she gave him more strength than he had before."[66] To be sure, the excessive deference paid to Godmother was, occasionally, a skillfully deployed tactic directed toward procuring funds—a brilliant and lucrative use of the "mask." We cannot overlook, however, the potentially humiliating and disempowered positions in which these artists found themselves once they became associated with Godmother and other patrons. After all, patronage, at its foundation, is a power relationship based on dependency and, often, submission.[67]

For Hughes, patronage was a necessary element of his artistic career, but ultimately, it was psychologically damaging. He received aid from a number of wealthy whites: Amy Spingarn, the wife of NAACP officer Joel Spingarn, provided money for his education at Lincoln University; Van Vechten facilitated Hughes's efforts at publishing his volumes of poetry; and Mason provided him with funds to take care of his needs while he was writing. Introduced to each other in 1927, Hughes and Mason immediately became very close, with Mason giving him gifts in addition to a monthly stipend of $150. Hughes also spent many weekends, while he was enrolled at Lincoln, in Mason's Park Avenue apartment, occasionally escorting her to various cultural events. Their relationship, which lasted for three years, however, was soaked with power and dependency. Godmother's gifts and requests for strict accounting of Hughes's expenditures created much anxiety in the young writer, which manifested alternately in infantile deference, subtle rebellion, and, as with his father, psychosomatic illness. Mason's expectations that Langston provide her with itemized statements of his expenses reminded him of his father's "eternal bookkeeping."[68] His relationship with his primary benefactor came to a head in the spring and summer of 1930, shortly after he finished his first novel, Not without Laughter.

Hughes's friendship and artistic relationship with Godmother collapsed as she was financing a joint effort between Hughes and Hurston to write a folk play. She had put them up in an apartment in New Jersey and paid for the typing services of Louise Thompson. Hughes had recently returned from Cuba, where he had been on an artistic expedition. In response to Mason's charges that he was not being productive enough after his trip, Hughes, in a letter he never sent, attempted to psychically break the bonds of power and dependency that connected the patron and the artist. "In all my life I have never been free," he wrote. "I have never been able to do anything with freedom, excep[t] in the field of my writing." Although the letter ended in a predictably obsequious tone, Langston lashed out at the dictatorial nature of his patron: "For the sake of my physical body I have washed thousands of hotel dishes, cooked, scrubbed decks, worked 12 to 15 hours a day on a farm, swallowed my pride for the help of philanthropy and charity—but nobody ever said to me 'You must write now[.] You must finish that poem tomorrow. You must begin to create on the first of the month.[']"[69] In his autobiography, Hughes alluded to the power of Mason, although he suggested that the break was ultimately his failure to please her with his writing, not his need for independence. For several months, he attempted to get back into her good graces. Unfortunately, this was one bridge that, with malicious intervention on the part of Locke and Hurston, burned beyond repair.[70]

The letter that Hughes never sent was a rejection of Godmother's Taylorist methods and, similar to his refusal to follow his father's choices, a repudiation of the marketplace. Hughes's psychic break from Godmother was an assertion of independence, a declaration that his ability to create would remain his. I do not want to overstate the significance of this manifesto in shaping his gender identity. However, he associated independence with his feeling that he was a man. This is clear in his recounting of his decision to take to the sea at the age of twenty-one. One thing he was leaving behind as the ship pulled out of port was "the feeling of always being controlled by others." Or, as he expressed this in another way: "I felt that nothing would ever happen to me again that I didn't want to happen. I felt grown, a man, inside and out."[71]

Other members of the Renaissance articulated the significance of independence as well. Wallace Thurman argued that independence was at the heart of the arts movement and, indeed, gave credit to the nationalism of Marcus Garvey for laying the groundwork. "Garvey," according to Thurman, "did much to awaken 'race consciousness' among Negroes, much to make the black masses aware of their latent possibilities for depending more upon themselves and less upon their 'white folks.'" He continued that "the alleged Negro renaissance . . . owes much to Garvey and to his movement."[72] The entire idea that African Americans and African Caribbeans were entering an era of the New Negro when, in addition to becoming cultural producers rather than just cultural consumers, they were creating art and literature free of white influence, was predicated on the masculinist concepts of production and independence. The irony that there were several talented women — who were asserting their own independence from men — involved in the Renaissance, is matched by the irony that neither the artists nor the leadership could sustain a movement completely independent of white influence. This concerned Locke to such an extent that he wrote to Van Vechten, "You know the paradoxical circumstances that make it logical and necessary to put ourselves forward as self-sponsored, and are, I am sure, broad enough to grant us that, for the sake of the future."[73]

As some artists jealously guarded their independence as central to the creative process, others relied on the idea that they were producers to negotiate the problematic artist-patron relationship and the "art versus propaganda" debate. Claude McKay, for example, conflated his artistic integrity, his pseudo-independence from white patronage, and his rejection of propaganda with production and, hence, his manhood. More often than not, he exuded a hypermasculinity when he railed against the Negro intelligentsia, or, as he and others called them, the "Niggerati." In one instance, however, he attacked the practice of patronage by asserting what he felt was the masculine nature of his cultural production. Nancy Cunard, the dilettantish heiress of the famous English shipping family, solicited an article from McKay for her anthology, *Negro*, and failed to compensate him. He reminded Cunard, who he felt still adhered "to the antiquated and aristocratic and very British idea that artists should perform for noble and rich people for prestige instead of remuneration," that this was a new age. McKay equated his "creative work" with his "common labor" and stressed that neither should be "exploited shamelessly." He informed Cunard that although he was "'romantic' about artists and creative work," his "romanticism is different from those nice people's who ask and expect artists to write, sing, act and perform in other ways freely and charitably for a Cause while they would not dream of asking the carpenter and caterer and others who do the manual tasks to work for nothing."[74] By invoking the idea of production, McKay unlinked the artist from the patron system. The idea that the artist exchanged his labor for financial backing mitigated, for McKay, the exploitative potential of the artist-patron relationship.

McKay reserved his most virile posturing for the older black literary establishment. His attacks upon this group usually revolved around the issue of propaganda versus art for art's sake and no one was immune. In one letter to Jackman, McKay referred to the front men of the Renaissance—including sociologist Charles S. Johnson, Du Bois, Locke, and White—as "rotten bastards," "little men with literary ambitions themselves and all [are] afraid of 'art' and forthright artistic expression, dependent as they all are on some sort of white philanthropy." It was against this literary establishment that the younger generation needed to rebel.[75] McKay's vitriolic reaction to the older members of the Renaissance was not unwarranted; his unromantic portrayal of working-class African Americans and African Caribbeans provoked much criticism from not only the literary elite, but from respectable black society as well. As James W. Ivy, editor of the socialist *Messenger*'s book page, wrote to McKay concerning *Home to Harlem*: "Here in America the darkies are yelping because of the milieu you described. 'Why the bulldykes, the faggots?' they ask. There has appeared a diatribe against your book in some nigger paper almost every week from the date of its release."[76] Blacks were not interested, from McKay's perspective, in artistic realism or anything that was not propagandistic. "Although I have strong social opinion I cannot mix up art and racial propaganda," he wrote to Locke. "I must write what I feel[,] what I know[,] what I think[,] what I have seen[,] what is true [and] your Afro-American intelligentsia won't like it." Indeed, McKay was adamantly opposed to anything that smacked of propaganda and he warned Hughes that to write "'propaganda stuff for the Crisis or cheap stuff to buy a meal'" would be "cruelly prostituting your highest natural gift."[77] In other words, independence from the dictates of respectable society, the aesthetic demands of white patronage, and the political agenda of the middle-class black leadership was the hallmark of the "true" black artist.

These issues found their most heated and gendered articulation in the tempestuous relationship between McKay and Locke. The iconoclastic artist and the decorous philosopher developed an antagonistic bond over the course of the 1920s. The source of the friction usually concerned Locke's editorial practices. When he decided not to include McKay's poem "Mulatto" in the *Survey Graphic*, for instance, McKay angrily shot back, "It isn't the 'Survey' that hasn't guts enough. It is *you*." Dismayed at the lack of militancy on the part of the black literary establishment, McKay offered a negative assessment of the nascent movement. "No wonder Garvey remains strong despite his glaring defects," he wrote. "When Negro intellectuals like you take such a weak line." McKay, using a tactic of the Garveyite intellectuals, feminized the black intellectual and literary elite—he called Locke "a dyed-in the wool pussyfooting professor"—and, in effect, linked masculinity to militancy and independence.[78] McKay and Locke had another falling out over *The New Negro*. One of his poems, "The White House," had been published in the *Survey Graphic* as "White Houses." Even though McKay had corrected Locke on the title, the poem appeared in *The New Negro* as it had in the *Survey Graphic*. Locke's editorial dishonesty infuriated McKay and he responded not by questioning Locke's manhood but, rather, by stressing his own. He did this by locating his aesthetic pursuit within the paradigm of production. "If you understand how an artist feels about *the word* that he chooses above *the words* to use," he railed, "—if you know that artistic creation is the most delicate of all creative things—if you [want] to pit it against how a craftsman—a goldsmith—an engraver—might feel about someone changing his design—then you will understand how I feel about 'The White House.'" In a letter some months later concerning the same issue, he explicitly connected his creative self to his gender identity. "I am a man and artist first of all," he reminded Locke. "The imprisoning quality of my complexion has never yet, and never will, move me to bend to flunkeyism and intellectual imprisonment with the sorry millions that are likewise tinted."[79] McKay expressed a similar sentiment, although in more forcefully gendered language, through his character Ray in *Banjo*. "However advanced, clever, and cultivated you are," Ray says to an acquaintance in Marseilles, "you will have the distinguishing adjective of 'colored' before your name. And instead of accepting it proudly and manfully, most of you are soured and bitter about it—especially you mixed-bloods" (201).

The younger generation of artists saw in the Renaissance the goals of independence and self-determination. This manifested not only in reservations about entering into relationships with white patrons, but in opposition to the heavy-handed propaganda line taken by much of the black middle class and some older, conservative critics and writers associated with the movement. Moreover, these sentiments were often articulated in masculinist language, or, at least, the concepts of independence and production worked to reinforce the gender identities of several of the artists. As they rejected the bourgeois manliness of what they felt to be a corrupt, market-driven culture through an embrace of "the primitive," they simultaneously clung to older notions of manhood, rooted in the producer ideal of the nineteenth century. The "newest Negroes," in effect, were reinforcing traditional European and Anglo-American models of manhood even as they were attempting to replace them with a more modern masculinity, one with closer links to physicality and that was independent of the marketplace, producer values, and respectability.

■ Wallace Thurman, in a draft of his unfinished book *Aunt Hagar's Children*, provided an assessment of the younger black artist involved in the Renaissance: "He believes it to be the duty of those who have the will to power in artistic and intellectual fields to shake off psychological shackles, deliberately formulate an egoistic philosophy, develop a cosmopolitan perspective, and soar where they may, blaming only themselves if they fail to reach their goal." He took a starkly different position on the importance of group consciousness than the older generation of New Negroes, including the hard-lined propagandists of the Renaissance and the nationalist Garveyites. "Individual salvation," he wrote, "may prove a more efficacious emancipating ag[en]t for his generation and for those follow[ing] than self[-]sacrifice or morbid resentment."[80] Like Locke some years earlier, Thurman wrote of the generic participant of the Renaissance in gender-specific language. "He" and "his generation" were charting a new direction for black culture and, ultimately, the ways in which blacks defined themselves. Of course, this says less about the reality of the Harlem Renaissance than it does about Thurman himself. Women were engaged in the cultural production of the 1920s and the same debates that surrounded primitivism, patronage, and propaganda. What I have tried to suggest is that the ways in which the male artists engaged in these discussions says something about how they thought about themselves as men—more specifically, as black men. Moreover, their masculine identities figured heavily in the ways they thought of themselves as artists.

Until recently, the historiography of the Harlem Renaissance has been dominated by the "paradigm of failure." Work within this vein has tended to look at the institutional and political character of the movement. It has highlighted the political agenda of the movement's leadership, which stressed that superior cultural production by blacks would lead to their social integration into the American political and economic mainstream; in the words of David Levering Lewis, the Renaissance was an attempt to achieve "civil rights by copyright." According to these histories, the movement failed due to either the lagging interest of white patrons by the 1930s, the paradox of attempting to solve the real socioeconomic problems of the Depression through arts and letters, and the lack of financial support from the black middle class.[81] Recent work on the Renaissance has attempted to transcend the interpretations of the movement's efficacy by locating it in the broader context of American modernism.[82] These two paradigms are not irreconcilable. It is clear that the leaders and sponsors of the Renaissance attached a political agenda to the creative self-expression of blacks that ultimately was not terribly successful; at the same time, however, the actual act of producing literature and art held greater meaning for the lives of the artists. That meaning was present in not only the racial self-definition these artists were engaged in; it was present in the new models of manhood that were being articulated in the cultural production of the period.

In their discussion of the artistic process as well as in their art, the younger Harlem literati participated in the construction of alternative definitions of masculinity that were replacing older models of Victorian manliness. Through their celebration of the "primitive" characteristics of African and black folk culture as opposed to the spiritually enervated, less virile bourgeois culture of the West, younger artists posited a more modern, healthier masculinity that was defined by the body, sexual desire, and an ethos of consumption. They did not completely abjure more traditional notions of manhood, however, as is evident in their adherence to the ideas of independence and production. Older participants in the Renaissance stressed production as a masculine act — in opposition to the stereotype of blacks as infantile, feminine consumers — as did the younger artists. Independence from both white patrons and the respectable black middle class also figured prominently in the politics of the arts movement. In the end, the "Newest Negroes," like the generation that came before them, were incapable of completely transcending the hegemonic definitions of manhood put into place by the American middle class.

6

A Tempestuous Spirit of Rebellion

In the winter and spring of 1925, two of the most important educational institutions for black people in the United States experienced tumultuous unrest on their campuses. Students at Fisk and Howard Universities—in Nashville, Tennessee, and Washington, D.C., respectively—"struck" against their respective administrations, ultimately contributing to the resignation of both schools' presidents. The strikes were not atypical of the black college experience in the 1920s. Indeed, the disturbances at Fisk and Howard were but a small part of a much larger phenomenon. Between 1914 and 1929, at least eleven other historically black colleges and universities endured protests in which a segment of their student bodies registered their dissatisfaction with the state of higher education that was available to them by walking out en masse. Strikes lasted anywhere from a couple of days to, in the case of Fisk, two months, and strike activities ranged from students boycotting classes and participating in generally disruptive protests to actually withdrawing for the term and returning home.[1]

Like their white counterparts at universities such as Brown and Tennessee, black college students were challenging the stifling environments of campuses, in which young men and women did not have access to the school's governmental processes and were subjected to draconian rules and regulations.[2] In addition to contesting the *in loco parentis* philosophy of education, students at Fisk, Howard, and elsewhere were also taking on administrative policies that were deeply rooted in American racial ideologies, specifically with respect to the education of blacks in a caste society. Black college students were rebelling against entrenched administrations that advocated industrial education over instruction in the liberal arts; school authorities that either tolerated or actively encouraged segregationist policies on campuses; and, in general, organizations and individuals that practiced "missionary paternalism" through their philanthropy. As Alain Locke noted in 1925, "Negro youth" were rebelling against "an autocratic and conservative tradition of management." Locke suggested that the campus uprisings were manifestations of the same postwar radicalism that contributed to nationalist movements of independence and workers' movements against capital. "Like its analogue, the nationalist university or the class-conscious group," Locke wrote, "the Negro college of the present day requires and demands, if not group exclusiveness, at least group management and the conditions of self-determination—in brief, spiritual autonomy." Indeed, Locke, like his contemporaries and later historians, placed the student strikes squarely within the racially conscious boundaries of the New Negro era. The rebellions, according to Locke, were the result of "a feeling of racial repression and the need for more positive and favorable conditions for the expression and cultivation of the developing race spirit."[3]

While the activities of black college students were certainly in tune with the emergent political militancy of such organizations as the Universal Negro Improvement Association (UNIA), the Brotherhood of Sleeping Car Porters and Maids, and—relative to the black and white advocates of industrial education—the National Association for the Advancement of Colored People (NAACP), and while the race consciousness of black college students owed a great deal to the cultural vitality of the Harlem Renaissance, the campus uprisings should not be seen solely within the context of the New Negro era. In significant ways, the unrest among black students should be situated within the emergent youth culture of the 1920s. As we saw in chapters 4 and 5, younger African Americans and African Caribbeans began to reject the bourgeois conventions of respectability that shaped their parents' generation's precarious claim on middle-class status within a caste society. As these challenges were made in the realms of jazz culture and the artistic production of the Harlem Renaissance, so too were they made on the college campus.

Although the rebellions were expressions of discontent toward the pedagogical missions of black colleges and the lack of input available to students—a quest for self-determination in Locke's estimation—they were also reflections of a refusal to conform to the disciplinary nature of the "missionary paternalist" model of education. Among other things, young men and women incorporated into their protests against their respective administrations a call for the end of compulsory chapel attendance; mandatory participation in military training; strict dress codes; bans against the consumption of alcohol and tobacco; prohibitions against playing, listening, and dancing to jazz and the blues; and strict surveillance of male-female socializing. On the campus of Fisk University, the student uprisings also challenged the administration's ban on fraternities and sororities. They were, in other words, rebelling against the imposition of late-Victorian standards of morality at a time when the ascendancy of consumer culture was increasingly undermining the importance of producer values and respectability among the American middle class. At stake for younger middle-class blacks in these confining environments was the desire and ability to control their own bodies, the freedom to consume and experience bodily pleasure without fear of being punished. Although these stakes were equally important for young women—and their campus experiences and participation in the student uprisings will be dealt with here—this chapter focuses on what the campus cultures and student activism in this period meant for men.

The "missionary paternalist" model of education prescribed ideal gender conventions and relied on mechanisms of control to reinforce those prescriptions. For male students, those mechanisms of control, which were predicated on the disciplining of the body, included mandatory military education, curtailment of their consumption and leisure practices, and, in the case of Fisk, the absence of social fraternities on campus. The students' resistance to these disciplinary regimes reflected a fundamentally different gender identity formation in which the self-controlled, and externally controlled, body was no longer paramount. Indeed, the exuberant body supplanted the disciplined body in the ways that these young men thought about, and performed, their manhood. To the extent that modern definitions of masculinity revolved less around character, production, and respectability and more around bodily virtuoso and sexual virility, the student strikes in the 1920s represented the ascendancy of these new definitions among college-bred, black middle-class youth.

In 1900, in addition to Hampton and Tuskegee Institutes, Fisk and Howard Universities were the most prestigious and well-known black educational institutions in the United States. Established in the aftermath of the Civil War by northern missionaries and funded, in part, by the federal government through the Freedmen's Bureau, the initial mission of Fisk and Howard was the education of newly emancipated slaves.[4] Fisk opened in January 1866 as a primary and normal school. First-year enrollment was robust, with daily attendance averaging one thousand and comprising a spectrum of the black community—male and female, children, adults, and the elderly. Within a year and a half, Tennessee's provision of free, albeit segregated, public education to its citizens allowed Fisk to move toward the status of a higher educational institution: Fisk University was incorporated in the summer of 1867; the trustees opened a normal department in the fall to train teachers; and, in 1869, a theology and college department were added. Howard began primarily as a normal school in May 1867 although its charter also listed collegiate, theological, law, medical, and agricultural departments. Like Fisk, Howard provided elementary instruction to local residents and college preparatory work for both Washingtonians and nonlocal residents. In addition to educating the diverse black community, Howard opened its doors to whites, thereby eliciting the charge from some quarters that it was advocating racial "amalgamation."[5]

Through the last quarter of the nineteenth century, both institutions—despite periods of financial instability—emerged as leading black liberal arts universities.[6] All the more important, their evolution as classical higher educational institutions took place within an environment that was generally hostile to liberal arts training for people of African descent. A majority of white southerners, and especially the landowning elite, opposed classical education for blacks. Although the rationale of such opposition—for those who chose to elevate it above a fundamental denial of black humanity—was that instruction in areas such as classical languages and natural sciences was ill conceived and useless for a people only barely removed from slavery, the motivation was clearly driven by a fear that education would foster an intractable agricultural work force. The extent to which blacks should be educated, they argued, was in the trades: carpentry, painting, gardening, dressmaking, cooking, and so forth. This racial ideology masquerading as educational philosophy was supported and advanced by many missionaries, southern reformers, individual philanthropists and philanthropic organizations, and conservative black educators. Northern capitalists such as George Foster Peabody, Julius Rosenwald, and John D. Rockefeller Jr. provided money through a variety of organizations—the General Education Board, Southern Education Board, and Phelps-Stokes Fund to name a few—to support the industrial educational programs that were modeled on Hampton and Tuskegee Institutes and advocated most prominently by Booker T. Washington. The relationship between these various groups meant that any effort to promote liberal arts education among blacks in the southern United States would need to be a Herculean one.[7]

The administrations of both Howard and Fisk grappled with the question of whether, and in what proportion, to educate the "head" or the "hand." From Howard's inception, manual labor was part of the curriculum. Initially, it was primarily a way to allow poor students to earn money to pay for their tuition and living expenses. There was a more overtly economic objective to industrial education as well in the early years of the university. Entrepreneurs involved in the day-to-day functioning of the school hoped that industrial education would provide them with cheap labor. Between 1867 and 1869, masonry and bedding factories operated on campus. Members of the liberal arts faculty were understandably leery of industrial education and, to the extent that it interfered with their own curriculum, sought to discourage it. Still, as late as 1903, Acting President Teunis S. Hamlin reminded the Board of Trustees of the importance of industrial education when he argued that the "liberally educated man is vastly improved as a breadwinner, and as a member of society, by knowing how to use his hands." Industrial education at Howard underwent a number of different incarnations through the first two decades of the century. After coming under control of the Teachers College between 1905 and 1913, it was reorganized in the Manual Arts and Applied Sciences College until 1919. After that, it joined engineering, architecture, art, and home economics in the College of Applied Sciences.[8]

The administration and faculty of Fisk similarly struggled with the role that industrial education would play in their overall pedagogical approach. Students who boarded at Fisk were required to work at least one hour per day at a number of different jobs, particularly custodial work. Having students work fulfilled objectives that were both utilitarian and idealistic. The policy allowed the university to avoid hiring outside workers, thereby reducing labor costs. Those savings were then passed on to students as lower boarding fees. But employing students was also geared toward producing men and women of substance through the instillation of producer values. "This arrangement," the 1900–1901 catalog stated, "conducive to good health and right habits, renders it possible to keep the price of board at a lower rate than could otherwise be done."[9] As the statement suggests, the labor of students was beneficial to both the university and its charges. But this commitment to the Protestant work ethic did not translate into a wholesale adoption of industrial education. Despite the fact that one of Fisk's primary benefactors, the American Missionary Association, was a prominent champion of vocational instruction, early administrations resisted abandoning a commitment to liberal arts as much as they could. The extent to which Fisk incorporated industrial education into its curriculum was generally determined by its financial situation. In the mid-1880s, for instance, the university accepted money from the John F. Slater Fund, a philanthropic organization that promoted industrial education, to offer domestic science and printing classes to its students. The decision to accept Slater funding was a pragmatic one, as it allowed the university to use external resources to produce the school's newspaper. Hard financial times in the first decade of the twentieth century forced the Fisk administration to integrate industrial education more fully into the curriculum. A grant from the Slater Fund in 1905 led directly to the creation of a department of applied sciences. Even as the university recognized the hegemony of industrial education, however, the administration continued to subordinate it to the goals of providing a liberal arts education to black youth.[10]

Despite the pressures to incorporate industrial education into their overall pedagogical philosophy and practice, officials at Fisk and Howard successfully charted a course for their institutions toward classical higher education. In a 1910 report for the Slater Fund, the two were listed, along with Atlanta University, Virginia Union University, and others as "First-Grade Colored Colleges." They were the only two schools with over one hundred "first-grade" college-level students and the only two in which the college-level students constituted at least a quarter of the total student population.[11] Seven years later, a report for the Federal Bureau of Education recognized them as the only two black schools that provided their students with postsecondary level instruction.[12] By the mid-1920s, both schools had firmly established liberal arts components. Half of Fisk's student body, which numbered roughly six hundred, matriculated in the college department. Howard was even more established, with three times as many students; more than 150 professors; graduate programs in law, medicine, dentistry, and theology; and undergraduate degrees in arts and sciences, business, education, home economics, and architecture and engineering.[13]

The fact that both universities' administrations and faculties cast their lots with liberal arts education did not mean that they were solely concerned with the professionalization of black youth. Even as they elevated the education of the "head" over the "hand," they were as concerned with the "heart," or moral education, as schools whose main educational objective was vocational-driven.[14] The missionary educational philosophy, which drew on both the "civilizing mission" ethos of patrician nineteenth-century New England reformers and the environmentalist explanations of racial inequality advanced by twentieth-century progressives, started from the premise that blacks were in dire need of instruction in the moral precepts of the dominant culture. Underlying this premise was the idea that the oppressive system of slavery had prevented African Americans from acquiring the necessary traits to survive and prosper as free-willed subjects in the United States: mainly, commitment to work ethic, devotion to family, and respect for the law. To their credit, missionary educators and progressive reformers attributed this group deficiency to environmental factors rather than inherited biological traits. Their rejection of biologically determinist explanations of the status of blacks, however, did not translate into a fundamental questioning of racial inferiority theories. The idea that African Americans suffered from a group pathology, environmental or otherwise, was the starting point of most conversations about the role of education in the black community. Missionary educators argued that schools such as Fisk and Howard would produce individuals who would strip away the pathology of black communities by delivering a "gospel of manners and morals."[15]

The administrations of both Fisk and Howard prided themselves on providing black youth with a sound liberal arts education as well as moral instruction. Fisk's mission statement, for instance, claimed that it "aim[ed] to be a great center of the best Christian educational forces for the training of the colored youth of the South, that they may be rightly disciplined and inspired for leaders in the vitally important work that needs to be done for their race in this country and on the continent of Africa." In promoting "an intelligent and earnest missionary zeal" among its students, the university required daily attendance at chapel, including a Wednesday night prayer service. The administration also encouraged the activities of several religiously oriented student organizations, the most prominent of which were the Young Men and Young Women's Christian Associations (YMCA and YWCA), Society of Christian Endeavor, White Cross League, and a Young People's Christian Temperance Union.[16] Officials at Howard identified the university as "distinctly Christian in its spirit and work." Students at Howard also had to attend chapel on Sundays and were encouraged to participate in daily chapel services and semiweekly evening prayer meetings. Like Fisk, Howard fostered the presence of pious associations such as the YMCA and YWCA and the Young People's Society of Christian Endeavor.[17]

But moral education expanded beyond the promulgation of the Gospel; it also involved the inculcation of late-Victorian bourgeois values. The instillation of character, respectability, and producer values was a primary objective of education at Fisk and Howard. To be sure, university officials expected students to arrive already possessing "good moral character," with, in many cases, written testimony to that effect. And administrators and faculty loathed the idea that some people might think of their venerable institutions as places they could send their wayward children in order to be reformed. Howard officials, for instance, reminded potential students and their parents that the school "aims to attract students of purpose and ability, and withal, of high moral standard. It is, therefore," they continued, "no place for those who are so lacking in self-control as to be in constant need of parental restraint or of the usual supervision of the school room."[18] Fisk's administration stressed the role that "character" played in determining which students received financial aid. "Satisfactory evidence is required that the student is worthy; that he has done the best practicable to help himself; that he practices proper self-denial and economy, and that he is willing to render such

service to the University in return as is required of him," the university's catalog informed prospective students. "It is believed to be better for the student
to earn the help as far as he can. Rightly given, help encourages and stimu-
lates independence, self-reliance, and manhood; unwisely rendered, the result may be exactly the reverse."[19] Despite the emphasis they placed on the
necessity of prospective students already possessing good character, officials
still stressed the "character building" aspect of their respective universities.
Lyman P. Powell argued that Fisk "is an institution for the training of the entire personality." In addition to receiving sound academic training, students
were exposed to rigorous cultivation of the moral self. "The Fisk road runs
through the mind," Powell wrote in the university's newspaper. "But no mind
can be properly developed in separation from the soul. If the standard college
catalog seems to stress the intellectual, it is because there must be specialization. Not even a college catalog can concentrate on everything. It is at best
a blue-print of personal development with room for the individual to fill in
the spaces commonly called character." The importance of building character among black youth was a mantra that was heard in all quarters of the
university community—from presidential speeches and fund-raising letters
to lectures at YMCA meetings and newspaper articles.[20]

The "character-building" discourse was gendered and racialized in a number of different ways. Of course, the development of "Christian manhood
and womanhood" was an objective of both universities and this did not di-
verge a great deal from the objectives of white colleges and universities that
had denominational affiliations. But educators at Fisk and Howard deployed
a rhetoric that was grounded in, and evoked, deeply racialized meanings of
manhood. The indispensability of moral education, they implied, lay in its capacity for instilling in black men the qualities and traits that were necessary
for attaining Victorian manliness. To be sure, young college-aged men of all
races were considered to be potential "savages." One individual, writing in
the Atlanta Journal in 1920, speculated that most young men went to college for
hedonistic reasons. "They regard it as an escape from parental supervision,"
he wrote, "and a chance to spend a little of dad's money without his direct
advice or assistance. In a word, the average undergraduate regards college
as an opportunity to assert his individuality, which is essentially a barbaric
individuality."[21]

The same discourse, when uttered in the context of educating young black
men, however, played on and reinforced racialized parallel constructions of
savagery and black masculinity. For instance, in promoting the "Charactar-
producing [sic] impact of such a great Christian School as Fisk," a fund-
raising letter written during World War I invoked black men as potential

threats to the well-being of the nation. The letter warned potential benefactors of devoting too much attention to the war in Europe at the expense of "the ever present and increasing Crisis of the Black Man at our door." The letter juxtaposed graduates of Fisk, presumably men of character, with the black soldiers who were executed for their participation in the Houston mutiny. The comparison implied that a moral education at Fisk would have prevented the soldiers from participating in a race riot that led to the deaths of seventeen whites and two blacks. The letter reminded those who were open to the idea of providing a liberal education to African Americans that "Fisk stands in the heart of the Great Black Belt facing this Crisis of the Black man, striving to convert a National Menace into an Asset and a Blessing."[22] The awkwardly veiled message of the letter was that Fisk acted as perhaps the last barrier between northern, middle-class whites and a southern black population that was, for the most part, poor, male, angry, and, in the context of war and migration, increasingly mobile. By providing financial backing to an institution that stimulated intellectual and moral growth among blacks, middle-class whites with a reformist bent could help ensure that the "race problem," as it was currently constituted in the South, would not travel beyond the Mason-Dixon line. Indeed, the following year, Fayette A. McKenzie, the white president of Fisk, discussed the educational philosophy of his institution in such a way that it must have put a great number of white Americans at ease. "We are a military institution," he averred. "Not that we have been absorbed by the military, but that the essential principles of efficiency exemplified in the military have been absorbed into the university. These principles include concentration of effort, unremitting toil, elimination of all unnecessary activities and motions, regular and insistent schedule of life, promptness, accuracy, reliability, thoroughness, instant and complete obedience."[23] By invoking the martial spirit of pedagogy, McKenzie also suggested that black youth were being molded into acquiescent cogs in the machine of industrial and corporate capitalism. In addition to academic training, then, young African American and African Caribbean immigrant men and women at Howard and Fisk were exposed to a moral education that, in many ways, revolved around bourgeois social and gender conventions.[24]

One significant element of the moral education advocated at these institutions was physical culture. Both educators and students expressed some concern that college-aged youths were devoting too much of their time and energy on academic subjects at the expense of their physical constitutions. "We are constantly priding ourselves on our ability to demonstrate the supremacy of mind over matter," a Fisk junior wrote in 1916, "and as an evil by-product of this demonstration we are becoming wiser but weaker." The author stressed the need for a holistic education. Physical activity would increase one's mental capacity which, subsequently, would improve one's cultural dexterity: "the value of athletic training lies in the wise development of the body in order that the mind may be free to devote its attention solely to the cultivation of those tastes which make for real, genuine culture and refinement." An article in Howard's *University Journal* articulated a similar sentiment when it declared that "no other phase of college work exercises such a tremendous force for systematic development as do well-regulated athletics."[25] The emphasis students and administrators placed on physical culture was present in organized sports on campus. Both universities fielded football, baseball, basketball, and track teams. Cricket was also a mainstay of the Howard athletics program, indicating a significant presence of African Caribbean students. An intramural Cricket Club was organized in the spring of 1906 and apparently consisted primarily of professional students in the medical and theological departments. By 1909, a university team was competing against cricket clubs and other colleges, including Lincoln University and Haverford College.[26]

Some educators, however, expressed ambivalence toward the presence of organized sports on campus. They expounded upon the danger of allowing competition to become the predominant organizing principle of college athletics. The objective of organized sports, they argued, should not solely be the vanquishing of one's opponent. Rather, athletics, as part of a moral education, should be geared toward providing young people with character. To that end, educators argued that college athletics should consist of amateurs as opposed to professionals, whose presence on college teams in the early twentieth century constituted a major problem. They insisted that academic work take priority among student athletes. President McKenzie urged the Board of Trustees to adopt a policy that required all athletes to have matriculated at least one year and to have good academic standings. He also rejected the use of athletic scholarships. Moreover, the raison d'être of college teams should be to promote the athlete's "permanent health and happiness" instead of the college itself—a rationale behind college sports that is more pervasive at the turn of the twenty-first century but that existed in the early part of the twentieth as well.[27] University officials clearly situated the value of organized sports within the realm of moral education and not the boosterism that would mark college sports later in the century: even football in the late-nineteenth and early-twentieth centuries was viewed more as a sport that was predicated upon, and designed to instill, rationality and efficiency.[28]

Perhaps the most disciplinary aspect of moral education—and certainly the most controversial by the 1920s—was military training. From the beginning, both institutions subjected their students to regimented lifestyles, although officials at Howard subscribed to a more explicitly martial logic than officials at Fisk. Howard's initial organization included a Military Department but it was abolished in 1874 due to lack of students. Even so, student life was structured militarily into the 1870s. Male students, in particular, woke to reveille; complied with room inspections; wore military-style uniforms; marched to and from meals, classes, and religious services; saluted members of the administration and faculty; drilled in the evening; and responded to "lights out" calls at night.[29] Even though educators at Fisk sought to regulate the most mundane of student activities—including requiring students to wake up and go to bed at the same time and keep neat rooms—the lives of boarding students were organized more along familial lines. The fact that students and teachers lived together in the same residence halls and ate together in a common dining hall encouraged both to characterize the boarding arrangements on campus as being akin to living in a home.[30]

By the turn of the century, the idea of incorporating a martial component into the overall pedagogy resurfaced and, by World War I, had become institutionalized through each campus's partnership with the U.S. armed forces. Initially, plans for "militarizing" student life at Howard emerged out of a concern that the overall physical condition of the male students was deficient. "Defective physical training and carriage of the body mark most of our young men," Acting President Teunis S. Hamlin reported in 1903. "They come from homes in which this has not been considered. No method of correcting this; of giving that erect figure, and free fine movement of the body on which so much depends for both health and effectiveness, is comparable to military drill." One year later, Howard's Board of Trustees unanimously approved a committee report to institute military drill with equipment obtained from the War Department.[31]

As the United States became involved in the First World War, both Howard and Fisk, like other campuses across the country, became even more militarized. From the beginning of American involvement, officials and students at both schools enthusiastically supported the war effort. Howard students were instrumental in the creation of the Central Committee of Negro College Men, an organization that, along with a divided NAACP, successfully lobbied the War Department to establish a black officers training camp in Des Moines, Iowa.[32] The campus itself became a veritable extension of the army. Between November 1917 and April 1918, the School of Manual Arts and Applied Sciences provided radio instruction to over 130 drafted and enlisted African American men, most of who ended up serving with the 325th Field Signal Battalion. The School of Manual Arts was also involved in the creation of a National Army Training Detachment on campus. From May to September 1918, the detachment offered courses in radio operation, carpentry, and electrical mechanics to 450 soldiers. The summer of 1918 also saw the institution of the Student Army Instruction Camp on campus, which, as part of the larger Student Army Training Corps (SATC), trained students and faculty members from different colleges to set up SATC units on their respective campuses. In conjunction with the War Department, colleges set up SATC units for undrafted high school and college students who wished to get both the benefits of military training and a standard academic education. Membership in SATC did not constitute a deferment; rather, it allowed students to continue studying while they waited for their "number" to be called. The SATC cadet received military training—in the form of drilling, marksmanship, and "other outdoor training"—and, through academic instruction, was "given an opportunity to specialize in a branch of training designed to fit him to become an officer of field artillery, medical or engineer officer, or an expert in some technical or scientific service." Once an SATC cadet's draft number was called, the president and commanding officer at his college conferred and made a recommendation as to whether the cadet should be allowed to continue regular academic study, enrolled in an officer training camp, assigned to support staff, or enlisted in a regular division. In the late summer and fall of 1918, Howard's SATC units consisted of 750 young men. Fisk accommodated six hundred SATC cadets, many of who were passing through temporarily on their way to other schools for vocational training.[33]

World War I changed both campuses dramatically. Young men and women both felt the impact of national mobilization. Female students at Howard organized auxiliary units of the Red Cross and Soldiers' Comfort Society and participated in the Circle for Negro War Relief. Moreover, when the university was forced to cancel classes due to the influenza epidemic in the fall of 1918, female students were organized into a Girls' Battalion. Young women wore uniforms, drilled like their male counterparts, and heard lectures "on phases of military life." The primary objective of the Girls' Battalion was to establish a disciplinary regime so as to prevent the spread of the influenza virus. Once classes resumed, the Girls' Battalion was disbanded.[34] Life at Fisk became similarly regimented. Students, even those not in SATC units, marched to and from classes, meals, and chapel services. A sentry on campus required students and faculty members to show passes to get around. All of these changes jolted one of the staff members into the realization that "Fisk campus is in reality a 'military camp.'" The university's administration was forthright about the militarization of the campus. In response to a parent of a female student who was concerned about the sudden influx of

The Student Army Training Corps of Howard University. (From Howard University
Record, April 1919; courtesy of the Moorland-Spingarn Research Center)

young men associated with SATC, McKenzie assured him that Fisk's campus
would remain a bastion of probity. "Life must move in fixed grooves," McKenzie wrote. "The boys will live a highly educational military life, a masculine
life, centered about Bennett Hall. The girls will live an equally efficient, busy
school life, centered about Jubilee Hall. Groups must move as groups, if we
are to be efficient on a crowded campus." The respectability that McKenzie
and Fisk officials sought to nurture among the students was matched only by
their desire to enforce a disciplined conformity upon them. "This is a time,"
he continued, "when every patriotic citizen must fall into line and into step
without delay and without complaint."[35]

If the war generated similar feelings of American nationalism among officials at Howard and Fisk, demobilization produced quite different sentiments
and, consequently, each university had a qualitatively different relationship
with the federal government after the war. Howard continued its close partnership with the federal government and, specifically, the War Department.
In February 1919, Howard officials established a Reserved Officers Training
Corps (ROTC) program on campus. Participation in ROTC, which was administered by the Department of Military Training, was mandatory for male students for the first three years and fulfilled physical education requirements.[36]

In distinct contrast, President McKenzie had a fundamentally negative evaluation of his university's partnership with the military. Although he acknowledged that the militarization of the campus contributed to a more efficiently functioning institution, he ultimately reproved the presence of SATC units on university grounds. McKenzie's main criticism of the military was its refusal to cede authority to university officials. As a result, SATC cadets were not accountable to the school's rules and regulations. The cadet's independence, in addition to the military officials' inability—or willing refusal—to "set up satisfactory moral standards," led to rampantly indecorous behavior on the campus, including smoking and profanity. "Institutions that have always held that immorality meant instant expulsion have been debarred the right to maintain their rule and have been obliged to hold their tongue while the military have tempted the youth by prophylactic treatments to enter upon careers of vice," McKenzie ruefully noted shortly after the war ended. "Whatever be the wisdom of such treatments in a regular army camp, it has no excuse upon a college campus." The behavior of cadets, and the disinclination of officers to police that behavior, was only one of McKenzie's grievances. In a perspicacious observation—one that anticipated the New Negro's disaffection with the government following the war—McKenzie argued that the federal government was failing to adequately compensate African Americans for their national sacrifice. "When the immediate aim of efficient fighters was no longer its aim, the Government sought to free itself from its financial obligations and forgot what havoc it would work in the lives of many, many young men," he charged even before many black soldiers began to return from Europe. "A moral obligation kept would in the long run have proved a national gain. Thousands, disappointed and demoralized, have gone out permanently indifferent to the higher types of opportunity." For these reasons, he reported to the Board of Trustees in January 1919, he did not feel that establishing an ROTC unit on campus was prudent. From the beginning, however, McKenzie had demonstrated a circumspect approach to the efficacy and appropriateness of a martial pedagogy. "By the very constitution of man and society," he wrote one month earlier, "the military organization cannot be an end in itself, but is the instrument of those other ideas, ideals, and purposes which rank higher in the universe of God. Force must ever be the servant of intelligence and conscience," he continued, "of morality and religion, or it becomes satanic and self-destructive." [37] In considering the suitability of organizing education along military lines, McKenzie clearly believed that the "military idea" was only the means by which moral education might be imparted to youth.

Military training, along with organized athletics, were elements of moral education that credited physical exertion and disciplined activity with "character-building" powers. Counterposed with these "positive" forms of "character-building" were the "negative" forms of "character-building," which primarily consisted of rigid systems of rules and regulations. The efforts to compel students to conform to "true Christian living" was, in many cases, nothing more than the policing of every aspect of the students' lives.[38] Respectable comportment—which ranged from adhering to dress codes to abstaining from the consumption of alcohol and tobacco to avoiding being alone with someone of the opposite sex—was required of Howard and Fisk students both on and off campus. Fisk's catalog for the 1900–1901 school year reminded students that they were "subject to the discipline of the University for immoral or unworthy conduct during absence from the institution." Similarly, Howard's 1922 student manual cautioned undergraduates of their liability "for misdeeds during vacation as well as in term time." Depending upon the severity of the infraction, disciplinary action included reprimands, probation, suspension, and expulsion.[39]

The management of student fashion was a significant aspect of moral education although, from all indications, it mattered more to officials at Fisk than to those at Howard. Whereas Fisk maintained a rigid dress code, the extent to which students at Howard had to conform to particular fashion guidelines was the policy—ironically, drafted by student leaders—that mandated first-year students to wear caps during their first few quarters.[40] To be sure, Howard administrators and professors were concerned that their students dress in a respectable manner so as not to damage the "good moral reputation of the institution"; Fisk's policy concerning student dress, however, was so much more draconian that it made Howard's seem downright permissive. Dress codes at Fisk were directed mainly at women. They were required to own two modest shirtwaist suits and they were not allowed to wear clothing with "elaborate and expensive trimmings" or that was made of lace, silk, satin, chiffon, velvet, or corduroy. Moreover, women were prohibited from wearing gaudy jewelry. "The clothing of students must be becoming, plain and substantial," Fisk's catalog stated. "Those who bring articles considered by the Dress Committee to be unsuitable, extravagant or unnecessary will be required to lay them aside while in the University."[41]

In their discussions of youth and fashion, educators at Fisk articulated a belief that dress was an indicator of individual character and vice versa. As the 1919 catalog unequivocally stated, "plain living with us is a sign of high thinking." In a sense, there was a noble sentiment behind Fisk administrators' insistence on "plain living." Given the diverse socioeconomic backgrounds of its students, officials at Fisk sought to avoid an environment in which the consumption patterns of more affluent students might embarrass those of less means. "The high costs of college life elsewhere are found in clothes and other personal expenditures largely for show and frivolity," McKenzie reported to the Board of Trustees in 1920. "Those costs have risen in the past and continue to rise because of the competing ambitions of the students in an atmosphere which exerts no restraining pressure. If the great mass of worthy poor are to have intellectual privileges at Fisk it will be necessary to continue the rigid control which almost eliminates the expenditures for adornments, flowers, banquets, receptions, dances, fraternities, etc." To prevent such a competitive environment, Fisk officials strongly urged students' parents to not send large amounts of "pocket money."[42]

But beyond seeking to level the field among middle- and working-class students, the strictures placed on fashion at Fisk were influenced by the connection educators perceived between dress and disposition. Fisk officials took pride in the fact that the institutions' dress code was both a reflection, and a facilitator, of its students' good character. An article for the school newspaper, for instance, pointed out that the university "several years ago began a quiet crusade against everything in the dress of its students which seemed at war with good health and the requirements of good taste."[43] As educators drew a correlation between "good taste" and personal integrity, so they mapped out a relationship between "bad" taste and questionable character. At one disciplinary hearing concerning a female student who left the campus without permission, her overall integrity was called into question when the investigative committee reported on her fashion habits. Even though she received a slap on the wrist, the student's reputation was impugned by the "damaging" revelation that "when she first appeared at school she wore dangling ear rings."[44]

Nor was it only young women's fashion that concerned educators. Officials at Fisk attached an equal amount of importance to the sartorial style of men. In an address in 1921, McKenzie discussed men's fashion and its lack of significance in determining success. He quoted from an article written by the vice president of Illinois Agricultural College, which appeared in the *Saturday Evening Post*. " 'The college student in general. . . .' " McKenzie quoted,

"affects peculiarities of dress and manner. This, too, is primitive, for the instinct belongs to the period of adolescence, not of manhood. It would be humiliating for him to be told that in this particular respect he closely resembles the Mexican laborer whom we opprobriously term 'the greaser,' except that the latter is rather more successful in the effects. Like the Mexican and the feathered Indian, this youngster wants to be seen and heard, whereas the successful man of the world moves about inconspicuously and you would never recognize him by any outward and distinguishing mark. *The real world is too busy to pose and too well bred to attract attention."* [45]

McKenzie's negative assessment of young men who postured flamboyantly juxtaposed the archetype of the modest Victorian gentleman with its racialized antitheses: working-class Mexican Americans and Mexican immigrants, and the stereotypical, premodern Native American. Others invoked a gendered and sexualized criticism of young men's fashion in the early 1920s. When Fisk seniors requested that the school standardize the design of a class ring and pin, an administrative committee was set up to study the question. The consensus of the committee was that there should be standardization but the committee was ultimately critical of the practice of men wearing rings, as it was evocative of "the dandy or the lady-like man." [46] Even though Fisk's dress code was directed primarily at female students, officials evinced a specific apprehension around the fashion tastes of the young male scholars. For them, modest dress was one of the hallmarks of Victorian manliness—a model of manhood to which they expected Fisk students to aspire, even in the face of the changing consumer tastes of the Jazz Age. [47]

The policing of social interaction between male and female students also characterized the disciplinary regimes of Howard and Fisk although, like their approaches to dress, the officials at the latter institution were much more uncompromising than officials at the former. Administrators and faculty members at Fisk sought to superintend the contact between young men and women in the areas of extra-curriculum and leisure. Most clubs and literary societies, for instance, were gender segregated and some forms of physical recreation, although coeducational, were considered by officials to be potentially dangerous venues for socializing between the sexes. [48] Perhaps the most feared—and consequently, the most regulated—interaction between men and women was in the realm of leisure. Concern over student propriety extended to the relationships between students as well as the relationships between students and local residents. On campus grounds, the leisure activities of students were heavily monitored. Students attended parties, or evening socials, that were chaperoned and at which, until quite recently, dancing had not even been countenanced. [49] Students had to observe curfews and prescribed hours for visiting with students of the opposite sex—always under the eye of the residence hall's matron. Fisk's dean of women even went so far as to discourage the giving of elaborate or expensive gifts, as it might lead to a certain "obligation" on behalf of the recipient. The dean's implication was that the "obligation" might be sexual in nature. "No young man should give the least article of wearing apparel to a young woman, not even a dainty scarf nor pair of gloves," she wrote. "This privilege comes after he has pronounced the words at the altar, 'With all my worldly goods I thee endow.'"[50] One professor at Fisk, who was critical of the school's excessive discipline, complained of the draconian rules that resulted in suspensions and expulsions for what, to his mind, constituted fairly innocent behavior. "It is forbidden for two students of opposite sex to meet each other without the presence and permission of the dean of women or of a teacher," he noted. "A girl and boy could be sent home for walking together in broad day light, on the sidewalk from Livingstone Hall to Jubilee [the male and female dormitories respectively]. A young lady may be sent home for casting a smile from a window to a youth below."[51] The professor's last comment may have been hyperbolic but he captured the general spirit of the school administrators' position on male-female interaction. Moreover, they discouraged the development of student relationships with individuals in the surrounding community. As pointed out earlier, female students were prohibited from leaving campus without permission. Male students, although having greater mobility, were still held accountable for their actions off campus. One young man, for instance, was expelled for having "wrongful relations with a girl in the neighborhood." McKenzie expressed the rationale behind the expulsion to the students' parents: "Permit me to hope that this experience may result in the final great good of your son. It would be a great benefit to him if a way could be found by which he might remain close to you until he has re-established his strength of character and his reputation with the world."[52]

Howard officials were similarly concerned with the interaction between male and female students. There were specific hours when female students could receive gentlemen callers, and parties were diligently chaperoned by faculty members and administrators. Students were also prohibited from marrying. Those who did were expelled and could be "readmitted only by the vote of the Faculty."[53] Like Fisk, the rules and regulations regarding the behavior of female students were more exacting than those regarding the behavior of men. Women were not allowed to spend a night off campus except during the holidays, provided that their parents sanctioned it. They were permitted to drive or "motor" only with the consent of the matron and only under chaperonage. The disparity between the rules directed toward men and those directed toward women was the cause of some critical commentary on the part of female students at Howard. One student ridiculed the cumbersome regulations that set up matrons as intermediaries and that made fairly innocent communication between men and women virtually impossible. She criticized the prohibitions against male and female students socializing outside of the residence halls as being disproportionately punitive to women. "The rule doesn't hurt the fellows much," she rightly complained. "They can ramble on down into the city, get their girls, bring them right up on the campus, and sit down and talk to them as long as they please. The girls alone really suffer. True, they don't come here to talk to the boys; nor do they come here to sit on the campus, nor gossip about in one another's rooms. But if we are to be held to just exactly what we come here to do life would be monotonous indeed." In the end, the student argued that as Howard was "modernizing" in the areas of infrastructure, academics, and athletics, so should it modernize in the "field of social discipline."[54]

The rationale behind such strict "social discipline" varied. In his critical assessment of Fisk's disciplinary regime, Professor Alphonse D. Phillipse suggested that racial ideologies of black sexuality were behind most of the regulations directed toward managing male-female socializing. "A few teachers," he wrote, "claim that the Negro is, by heredity, more inclined to looseness in sexual relations than the whites, and require stricter supervision."[55] Even though longstanding notions of the hypersexual nature of people of African descent may have influenced official policy, the Victorian regime of moral discipline was applauded by many parents. "The rules and regulations at Fisk are entirely satisfactory to us," Dr. and Mrs. A. W. Davis wrote, "and we think to all parents who are striving to bring their daughters up as pure Christian young women who may be an asset to our race." D. W. Sherrod, who graduated in 1892, concurred with the continued vigilance with which faculty members and administrators policed the behavior of young black men and women. "I have never known the time that Fisk University allowed the association of the male and female students on the campus and highway," Sherrod wrote. "It was not the case during my school days, and I do not believe such liberties now should be allowed." Another set of parents stated quite bluntly, "We do not send our children to school to court."[56]

Educators were just as rigorous in their policing of other behavior. Officials at both schools considered the consumption of alcohol and tobacco, particularly among male students, to be an especially acute problem. Fisk expressly prohibited the "use of ardent spirits as a beverage, and . . . tobacco" in the university catalog, while Howard forbade students from going to "poolrooms, gambling houses and places of corrupting influence or evil resort."[57] These regulations were supplemented by sermons, editorials, and efforts to provide more wholesome outlets for students' energies. One editorial in the Fisk Herald, for instance, conflated the dangers of alcohol with the destruction being waged in Europe. Referring to both war and alcohol as an "ill wind," the editorial argued, "if alcohol makes men less efficient in time of war, is it reasonable to suppose that it will not make them less efficient in time of peace? Away with alcohol now and forever." During the same month, Fisk students attending chapel heard a sermon on "Our Responsibility in the Liquor Question," which referred to alcohol as a "deadly, demoralizing poison."[58] Administrators at Howard attempted to deal with the alcohol problem—which manifested in the annual confiscation of approximately one hundred bottles of liquor from the men's dormitory—by increasing surveillance and providing more social activities for men. In 1914, the administration hired a married couple as "custodians" of the men's dormitory, Clark Hall, and authorized the campus YMCA to manage a pool table for the enjoyment of the male students.[59] Despite these efforts to prevent the consumption of alcohol, and to a lesser extent, tobacco, officials still had to utilize disciplinary measures against students—especially at Fisk.[60]

Students at Fisk were also subjected to more rigid precepts than those at Howard when it came to what kinds of music they could play and listen to on campus. Educators were particularly critical of ragtime. Professor J. W. Work recognized the intrinsic melodic quality of ragtime but found the environment that it produced to be especially vexatious. "All the beauty and power of syncopation and rhythm, are degraded by the company they keep—they are associated with cheap vulgarity, senseles [sic] ugly, harmful dances, silly and debasing words," Work lamented. "What profanity is to language, what baseness is to human life, what drunkenness is to human character ragtime is to music." Work drew a link between the appreciation of ragtime and poor character. He explicitly questioned the integrity of those who listened to this vernacular music: "Do you know a devotee of ragtime? Would you trust him in any important matter? Do you not find him trifling, giddy, light and unreliable? Just as he does in the ragtime dances, he 'dog walks[,]' he 'dips[,]' he 'turkey trots,' he 'tangoes[,]' and he hesitates all through life—he goes with no certain or consistent gait." Work's distaste for ragtime was not merely idiosyncratic; it was, more or less, official policy of the school as the playing of ragtime on "university pianos" was strictly forbidden.[61] There is no indication that there were similar prohibitions against ragtime at Howard, although officials proscribed students from frequenting places where ragtime or jazz might be played, such as pool halls, gambling dens, and brothels. Moreover, they sought to instill an appreciation for classical choral and orchestral music in their students through the creation of campus musical societies.

In his report to the Board of Trustees on the 1919–20 school year, President McKenzie articulated the overarching rationale behind the university's pedagogical philosophy. "It is an intensive program that we propose," he wrote. "It cannot be carried through without a fearful elimination of student material unless we can protect the majority by such a control of their time and methods as will make their every activity contribute to health, to vigor, to speed, and to efficiency. . . . Non-efficient habits in non-scholastic hours," he concluded, "may render the imparting of efficient scholastic habits practically impossible." [62] McKenzie's summation of the educational praxis of Fisk succinctly revealed its late-Victorian cultural core. According to McKenzie, the pedagogical mission of the institution—and here, the same might be said of Howard—was to redirect the puerile energy of youth into productive channels. Part of this project involved the inculcation of bourgeois gender conventions through the promotion of producer values and respectability. Implicit in this discourse, however, was the presupposition that black youth were barely capable of acquiring self-control. Paradoxically, it was the duty of the university to see to it that they maintained that self-control through external, coercive mechanisms. In the case of male students, these mechanisms geared toward bodily discipline included physical culture, military training, and proscriptions against certain consumption and leisure practices. As the 1920s progressed, and as black middle-class youth were confronted more and more with consumer culture and the more permissive gender conventions that marked the postwar period, their resistance to the disciplining of the body escalated. By the middle of the decade this resistance culminated in a rash of student strikes.

■ Between February and May 1925, the student bodies of Fisk and Howard expressed their discontent with their respective administrations by striking. The animus that many, but certainly not all, students harbored toward university officials had been incubating for at least a couple of years but intensified, and later culminated in concerted actions by student leaders that ultimately contributed to the resignation of both presidents. In addition, the actions by students were part of larger campaigns—by alumni of both schools and, in the case of Howard, the faculty—directed against the administrations. Howard's president, James Stanley Durkee, maintained his position for nearly a year after the strikes—and more than a year longer than McKenzie—but, by the spring of 1926, the missionary paternalism that both men represented was clearly on its way out as an organizing principle of these institutions' educational missions.

McKenzie took over the reins of Fisk in 1915. The forty-three-year-old white academic had taught at a number of different schools—including a reservation school in Wyoming and as a sociology professor at Ohio State University—before arriving in Nashville. His commitment to raising the educational standards and the profile of the university as a liberal arts school was greeted with both enthusiasm and skepticism. The Fisk Herald captured this ambivalence when it published an editorial before McKenzie was officially installed. "It is indeed gratifying to know that our president-elect is a believer in the higher education of the Negro," the editorial stated. "The ideas and opinions which are held by a man at the head of a university like Fisk will largely determine whether the institution will move forward or backward. If he is not a thorough believer in the principles for which the school stands, if he himself is at heart a 'Negro hater' nothing could be expected but retrogression, as far as his influence is concerned."[63] By many standards, McKenzie did indeed move Fisk forward. Through the expansion of the curriculum and the elevation of instructional and evaluative standards that occurred under his watch, Fisk was recognized by other schools as a bona fide institution and its students' applications, both as transfers and graduates, were considered by most non-southern white universities. Additionally, Fisk became an associate member of the highly respected Carnegie Foundation. McKenzie also reestablished Fisk as part of the larger community by promoting the service component of the university's mission. Through his contacts with Nashville's business community and the efforts of several faculty members—most notably social work professor George E. Haynes—Fisk rendered assistance to local blacks and whites in the areas of disease prevention, housing, and social welfare. Finally, McKenzie increased the endowment of Fisk through fund-raising that solicited money from philanthropic and local civic organizations.[64]

Despite his efforts at transforming Fisk into a first-class liberal arts university, McKenzie's position on the "race question" and his despotic control of the institution alienated many of the students as well as the larger black community. Prior to McKenzie's presidency, tension had existed between Fisk's administration and more radical black Nashvillians who rejected the accommodationist stance of black conservatives. The source of the tension lay in the belief that, as a white-controlled institution, Fisk was not sufficiently connected to the black community. This was reflected, many black Nashvillians argued, in the continued appointments of white presidents and the observance of segregation at university events. McKenzie, a moderate when it came to race relations, did little to alleviate the tension when he became president. He opposed Jim Crow but did not support political protest against the battery of social customs that kept blacks in the position of second-class citizens. In order to curry favor with white business and civic groups, he upheld segregationist policies at events on campus that attracted whites who were not affiliated with the university.[65] Tied to his conciliatory posture toward southern racial politics—and most directly related to the lives of students—was a repressiveness that sought to contain any hint of radicalism or, indeed, any sense of autonomy among the student body. One of his first moves, for instance, was to suspend the student newspaper, the *Fisk Herald*, in the winter of 1915–16 and fold it into the alumni newspaper, the *Fisk University News*. His reasoning was that the *Herald* had been operating in the red for some time and that the *University News* was better equipped to handle the financial burden of publication. His efforts to convince critics that it was merely a matter of money and that students would still have a "voice" on the alumni newspaper were unsuccessful.[66] In addition to the strict code of discipline that he continued to enforce, McKenzie quashed an effort by local residents and students to form an NAACP chapter on campus and directed the school librarian to purge the library's copies of the *Crisis* of all radical material.[67]

By the early 1920s, there was sufficient discontent among students that they began to form grievance committees. One such committee was able to secure a series of meetings in 1921—with the reluctant permission of McKenzie, to be sure—with William N. DeBerry, an alumnus and member of the Board of Trustees. The bulk of the complaints were directed at the rigid system of rules and regulations which subjected "upper classmen with good records in deportment, along with all other students" to "a sort of schoolboy discipline" and did not allow them "to be placed on their honor." They were also critical of the ban on college fraternities and the segregationist policies on campus. DeBerry, who had to expel McKenzie from one of the meetings after he surreptitiously entered the room through the back, found that the campus was in the grips of "a policy of suppression and intimidation against which there was a tempestuous spirit of rebellion."[68]

Three years after DeBerry's series of meetings, W. E. B. Du Bois, an alumnus of Fisk, delivered an address at his alma mater. In Nashville to attend his daughter Yolande's graduation, Du Bois gave a speech to Fisk alumni in the campus chapel. He took the opportunity to deliver a blistering shot across the bow of the McKenzie administration. "I have known and been connected more or less intimately with many colored institutions of learning," he stated, "but I have never known an institution whose alumni on the whole are more bitter and disgusted with the present situation in this university than the alumni of Fisk University today." Du Bois was critical of Fisk's administration on primarily two points. He argued that the university officials' clamoring for philanthropic assistance—which necessitated a capitulation to the benevolent racism of the "liberal white South"—led to segregationist policies on campus. Moreover, the administration's effort to contain student "self-expression" resulted in disciplinary methods that were "medieval and long since discredited." Du Bois couched this criticism in explicitly gendered language. "Thus self-expression and manhood are choked at Fisk in the very day when we need expression to develop manhood in the colored race," he intoned. "We are facing a serious and difficult situation. We need every bit of brains and ability that we have for leadership. There is no hope that the American Negro is going to develop as a docile animal. He is going to be a man, and he needs therefore his best manhood. This manhood is being discouraged at Fisk today and ambition instead of being fostered is being deliberately frowned upon." The second major criticism Du Bois leveled was against the lack of alumni involvement in university governance. He called for greater alumni representation on the Board of Trustees and concluded his scathing address by encouraging Fisk graduates to support the unofficial boycott of the school—which he suggested consisted of black students either initially enrolling in, or transferring to, other schools such as Howard—until administration policies changed.[69]

Du Bois's controversial address, while certainly not the first expression of discontent toward the McKenzie administration, intensified people's indignation. In order to press his case, Du Bois solicited statements from Fisk alumni, students, and faculty members. Individuals wrote to him complaining of the strict disciplinary code, the acquiescence to segregationist practices, and the repressive policies regarding student activities. Elmer J. Ortman, president of LeMoyne Junior College and a Fisk alumnus, concurred with Du Bois's criticism. "It said what a lot of people had been saying privately and thinking," he wrote. "Truth will arise—and woe is the little man who tries to sit on the lid. I am pleased I left when I did."[70] As Du Bois and the Committee of the Fisk Club of New York were gathering support for their campaign, so was McKenzie. Shortly after Du Bois's speech, McKenzie requested a vote of confidence for his presidency from the Board of Trustees. The Board responded with a letter of endorsement that was signed by all except two members: Dr. Thomas Jesse Jones, who was in Africa at the time, and DeBerry, who, after having extended discussions with students three years earlier, was beginning to show a lack of confidence in the McKenzie administration.[71]

Initially, students were reluctant to join the crusade against McKenzie. As one of the more outspoken student leaders, George Streator, assessed of the mood on campus, students were afraid to speak out against the president for fear that they might be "blacklisted" by the faculty and administration. The repressive atmosphere led many students to hold their tongues. "Today around Fisk the official air is[,] of course, anti-DuBois," Streator wrote to a former faculty member who was sympathetic to the movement to oust McKenzie. "To be in the 'band-wagon' and still be assured of little favors like good marks, appointments when graduation comes, etc., one must either swallow his manhood and conscience in silence, or suffer the penalty of expulsion or failure to graduate."[72] By the fall of 1924, the repressive structures and the environment of fear that they produced were cracking. A group of students submitted a statement of grievances to the Board of Trustees in October. The complainants pointed out the existence of arbitrary and unwritten rules of conduct; the absence of forums for the expression of students' voices, such as an undergraduate council and a student newspaper; the strict supervision of student activities; an environment of distrust, which produced a "wide-spread system of spying" and the inspection of students' mail; the replacement of qualified black faculty members with ill-equipped, conservative southern whites; and the capitulation of McKenzie to "southern white prejudices." They concluded the declaration by unequivocally calling for either the resignation or firing of McKenzie. "If the above accusations are substantially true, they cannot be answered by minor changes or reforms," they boldly wrote. "They call for the severing of Fayette McKenzie from the presidency of Fisk and for a system of alumni representation on the board of trustees."[73]

The campaign against McKenzie gained momentum in November as student protests increased. "The students are dissatisfied and thank God they are beginning to express their dissatisfaction," a senior wrote to Du Bois. He informed Du Bois that students were registering their discontent by acting in an "irreverent" manner during chapel exercises and staging demonstrations on campus grounds. One such rally lasted from 6 P.M. to 1 A.M. with students chanting, among other things: "Hey Boys! Who Boys? Du Bois. Down with McKenzie." Even students from Meharry, the black medical school that was affiliated with Fisk, became involved in the protests. "At the football games," Streator wrote, "they gave rousing cheers for Du Bois and yelled down with the Fisk parasites and job-holders! Give us men on your faculty."[74] These demonstrations, in addition to a boycott of classes carried out while trustees were on campus for Founder's Day ceremonies, forced the administration to respond to the students' grievances. At the Board's meeting, a committee consisting of seven students presented an additional list of complaints against the administration and requested several changes in the university policies. They asked for the right to have fraternities and sororities, a student council and publication, and an athletic association on campus. They called for less stringent dress codes and rules regarding interaction between the sexes, including the right for men to escort women to movies held on campus. They also demanded changes in the fundamental way in which the administration treated students. One of the requests was "that the faculty refrain from constantly watching the students on the grounds that it creates resentment and ill-feeling between the groups."[75]

In its articulation of student grievances, the committee met with limited success. One trustee felt that the committee "could not have done it in a more effective manner" and the president of the Board was "deeply impressed and pleased with the fair and manly way in which the students had conducted their case." Although there was some disagreement among the Board—particularly with respect to the presence of Greek-letter organizations on campus—the trustees ultimately agreed to the creation of a student council, an athletic association, an alumni committee, and a slight modification of the dress code.[76] The success was short-lived, however. McKenzie either dragged his feet or directly refused to implement many of the students' requests. In late January 1925, he more or less shut the door on reform at Fisk when he stated to reporters that "a complete ignoring of the charges made against the administration will be the policy of the Board of Trustees of Fisk University." Moreover, in early February, he staged a series of talks in the chapel essentially informing the students that the administrative policies would remain in place and that anyone who did not agree with them could withdraw.[77]

On the night of his last talk, 4 February, the campus erupted. Reportedly, approximately one hundred male students disregarded curfew and marched around campus, banging trash cans, breaking windows, and chanting "Du Bois! Du Bois!" and "Before I'd be a slave!" In response, McKenzie called out the Nashville police. Dozens of white police officers arrived on campus and, with a list of names provided by McKenzie, arrested the seven students who comprised the committee that met with the Board of Trustees in November. The students were charged with a felony, which, according to Du Bois, was an unbailable offense. At the students' trial, it was discovered that some of the students were not even on campus during the "riot." This revelation, in conjunction with McKenzie's admission that he did not actually have any proof that the students were involved, forced him to request that the felony charges be dropped. The students were instead found guilty of disorderly conduct and given suspended fines. When the students' counsel threatened to sue McKenzie for false prosecution, he agreed to a plan in which the guilty verdicts were nullified by the court and the students were given honorable dismissals. The incidents of early February mobilized both the Nashville community, which was aghast at the deployment of the city police, and the students. Three-quarters of the student body began a general strike and commenced a boycott of classes. With student attendance below 50 percent, alumni refusing to give money, and trustees privately, if not publicly, beginning to question his ability to run the school, McKenzie resigned on 16 April 1925.[78]

Supporters of McKenzie framed the student unrest in a number of different ways, at once making them pawns of black radicals and reducing their grievances to selfish, racially motivated rants. Du Bois, for instance, was blamed for undue "evil influence" on the students. Mrs. Arch Trawick, a white trustee from Nashville, pointed out to a Fisk patron that the "Negro radical leader" had the "support of a number of Negroes who are like minded in resenting authority and discipline in college administration, and inter-racial cooperation in the life of the South." As such, she suggested to another donor, "it was easy for him to inflame young, impressionable students, to make them feel sorry for themselves, and to rouse them to a course of violence and lawlessness."[79] In addition, McKenzie and others adamantly argued that the student and alumni movement against his administration was a misguided and racially conscious effort to eradicate white influence from the education of blacks. "It is . . . of little concern whether I resign or not," McKenzie wrote to Paul Cravath, president of the Board of Trustees shortly after Du Bois's speech, "but it is a matter of great concern to the university if its policies can be subjected to personal whims and prejudices. The goal all this approaches is the removal of white people from Negro education." Opponents of the McKenzie administration were particularly cognizant of the strategy to paint them as self-serving nationalists and its significance in terms of public relations. Streator, for instance, wrote that "the McKenzie forces are trying like everything to make it appear that the Northern alumni are a bunch of hot-headed radicals opposed to everything white, whether good or evil."[80] Du Bois and others took pains to assuage those concerned that the campaign against McKenzie was not a "question of color or race," but, rather, an issue of the repressive and outdated nature of the pedagogical practices of missionary paternalism.[81]

Another strategy of delegitimizing the student strike—and one that was particularly deployed by students' parents—was to cast it as not only a rebellion against the Fisk presidency, but a rebellion against bourgeois social conventions. Parents sought to reaffirm the necessity and desirability of the same missionary paternalism that was so fervently criticized by the opponents of McKenzie. One individual reduced the protests to the activities of a fringe group of students who were incapable of imbibing the discipline and self-control that educators sought to instill:

> When I went to school students were sent there to get an education so as to be of some service to humanity and they needed it in efforts. Now, in some instances, parents send a child to college to reform it, because they cannot manage the child. A few of this type can wreck a whole school

if they once get control of the student body. This is the class that starts school strikes that end in riots. They are moral cowards and while looking for immediate advantage shut out the sun light of eternal principle. . . . You have not, as I see it, had a strike or a riot—simply a few students who cannot stand discipline [and] who don't know that there can be no real education without discipline, and have aroused the whole school to their tomfoolery.

In charging that its core consisted of "moral cowards" who were looking for "immediate advantage," this critic of the strike argued that the movement against McKenzie was engineered by youth who were antipathetic toward the moral education offered by Fisk. The reference to "immediate advantage" also suggests that the critic was characterizing the students' resistance toward "discipline"—or the conformity to producer values—as the result of their immersion in a consumer culture that encouraged self-gratification rather than self-denial.[82]

Other parents expressed this concern more explicitly. Although Dr. and Mrs. A. W. Davis found the actions of the Nashville police on the night of 4 February regrettable, they were even more chagrined at the actions of the students during the strike. "While out at Fisk last Tuesday and seeing the boys loitering on the steps and campus of Jubilee Hall, some in the hall, smoking, with hats on, we wondered what could these boys who forgot to act as gentlemen in a crisis like this do with a student council if they had one." One father, squarely throwing his support behind McKenzie, captured the generational and cultural divide, in terms of the shift from Victorian asceticism to postwar consumerism, that he felt the strike represented. "Those of us who have had the good fortune to come under some 'Puritanical' rule, thank God for it," he wrote, "for, while such training does not seem to have made us less courageous than some others, it does appear to have ever kept us within the law. As long as you and Fisk University stand against smoking, gaming, and debauchery of the young men students and against spectacular and suggestive dress and actions in the young ladies, so long will the Negro race continue to look upon Fisk as a beacon of light."[83] As all of these letters suggest, more than the presidency of McKenzie was at stake. The strike represented, for an older generation of middle-class blacks, the unbottling of youthful iconoclasm. To the extent that the strike and its forced resignation of McKenzie resulted in a number of changes on the campus—such as a more relaxed dress code, the granting of dancing privileges, and the removal of the ban on Greek-letter organizations—the iconoclasm of black youth at Fisk was tied to the ascendancy of consumer culture.

A little less than one month after McKenzie resigned, students at Howard struck against their administration. In many respects, the revolts at Fisk and Howard were worlds apart. As discussed earlier, students at Howard matriculated in a somewhat more permissive environment. They endured no rigid dress code, they were subject to less strict regulations involving male-female socializing, and fraternities and sororities had enjoyed a presence on campus for almost two decades.[84] Moreover, the student body possessed a student council and had a "voice" in the university publication. Still, as at Fisk, the strike at Howard was generated by discontent over the vestiges of late-Victorian moral education.

Stanley Durkee, born in Canada and educated in New England, became the president of Howard in 1918. A white Congregationalist minister with a doctorate from Boston University, he fell firmly in the moral education camp. In his inaugural address, he discussed the importance of building character in students. "The acquisition of knowledge is . . . a secondary and subordinate end; the school's essential task is to make citizens capable of self-support and capable of devotion to humanitarian causes," he reasoned. "Character, moral courage, energy, and a sense of civic duty are qualities that are more vital than mere information." In addition to being in the missionary paternalist tradition, he was, from a purely organizational sense, an efficient administrator. Durkee revamped the administrative structure of the institution, creating a registrar's office, combining the offices of the secretary and treasurer, and forming a faculty council.[85] Durkee's restructuring involved centralizing power within his office, a move that alienated deans, who had enjoyed an autonomous and authoritative position within a strong dean/weak president system since 1889. Durkee also came into conflict with various professors, mainly around the issues of curriculum, salaries, and promotions. By the mid-1920s, he was seen by faculty members, deans, and alumni as somewhat of an autocrat who wielded his power arbitrarily and without the racial sensitivity necessary to head a historically black university.[86]

While Durkee's management style led to an acrimonious relationship between his office and the faculty, his stance toward the student body was less imperious. He was receptive to the grievances of students and responded to their concerns in an equitable manner—even though he often did so only after he was pressured to by either the faculty or the students themselves. Durkee's first taste of student discontent came in 1922 when undergraduates protested against compulsory chapel attendance policy. A "compulsory chapel must go" campaign ensued after the suspension of a handful of students from the School of Applied Sciences for having more than the maximum number of unexcused absences from noon chapel service. Signs demanding the cancellation of mandatory attendance plastered the campus and over seventy students from the School of Applied Sciences threatened to withdraw if the administration continued to enforce the policy selectively. After faculty members voted to endorse voluntary attendance and cautioned Durkee that they might press the argument in Congress that compulsory chapel was a violation of the separation of church and state doctrine, the president and the Board of Trustees nullified the ordinance. The president again yielded to student demands when, in the face of a threatened strike, he authorized the student council to "revise its charter" so that it would have a greater role in extracurricular affairs and disciplinary matters. In March 1924, the student council's attempt to exercise its expanded authority laid the foundation for direct conflict between the student body and the president. The council recommended that mandatory military training be abandoned as a university policy. It further called for the forced resignation of six white professors who, students felt, were "too 'old-fogey' and out of date" and were simply collecting paychecks. The heretofore accommodative president was unwilling to consider the students' requests. As one of the leading historians of the student revolts argues, "abolition of compulsory ROTC might endanger the university's annual congressional appropriation, and the exclusion of whites simply because of their color ran counter to the university's historic opposition to racial discrimination."[87]

A little more than a year later, students renewed their protests against military training. To be sure, there had always been some resistance to ROTC, especially among African Caribbean students who "claimed vigorously and not without reason, that not being citizens of the United States, they were neither desirous nor bound to take military training in any branch of the United States army whatsoever."[88] The campaign against compulsory military training was specifically directed toward the "twenty-cut rule," which mandated the expulsion of any student who had twenty combined unexcused absences between military training and physical education. To the extent that it involved a remonstration against ROTC, the activism of the Howard students was part of a larger campaign that was occurring on campuses across the nation. The Howard protest was sparked by the expulsion of five students on 5 May. On 6 May, the student council communicated to the administration its demands that the students be reinstated "within 48 hours." The following day, 602 students from the College of Liberal Arts, the School of Education, the School of Commerce, and the Junior College signed a strike pledge. After reviewing the attendance records and finding inaccuracies, the faculty voted to reinstate the students. Sensing that there was a swell of discontent among the students, the student council pressed for the nullification of the rule on principle. The faculty refused to abolish the policy and the students began a boycott of classes that virtually shut the campus down for eight days.[89]

What began as a protest against mandatory attendance policy in military training and physical education quickly evolved into a larger indictment of black education in general and the Durkee administration in particular. The students did not take the opportunity to link their protest with that of the alumni, who had been questioning Durkee's ability to run Howard because of his "dictatorial" and arbitrary use of power and the fact that he was also the president of the Curry Graduate School of Expression, an institution in Boston that did not accept blacks. Nor did they, as a whole, endorse the faculty's struggles with Durkee over salaries and promotions, although the student council did propose that they affiliate with the faculty council, the chief bargaining unit of the professors and member union of the American Federation of Labor.[90] However, by the fourth day of the strike, which now numbered some eight hundred students, they were articulating a number of grievances that struck at the very heart of the missionary paternalist model of education. Among them was the complaint that the mandatory attendance policy "placed R.O.T.C. drill and physical education as subjects of major importance, and academic subjects of comparative minor consideration." Moreover, they insisted that Howard was the "only class A school that requires four years of physical education." In an effort to address this problem and end the strike, the faculty, students, and alumni agreed to an arbitration process that would survey the weight given military training and physical education at other institutions. Students complained of the lack of "adequate sanitary facilities" with respect to physical education and the laxity with which attendance records were kept. They also criticized the administration for levying an "unexplained" eight dollar increase in tuition and curtailing the authority of the student council. Finally, in a vein similar to the Fisk protest, the students complained of a rule that forbade "coeds to attend moving pictures on Sunday with male escorts."[91]

By Fisk standards, the uprising at Howard was relatively tame. There was very little disorderly conduct on the "hilltop," as Howard's campus was affectionately called. During the strike, students posted signs with slogans such as "Don't Be an Uncle Tom" and "What Is This Going to Be—An Army or a University?" Striking students sought to prevent their classmates from attending classes by setting up human blockades around campus buildings and there were peaceful rallies and meetings throughout the week. Despite Durkee's warning that he would call out the police to "maintain order at all costs," there were no incidents similar to what happened at Fisk on the night of 4 February. Indeed, the students and the police handled themselves with the utmost professionalism. There were so many students at a meeting held in the Dunbar Theater near the end of the strike, for instance, that officials from the police and fire departments were called out to enforce the maximum occupancy regulations. The *Washington Post* captured the utter ordinariness of the interaction: "Capt. Doyle of the Eighth Precinct, with another policeman, appeared and asked that he might address the students. He was given the order of business by the chairman of the student council and informed that if he would state the purport of his remarks to the chairman a place might be found for him. This he declined to do and he was ruled out of order." The reporter failed to note the officers' reactions but they clearly did not respond to the students in an authoritarian style—nor, unlike at Fisk, was the environment conducive to such a response.[92]

As a Howard alumni committee was attempting to resolve the strike through arbitration, the faculty and administration were trying to end the strike through other means. On 11 May, the faculty met with members of the student council for three hours. The students balked at the faculty's proposition that they would address the student grievances only after the strike was called off. After a four-hour meeting the following day, the faculty decided to play hard ball with the students. They informed the president of the student council that unless the strikers ceased their blockades by the 13th and return to classes by the 14th they would be subject to suspension from the university. The faculty distributed excuse slips to students and informed those who were prevented from attending classes by the strikers to sign them so as not to be mistaken for the disruptive students. The student body quickly responded to the faculty's tactics with a show of solidarity. Female students from Miner Hall, for instance, "met by classes and voted solidly to accept suspension when it comes and go home." Leaders of the student council, moreover, suggested that all the students, especially the striking ones, sign the excuse slips "so that the faculty . . . will receive this morning answers purporting to be from the entire student body." With the news of the faculty's move and the students' countermove, the alumni committee kicked into high gear. In a "stormy" meeting that lasted for four hours on 13 May, the faculty, administration, and student council agreed to a resolution of the strike. By agreeing to return to classes, the students were able to secure promises from the university that no striker would be punished or reported as cutting classes; that the faculty would reassess the mandatory attendance policy and would not enforce the "twenty-cut rule" until the reassessment was complete; and that even if the "twenty-cut rule" was sustained, it would not apply to the current class since it had only been implemented in mid-year. On 14 May, students began attending class and, as the *Washington Post* declared, "Howard university [*sic*] returned to its normal state." [93]

In assessing the end of the student uprising, the *Washington Post* essayed to interpret the mindset of the strikers: "The students, upon representation that their determination to depart would wreck the university, agreed that the principle for which they were fighting was not large enough to be the cause of such disaster." [94] Indeed, the challenges to the Durkee administration fell upon the shoulders of the faculty and alumni, the latter of whom, meeting in Atlantic City in August, drafted a letter calling for the ouster of the president. The grievances primarily dealt with what was considered to be Durkee's "unfitness, mismanagement and misconduct in office" when it came to his dealings with the faculty and the alumni. Interestingly, only one of the eight points of contention dealt with Durkee's relationship with students, and, furthermore, only in a tangential way. "In his management of the University," the alumni committee wrote, "Dr. Durkee has pursued an arbitrary and dictatorial policy and manner, supported by a system of espionage and intimidation, and has established among teachers and students an unenviable reputation for personal suspicion, unreliability of personal word, reliance upon rumor without fair investigation, and personal animus and bias." [95] The charges, and particularly the public press they were receiving, were sufficient to warrant an investigation by the Board of Trustees. After hearing testimony from witnesses opposed to the administration—including such prominent faculty members as dean of liberal arts Kelly Miller, history professor Charles Wesley, and philosophy professor Alain Locke—and Durkee's defense, the Board found "that none of the charges against President J. Stanley Durkee has been sustained by adequate or convincing evidence." It further delivered a statement of unconditional support for the administration. Still, as historian Raymond Wolters notes, "Durkee could see the handwriting on the wall." With such vehement opposition amongst the faculty and alumni, he decided to accept the pastorate of Plymouth Congregational Church in Brooklyn and tendered his official resignation on March 25, 1926.[96]

Unlike the Fisk rebellion, then, the actions of Howard students did not lead directly to the resignation of the president, although it is safe to say that the fact that he had lost confidence among the students placed Durkee in a weak position from which to take on the alumni and faculty. Another fundamental difference between the Howard and Fisk strikes was their scope. Fisk students rebelled against, among other things, the authoritarian regime of McKenzie, which included strict disciplinarian codes, while Howard undergraduates took aim at specific policies regarding military training and physical education. Still, the revolts on both campuses were similar in two respects. On the one hand, they reflected a certain masculinist posturing. The primary targets for Howard students were parts of the curriculum that directly affected male students, while opposition to McKenzie—by both Fisk students and Du Bois—used rhetoric that framed the strike as an effort to assert the race's manhood and honor. On the other hand, both strikes represented the same overarching desire among middle-class black youths to free themselves of the stifling missionary paternalism that characterized their educational institutions. The ways in which these desires became manifest in new models of masculinity and femininity—and the links between these models and consumer culture—is apparent once we look at student life on these campuses in the aftermath of the uprisings.

In the winter of 1927, Fisk officially inaugurated McKenzie's successor, Thomas Elsa Jones. A Quaker from Indiana, Jones received a bachelors and masters of divinity from Hartford Theological Seminary. After doing missionary work in East Asia, he was working on his Ph.D. at Columbia University when he was asked to take over Fisk's presidency. At his inaugural ceremony, Harold S. Brown, president of the senior class, expressed optimism toward Jones and the post-McKenzie era. "We are indeed appreciative, President Jones," Brown remarked, "that you do not judge twentieth century youth in the light of mid-victorian [sic] ideals. Public opinion is almost certain to aim much criticism at you for some of your recent steps, but we will cooperate with you to the nth degree that your actions may be vindicated, and that the veritable army of 'I told you so's' may be forced into the background." The "recent steps" to which Brown referred were a relaxing, or complete overturning, of many of the rigid regulations that characterized the administrations of McKenzie and earlier presidents. Almost immediately, Jones instituted new policies that endorsed respectable male-female socialization, allowed dancing on campus, modified the dress code, permitted smoking among male students, liberalized compulsory chapel, and paved the way for the establishment of Greek-letter organizations.[97]

Optimism was high with regard to the new president—who one student claimed was "a supporter both of the youth movement and the student friendship movement"—and the new opportunities to express the youth culture of the postwar period. Students responded to this new atmosphere, however, with a measured sense of propriety. Both at Fisk and Howard, black middle-class youths were indulgent of the more permissive environments that allowed dancing, listening to vernacular music, smoking, "courting," dressing in modern fashions, and joining fraternities. But many were also careful to enjoy the new luxuries of consumption and leisure within the bounds of respectability. In other words, the campus cultures in the poststrike era were marked by, to risk employing a hackneyed historical term, change and continuity.

One of the areas in which students, especially those at Fisk, found more freedom was fashion. In the Jones era, a committee composed of faculty members and female students drafted new regulations that removed many of the earlier restrictions regarding women's dress. The committee still encouraged women to dress modestly, but the earlier *proscriptions* against women wearing expensive materials and gaudy colors merely became *prescriptions*. One student, writing for the college newspaper, remarked on the sartorial emancipation of women at Fisk and the impact that these new fashion habits had on male students and the interaction between the sexes:

> In their mad desire to gain the favor of the fair ones, some of the men go to great extremes. A few of them whose wardrobes are large, dress for breakfast, dress again for lunch, and a third time, dress for dinner. These 'beau brummels' have the latest thing from Fashion Park, Hickey Freeman, and other noted clothiers. It is a wild pace that they have set. If your father does not own an oil well, or two or three plantations, you cannot keep up. And oh dear! most of the men use powder. But horror of horrors, some are suspected of using rouge! Can you imagine it? And yet they call each other men. What a compliment, what a compliment.

Even though the depiction of some male students as foppish dandies questioned their manhood, the editorialist reaffirmed their presumed heterosexuality when he attributed their behavior to an effort to attract women. He argued that the "comely and elusive beings that reside in Jubilee Hall" were the cause of the fashion excesses of male students. Women, too, dressed in a different outfit for each meal of the day and, moreover, did so in the more trendy fashions. "The latest thing in hosiery and boots are displayed on every feminine leg and foot," he wrote. "Powder, paint, silk dresses, sheer silk stockings, shoes, etc., are women's implements of war on man. Since these wars of the women are usually so successful, why blame them [men, for dressing extravagantly]?" Ultimately, the student suggested, the fashion "wars" on campus were part and parcel of the relaxed environment with respect to male-female socialization. "After the short stroll in the twilight, the students betake themselves to various places and things," he noted. "Some to study, some to frivolity, and some to bed."[98]

As the editorial suggested, another area in which students experienced more freedom was in the social interaction between young men and women.

New attitudes toward the commingling of the sexes—certainly influenced by post-Victorian "sexual liberalism"—emerged on both campuses and became manifest not only in the everyday interaction of men and women, but in particular stances toward dancing and vernacular music.[99] That a more open environment regarding sex existed on black college campuses by the second half of the 1920s is perhaps best represented in a relatively frank discussion of "modern youth and the sex problem" that appeared in Fisk's newspaper. The unnamed author challenged the repressive sexual mores that "were handed down by our forefathers" and suggested that the lack of sex education, coupled with a sexual double standard that was applied to men and women, created a generation that labored under a "sense of shame and a spirit of taboo" when it came to sexual matters. Young college men who were reared in cloistered environments arrived on campus eager to satisfy a "curiosity long held in abeyance by overzealous and puritannical [sic] parents" and, as a result, approached their interactions with the opposite sex "with a daring only equalled [sic] by [their] ignorance." Similarly, young women were "shielded from the actualities of life by an almost insurmountable barrier of prejudice engendered by a religious belief in a double standard which decrees that there are phases of life around which an impenetrable wall must be maintained for the sake of preserving the goodness and purity of women." With the repressiveness that characterized their childhood, adolescence, and young adulthood, was there any doubt that, once unleashed, these youths would behave with a certain amount of sexual recklessness, the author questioned. "It is not a question of 'flaming youth,'" the editorialist opined, "but who set them afire."[100]

More tolerant postures toward the sexuality of youth obtained among officials at both Fisk and Howard after the strikes. Because students at Howard had always been in a somewhat more permissive environment than students at Fisk, the new attitudes amounted to minor adjustments for the former while, for the latter, they constituted a veritable sea change. For instance, the debate on whether to use colored or white lights at student socials on Howard's campus barely generated discussion among the student body— although it did warrant a vote by the Faculty Committee—whereas at Fisk, articles abounded as to whether or not dancing between the sexes should be allowed on campus.[101] Herbert Shaw, a junior at Fisk, argued that dancing, what he considered to be a "wholesome form of recreation," should be permitted by university officials. He not only pointed out that dancing was a time-honored cultural practice in all forms of society; he went on to suggest that the continued ban at Fisk would force students to seek out dance opportunities in less than ideal environments. "A restriction upon a legal free action makes of that action a 'badge of freedom,' " he argued. "An institution which drives from its presence a thing that is desired by its inmates drives the obtainment of that thing into places where the result of that thing will be in no wise as good as it would be if that thing were rightly obtained in the right place." Apparently, Fisk students had been fulfilling their desire to dance for some time. Another editorial, praising the administration for rescinding the dance law in November 1926, reminded readers that "students have resorted to all manner of subterfuge to get around the old dance law whose indefiniteness in wording offered excellent opportunities for technical misinterpretation. This had as its result obvious violation in the form of 'bootleg' dances. Quite naturally these affairs were inadequately chaperoned." But the sanctioning of dancing on Fisk's campus did not translate into the sanctioning of ignominious behavior. While commending the relaxation of dance rules, the editorialist admonished the student body to act responsibly and respectably. "In our rejoicing we are not blind to the dangers that lurk in the future," he wrote. "Another responsibility has been placed on the shoulders of the students. We have asked for dancing; we have been granted it. We must not give occasion for regret." [102]

With the marked change of attitudes toward dancing came a more relaxed position on what kinds of music could be played, and listened to, on campus. Again, however, as jazz and blues found an eager audience on the grounds of Howard and Fisk, some students took a fairly circumspect approach to these vernacular forms of music. Jazz and blues were the subject of intense debate among the students at Fisk. John Hewlett, for instance, puzzled over the absence, to any great degree, of jazz on campus given that firstly, it "arose out of the music of the American Negro" and secondly, it had enjoyed recent popularity in Europe. In advocating for the appreciation of jazz by the Fisk community, Hewlett posited an essentialist argument that would have made Claude McKay and Langston Hughes proud. "There is a subtle unconscious philosophy underlying all our jazz and blues songs—that peculiar experience of making laughter and joy the reaction to sorrow instead of tears," he wrote. "It is this making fun of one's sorrows by dwelling on them that is characteristically and distinctively Negroid." Hewlett was perhaps responding to an earlier article in the school newspaper that was critical of jazz. The article was a recounting of a lecture by Harvey Waugh, chair of Fisk's Music Department. Although Waugh felt that he could "learn to look for beauty rather than sensuousness," he nonetheless criticized jazz for its primitivist simplicity. "I do not condemn all jazz, for there is some of it that does contain beauty of melody and originality," Waugh conceded. "But when we hear the thump thump of bass notes in a barbaric emphasis of rythm [sic] and turn our ears away from musical forms that take a little thinking, then we might just as well say that one should read all Elinor Glyn and none of Dickens."[103]

There was a similar debate around vernacular music at Howard. One article criticized the practice—primarily at parties hosted by fraternities—of setting the school song to a syncopated jazz beat. Another article, although in a tone of resignation that recognized the popularity of jazz, was nonetheless critical of certain by-products of the new music. "Now, in the matter of dancing," the article stated, "Howard University is greatly influenced by the type of dancing that is characteristic of Washington groups. Sometimes students are seen dancing 'cheek to cheek,' wrapped in each other's arms. Then too, the 'Charleston cutout,' the latest and most popular of modern freak dances, is sometimes danced as well [as] several other contortionist steps called dances. . . . We cannot expect young people of today to dance the 'Virginia Reel' and like dances," the editorial concluded, "but modern dances can at least be graceful." The article further lamented the effects that jazz was having on the leisure practices of young men and women. It attributed to jazz ostentatious fashion styles and the growing custom of attending parties in single-sex groups, instead of young ladies being escorted by respectable gentlemen.[104]

The consumption of alcohol and tobacco also produced a vigorous debate on the campuses of Fisk and Howard. Given that the Eighteenth Amendment and the Volstead Act were the laws of the land throughout the 1920s, both institutions' official position regarding alcohol remained squarely behind prohibition, although some students were openly questioning its efficacy by the end of the decade.[105] Smoking was an issue that was more open to debate. In the early months of 1927, Fisk's administration responded to demands by male students for the right to smoke on campus by setting up a special room in the Chocolate Shop. As part of this policy, students caught smoking anywhere else on campus, including their dormitory room, were in jeopardy of losing their right to board at Fisk. Despite the accommodations provided by the administration, students pressed for a greater relaxation of rules, including, first, the creation of special smoking rooms in the men's dormitories and, later, the right to smoke on the campus walkways and public streets adjacent to the campus. One individual suggested that smoking had become such a common habit among the male students that "if the administration were to attempt to enforce the present rule regarding smoking in the dormitory, nearly eighty per cent of the men would be penalyzed [sic] for infringement." He went on to suggest that the restrictions placed on the consumption of a legal product were tantamount to a contravention of students' rights. "In conclusion," he intoned, "I suggest that the faculty revise the present rulings regarding smoking. Revise them with the realization that we are men." Despite the gendered rationale behind his argument, some students also contended that female students should be allowed to smoke. An editorial in the *Greater Fisk Herald*, speculating that upwards of 75 percent of Fisk women smoked, suggested that accommodations be made for them so that they would not have to puff secretly in their room and run the risk of inadvertently starting fires. Notwithstanding these arguments, the administration continued to prohibit public smoking by men and any smoking whatsoever by women until 1935.[106]

The consumption and leisure practices that, if not ushered in, were certainly legitimated by the student rebellions of 1925, led to a fair amount of consternation among students themselves. George Streator, one of the leaders of the Fisk strike, pointed out, in ridicule, smokers who recklessly discarded their butts in their rooms; "young gallants who believe in giving the ladies an extra advantage of their company by taking those needlessly long strolls about the campus"; and "those simple young sheiks who like to brag about their proficiency in the 'Charleston' and their ability with the flask." He reminded students that these were "worthy examples of collegiate light-mindedness." Another editorial in the *Herald* stressed the need to improve athletics through a physical education department. Athletics, according to the editorialist, would "do much to lessen the number of Romeos that trouble the campus in spring time. The Fisk men are beginning to show a falling of[f] in the dignified carriage that should characterize a college man."[107] At Howard, too, students complained that some undergraduates were "carrying our social life too far." Prompted by a "scandal" in which a coed stayed out all night without a chaperone, the student newspaper ran an article criticizing the personal behavior of students when it came to the opposite sex. Although the article indirectly rebuked young men for not upholding "their responsibilities of the protection of womanhood," it suggested that women were ultimately at fault. "The average fellow," the article stated,

> goes just as far as the female permits him to and checks up on his behavior only when he becomes conscious of indignation on her part. If she doesn't like him to smoke, he will stop smoking; if she doesn't like slang he will stop using it. But on the other hand, if she encourages and admires the beast in man he gladly permits his beast instinct to predominate. There is no doubt that there are many things that women do to please men, such as dress, bobbed hair, and love letters, but for the more intimate social relationships the average man adjusts himself to the type and social standards of the girl he admires.

The article elicited one response that sought to redirect the blame. A self-described feminist wrote a letter to the editor suggesting that, in fact, women were not responsible for men's behavior. "It was the honor of these men who invited and escorted ladies to a party to see that they return in a respectable condition," she wrote, referring to the scandal that sparked the original editorial. "This, any man would demand for his sister, and yet you take someone else's sister to disgrace. Now is this manly? I am not totally excusing these girls," the letter writer continued, "yet, after all is said and done, the responsibility for her honor rests with you." [108] Streator's condemnation of the "young gallant" and the "sheik," the *Herald*'s reproach of the "Romeo," and the exchange in the *Hilltop* are indicative of a number of things. First, that these criticisms were leveled suggests that, to a greater degree than before, students on these campuses were rejecting the late-Victorian, bourgeois social conventions that educators at these institutions sought to maintain. Second, and just as significantly, that these criticisms were leveled points to the fact that these challenges to the social and gender conventions of an earlier generation did not represent, or culminate in, a neat and clean break. Rather, many within the generation that came of age in the postwar era still adhered to older and increasingly outdated notions of respectability and producer-ist models of manliness even as they existed within a consumer culture that encouraged an alternative model of masculinity.

The last, and perhaps most contentious, area of college life in which this ambivalence showed itself was the presence of Greek-letter organizations. Again, as in other areas of leisure, Howard students operated in a less repressive environment than undergraduates at Fisk. Fraternities and sororities had been on Howard's campus since 1908 and, despite some trepidation on the part of university officials to endorse "secret societies," they enjoyed a fairly lofty position within the university community. The *University Journal*, for instance, reported on the establishment of a chapter of Alpha Phi Alpha by remarking that "it bids fair to become quite a factor in the student life at Howard, for it is fraternal and has noble purposes." Another article, speaking about fraternities in general, argued that they "aim[ed] to promote brotherhood among its members, aid the weak and discountenance evil." By the middle of the second decade of the twentieth century, five undergraduate fraternities and sororities and at least two professional Greek-letter organizations were present on campus and, with the blessings of the administration, were a fundamental part of college life.[109] In contrast, prior to McKenzie's departure, many male undergraduates joined fraternities at Meharry while female students had the option of joining sorority chapters located in Nashville. In an effort to promote school loyalty, President Jones and a committee

Fisk University's Lampados Club, pledges to Omega Psi Phi Fraternity. (From Lighthouse, 1930; courtesy of Special Collections, Franklin Library, Fisk University)

consisting of faculty members and students recommended that Greek-letter organizations be allowed on campus. By the spring of 1927, the *Herald* boasted of the presence of Greeks in student government, college athletics, and the newspaper itself. By 1929, thirty-five of the sixty-six members of the graduating class belonged to Greek-letter organizations.[110]

Despite the relative success fraternities and sororities had in becoming embedded in the institutional life of Fisk and Howard, there was hardly any consensus regarding the benefits that these organizations brought to the university community. Supporters of the Greek system argued that they facilitated the development of character and respectability among young adults, and that their emphasis on scholarship and success was wholly in keeping with the college mission. As one Fisk student asked, "What better examples of college culture and ideals of manhood can be emphasized than those that characterize fraternity men?" The interrogator conceded that there were "objectionable features to Fraternities such as socialism, commercialism, and favoritism" but went on to argue that, to the extent that these existed, they were bastardizations of the original fraternity ideal.[111]

Although socialist tendencies were rarely pointed out as flaws of the Greek system by its critics, the charges of "favoritism" and "commercialism" were. Opponents of fraternities and sororities argued that they constituted a set of cliques in which "connection" replaced merit as the ultimate determinant of success. There was a concern among many who held this position that the involvement of Greeks in campus politics would undermine the democratic and inclusive spirit of student governance. One Fisk student, lamenting that fraternities "have shown such a mean, nasty spirit of non-cooperation in the past," noted that Greeks running for positions on the student council exploited their membership in the fraternity in order to garner votes. "Such conduct not only shows a baseness of principle of the fraternity involved," he remarked, "but also a desire to dominate the student body instead of to serve."[112] Others argued that the Greek-letter organization fostered fidelity to a very narrow group instead of encouraging loyalty to the larger university community. One student at Howard expressed chagrin at the exclusiveness and isolation that characterized the Greek system. "Fraternities are supposed to represent the highest manhood and scholarship in the university," the article reminded its readers. "They are supposed to be a PART of the University and consequently secondary to it. But it is long since the fraternities made their choice upon scholarship; since the University was the primary consideration; since the slogan was 'school' first—fraternity second." The article noted that "it is high time for our fraternal organizations to get away from the stereotyped snobbishness and come together into a big 'oneness' of purpose, a bigger and better Howard."[113]

Charges of "commercialism" were also aimed at Greek-letter organizations. Reports of extravagant dances and entertainments fed into these charges as did the public spectacle of being "on line"—or going through the hazing process in order to become a member. Van Taylor, a Howard student, criticized going "on line." In an article replete with florid, overblown language, Taylor lambasted the "kingdom of Fraternalism" and its tradition of "Hell Week":

Ye Gods of Brotherhood, and Shades of departed spirits, but what manner of desire is this that will lead young men to turn their backs on the carefully cultivated ideals of a lifetime; that will force them to deny even the Lady Fair of their hearts and with utmost disrespect for the conventions of society array themselves in garb of various hue? Thrust their manly but unshaven chins high into the air on one day, and the very next bow their heads in meek submission, and bark even as the lowest canine of the street, at the demand of one who has experienced [all?] the pangs of humiliation thru which he is just passing?

Taylor's turgid attack on fraternities evinced a longing to return to a golden age in which Victorian manliness was the normative model of manhood. His particular use of language—"carefully cultivated ideals," which was evocative of character, and "Lady Fair," which, by implication, posited black middle-class youths as knights-errant, icons of Victorian manliness in children's popular literature and historical romances—reflected a sense of mourning for a specific style of respectable manhood that was increasingly giving way to one in which transgressing social norms through spectacular public performance was itself becoming the norm. For Taylor, the modern college fraternity man was the antithesis of the stoic, self-controlled Victorian gentleman.[114]

To be sure, Greek-letter organizations did more than throw parties and organize public rituals of initiation that placed an emphasis on the spectacular performance of the body. Fraternities and sororities raised money for scholarships, sponsored activities for the edification of the entire campus, and continued to encourage academic excellence. Still, by the end of the decade, Greek-letter organizations were associated with social climbing, group exclusion, and personal gratification. That these perceived characteristics were inextricably linked to the emergence of a larger consumer culture in which the personal use and bodily display of commodities became constitutive of individual and group identity is apparent in a statement made by Du Bois at Howard's commencement in 1930. "Our college man today is, on the average," he charged acerbically, "a man untouched by real culture. He deliberately surrenders to selfish and even silly ideals, swarming into semiprofessional athletics and Greek letter societies, and affecting to despise scholarship and the hard grind of study and research. The greatest meetings of the Negro college year like those of the white college year have become vulgar exhibitions of liquor, extravagance, and fur coats. We have in our colleges a growing mass of stupidity and indifference."[115] Du Bois's conflation of materialism, academic laziness, and participation in extracurricular activities such as fraternities was emblematic of a concern, shared by older blacks, that middle-class black youths were becoming too embedded within American consumer culture.[116] There is an unmistakable irony in Du Bois's criticism of black youth. Only five years earlier, he was spearheading a movement against the missionary paternalism of black colleges, a movement through which black students articulated their own desires to participate in consumer culture. Whether or not he perceived the explicit connection, by the end of the decade, Du Bois was chagrined at the transformation of black middle-class youth culture and its attendant gender conventions, which he, in part, unintentionally and implicitly endorsed.

■ The struggles that students engaged in to expand their autonomy were not just attempts to enjoy the personal and psychological benefits of consumption. Rather, black youths at Howard and Fisk Universities sought to free themselves of the stifling social conventions that characterized the pedagogical philosophy of missionary paternalism and their parents' claims to respectable, middle-class status. Embedded within their challenges to the administrations of their respective institutions was a transformation of the very organizing principles of middle-class identity: freedom to consume supplanted adherence to producer values; self-expression displaced respectability; and personality replaced character. This is perhaps best captured by an editorial in the *Greater Fisk Herald* in 1929 that commented upon a talk delivered at the campus chapel in which the speaker argued that "the struggle for personality is one of the strongest motives for existence." The editorial went on to sum up the message: "Where there is no striving for the development of personalities, there is retrogression. Study the lives and biographies of some of the great personalities of the world and see how they have achieved a personality and then try to make one for yourself, for the making of personality is the making of the individual." [117]

As the 1920s came to a close, a consumerist model of masculinity had become firmly ensconced in the campuses of black colleges. To be sure, this new model—and its performance through various modes of youth culture—was characteristic of a larger transformation of gender conventions among the American middle class, black and white. In the case of African American and African Caribbean young men, the struggles that they engaged in over the right to consume and participate in certain forms of leisure were aimed at asserting a bodily exuberance in the face of the bodily discipline that was represented by physical culture, military training, and the moral education philosophy of higher educational institutions. In this sense, they were reconfiguring the relationship between the body and manhood. A physically fit body was no longer primarily an indicator of good character, as Garveyites and devotees to physical culture argued. Rather, a physically fit body was an end in itself. Or if it was a means it was, along with the consumer goods one owned, a means to enhance one's image in the eyes of others. Bodily virtuoso and sexual virility, then, were more important in determining one's manhood than character and respectability. Even as older middle-class blacks and even some black youth lamented this transformation, there was an inevitability about it given the confluence of the currents of consumer, youth, and jazz cultures. A Fisk student expressed the ineluctable character of the transition. "The question in our minds," the student insouciantly queried, "is why so much row about the wickedness, cussedness and general liberty of the younger generation. . . . Youth has appeared and ever will appear wild to the preceding generations, and to find an explanation for this attitude is to find an explanation of why an explosion explodes as it explodes."[118]

Conclusion
The Respectable and the Damned

In 1925, the noted African American sociologist E. Franklin Frazier contributed an essay to *The New Negro* on Durham, North Carolina, a city he considered to be the economic center of black America. In this early sketch from his lifelong effort at documenting "the rise of a new middle class" among the black population in the United States, Frazier initially praised the efforts of this industrious group. The gendered language he employed was suggestive of Garveyite and Masonic rhetoric. "No longer can men say that the Negro is lazy and shiftless and a consumer," Frazier wrote. "He has gone to work. He is a producer. He is respectable. He has a middle class." Frazier delineated this process of class formation not only by highlighting the relationship between production and respectability, but by emphasizing the polarity between the nascent black middle class and its working-class brethren. Middle-class blacks' "lives are as free from the Negro's native love of leisure and enjoyment of life as [Benjamin] Franklin's life," he argued. "Hard work was their rule. We see them assuming the rôle of promoter and organizer. And finally we find them in the rôle of the modern business man."[1] Thirty years later, Frazier took a much more critical posture with respect to the black middle class. Indeed, he lamented that the generation coming of age in the 1920s and beyond had departed significantly from the "canons of respectability" that shaped the traditional black elite and the "old middle class." The new generation of this "emerging black bourgeoisie," Frazier argued, was characterized by "conspicuous consumption," unrespectable social conduct, and scandalous "sex behavior." Although Frazier directed the bulk of his criticism at the black middle class of the 1940s and 1950s, he located the initial departure from the traditional values of industry, thrift, temperance, and respectability in the events of the 1920s, when black college campuses were in upheaval and blacks were moving to northern, urban areas in great numbers.[2]

Frazier's voice was one among a chorus of voices that was growing ever critical of black middle-class youth. As we saw in the final chapter, W. E. B. Du Bois's commencement address at Howard University in 1930 criticized a "growing mass of stupidity and indifference" and an increasing preoccupation with consumer goods and leisure on black college campuses.[3] Along with the irreverence many of these critics associated with jazz and consumer culture, the younger generation also evinced a certain "pagan" character. Francis J. Grimké, a member of the Washingtonian black elite, Presbyterian minister, and NAACP official, for instance, wrote to James Weldon Johnson, one of the composers of "Lift Every Voice and Sing," the National Negro Anthem, complaining of the spiritual laxity of younger blacks. "We need, as a race, men of prominence, men in high places, who believe in God, and in the Bible, and in Jesus Christ," he declared, "in order to help stem the tide of atheism, infidelity, and irreligion that is setting in more and more in this age in which we are living. One of the things that particularly interested me in your splendid Anthem, was that it reflected the training under which you were brought up in a Christian home, with parents such as you had, a godly father and mother."[4]

Sometime before he died at a tragically young age, Wallace Thurman, reflecting on the Harlem Renaissance and the older black middle class's less than positive response to the younger literati's cultural production, succinctly captured the low esteem in which he and many others were held by the older generation. "Negroes stood by," he wrote, "a little subdued, a little surprised, torn between being proud that certain of their group had achieved distinction, and being angry because a few of these arrived ones had ceased to be what the group considered 'constructive,' having in the interim, produced work that went against the grain, in that they did not wholly qualify to the adjective 'respectable.'" Indeed, as if to underline Grimké's lamentation, Thurman labeled this latter group—in which he included himself—as the "damned."[5]

Not all older middle-class blacks looked at the Jazz Age generation as hopelessly mired in the hedonism of the postwar era; but by and large, they were attentive to the fact that black middle-class youths were rapidly jettisoning the Victorian framework of values that had structured their parents' gender and class identities. When Rodney L. Curtis, worshipful master of Joppa Lodge No. 55, located in Manhattan, gave his farewell address in 1930, he spoke of the need to come to grips with this fundamental shift in the worldview of younger blacks. Alarmed at the dwindling numbers of black men joining the ranks of Prince Hall Freemasonry, Curtis implored his brothers to take steps to transform the Craft into a fraternal body that could engage the minds and serve the needs of the younger generation. "We should ever be mindful of the fact that mysticism like religion does not appeal to the present trend of mind as of years gone by," Curtis counseled his lodge. "Therefore we must shape our side lines to meet the demands of the modern mind by improving strongly upon our social side and also our intellectual and charitable side." Curtis's assessment of the order—along with concern raised elsewhere about the "lax attendance" of younger Freemasons at lodge meetings—suggests that fewer and fewer younger African American and African Caribbean men were attracted to an institution through which many of their fathers had achieved and enacted a respectable manliness. The decline in numbers may have been concomitant with the growth of Greek-letter organizations. But Curtis's reasoning that adherence to an antiquated tradition of mysticism failed to attract potential members indicates the possibility that abstract principles such as character and production—embedded within the legends, doctrine, and rituals of the order—no longer resonated with younger black men as markers of manhood.[6]

The concerns raised about black youth by Frazier, Du Bois, and Grimké, reflect not only the gap that so commonly occurs between generations throughout history; they also reflect the specific cultural transformation that characterized the United States's metamorphosis from a producer- to a consumer-oriented society in the early twentieth century. This shift from an ethos of production to one of consumption, from character to personality, from self-denial to self-expression and self-fulfillment, produced cultural reverberations within the black middle class. These reverberations are evident in the denunciations of the youth culture that was associated with the Jazz Age— a constellation of styles, aesthetics, and manners whose very logic was predicated upon a rejection of the producer values of late-Victorian society. These cultural repercussions, moreover, held significant implications in terms of gender identities and relations within the black community. As younger African American and African Caribbean men increasingly participated in the creation and maintenance of a vibrant, modern Jazz Age culture—through particular modes of consumption and leisure practices, and through the cultural production of the New Negro era—they articulated meanings of manhood that differed radically from those of an earlier generation of black middle-class men. The commitment to manliness so evident in the lives of Prince Hall Freemasons and Garveyites hardly held the same kind of currency among younger middle-class blacks. By the mid-1920s, young black men in speakeasies in Chicago and Los Angeles, literary salons in Harlem and Greenwich Village, and student unions in Nashville and Washington, D.C., were expressing discontent with the stifling gender conventions that undergirded their parents' claims to bourgeois status as well as black nationalists' assertions of self-determination.

Of course, the supplanting of the normative model of manliness by a modern ethos of masculinity within the middle-class black community paralleled a similar shift among middle-class whites. The hegemonic nature of dominant cultural ideas of manhood—clearly informed by Anglo-American bourgeois gender conventions—ensured that this would be so. What I have tried to do here, however, is recognize the hegemonic power of white manhood while locating African American and African Caribbean men as agents within these hegemonic gender conventions. In doing so, I acknowledge that black men engaged in their gender identity formation in relation to, and in tension with, the dominant culture and its gender ideals. Black men, in other words, were not merely screens on which white men projected their anxieties about manhood. Nor did black men reduce their gender identity to a measure of their political and economic citizenship or an expression of resistance to the various forms of marginalization to which they were subjected. African American and African Caribbean men in the first three decades of the twentieth century imagined and performed a gendered self in a number of different sites, through a number of different modalities (including work, leisure, cultural production, organizational life, love and sex), and within a web of relations that consisted of whites, black women, and black children. In that sense, this book also recognizes that changing conceptions of manhood shaped the relationships between black men and black women and among black men themselves—relationships that were as rooted in notions of difference and the reality of power as were the relationships between blacks and the dominant culture.[7]

Notes

Abbreviations

ADP	Aaron Douglas Papers, SCRBC
ALP	Alain Leroy Locke Papers, MSRC
ASP	Arthur Schomburg Papers, SCRBC
Beinecke	Beinecke Rare Book and Manuscript Library
BOT/HU	Records of Meetings of the Board of Trustees of Howard University, HUA
CBL	Universal Negro Improvement Association's *Constitution and Book of Laws*
CCP	Countee Cullen Papers (microfilm), SCRBC
CMC	Claude McKay Correspondence, JWJMC
CVVP	Carl Van Vechten Papers, NYPL
CVVP-Black	Carl Van Vechten Papers (Black Correspondence), JWJMC
FMC	Fayette A. McKenzie Presidential Collection, FUSC
FUSC	Special Collections, Franklin Library, Fisk University, Nashville, Tenn.
HUA	Howard University Archives, Washington, D.C.
HWC	Harry A. Williamson Collection on Negro Masonry, SCRBC
JBP	John E. Bruce Papers, SCRBC
JTP	Jean Toomer Papers, JWJMC
JWJMC	James Weldon Johnson Memorial Collection, Beinecke
JWJP	James Weldon Johnson Papers, JWJMC
LHP	Langston Hughes Papers, JWJMC
MGMC	Marcus Garvey Memorial Collection, FUSC
MSRC	Moorland-Spingarn Research Center, Howard University, Washington, D.C.
NAACP	National Association for the Advancement of Colored People
NYPL	New York Public Library, New York, N.Y.
OES	Order of the Eastern Star
ROTC	Reserve Officers Training Corps
SCRBC	Schomburg Center for Research in Black Culture, NYPL
UNIA	Universal Negro Improvement Association
WEBDP	W. E. B. Du Bois Papers (microfilm), Alexander Library, Rutgers University, New Brunswick, N.J.

Introduction

1. Hilkey, *Character Is Capital*, 1–12 (quote on p. 5). Also see Rotundo, *American Manhood*, esp. 18–25; Coben, *Rebellion against Victorianism*, 3–35. One could argue that these definitions turned not only on gender, but race and ethnicity as well.

2. Testi, "Gender of Reform Politics," 1509–12; Paula Baker, "Domestication of Politics"; Rotundo, *American Manhood*, 217–21.

3. Hoganson, *Fighting for American Manhood*, 1–14; Bederman, *Manliness and Civilization*, 170–215; Rotundo, *American Manhood*, 232–39; Kaplan, "Black and Blue on San Juan Hill"; Rydell, *All the World's a Fair*.

4. Quoted in Scott, *Negro Migration*, 169.

5. Higginbotham, "African-American Women's History," 260–62. On unisex toilets, see Scott, *Negro Migration*, 22. For an excellent discussion of segregation and gender, see Gilmore, *Gender and Jim Crow*.

6. As Jacqueline Jones reminds us, however, at the turn of the century, 90 percent of blacks within the United States lived in the South and 80 percent of southern blacks lived in rural areas, where Jim Crow was extensively embedded in social relations. See Jones, *Labor of Love*, 80.

7. Chateauvert, *Marching Together*; Du Bois, *Souls of Black Folk*, 37; Barkley Brown, "Negotiating and Transforming the Public Sphere"; Higginbotham, *Righteous Discontent*; Gaines, *Uplifting the Race*; Mitchell, "'The Black Man's Burden.'"

8. James, *Holding Aloft the Banner*, 12, 16–23, 32–38, 41–43, 358; Holt, *Problem of Freedom*, 145–46, 345–79; Watkins-Owens, *Blood Relations*, 12–15.

9. Harris, *Harder We Run*, 55–56; Earl Lewis, "Expectations, Economic Opportunitites." For overviews of black migration during this period, see Henri, *Black Migration*; Marks, *Farewell—We're Good and Gone*.

10. Gatewood, *Aristocrats of Color*, 332–43; Grossman, *Land of Hope*, 129–30; Trotter, *Black Milwaukee*, 80–81. The classic study of the "new" black middle class is Frazier, *Black Bourgeoisie*.

11. Trotter, *Black Milwaukee*, 83; Gaines, *Uplifting the Race*, 13–17. Also see Neilson, *Black Ethos*, 68–76.

12. Trotter, *Black Milwaukee*, 80–110; Grossman, *Land of Hope*, 128–30; Earl Lewis, *In Their Own Interests*, 38–46.

13. Brereton, "Society and Culture in the Caribbean," 90–92.

14. James, *Holding Aloft the Banner*, 38–41, 70, 81. On the percentage of "better-educated classes" among total island populations, see Watkins-Owens, *Blood Relations*, 12–15.

15. Susman, "'Personality' and the Making of Twentieth-Century Culture," in Susman, *Culture as History*, 271–85. Susman's classic formulation of the transition from a culture of character to a culture of personality predated most of the scholarship on the social construction of masculinity but it is central to understanding the transformation from manliness to masculinity. See Rotundo, *American Manhood*, 282–86, who

characterizes this transition as one of "self-made manhood" to "passionate man-hood"; Bederman, *Manliness and Civilization*, 10–20, who defines the shift as one of "civilized manliness" to "primitive" or "natural masculinity." Also see Pendergast, *Creating the Modern Man*, 1–18; Erenberg, *Steppin' Out*, 237–38.

16. Scott, "Gender." This distinction between identity and convention is influenced by Elizabeth Fox-Genovese. In her work on gender in the antebellum South, she writes: "Gender conventions direct fundamental human impulses into socially acceptable and useful channels and thereby serve the needs of individuals as well as of so-ciety. They derive as much from custom and practice as from ideology. Influenced both by tradition and circumstances, they constitute compelling ideals dissemi-nated through literate, visual, and oral cultures. They figure among society's most influential and binding elements, for, in telling people how to be men and women, they tell them how to relate to society." See *Within the Plantation Household*, 194.

On the performative dimension of gender—or gender as process—see Butler, *Gender Trouble*, who notes that gender is, in part, "the repeated stylization of the body, a set of repeated acts within a highly rigid regulatory frame that congeal over time to produce the appearance of substance, of a natural sort of being" (33); Uebel, "Men in Color: Introducing Race and the Subject of Masculinities," in Stecopoulos and Uebel, *Race and the Subject of Masculinities*, who argues that "racial and gender iden-tities emerge as dynamic performances scripted, rehearsed, and (re)enacted in the presence of one another" (5); and Bederman, *Manliness and Civilization*, who notes that masculinity is the "cultural process whereby concrete individuals are consti-tuted as members of a preexisting social category" (7).

17. Segal, *Slow Motion*, esp. 114; Connell, *Masculinities*, 75; Bederman, *Manliness and Civili-zation*, 10–31; Fox-Genovese, *Within the Plantation Household*, 29.

18. In this sense, gender operates, like race, as a metalanguage. See Higginbotham, "African-American Women's History."

19. For critiques of sex role and psychoanalytic theories, see Connell, "The Big Pic-ture"; Segal, "Changing Men"; Donaldson, "What Is Hegemonic Masculinity?"; Scott, "Gender," 1061–64.

The social constructionist literature is vast and it might be helpful to men-tion only some of the representative works. See Rotundo, *American Manhood*; Hilkey, *Character Is Capital*; Bederman, *Manliness and Civilization*; Kimmel, *Manhood in America*; Carnes and Griffen, *Meanings for Manhood*; Chudacoff, *Age of the Bachelor*; Gorn, *Manly Art*; Baron, "Other Side of Gender Antagonism"; Mangan and Walvin, *Manliness and Morality*.

20. Even the best scholarship that posits the centrality of race in constructions of manhood fails to attribute agency to black men. In Gail Bederman's brilliant ex-amination of the ways in which ideas of race and "civilization" shaped dominant definitions of manhood in the late nineteenth and early twentieth centuries, an

abstracted black masculinity hovers above the individuals who are articulating discourses of manliness and masculinity. These include two white men (G. Stanley Hall and Theodore Roosevelt), one black woman (Ida B. Wells), and one white woman (Charlotte Perkins Gilman). Bederman does discuss the legendary African American boxer, Jack Johnson, and how he manipulated the dominant cultural ideas of manhood, but his voice is not heard to the same extent as the others, which reproduces, on some level, his non-agency.

21. Connell, *Masculinities*, 76–77; Donaldson, "What Is Hegemonic Masculinity?," 644–47.

22. Kimmel, *Manhood in America*, 5 (original emphasis).

23. Ibid., 98, 230–31, 271.

24. Franklin, "Surviving the Institutional Decimation of Black Males"; Blake and Darling, "Dilemmas of the African American Male"; Hunter and Davis, "Hidden Voices of Black Men"; Ferguson, *Bad Boys*; Majors and Billson, *Cool Pose*; Westwood, "Racism, Black Masculinity"; Fiske, "Surveilling the City."

25. See Sale, *Slumbering Volcano*; Mercer, "Black Masculinity and the Sexual Politics of Race," in Mercer, *Welcome to the Jungle*, 131–70; Blount and Cunningham, *Representing Black Men*; Carbado, *Black Men on Race*; Carby, *Race Men*; Hatt, " 'Making a Man of Him' "; hooks, "Reconstructing Black Masculinity"; Harper, *Are We Not Men?*; Segal, *Slow Motion*, 168–204; Wallace, *Constructing the Black Masculine*.

26. See, for example, Black, *Dismantling Black Manhood*; Young, *Antebellum Black Activists*; James Oliver Horton and Lois E. Horton, "Violence, Protest, and Identity: Black Manhood in Antebellum America," in Horton, *Free People of Color*, 80–96; Bolster, " 'To Feel like a Man' "; Cullen, " 'I's a Man Now' "; Hine and Jenkins, *A Question of Manhood*; Booker, *"I Will Wear No Chain!"*; Estes, " 'I AM A MAN!' "; Pendergast, *Creating the Modern Man*.

27. Hunter and Davis, "Constructing Gender," 477. Of course, some scholarship does just this. See Duneier, *Slim's Table*; Dorsey, "Gendered History of African Colonization"; Gaines, *Uplifting the Race*; Gilmore, *Gender and Jim Crow*; Chateauvert, *Marching Together*; Mjagkij, "True Manhood." This is not an exhaustive assessment of the scholarship on black masculinity. There are several works that I have not mentioned, some of which are collections of essays using various approaches and, therefore, defy my categorization. See, for example, Belton, *Speak My Name*; Byrd and Guy-Sheftall, *Traps*.

28. See, for example, Carby, *Race Men*. My thinking about black masculinity in this way has been greatly influenced by Higginbotham, "African American Women's History."

29. Raymond Williams, *Marxism and Literature*, 110, 112–13. For a good discussion of cultural hegemony as an analytical tool, see Lears, "Concept of Cultural Hegemony."

Part One

1. "Death of Sir John Edward Bruce, Knight Commander of the Nile," *Negro World*, 16 August 1924; Burkett, *Black Redemption*, 149–53; Gilbert, *Selected Writings of John Edward Bruce*, 1–9.

2. "5,000 Bow at Bier of Duke of Uganda," [N.Y.?] *World*, 11 August 1924, MGMC, Box 8, Fol. 1, FUSC; "Death of Sir John Edward Bruce."

3. The following description is based on William Grimshaw's discussion of Masonic funeral rites. See *Official History*, 377–86.

4. Hill, *Marcus Garvey and UNIA Papers*, 1:lxi.

5. Ibid., 1:lx–lxiv; Stein, *World of Marcus Garvey*, 224–25; Tolbert, *UNIA and Black Los Angeles*, 96; Watkins-Owens, *Blood Relations*, 103–4.

6. Davis, *History of Freemasonry*, 21–39; Grimshaw, *Official History*, 69–77; Wesley, *Prince Hall*, 34–35.

   From Grimshaw's 1903 publication onward, the standard narrative of Hall's life had him born in Bridgetown, Barbados, in 1748 to an English father and a free woman of French and African descent. In 1765, he supposedly migrated to Boston where he was a leather worker and soap maker, a property owner and voter, and a Methodist minister. In 1977, Wesley's biography took Grimshaw to task for providing an erroneous portrait of Hall. Conceding the dearth of concrete evidence, Wesley makes the following judgments regarding Hall: he was most likely born in 1735; his nationality and parentage are unknown; he may not have been a minister; and he may have been a slave who was manumitted in 1770. Despite this important corrective, Grimshaw's original portrait, transmitted through earlier histories than Wesley's, continues to find its way into more recent histories of Prince Hall and black Freemasonry. For an interesting discussion of Grimshaw and Wesley, see Wallace, " 'Are We Men?' ", 399–405.

7. Grimshaw, *Official History*, 84–86, 90, 304–5. A note should be made here about the organizational and governmental structure of Masonry. Masonry is organized on the state and local level. Grand Lodges of states issue warrants to groups of Masons who wish to form a lodge (the required number is seven). In states that did not have Grand Lodges, Masons received charters from other states. For instance, the first lodges in California were chartered by the Grand Lodge of Pennsylvania. Once at least three local lodges existed within a state, they could convene to organize a Grand Lodge. There was one attempt in the mid-nineteenth century to create a national governing body of Prince Hall Freemasonry but it failed after three decades due to hostility toward centralization on the local and state level and the lack of precedent in European Masonic tradition. See Grimsahw, *Official History*, 193, 217; Muraskin, *Middle-class Blacks*, 39.

8. Muraskin, *Middle-Class Blacks*, 19–20; Carnes, *Secret Ritual and Manhood*, 24.

9. The antebellum ideology that held that in order for the republic to survive and

flourish, it needed a citizenry that was politically and economically independent. Economic independence, in the form of land ownership and/or skilled self-employment, would foster a virtuous public that would not be susceptible to the machinations of a corrupt, avaricious elite (merchant capitalists and slave owners) and the dependent, docile masses (wage workers and slaves). See Clawson, *Constructing Brotherhood*, 153; Roediger, *Wages of Whiteness*, 31–36; Denning, *Mechanic Accents*, 103–6.

10. Martin, *Race First*, 13–19; Vincent, *Black Power*, 151–61. Vincent suggests that there were 400,000 regular, dues-paying members, 750,000 occasional members, and 2 to 3 million people "in and around the movement." The number of branches in the United States, which exceeded 700 around 1926, suggests that the UNIA was second only to the Baptist and African Methodist Episcopal (AME) churches in terms of membership. For figures on the National Baptist Convention and the AME church in the early twentieth century, see Higginbotham, *Righteous Discontent*, 6.

11. Hobsbawm, "Introduction: Inventing Traditions," in Hobsbawm and Ranger, *Invention of Tradition*, 1, 9; Ryan, *Women in Public*, 20.

Chapter One

1. Freemasonry consisted of many different gradations. The original, and most common, branch of Masonry, called Blue Lodge Masonry, was comprised of the first three degrees: Entered Apprentice, Fellow Craftsman, and Master Mason. The fourth degree, Mark Master, was conferred under Royal Arch Masonry. York Rite (which included Knights Templar and Knights of Malta) and the Ancient Accepted Scottish Rite were similar forms of, respectively, English and continental Freemasonry that granted higher degrees, up to thirty-three. The Ancient Arabic Order of Nobles of the Mystic Shrine was open only to Knights Templar and thirty-second-degree Masons but was not an official branch of Freemasonry. See Grimshaw, *Official History*, 336, 356–57; Clawson, *Constructing Brotherhood*, 114–15, 232–33; Muraskin, *Middle-Class Blacks*, 283; Bullock, *Revolutionary Brotherhood*, 239–41.

2. Grimshaw, *Official History*, 336–42.

3. Ibid., 142, 200–205, 260–62; Nash, *Forging Freedom*, 51–52, 148–49; Gatewood, *Aristocrats of Color*, 40, 43–44; Foner, *Reconstruction*, 353.

4. Cook and Alexander quoted in Grimshaw, *Official History*, 195, 298, 300.

5. Muraskin, *Middle-Class Blacks*, 29. In the 1930s, the Improved Benevolent Protective Order of Elks of the World dwarfed Free and Accepted Masonic orders, particularly in New York City. See Westley Curtwright, "Civic Organizations," 6, Writers' Program, "The Negro of New York," reel 3, SCRBC.

6. For discussions of Freemasonry in the United States during the antebellum era, see Curry, *Free Black in Urban America*, 196–215; Horton, *Free People of Color*, esp. 42–43; Nash, *Forging Freedom*, 218–22; Wilder, *In the Company of Black Men*, 111–19. For discussions on twentieth-century black Masonry, see Muraskin, *Middle-Class Blacks*;

Grossman, *Land of Hope*, 92, 129; Watkins-Owen, *Blood Relations*, 71–74. For a study that spans both the nineteenth and twentieth centuries, see Loretta J. Williams, *Black Freemasonry*.

7. Muraskin, *Middle-Class Blacks*; Loretta J. Williams, *Black Freemasonry*.
8. Two recent works that provide a gendered analysis of Prince Hall Freemasonry are Wilder, *In the Company of Black Men*, and Wallace, "'Are We Men?': Prince Hall, Martin Delany, and the Masculine Ideal in Black Freemasonry, 1775–1865," in *Constructing the Black Masculine*, 53–81. There are also several good studies that explore the gendered meanings of fraternalism but limit their discussions to Anglo-American orders. See Clawson, *Constructing Brotherhood*; Carnes, *Secret Ritual and Manhood*; William D. Moore, "Structures of Masculinity."
9. Clawson, *Constructing Brotherhood*, 38.
10. Jeppe, "Masonic Resume of Louis Alexander Jeppe, 32°, Past Master No. 1 of Carthaginian Lodge, No. 47, F. & A.M. of Brooklyn, New York and R.W. Grand Orator of the M.W. Grand Lodge, Prince Hall, State of New York," program, 16 October 1925, in "Printed Material-New York," HWC.
11. Grossman, *Land of Hope*, 129; Muraskin, *Middle-Class Blacks*, 58–78.
12. Williamson, *Story of Carthaginian Lodge*, 5–7, 10, in "Printed Material-New York," HWC.
13. The following information on the class and ethnic backgrounds of the lodge's members is culled largely from minute books and state census records. Data from the lodge minutes is somewhat spotty due to the fact that records cover only the following years: 1904–08 and 1920–30. At every meeting in which an individual was proposed, the secretary was supposed to provide the following biographical information in the minutes: address, place of birth, age and occupation. Whether or not these prospective initiates had sufficient biographical records depended on the meticulousness of the secretaries, as some provided complete records and others provided only last names. The majority of the secretaries over the years fell between these two extremes, providing only partial information. See Hall of Carthaginian Record Book, 1904–30, "Masonic Records," vols. 1–6, HWC.

   Where possible, I have supplemented the records with data from the 1905 and 1925 New York State Census, Kings County, located in NYPL. Out of the 186 individuals for whom I have first and last names, there are 70 with complete records and 12 with partial, but sufficient, records (that is, having at least place of birth and occupation listed). Therefore, I am working with a sample of eighty-two people.
14. This observation is based on the fourteen prospective members for whom there is a specific island listed for their place of birth. The state census tended to only list either West Indies or British West Indies. The minutes were more specific. Of these fourteen, nine were from Barbados, two from Jamaica, two from Nevis, and one from Trinidad. On the English and Scottish influence on the culture of St. Thomas, a Danish possession until 1917, see Reid, *Negro Immigrant*, 74.

15. The nine professionals included four lawyers, an accountant, a minister, an architect, an engineer, and a mechanical dentist. Because neither the minute books nor the censuses indicated whether or not they were proprietors, the judgment that the following were entrepreneurs is speculative: two caterers, two realtors, a butcher, a pharmacist, a presser, a contractor, and an undertaker.

16. I am including messengers within the white-collar/managerial group because most worked in offices. On occasion, the specific type of office, such as "bank" or "Standard Oil," was listed in the minute books. Albert Hines, for instance, who was born in the British West Indies and applied for membership in September 1925, was listed as a messenger in the minute books but was listed as "office assistant" in the 1925 census. See Hall of Carthaginian Record Book, 1 September 1925, "Masonic Records," vol. 5, HWC; 1925 New York State Census, Kings County, reel 21, NYPL.

17. Among the thirteen semi- and unskilled laborers were four janitors, two elevator operators, two day laborers, two railroad employees, a driver, a bricklayer (note he was not listed as a mason), and a fireman. The skilled laborer, artisan, and artist group consisted of two musicians, a woodworker, a caretaker, a mechanic/blacksmith, an electrician, and a sign-painter.

18. Of course, the presence of blacks, regardless of ethnic or national background, in civil service was practically nonexistent. In the federal agencies in Washington in 1900, for example, black men made up only 4 percent of all male government clerks. See Aron, *Ladies and Gentlemen*, 30, 202 n. 57.

19. Grimshaw, *Official History*, 323–30.

20. These numbers are based on the censuses from 1910, 1920, and 1930. See Wilder, *Covenant with Color*, 125. Also see Connolly, *Ghetto Grows in Brooklyn*, 52–53, 76.

21. "Negro Masons Eager to Aid in Fight on Frauds," *New York World*, 13 June 1925, in "Clipping File," HWC.

22. "History of Prince Hall Lodge No. 38," *Seventy-fifth Anniversary of Prince Hall Lodge, No. 38, F. & A.M.P.H.*, souvenir program, 4 November 1956, "Printed Material-New York"; Harry A. Williamson, "Arthur A. Schomburg: The Freemason," typescript, 13 March 1941; "Lodge Problem of Color Settled," *World*, 22 June 1930, in "Clipping File"; "Report of Special Deputy Grand Master for Hijos del Caribe, U.D.," *Eighty-fifth Annual Session Proceedings of the Most Worshipful Grand Lodge of the Most Ancient and Honorable Fraternity of Free and Accepted Masons Prince Hall of the State of New York for the Year 1930*, 53–54, "Printed Material-New York." All in HWC. Also see Hoffnung-Garskof, "Migrations of Arturo Schomburg," 29–32; Wilder, *In the Company of Black Men*, 206.

23. Williamson, *Story of Carthaginian Lodge*, 21; Hall of Carthaginian Record Book, 30 May 1905, "Masonic Records," vol. 1, HWC; 1905 New York State Census, Kings County, reel 64, NYPL.

24. "Negro Masons," *Masonic Analyst* (1929), in "Clipping File," HWC. This was probably

not an uncommon practice. Earl Lewis has found the instance of a Chinese businessman joining a black Elk's lodge in Norfolk, Virginia. See *In Their Own Interests*, 42–43.

25. Dumenil, *Freemasonry and American Culture*, 13, 122–27.
26. Watkins-Owens, *Blood Relations*, 72.
27. Williamson to V. A. Thompson, copy, 28 September 1926, Box 5, Fol. 3, HWC.
28. *Members Due Book and By-Laws of Carthaginian Lodge, No. 47, F. & A.M. of Brooklyn, N.Y.* (1914), in "Printed Material-New York," HWC.
29. Address by R. R. Mims in *Proceedings of the National Congress of Free and Accepted Masons of the United States of America* (Pine Bluff, Ark.: "Echo" Job Print, 1893), 7, in "Printed Material," Box 15, Fol. 1, HWC. Ida B. Wells and Frederick Douglass made similar arguments in their pamphlet, *The Reason Why the Colored American Is Not in the World's Columbian Exposition*. See Bederman, *Manliness and Civilization*, 38–39.
30. Gaines, *Uplifting the Race*, xiv–xv, 1–5.
31. Address by Mims, 7.
32. Muraskin, *Middle-Class Blacks*, 1–85 (quote on 70, n. 69).
33. This understanding of class and gender has been influenced by the following work: Thompson, *Making of the English Working Class*, 10–13; Scott, "Women in *The Making of the English Working Class*," 68–90; Gaines, "Rethinking Race and Class." I have also benefited from Anne McClintock's reading of race, gender, and class as "articulated categories" because they "are not distinct realms of experience, existing in splendid isolation from each other. . . . Rather, they come into existence in and through relation to each other—if in contradictory and conflictual ways." See McClintock, *Imperial Leather*, 4–5 (original emphasis).
34. *Masonic Handbook of Most Worshipful Grand Lodge F. & A.M. of the State of Arkansas*, n.d., 20, "Printed Material," Box 15, Fol. 1, HWC.
35. Cited in Grimshaw, *Official History*, 228.
36. Clawson, *Constructing Brotherhood*, 145–77. Also see Rodgers, *Work Ethic in Industrial America*.
37. Grimshaw, *Official History*, 163.
38. For discussion, and a critique, of the doctrine of the self-made man, see Rotundo, *American Manhood*, esp. 194–96.
39. Hall of Carthaginian Record Book, 19 October 1926, "Masonic Records," vol. 6, HWC.
40. See the following minutes in Hall of Carthaginian Record Book, 15 October 1907, 18 February 1908, 4 October 1922, 21 November 1922, and 6 December 1927; *Members Due Book and By-Laws of Carthaginian Lodge*, 7; both in HWC.
41. For instance, the mandate of the Committee on Widows and Orphans included the following directive: "Show them that we are not stifles with vanity, that our charges and claims have value notwithstanding the general opinion that masons are selfish.

Whisper wise consul into their ears when ever you may think it wise and expedient." Addendum to 5 February 1929 minutes, Hall of Carthaginian Record Book, "Masonic Records," vol. 6, HWC.

42. "Address of Grandmaster John Wesley Dobbs at Special Communication of the Most Worshipful Union Grand Lodge Ancient Free and Accepted Masons, Jurisdiction of Georgia," 28 January 1933, "Printed Material," Box 15, Fol. 1, HWC; "Constitution of the Masonic Benefit Association," *Masonic Handbook*, 23–25. These figures are based on the Grand Lodge plans for Georgia and Arkansas and are prior to the Great Depression. Benefits varied according to place and time. Families of Texas Masons during the post–World War II period, for instance, received as much as $1,000 benefit payments. See Muraskin, *Middle-Class Blacks*, 137.

43. Muraskin, *Middle-Class Blacks*, 40, 135–36. For a general discussion of the mutual benefit dimension of fraternal associations, see Beito, "To Advance the 'Practice of Thrift and Economy'," 602–12.

44. Hall of Carthaginian Record Book, 16 March, 6 April, and 16 November 1926, 6 December 1927, 15 January 1929, "Masonic Records," vols. 5 and 6, HWC.

45. Because orphanages, and particularly the role of women's auxiliaries in these institutions, provide an interesting launching point for the discussion of the ways in which Masons incorporated the category of age and bourgeois notions of domesticity into their process of gender identity formation, they will be discussed in more detail in Chapter 3.

46. Hall of Carthaginian Record Book, 6 and 20 December 1921, 7 December 1926, "Masonic Records," vols. 3 and 6, HWC.

47. On black female business owners, see Gill, " 'Never Wanted to Do Anything but Hair.' "

48. Muraskin, *Middle-Class Blacks*, 157. Also see William D. Moore, "Structures of Masculinity," for a discussion of the gendered significance of temple building.

49. Sullivan and Martin quoted in "Masonic Temple to be erected . . . by the Prince Hall Temple and Home Association, Inc.," pamphlet, n.d. Also see "Celebration of the Laying of the Corner Stone for the Prince Hall Masonic Temple," announcement and program, 30 May 1926; both in "Printed Material-New York," HWC.

50. Hall of Carthaginian Record Book, addendum to 21 December 1926 minutes. Also see 7 September 1926 minutes. Both in "Masonic Records," vols. 5 and 6, HWC.

51. Quoted in "Masonic Temple to be erected."

52. "The New Masonic Temple," brochure, n.d., "Printed Materials," Box 15, Fol. 1, HWC.

53. Muraskin, *Middle-Class Blacks*, 168–69.

54. Address by Mims, 7–8; "Address of Grand Master John Wesley Dobbs," 9.

55. Higginbotham, *Righteous Discontent*, 185–211. Also see Gaines, *Uplifting the Race*, esp. 67–99.

56. "The study of Masonry leads man to the correct knowledge of God; the correct

knowledge of God leads to the true worship of Him, and the true worship of Him places man in harmony with all that is true and good, enlarging his powers for usefulness in every vocation, station, position, or condition in life, thereby fitting him for citizenship, in whom we find a true neighbor, a generous friend, and a clear-cut and well defined power in circumscribing his desires and keeping his passions in due bounds." Grimshaw, *Official History*, 5–6, 29–34.

57. "Report of Grand Secretary," Minutes of the Grand Lodge of New York, June 1912; Minutes of the Grand Lodge of New York, June 1913; both in "Masonic Records," vol. 2, HWC.

58. Hall of Carthaginian Record Book, 18 October 1927, "Masonic Records," vol. 6, HWC. But it was not just the image of the order that concerned Masons; a commitment to ethical behavior animated most Masons. As Grimshaw wrote: "A Mason is obliged by his tenure to obey the moral law; therefore, any violation of that law is a Masonic offense." *Official History*, 374–75.

59. Hall of Carthaginian Record Book, 19 October 1926, "Masonic Records," vol. 6, HWC.

60. "Notice: The Craft Take Warning," circular, n.d., "Printed Material-New York," HWC.

61. Address by Ellis, *Proceedings of the Fifty-Ninth Annual Communication of the Most Worshipful Prince Hall Grand Lodge F. and A.M. of Illinois and Jurisdiction, October 13–15, 1925*, "Printed Material," Box 15, Fol. 1, HWC.

62. "Grand Master's Address," and "Report of Grand Secretary," Minutes of the Grand Lodge of New York, June 1912, "Masonic Records," vol. 2, HWC.

63. Hall of Carthaginian Record Book, 6 December 1927, "Masonic Records," vol. 6, HWC.

64. "Grand Master's Address," Minutes of the Grand Lodge of New York, June 1913, "Masonic Records," vol. 2, HWC. The recounting of this legal battle is based solely on the Grand Lodge's account (even the judge's ruling is excerpted). After conducting some research in state Supreme Court case reports, I have not been able to find reference to *Miller v. Spencer*. However, there was precedence in state courts not intervening in the affairs of fraternal associations. For a similar case, see the decisions in *Kopp v. White* (1900), N.Y. Civ. Proc. Rep. 352, 65 N.Y. Supp. 1017, in Longsdorf, *Abbott's Digest*, 590–91.

65. Muraskin, *Middle-Class Blacks*, 125.

66. Two of the landmarks were "the right of every Mason to be represented in all general meetings of the Craft and to instruct his representatives" and "the right of every Mason to appeal from the decision of his brethren, in Lodge convened, to the Grand Lodge or General Assembly of Masons . . . a landmark highly essential to the preservation of justice and the prevention of oppression." See Grimshaw, *Official History*, 31–32.

67. Prince Hall Freemasonry, however, did not practice a policy of one person, one vote.

Only Master Masons were allowed to vote. Masons of the first two degrees, Entered Apprentice and Fellow Craftsman, could not vote on candidates' petitions because historically apprentices and journeymen had "no voice in receiving or rejecting material or workmen for the Temple." See ibid., 329.

68. Ibid., 318–19.

69. Ibid., 327.

70. This understanding of rituals has been influenced by Eric Hobsbawm, who writes that "heightened ceremon[ies] . . . surrounded the initiation of a man into the special group of his fellows, one designated to demonstrate its utter difference from other groups and to bind him to it by the strongest conceivable links." See Hobsbawm, *Primitive Rebels*, 154. Also see Dumenil, *Freemasonry and American Culture*, 32–42.

71. "Mysteries and Freemasonry," n.d., "Masonic Writings," Box 10, Fol. 5; Alphonse Cerza, *Masonic Information Please* (Riverside, Ill.: n.p., 1952), "Masonic Writings," Box 11, Fol. 1; R. W. Daniel O. Braithwaite, "General Instructions," 23 September 1929, 2, "Printed Material-New York." All in HWC.

72. Dumenil, *Freemasonry and American Culture*, 36–37; Clawson, *Constructing Brotherhood*, 81.

73. Grimshaw, *Official History*, 328.

74. "Mysteries and Freemasonry."

75. W. DeVoe Joiner, "Can the Craftsmen School Be Wrong?" 2 December 1934, 6, "Printed Material-New York," HWC.

76. On the construction of manhood within homosocial spaces, see Kimmel, *Manhood in America*, 7–8, 365 n. 11.

77. "The Lodge, technically speaking," William Grimshaw wrote, "is a piece of furniture made in imitation of the Ark of the Covenant, which was constructed according to the form prescribed by God himself, and which, after the erection of the Temple, was kept in the holy of holies, which also contained the Table of the Law." See Grimshaw, *Official History*, 319–20.

78. Ibid., 320–23; Harry A. Williamson, "Outline of Ideas for the Preparation of a Volume to be Known as 'The Book of Procedure,'" typed manuscript, n.d., "Masonic Writings," Box 10, Fol. 4, HWC.

79. Grimshaw, *Official History*, 330. For examples, see Hall of Carthaginian Record Book, 5 December 1905 and 7 January 1908, "Masonic Records," vol. 1, HWC.

80. *Masonic Handbook*, 10. Given the probably not uncommon practice of individuals impersonating Masons in order to receive financial support, the procedure was not unwarranted. In 1906, for instance, Carthaginian was visited by an individual claiming membership in a Floridian lodge. When he asked for pecuniary assistance "on account of unavoidable [trouble?] at home which he explained [he] had to flee from" the lodge turned the matter over to the Charity Committee. The committee contacted the lodge from which he claimed he hailed and several weeks later was in-

formed by the Florida Masons that the man was not only not a member of the lodge but that he had attempted the same ruse with them. See Hall of Carthaginian Record Book, 18 September and 30 October 1906, "Masonic Records," vol. 1, HWC.

81. Grimshaw, *Official History*, 324. For a description of a typical meeting, see Hall of Carthaginian Record Book, 6 June 1908 and 15 December 1925, "Masonic Records," vols. 1 and 5, HWC.

82. *Masonic Handbook*, 7–8; Grimshaw, *Official History*, 331.

83. Carnes, *Secret Ritual and Manhood*, 24–25.

84. *Masonic Handbook*, 9.

85. Ibid., 9. On the "stylization of the body," see Butler, *Gender Trouble*, 33.

86. For an excellent discussion of clothes as signifiers of group identity, see Kelley, "Riddle of the Zoot," 165–69.

87. "Report of the Fraternal Correspondent," 1 June 1931, 14a, "Masonic Writings," Box 10, Fol. 2, HWC.

88. Williamson, *Story of Carthaginian Lodge*, 3, 9. *Colored American* quoted in ibid., 9. Also see "Brief Historical Resume," in *Program of Nineteenth Anniversary of Carthaginian Lodge, No. 47, F. & A.M. Prince Hall*, 21 October 1924, "Printed Material-New York," HWC.

89. Williamson to Thomas H. Barnes, copy, 30 March 1932, Box 6, Fol. 8, HWC.

90. *The Centennial Celebration of the Most Worshipful Prince Hall Grand Lodge, F. & A.M. of Massachusetts, Boston, Mass., September 10–13, 1908*, program, "Printed Material," Box 15, Fol. 1; "Celebration of the Laying of the Corner Stone for the Prince Hall Masonic Temple," announcement and program, 30 May 1926, "Printed Material-New York"; both in HWC.

91. Grimshaw, *Official History*, 342.

92. "Ivanhoe Commandery Holds Re-Union Picnic," *New York Age*, 26 July 1906. For a discussion of the militaristic model of manhood the Knights Templar represented, see William D. Moore, "Structures of Masculinity," 108–68.

93. Williamson, *Story of Carthaginian Lodge*, 22. King was also a Mason and the deputy grand master of Liberia, which explains the ceremonial trappings of the banquet.

94. On Negro Election Day, see Wade, "'Shining in Borrowed Plumage'"; on Jonkunnu, see Burton, *Afro-Creole*, 47–89 and Stuckey, *Slave Culture*, 64–73; on black militias, see Barkley Brown and Kimball, "Mapping the Terrain."

95. On New York, see "Negro Masons Eager to Aid in Fight on Frauds," *New York World*, 13 June 1925, "Clipping File"; on Washington State, see W. Devoe Joiner, "Why Prince Hall Masonry?" in Joiner, comp., *The First Annual Report of the Research Committee of Lewis Hayden Lodge Number Sixty-Nine of the Most Worshipful Grand Lodge of the Most Ancient and Honorable Fraternity of Free and Accepted Masons [Prince Hall] of the State of New York, U.S.A.* (n.p., 1928), "Printed Material-New York"; both in HWC.

96. G. A. Kenderdine to Harry A. Williamson, 29 January 1930, Box 5, Fol. 15, HWC; Joiner, "Why Prince Hall Masonry?"

97. Grimshaw, *Official History*, 104; "The Right to Wear the Mason's Emblem," *Masonic Home Journal*, 16 February 1914, "Clipping File," HWC; Sadie Hall, "Negroes in Freemasonry," 10–11, Writers' Program, "The Negro of New York," reel 3; Claude McKay, "The Free Masonic Order of Negroes in New York," 2, ibid. Also see Dumenil, *Freemasonry and American Culture*, 10, 123; Loretta J. Williams, *Black Freemasonry*, 67–72.

98. "Lodges of Colored Masons in Colorado, Enjoined by Court," *American Co-Mason*, November 1929; "Negroes Forbidden Use of Shrine Emblem," unidentified news article; "Negro Shriners Win Suit," *American Co-Mason* (ca. 1929). All in "Clipping File," HWC.

99. Muraskin, *Middle-Class Blacks*, 195–96.

100. Freemasonry, Grimshaw wrote, "embraces the African, as well as the fairer Saxon. It welcomes within its fraternal fold the sons of every clime and country. No religious creeds nor political differences separate us. The Hebrew and the Christian, the subject and the citizen kneel at the same altar and receive the same light; we are all upon the same level — the king and peasant, the master and the servant throughout the world." See Grimshaw, *Official History*, 101–2.

101. John E. Bruce to the Editor of the *Negro World*, 29 April 1922, in "Clipping File," HWC. Also see Muraskin, *Middle-Class Blacks*, 197–98, 212–13, where he argues that this invocation of Egypt as the birthplace of Masonry "means that middle-class blacks accept white evaluations of what civilization and culture are (i.e., Pyramids 'yes,' Bantu villages 'no'), and gains its nationalistic and prideful quality of turning the tables on the dominant race only after the white man's ground rules have been accepted" (213).

102. "At Home Negroes Do Not See Lodge Fellowship," unidentified editorial, "Clipping File," HWC.

103. For an example of one Mason who became increasingly realistic with respect to the white policy of nonrecognition, see the following letters: Harry Williamson to the editor, *American Tyler-Keystone*, copy, 1 February 1913, Box 5, Fol. 5; Williamson to *Trestle Board*, copy, 7 February 1928, Box 4, Fol. 7; Williamson to Harry E. Davis, copy, 11 December 1935, Box 7, Fol. 7. All in HWC.

104. Grimshaw, *Official History*, 106. Also see Muraskin, *Middle-Class Blacks*, 202–5.

105. On black Masons alerting each other to the presence of bogus bodies, see Harry Williamson to George W. Wilson, copy, 23 September 1923, Box 4, Fol. 7. On black Masons providing assistance in legal suits against bogus bodies, see George W. Crawford to Williamson, 31 July 1931, and John P. Graham to Williamson, 31 March 1932, Box 4, Fol. 12. All in HWC.

106. Williamson to H. A. Collins, copy, 6 May 1935, Box 7, Fol. 11, HWC. Also see Davis, *History of Freemasonry*, 98–99.

107. Muraskin, *Middle-Class Blacks*, 39; "Bogus and Compact Masons," *Negro World*, 14

April 1923, "Clipping File," HWC; Davis, *History of Freemasonry*, 105–6. Also see n. 2 above.

108. Schomburg to Joseph Bartlett, Esq., 18 August 1921, Box 7, Fol. 2, HWC. Also see "Bogus and Compact Masons."

109. Schomburg to Bartlett, 18 August 1921, Box 7, Fol. 2, HWC.

110. "Open letter from the Committee of Investigation of Spurious Organization," Illinois Grand Lodge, 9 October 1918, "Printed Material," Box 15, Fol. 1, HWC. Also see Grossman, *Land of Hope*, 123–60, for a discussion of the class tension between Old Settlers and migrants.

111. Sherwood to Williamson, 14 January 1924, Box 7, Fol. 2, HWC.

112. Williamson, "Prince Hall Freemasonry: An illustrated lecture," typescript, n.d., HWC.

113. Joiner, "Why Prince Hall Masonry?"

114. Grimshaw, *Official History*, 23.

115. Gilmore, *Gender and Jim Crow*, 75.

Chapter Two

1. Garvey to Buxton, 27 August 1914, Anti-Slavery and Aborigines Protection Society Manuscripts, Rhodes House Library, Oxford, England. Reprinted in Hill, *Marcus Garvey and UNIA Papers*, 1:53–54. Also see Amy Jacques Garvey, "Marcus Mosiah Garvey, 1887–1940," typescript, n.d., Box 4, Fol. 1, MGMC, FUSC.

2. This is reflected in the historiography. Historical interpretations range from the UNIA as a working-class precursor of 1960s black radicalism to a movement caught up in, and unable to transcend, the cultural and social conventions of the Western bourgeoisie during the era of industrial capitalism and high imperialism. The literature on Garveyism is vast and will only be cited in part here. On the working-class interpretation of Garveyism, see Cronon, *Black Moses*; Draper, *Rediscovery of Black Nationalism*. On the Garvey movement as an early example of black radicalism and anticolonialism, see Martin, *Race First*; Vincent, *Black Power*; Rupert Lewis, *Marcus Garvey*; James, *Holding Aloft the Banner*. On the bourgeois elements of Garveyism, see Cruse, *Crisis of the Negro Intellectual*; Lawrence W. Levine, "Marcus Garvey and the Politics of Revitalization," in Levine, *Unpredictable Past*, 107–36; Moses, *Golden Age*; Stein, *World of Marcus Garvey*. For a study that successfully explores Garveyism as an internationalist ideology that was received, transformed, and then rearticulated on a local level, see Tolbert, *UNIA and Black Los Angeles*.

3. Hill and Bair, *Life and Lessons*, xviii–xlvii (quotes on xviii and xxiv). Also see Hill, *Marcus Garvey and UNIA Papers*, 1:xxxix–lxvi.

4. Garvey quoted in *Daily Chronicle*, 26 August 1915, in Hill, *Marcus Garvey and UNIA Papers*, 1:134.

5. "Fund Raising Appeal by Marcus Garvey," *Gleaner* (Kingston), 1 October 1915, in

Hill, *Marcus Garvey and UNIA Papers*, 1:155. For a discussion of Garvey's advocacy of the Tuskegee model, see Lively, "Continuity and Radicalism," 215–20.

6. "Active Members Wanted For the Universal Improvement Association of Jamaica," *Daily Chronicle*, November 1915, in Hill, *Marcus Garvey and UNIA Papers*, 1:168. Du Bois's classic critique of the Tuskegee model is in *Souls of Black Folk*, 30–42. For a thorough discussion of the political ideologies of the era, see Meier, *Negro Thought in America*, esp. 171–255.

7. Garvey to Casimir, 12 June 1920, J. R. Ralph Casimir Papers, Box 2, Fol. 3, SCRBC.

8. Universal Negro Improvement Association, *CBL*, 1918, UNIA Central Division Records, Box 1, Fol. a5, art. I, sec. 4, art. XII, sec. 4, art. VI, sec. 2, art. IV, sec. 3, and art. III, sec. 39, 39a, SCRBC; "The Great Convention," *Negro World*, 28 August 1920, in Hill, *Marcus Garvey and UNIA Papers*, 2:597.

9. The debate over the class dynamics within the Garvey movement is a vigorous one. Theodore Vincent reluctantly acknowledged that much of the UNIA leadership was middle class, although he qualified it by arguing that they were the "young renegades of that class." He provided an occupational breakdown which shows that the majority of UNIA leaders were ministers, professionals, and skilled laborers. See Vincent, *Black Power*, 105, 152. Judith Stein suggests that the local UNIA leadership came from the "middling strata" of upstart entrepreneurs, reflected in her close examinations of the UNIA chapters in Detroit, Cincinnati, Cleveland, and Gary, Indiana. See Stein, *World of Marcus Garvey*, 223–47, 275–78. Earl Lewis and Joe William Trotter Jr. argue that the UNIA locals in Norfolk, Virginia, and Milwaukee, respectively, created a leadership from the laboring classes. See Earl Lewis, *In Their Own Interests*, 73–74, and Trotter, *Black Milwaukee*, 125, 134–35.

10. James, *Holding Aloft the Banner*, 134–35.

11. "Africa for the Africans," *Washington Eagle*, n.d.; "Long Arm and High-Handed West Indian Business," *Norfolk Journal and Guide*, 21 August 1920; both in Box 8, Fol. 1, MGMC.

12. Reports by Special Agent WW, 22 February and 24 February 1920, RG 65, Records of the Federal Bureau of Investigation, File OG258421, National Archives, reprinted in Hill, *Marcus Garvey and UNIA Papers*, 2:219–21. Hill identifies WW as William A. Bailey in ibid., 2:170.

13. For example, at the 1922 annual convention, bickering broke out among African American and African Caribbean delegates over the efficacy of the vote. The argument degenerated into personal attacks between Garvey and J. W. H. Eason, "Leader of American Negroes." The "bloodshed" comment was apparently the assessment of Walter White and William Pickens of the National Association for the Advancement of Colored People. See Report by Agent Andrew M. Battle, copy, 18 August 1922; Report by Special Agent James E. Amos, copy, 9 August 1922; both in Garvey Investigative File, Box 11, Fol. 2, MGMC.

14. Ferris, "Dr. DuBois' [sic] Ten Mistakes," typescript copy, 10 February 1923, 5, Box 1, Fol. 8, MGMC; Burkett, Black Redemption, 65–70.
15. Unsigned letter to Hon. Harry M. Daugherty, copy, 15 January 1923, Box 9, MGMC. The letter is reprinted in Amy Jacques Garvey, Philosophy and Opinions, 2:294–300. The letter signers were New York businesspeople Harry H. Pace (record company executive), John E. Nail (realtor), and Dr. Julia P. Coleman (beauty industry executive); Robert S. Abbott, editor of the Chicago Defender; NAACP officials William Pickens and Robert W. Bagnall; George W. Harris, editor of the New York News and city alderman; and Chandler Owen, coeditor, along with A. Philip Randolph, of the Messenger. Also see Stein, World of Marcus Garvey, 166–68.
16. Edwards, "Division of Negro Sentiment," Globe, 4 August [n.y.], Box 8, Fol. 1, MGMC.
17. On Kinston, see "The News and Views of U.N.I.A. Divisions," Negro World, 2 June 1928; Stein, World of Marcus Garvey, 228. On Woodlawn, see R. B. Spencer to William J. Burns, copy, 29 August 1922; Report by Agent H. L. Morgan, copy, 5 October 1922; both in Garvey Investigative File, Box 11, Fol. 2, MGMC.
18. "The News and Views of U.N.I.A. Divisions," Negro World, 2 June 1928.
19. Report by Special Agent W. L. Buchanan, copy, 24 February 1922, Garvey Investigative File, Box 11, Fol. 1, MGMC.
20. Tolbert, UNIA and Black Los Angeles, 42, 51, 63.
21. Report by Agent A. A. Hopkins, copy, 17 November 1921, Garvey Investigative File, Box 11, Fol. 1, MGMC.
22. Tolbert, UNIA and Black Los Angeles, 62–67; Hill, Marcus Garvey and UNIA Papers, 2:650 n. 3.
23. Tolbert, UNIA and Black Los Angeles, 63–66, 75, 77.
24. Tolbert does not refer to any obvious antagonism between African American and African Caribbean Los Angelenos. According to the 1920 federal census, there were 287 Los Angelenos of Caribbean origin; out of that, 244 were of European ethnicity. By 1930, there were only 525 foreign-born blacks in Los Angeles. Of course, there is the possibility that observers of the split mistook Africans (of which there were 135 in Los Angeles in 1920) for African Caribbeans but, given the fact that the division's membership approached one thousand, it is difficult to believe that the numbers of foreign-born blacks had any significant impact on the chapter's dissolution. See U.S. Bureau of the Census, Abstract of the Fourteenth Census, 314–15, 380–81; U.S. Bureau of the Census, Fourteenth Census of the United States, 731; Reid, Negro Immigrant, 248. For a history of blacks in Los Angeles that also does not note the presence of African Caribbeans in the 1920s, see Sonenshein, Politics in Black and White, esp. 21–35.
25. Report by Agent A. A. Hopkins, copy, 17 November 1921, Garvey Investigative File, Box 11, Fol. 1, MGMC.

26. Unsigned letter to Hon. Harry M. Daugherty, copy, 15 January 1923, Garvey Investigative File, Box 9, MGMC.

27. Tolbert, *UNIA and Black Los Angeles*, 74.

28. Stein, *World of Marcus Garvey*, 26.

29. Quotes are from Garvey, "The Negro's Greatest Enemy," *Current History* (September 1923), reprinted in Amy Jacques Garvey, *Philosophy and Opinions*, 2:124. Also see Amy Jacques Garvey, "Marcus Mosiah Garvey, 1887–1940"; Ferris, "Dr. DuBois' [sic] Ten Mistakes."

30. Walkowitz, *Working with Class*, 5. Also see Gaines, *Uplifting the Race*, esp. 1–17.

31. Garvey, "Dissertation on Man," in Amy Jacques Garvey, *Philosophy and Opinions*, 1:24; Bruce, "Bruce-Gritisms," typescript, n.d., File B.MS. 11-26B, JBP.

32. "The 'Star' of Newport News under an Eclipse," *Negro World*, 25 October 1919; "Marcus Garvey, Rev. Dr. Eason, Rev. Dr. Smith, Rev. Dr. Cranston and Dr. Lewis Again Electrify Thousands in Liberty Hall," *Negro World*, 28 August 1920. Both in Hill, *Marcus Garvey and UNIA Papers*, 2:106, 616.

33. Maloney, *Some Essentials*, 13. In a letter to Arthur Schomburg, Maloney claimed that his book did not refer to the UNIA per se, but it is clear from the text that he was using the Garvey movement as an ideal model of twentieth-century black politics. Sections of his book had also been previously printed in the *Negro World*. See Maloney to Schomburg, 12 January 1924, Box 5, Fol. 31, ASP.

34. Rotundo, *American Manhood*, 222–46. On the importance of the frontier in constructing manhood, see Dubbert, *Man's Place*, 9–11.

35. Dubbert, *Man's Place*, 13–32; Rotundo, *American Manhood*, 222–27; Bederman, *Manliness and Civilization*, 16–17.

36. Rotundo, *American Manhood*, 209–21; Bederman, *Manliness and Civilization*, 13–14; Testi, "Gender of Reform Politics," esp. 1511–12.

37. Clyde Griffen puts it succinctly when he argues: "Middle-class men after the Civil War moved toward an accommodation with the emerging world of a bureaucratized corporate capitalism . . . and simultaneously moved toward compensatory ideas and fantasies of male independence, adventure, and virility." See Griffen, "Reconstructing Masculinity from the Evangelical Revival to the Waning of Progressivism: A Speculative Synthesis," in Carnes and Griffen, *Meanings for Manhood*, 191; Bederman, *Manliness and Civilization*, 12–13; Rotundo, *American Manhood*, 248–51.

38. Testi, "Gender of Reform Politics," 1517–19; Dubbert, *Man's Place*, 122–90. On the increasing importance of physicality in constructions of middle-class manhood, see J. A. Mangan's and James Walvin's introduction to *Manliness and Morality*, edited by Mangan and Walvin. For a discussion of hunting and imperialism, see John M. Mackenzie, "The Imperial Pioneer and Hunter and the British Masculine Stereotype in Late Victorian and Edwardian Times," in ibid., 176–98. On the military and imperialism, see Rotundo, *American Manhood*, 222–27, 232–44.

39. Garvey, "The Function of Man," in Amy Jacques Garvey, *Philosophy and Opinions*, 1:28.

40. *Negro World*, 17 March 1923, 4; "Garvey Proves Contention of a Government for Negroes in Africa as Only Solution of Negro Problem," *Negro World*, 3 March 1923.

41. Typed transcript of Washington, D.C., UNIA meeting, 24 July 1920, RG 65, FBI Records, File OG329359, National Archives; "Detailed Report of Sunday's Meeting at Liberty Hall," *Negro World*, 14 August 1920; both in Hill, *Marcus Garvey and UNIA Papers*, 2:452–53, 560–62.

42. Dubbert offers an insightful interpretation when he argues that urban areas, for male Progressives, became the frontier in the sense that they were environments which needed to be controlled through various reform measures. On the "masculinization" of reform during the Progressive era, see Dubbert, *Man's Place*, 130–36, and Testi, "Gender of Reform Politics."

43. Ferris quoted in *Negro World Convention Bulletin*, 3 August 1920, in Hill, *Marcus Garvey and UNIA Papers*, 2:507; Garvey, "Africa's Wealth," in Amy Jacques Garvey, *Philosophy and Opinions*, 2:67.

44. Amy Jacques Garvey, *Philosophy and Opinions*, 2:362; Stein, *World of Marcus Garvey*, 118; Bruce to King, 3 April 1920, and Bruce to Dossen, 3 April 1920, File BL 4-41, 4-40, JBP.

45. Commissioner Elie Garcia to President King, 8 June 1920; Marcus Garvey to King, 5 December 1923; both letters reprinted in Amy Jacques Garvey, *Philosophy and Opinions*, 2:363–64, 368. Also see photograph of second UNIA delegation in ibid., 2:367.

46. Amy Jacques Garvey, *Philosophy and Opinions*, 2:376–77, 388 fig.

47. Ibid., 2:379–80.

48. Ibid., 2:384. For a more detailed account, see Stein, *World of Marcus Garvey*, 209–22. I use the terms "colonization" and "civilizing mission" with some circumspection, given that the UNIA's positioning of Western blacks vis-a-vis Africans was fairly ambiguous. Two of the stated goals of the UNIA, for instance, were to "assist in civilizing the backward tribes of Africa" and to "promote a conscientious Spiritual worship among the native tribes." However, concerning African redemption, Garvey also warned that "any Negro who expects that he will be assisted here, there or anywhere by the [UNIA] to exercise a haughty superiority over the fellows of his own race, makes a tremendous mistake." See "Aims and Objects of Movement for Solution of Negro Problem" and "Africa for the Africans," in Amy Jacques Garvey, *Philosophy and Opinions*, 2:38, 1:71.

49. Amy Jacques Garvey, *Philosophy and Opinions*, 2:376, 393–94, 399.

50. For a discussion of self-culture, see Cawelti, *Apostles of the Self-Made Man*, esp. 80–90.

51. Ferris quoted in *Negro World*, 26 June 1920, in Hill, *Marcus Garvey and UNIA Papers*, 2:382. For a study that provides an insightful interpretation of the nationalist thought of Ferris, see Gaines, *Uplifting the Race*, 100–127.

52. See for example, "Universal Negro Improvement Association Fills Carnegie Hall at Historical Meeting," *Negro World*, 3 March 1923.

53. "Dissertation on Man," in Amy Jacques Garvey, *Philosophy and Opinions*, 1:24. For

a critique of the doctrine of the self-made man from different positions, see Rotundo, *American Manhood*, 194–96, and Lears, *No Place of Grace*, 15–18. On Garvey and self-made man ideology, see introduction to Hill and Bair, *Life and Lessons*, xxv–xxviii.

54. Bruce, "Address to Boston UNIA," handwritten document, 9 September 1923, File B.6-75, JBP; Brooks quoted in typed transcript of Washington, D.C., UNIA meeting, 24 July 1920, RG 65, FBI Records, File OG329359, National Archives, in Hill, *Marcus Garvey and UNIA Papers*, 2:451.

55. Flyer for Negro Factories Corporation, RG 65, FBI Records, File OG329359, National Archives, in Hill, *Marcus Garvey and UNIA Papers*, 2:657 (original emphasis).

56. Bruce, "Address to alumni of Virginia Theological Seminary," typescript, 27 October 1914, File B.6-75, JBP; Amy Jacques Garvey, *Philosophy and Opinions*, 1:9.

57. "Garvey's Surgeon General Seems to Be Out of Job," *Tribune*, 4 August 1922, Box 8, Fol. 1, MGMC. Also see "Money Rows Split Garvey and Aids; Gibson Loses Job," *New York World*, 4 August 1922, Box 8, Fol. 1; Report by Agent Andrew M. Battle, copy, 10 August 1922, Garvey Investigative File, Box 11, Fol. 2; both in MGMC.

58. See "Eason is Dropped as Negro Leader," *World*, 24 August 1922, Box 8, Fol. 1, MGMC; "Convention Reports," *Negro World*, 2 September 1922, in Hill, *Marcus Garvey and UNIA Papers*, 4:944–45, 953, 979–88. Shortly after his impeachment and expulsion, Eason formed a rival anti-Garveyite organization, the Universal Negro Improvement Alliance. During the fall and early winter of 1922, he agitated against Garveyism and sought to draw members from the UNIA to his own association. On 1 January 1923, Eason was shot in New Orleans. Before he died, he identified two local Garveyites, Constantine Dyer and William Shakespeare, as the gunmen. Garvey's involvement in the assassination of one his most vociferous critics has been covered in detail by historians of the UNIA. Eason had agreed to become a witness in the government's mail fraud case against Garvey, which could have provided the UNIA president-general the motive for calling for his assassination. Although federal and local law enforcement agencies believed that the three alleged gunmen (the two whom Eason identified and Esau Ramus, who was later implicated by the wife of Dyer) were acting on the orders of Garvey, no one was ever convicted of the murder. And, as Judith Stein persuasively points out, no convincing evidence exists that the three were working at the behest of Garvey. See Stein, *World of Marcus Garvey*, 171–85; Martin, *Race First*, 318–19; Burkett, *Black Redemption*, 55–56; Hill and Bair, *Life and Lessons*, 381–82.

59. "Instructions for Members of the Universal Negro Improvement Association," *Negro World*, 29 March 1924.

60. Mosse, *Nationalism and Sexuality*, 1–9; Rodgers, *Work Ethic in Industrial America*, 16; Gorn, *Manly Art*, 56–68. For important works on African Americans and respectability, see Higginbotham, *Righteous Discontent*, esp. 185–229; Gaines, *Uplifting the Race*; Barkley Brown and Kimball, "Mapping the Terrain." Victoria Wolcott argues that, at least in the case of interwar Detroit, respectability was a discourse that was

deployed primarily by middle-class female reformers and that, by the 1930s, it had given way to a more masculinist discourse of self-determination and self-defense. My reading of respectability is that it was certainly gendered but encompassed specific notions of manhood as well as womanhood and, moreover, was not antithetical to the self-determinationist discourse of the Garvey movement. See Wolcott, *Remaking Respectability*.

61. Gatewood, *Aristocrats of Color*, 186–90, 193–95; David Levering Lewis, "Parallels and Divergences," 543–52.

62. "Interesting Interview Given by Mr. Ware on Migration of the Negro," *Negro World*, 22 September 1923.

63. Leadett, "The Obligations of Motherhood," *Negro World*, 29 March 1924.

64. On the role of respectability in nationalist rhetoric, see Mosse, *Nationalism and Sexuality*, and Stoler, *Race and the Education of Desire*, esp. 95–136.

65. John Houghton, "The Plight of Our Race in Harlem, Brooklyn and New Jersey," *Negro World*, 21 April 1923; Hubert J. Cox, "The Highway to Success," *Negro World*, 10 November 1923; Le Van, "Dollars — 14 Billion," *Negro World*, 8 September 1923.

66. N. G. G. T[homas]., "The Way of the World," *Negro World*, 15 December 1923; *Negro World*, 18 August 1923. On the availability of alcohol in Harlem during Prohibition and the response of the mainstream clergy and press, see Anderson, *This Was Harlem*, 145–48.

67. "The Intoxication of Jazz," *Negro World*, 3 March 1923. For a discussion of the negative response to jazz in the early twentieth century, see Lawrence W. Levine, "Jazz and American Culture," in Levine, *Unpredictable Past*, 172–88.

68. "Our Negro Bands," *Negro World*, 8 September 1923; Martin, *Race First*, 27. Robert Hill partially quotes Garvey from a 1938 issue of *Black Man*: " 'Spiritual and Jazz Music are credited to the Negro,' Garvey conceded, but 'it was simply because we did not know better music.' " See Hill, *Marcus Garvey and UNIA Papers*, 1:li.

69. For examples of Garveyite prescriptive literature on sex, see Houghton, "Plight of Our Race"; Reverend J. C. Cake, "Sex Truths," *Negro World*, 19 May 1923; and James W. Streeter, " 'One Girl in a Million,' " *Negro World*, 24 February 1923. For a more detailed discussion of sexuality and homophobia in Garveyite discourse, see Summers, " 'This Immoral Practice.' " For an excellent discussion of the eugenic dimensions of Garveyite discourse on racial reproduction, see Mitchell, "Adjusting the Race," esp. 331–48. On Anglo-American and European nationalism, see Bederman, *Manliness and Civilization*, esp. 77–120; D'Emilio and Freedman, *Intimate Matters*, 202–21; De Grazia, *How Fascism Ruled Women*; Bridenthal, Grossman, and Kaplan, *When Biology Became Destiny*; Haeberle, "Swastika, Pink Triangle, and Yellow Star," 365–79.

70. As Michele Mitchell persuasively argues, however, black women tended to be targets of the UNIA's sexual policing more than men. See Mitchell, "Adjusting the Race," 307–53.

71. Thomas, "The Way of the World," *Negro World*, 15 December 1923; "Lincoln Defeats

Hampton, 13–6," *Negro World*, 9 November 1929. Both Lincoln and Hampton were historically black colleges.

72. For descriptions of UNIA meetings, see interviews with Ruth Smith and Thomas Harvey, in Smith-Irvin, *Footsoldiers*, 59, 26.

73. UNIA, "Rules and Regulations for Universal African Legions of the U.N.I.A. and A.C.L.," CBL, arts. I–VI (hereafter cited as UAL-CBL). Also see Rupert Lewis, *Marcus Garvey*, 68.

74. Enclosure to British Military Intelligence Report, 10 February 1920, RG 165, Records of the War Department, General and Special staffs, File 10218-364-20-190X, National Archives; Report by Special Agent Jones, 9 February 1920, RG 65, FBI Records, File OG185161, National Archives. Both reprinted in Hill, *Marcus Garvey and UNIA Papers*, 2:213–14, 202.

75. Nesbitt, "The Worth and Possibilities of Training," *Negro World*, 7 July 1923; John Charles Zampty (1974), interviewed by Smith-Irvin, in *Footsoldiers*, 47.

76. UAL-CBL, art. III, sec. 3, art. VIII, art. XIV, sec. 1; Thomas Harvey (1975–76), interviewed by Smith-Irvin, in *Footsoldiers*, 24.

77. UAL-CBL, arts. XXII and XXV.

78. For discussions of the military's role in constructing middle-class notions of manliness, see Rotundo, *American Manhood*, 232–39, and Donald J. Mrozek, "The Habit of Victory: the American Military and the Cult of Manliness," in Mangan and Walvin, *Manliness and Morality*, 220–39. On war and the military and working-class definitions of masculinity, see Gorn, *Manly Art*, 159–64.

79. UAL-CBL, arts. I and XVIII.

80. Major H. Vinton Plummer, "Legion Notes of Interest," *Negro World*, 1 November 1924.

81. Hill, *Marcus Garvey and UNIA Papers*, 1:xxxix–xli; Rodgers, *Work Ethic in Industrial America*, 14–15, 153–55.

82. On the connection between autonomy and masculinity among the antebellum working class, see Roediger, *Wages of Whiteness*, esp. 43–64. For broader discussions, see Rodgers, *Work Ethic in Industrial America*, 30–64, and Gorn, *Manly Art*. On competence and skill in constructions of working-class masculinity, see Baron, "Other Side of Gender Antagonism"; Boyle, "The Kiss"; Maynard, "Rough Work and Rugged Men," 159–60. For a discussion of mutuality, "acquisitive individualism," and masculinity, see Montgomery, *Fall of the House of Labor*, 17, 22–44.

83. On both the general exclusion of black laborers from unions and the Garveyite position on the labor movement, see Harris, *Harder We Run*, 39–50, 70–71.

84. See Montgomery, *Fall of the House of Labor*; Kessler-Harris, "Treating the Male as 'Other.'"

85. Harvey interview (1975–76), in Smith-Irvin, *Footsoldiers*, 24.

86. CBL, art. V, sec. 3; Johnson, *Black Manhattan*, 254; Amy Jacques Garvey, *Garvey and Garveyism*, 65. On black elite debutantes, see Gatewood, *Aristocrats of Color*, 229–30.

87. "Third Court Reception a Roaring Success," *Negro World*, 30 August 1924; Hill, "Making Noise," 182.

88. Ruth Smith remembered that her Detroit local "participated with the city in general" in Armistice Day parades. See Smith interview (1987), in Smith-Irvin, *Footsoldiers*, 61.

89. "Fourth Convention of Negro Peoples Opens in New York Amid Great Splendor," *Negro World*, 9 August 1924; "Garvey Reviews Big Negro Parade," *New York Times*, 2 August 1924, 10:1.

90. Amy Jacques Garvey, *Garvey and Garveyism*, 46.

91. Roberson, "The Soldiers of Our Legion and Their Work," *Negro World*, 16 August 1924.

92. Gaskin, "Boys, Salute the Flag, the Red, Black, Green," *Negro World*, 5 July 1924, 10; Ash is quoted in British Military Intelligence Report, 7 January 1919, RG 165, War Department Records, File 10218-364-18-190X, National Archives. Reprinted in Hill, *Marcus Garvey and UNIA Papers*, 2:181.

93. Amy Jacques Garvey, *Garvey and Garveyism*, 46.

94. For images of blacks in popular culture, see Donald Baker, "Black Images"; Bogle, *Toms, Coons, Mulattoes*; Hatt, "'Making a Man of Him'"; Lemons, "Black Stereotypes"; Rydell, *All the World's a Fair*; Lott, *Love and Theft*.

95. On cultural counterappropriation, see Kobena Mercer, "Diaspora Culture and the Dialogic Imagination: The Aesthetics of Black Independent Film in Britain," in Mercer, *Welcome to the Jungle*, 53–66.

96. Hill, "Making Noise," 194–201.

97. Similar to the "oppositional style" that Richard D. E. Burton argues marks African Caribbeans' participation in cultural forms such as cricket and carnival, the public rituals of Garveyites "challenge[d] the dominant order on the latter's own terrain, turning its cultural and ideological 'weapons' against it, and while victory over the other on the other's own terms enable[d] the dominated to get their frustration out of their system, the System itself survive[d] — strengthened, not weakened by its merely symbolic defeat." See Burton, *Afro-Creole*, 185–86 (original emphasis).

98. Mark C. Carnes, "Middle-Class Men and the Solace of Fraternal Ritual," in Carnes and Griffen, *Meanings for Manhood*, 37–52; Rotundo, *American Manhood*, 227–32; Bederman, *Manliness and Civilization*, 71–75; Clark and Nagel, "White Men, Red Masks."

99. Garvey quoted in *Negro World*, 8 May 1920, in Hill, *Marcus Garvey and UNIA Papers*, 2:301. In October 1919, Garvey was shot by George Tyler but escaped serious injuries. Although the incident was attributed to an unpaid loan, Garveyites suspected that Tyler had been part of a larger conspiracy. These suspicions intensified when Tyler "leapt" to his death before an investigation or trial began. See Martin, *Race First*, 12; Stein, *World of Marcus Garvey*, 79–80.

100. Garvey quoted in typed transcript of Washington, D.C., UNIA meeting, 24 July

1920, RG 65, FBI Records, File OG329359, National Archives, in Hill, *Marcus Garvey and UNIA Papers*, 2:454–55.

101. Regarding the discourse of "civilization," Bederman writes that "as effective as 'civilization' was in its various ways of constructing male dominance, it was never totalizing. People opposed to white male dominance invoked civilization to legitimize quite different points of view." *Manliness and Civilization*, 23.

102. "Speech Delivered at Madison Square Garden, New York City, N.Y., U.S.A., Sunday, March 16, 1924," in Amy Jacques Garvey, *Philosophy and Opinions*, 2:119–20. For a discussion of the effects of World War I on black intellectuals' perceptions and assessments of European culture and values, see Moses, *Golden Age*, 220–50.

103. Fullinwinder, *Mind and Mood*, 1–46; Moses, *Black Messiahs and Uncle Toms*, 1–16.

104. The role of religion in the UNIA is a complex issue and has received extensive scholarly treatment. See Burkett, *Garveyism as a Religious Movement*, esp. 111–94; Burkett, *Black Redemption*; Moses, *Black Messiahs and Uncle Toms*, 132–38; Lively, "Continuity and Radicalism," 210–20.

105. "The Position of the Universal Negro Assn. Stands Unchallenged," *Negro World*, 17 March 1923, 2; "The Views of the U.N.I.A. on the Race Problem Are Upheld," *Negro World*, 24 March 1923. For a biography of Poston, see Hill, *Marcus Garvey and UNIA Papers*, 3:694 n. 1.

106. Diggs quoted in Moses, *Black Messiahs and Uncle Toms*, 135.

107. "God as A War Lord," in Amy Jacques Garvey, *Philosophy and Opinions*, 1:44; "Garvey Proves Contention of a Government for Negroes in Africa as Only Solution of Negro Problem," *Negro World*, 3 March 1923.

108. Amy Jacques Garvey, *Philosophy and Opinions*, 1:9.

109. Bell, "The Christian Spirit in Race Redemption," *Negro World*, 11 August 1923, reprinted in Burkett, *Black Redemption*, 143–47. Also see Susan Curtis, "The Son of Man and God the Father: The Social Gospel and Victorian Masculinity," in Carnes and Griffen, *Meanings for Manhood*, 67–78.

110. See reports by Young and Gibson in *Negro World Convention Bulletin*, 7 August 1920, in Hill, *Marcus Garvey and UNIA Papers*, 2:514–16, 518, 523. Also see Burkett, *Garveyism as a Religious Movement*; Moses, *Black Messiahs and Uncle Toms*, 133–37.

111. Bruce, "Editorial Notes," 19 July [1920?], File B.9-31, JBP. The longstanding cultural stereotypes of the church as a feminine space and the ministerial profession as an effeminate occupation made the black clergy an easy target for the UNIA. These attacks drew on stereotypes in the truest sense of the terms, as black churches tended to be the most independent institutions in black communities. The authoritative study of the feminization of the nineteenth-century American church is Douglas, *Feminization of American Culture*, esp. 80–117. Also see Rotundo, *American Manhood*, 170–72.

112. Maloney, *Some Essentials*, 128, 126.

113. Amy Jacques Garvey, *Philosophy and Opinions*, 1:38, 29.

114. For an essay that is critical of both Garvey and Du Bois, see Richard B. Moore, "Critics and Opponents."

115. Garvey, "W. E. Burghardt Du Bois as a Hater of Dark People," in Amy Jacques Garvey, *Philosophy and Opinions*, 2:310–20.

116. Sheppard, *Mistakes of Dr. W. E. B. Du Bois*, 11, 15, 26–28.

117. Garvey quoted in Amy Jacques Garvey, *Philosophy and Opinions*, 2:181.

118. Bruce, untitled typescript, n.d., pp. 4–6, File B.9-107, JBP.

Chapter Three

1. "Configuration of practice" is sociologist R. W. Connell's term. See *Masculinities*, 72–73.

2. For discussions of respectability and black middle-class women, see Higginbotham, *Righteous Discontent*, 185–229; White, *Too Heavy a Load*, 69–78; Chateauvert, *Marching Together*, 11, 138–62; Barkley Brown, "Negotiating and Transforming the Public Sphere," 144–45; Shaw, *What a Woman Ought to Be*, 13–40; Wolcott, *Remaking Respectability*, 11–92; Hine, "Rape and the Inner Lives of Black Women"; Mitchell, "Silences Broken, Silences Kept."

3. "Preexisting social category" is Gail Bederman's term. See *Manliness and Civilization*, 7.

4. Maloney, *Some Essentials*, 24–25.

5. White, *Too Heavy a Load*, 21–55 (quote on p. 42). Also see Gilmore, *Gender and Jim Crow*, 147–224.

6. "Brief Historical Resume of Carthaginian Lodge, No. 47, F. and A.M.," *Nineteenth Anniversary of Carthaginian Lodge, No. 47, F. & A.M. Prince Hall Masons*, pamphlet, 21 October 1924, 7; Williamson, *Story of Carthaginian Lodge*, 19, 26; both in "Printed Material-New York," HWC.

7. Williamson, *Story of Carthaginian Lodge*, 26; "8 Big Acts — Vaudeville and Dance Will be Given by the Ladies of Carthaginian Auxiliary," advertisement, 21 April 1909, in "Printed Material-New York," HWC.

8. *The Centennial Celebration of the Most Worshipful Prince Hall Grand Lodge, F. & A.M. of Massachusetts, Boston, Massachusetts, September 10–13, 1908*, program, "Printed Material," Box 15, Fol. 1; *The Diamond Jubilee of the Most Worshipful Grand Lodge, F. & A.M. Prince Hall Masons, State of New York, May 30–June 4, 1920*, program, "Printed Material-New York"; both in HWC.

9. Williamson, *Story of Carthaginian Lodge*, 19, 26.

10. Hall of Carthaginian Record Book, 4 December 1923, "Masonic Records," vol. 3, HWC.

11. Carnes, *Secret Ritual and Manhood*, 81–85; Clawson, *Constructing Brotherhood*, 185–91; Dumenil, *Freemasonry and American Culture*, 7.

12. "Address of Grand Patron Thornton A. Jackson, 33°, at the Second Annual Communication of the Grand Chapter of the District of Columbia and Jurisdiction, 23 May 1893," reprinted in Sue M. Wilson Brown, *History of the Order*, 15; Clawson, *Constructing Brotherhood*, 202; Dumenil, *Freemasonry and American Culture*, 33, 37, 40.

13. "Address of Grand Patron Thornton A. Jackson," 15–16. Because chapters of the OES were "adopted" by Masonic lodges, there was an erroneous conflation of the Rite of Adoption, a creation of Dutch and French Masons, and the OES, an American institution. American Masons may have made the connection between OES and the continental European lodges of adoption because of the confusion over the word adoption. In Europe, "adoption" was used to define the relationship of women to Masonry as a whole. Women were adopted into lodges, whereas men were "made" Freemasons. The European lodges that initiated both men and women were not adopted by single-sex Masonic lodges per se. In the OES, these chapters were adopted by Masonic lodges, therefore leading to the tendency to equate the two separate Masonic traditions. On the history of European lodges of adoption, see Jacob, *Living the Enlightenment*, 120–42. For an example of the conflation, see Grimshaw, *Official History*, 359.

14. "Address Delivered by Mrs. S. Joe Brown before Ninth Biennial Conference, Pittsburgh, Pennsylvania, August 1924," reprinted in Sue M. Wilson Brown, *History of the Order*, 37.

15. Sue M. Wilson Brown, *History of the Order*, 19–20.

16. "Address Delivered by Mrs. S. Joe Brown," 37–38. There is no evidence that, as of 1924, there were any subordinate or Grand Chapters in the Caribbean or South America.

17. Sue M. Wilson Brown, *History of the Order*, 47; White, *Too Heavy a Load*, 146; Giddings, *When and Where I Enter*, 138, 177; Invitation for banquet in honor of C. D. B. King, Mrs. C. D. B. King, and Dr. Nathaniel H. B. Cassell, New York City, 22 September 1919, in "Printed Material-New York," HWC.

18. *Constitution and By-Laws of Eureka Grand Chapter, O.E.S., State of New York*, 1927–28, 12–13, 16, in "O.E.S. Constitutions, 1927–1938," HWC.

19. Eato's address, given in 1903, is reprinted in unidentified typescript, in "Order of the Eastern Star-Eureka Grand Chapter," HWC.

20. Grimshaw, *Official History*, 360.

21. Clawson, *Constructing Brotherhood*, 195, 199.

22. Patricia Hill Collins discusses the function of "controlling images" as they relate to black women within dominant cultures: "In order to exercise power, elite white men and their representatives must be in a position to manipulate appropriate symbols concerning Black women. They may do so by exploiting already existing symbols, or they may create new ones relevant to their needs." But white elite males are not the only ones who can traffic in these symbols. Collins also suggests that "the question of the role of Black institutions [including the family] as transmitters of control-

ling images of Black womanhood merits investigation." See Collins, *Black Feminist Thought*, 67–90.

23. On domesticity as a platform for achieving citizenship rights, see Chateauvert, *Marching Together*, 2–3. An example of the importance of domesticity is the fact that the "international matron" and official historian of the OES in 1924, Sue M. Wilson Brown, identified herself as Mrs. S. Joe Brown, published the official history under the same name, and represented herself as the wife of S. Joe Brown throughout the text.

24. Taylor, *Veiled Garvey*, 64 (original emphasis).

25. *Constitution and By-Laws of Eureka Grand Chapter*, 5–6; *Constitution and By-Laws of the United Grand Chapter Order of the Eastern Star for the State of Missouri and Jurisdiction*, 1920, 11, in "O.E.S. Constitutions, 1904–1940," HWC.

26. *Constitution and By-Laws of Eureka Grand Chapter*, 6; *Constitution and By-Laws of the United Grand Chapter*, 13–14.

27. Clawson, *Constructing Brotherhood*, 202.

28. *Gleaner*, 23 October 1914; *Daily Chronicle*, 26 August 1915; both articles reprinted in Hill, *Marcus Garvey and UNIA Papers*, 1:82, 135.

29. "UNIA Meeting in St. Ann's Bay," *Jamaican Times*, 13 November 1915, in Hill, *Marcus Garvey and UNIA Papers*, 1:162–63. Amendment in text.

30. Robert A. Hill suggests that Garvey turned to race purity as "the basis of the UNIA's search for legitimacy" only in 1921. See Hill, *Marcus Garvey and UNIA Papers*, 1:lxxx–lxxxiv.

31. See Appendix III in ibid., 1:552–59.

32. Bair, "True Women, Real Men," 155, 157; Universal Negro Improvement Association, CBL, 1918, UNIA Central Division Records, Box 1, Fol. a5, art. III, sec. 2, 5, 9, 11, SCRBC.

33. CBL, article VI, sec. 1 and art. V., sec. 1. The potentate also had to be an African.

34. UNIA, "Rules and Regulations Governing the Universal African Black Cross Nurses," CBL, art. II and art. III, sec. 1. (Hereafter cited as BCN-CBL.) Also see Rupert Lewis, *Marcus Garvey*, 68.

35. BCN-CBL, art. V, sec. 3; Bair, "True Women, Real Men," 157. As Darlene Clark Hine also points out, nursing, in the black community as a whole, was important in that it was one of the few routes available to working-class black women who sought "dignified employment" and a "middle-class lifestyle." See Hine, *Black Women in White*, xv.

36. BCN-CBL, art. IV, sec. 1, 2, 5; Bair, "True Women, Real Men," 157. For an example of nurses' training activities, see "Black Cross Nurses Have a Training School," *Boston Chronicle*, 18 June [n.y.], clipping, Box 8, MGMC.

37. UNIA, "Rules and Regulations for Juveniles," CBL, art. IV, sec. 1.

38. Ibid., articles I and II; "Philadelphia Juveniles," *Negro World*, 3 November 1923. The UNIA also provided higher education to young Garveyites in the short-lived Uni-

versal Liberty University, located in tidewater Virginia, which lasted from 1926 to 1929. See "Universal Liberty University Circular of Information," n.d., in Ralph J. R. Casimir Papers, Box 2, Fol. 2, SCRBC; Martin, *Race First*, 36–37.

39. Cott, *Groundings of Modern Feminism*, esp. 3–10, 16–20; Kessler-Harris, *Out to Work*, 217–49, quote on p. 228.

40. Jones, *Labor of Love*, 152–82, quote on 164; Kessler-Harris, *Out to Work*, 237–38; Shaw, *What a Woman Ought to Be*, 135–37.

41. Marcus Garvey, for instance, told a Philadelphia audience that one of the benefits of nation-building would be the opportunity for black women to "leave the white man's kitchen and go into your home as the wife of a big Negro banker or a corporation manager." See "Hon. Marcus Garvey, Foremost Orator of the Race, Delivers Brilliant Speech in Philadelphia," *Negro World*, 1 November 1919, in Hill, *Marcus Garvey and UNIA Papers*, 2:96.

42. Rotundo, *American Manhood*, 255–62, quotes on pp. 258–59. Also see Bederman, *Manliness and Civilization*, 77–120, and Kimmel, *Manhood in America*, 117–41, 157–71.

43. Rotundo, *American Manhood*, 262.

44. Anderson, *Education of Blacks in the South*, 148–50, 186–88.

45. Dollard, *Caste and Class*, 173–87; Mjagkij, "True Manhood," 140.

46. For a discussion of the infantilization of blacks in social science scholarship at the turn of the century, see Fredrickson, *Black Image in the White Mind*, esp. 283–91.

47. Sue M. Wilson Brown, *History of the Order*, 37–38, 54.

48. Thomas H. Samuels, *Ritual for the Order of Bees For Boys and Girls (Independent): A Royal and Exalted Degree For the Juvenile Department of the Ancient and Honorable Fraternity of Free and Accepted Masons and Adopted Rites with Appropriate Ceremonies* (Chicago: T. H. Samuels, 1922), 8, in "Printed Material," Box 15, Fol. 1, HWC. It is not clear whether there were several chapters in Illinois or just one in Chicago.

49. Samuels, *Ritual for the Order of Bees*, 7–8, 23–24, 26.

50. Even though boys and girls held executive positions within the Order of Bees, the "supreme king bee" and his "royal counselors" (grand officers of Prince Hall and OES) wielded the ultimate decision-making power. See ibid., 24–25.

51. David D. Richards to Harry A. Williamson, 20 April 1927, Box 7, Fol. 11, HWC.

52. Harry Williamson to Arthur M. Millard, 22 July 1923, Box 5, Fol. 2, HWC.

53. See 1938–39 correspondence between Williamson and Millard, Box 5, Fol. 2; Williamson to Hilton L. Mayers, Box 6, Fol. 10; Williamson to James Yearwood, Box 7, Fol. 3; Williamson to Harry E. Davis, Box 7, Fol. 7; all in HWC.

54. Address excerpted in unidentified typescript, in "Order of the Eastern Star-Eureka Grand Chapter," HWC.

55. Sue M. Wilson Brown, *History of the Order*, 58; "Address of Grandmaster John Wesley Dobbs at Special Communication of the Most Worshipful Union Grand Lodge Ancient Free and Accepted Masons, Jurisdiction of Georgia," 28 January 1933, 6–7, "Printed Material," Box 15, Fol. 1, HWC.

56. Sue M. Wilson Brown, *History of the Order*, 59–60.

57. OES chapters participated in the anti-lynching campaigns of the early 1920s by passing resolutions in support of the NAACP, contributing money to its Anti-Lynching Fund, and writing to U.S. senators urging passage of the Dyer Anti-Lynching Bill. Sue M. Wilson Brown, *History of the Order*, 51.

58. "Address of Grandmaster John Wesley Dobbs," 6.

59. Whitby's address in Sue M. Wilson Brown, *History of the Order*, 59–60.

60. Sue M. Wilson Brown, *History of the Order*, 57.

61. As international matron, Brown gave an address at the 1924 Inter-state Conference in which she stated: "And while I would not suggest the taking of our Order into politics, yet in this new day our women everywhere should be urged to make use of their right of suffrage where they are permitted to do so and that they vote not to fail to place in office men and women who will safeguard the interest of our group as well as the public in general." Sue M. Wilson Brown, *History of the Order*, 38.

62. Deborah White discusses this in the context of black clubwomen. See *Too Heavy a Load*, 37–49.

63. "Marcus Garvey Introduces Officials of U.N.I.A. to Vast Audience in the Star Casino," *Negro World*, 11 September 1920; "Jubilee of Universal Negro Improvement Association," 30 October 1919, typed stenographer's report, RG 65, Records of Federal Bureau of Investigation, File OG185161, National Archives. Both reprinted in Hill, *Marcus Garvey and UNIA Papers*, 2:653, 125.

64. Bair, "True Women, Real Men," 159. On the domestic ideal among the white bourgeoisie between 1880 and 1920, see Coontz, *Social Origins of Private Life*, 251–83; Margaret Marsh, "Suburban Men and Masculine Domesticity, 1870–1915," in Carnes and Griffen, *Meanings for Manhood*, 111–27. On the domestic ideal among the black elite and emerging middle class, see Gaines, *Uplifting the Race*, 78–80; Gatewood, *Aristocrats of Color*, 190–94. For an overview of literature on separate spheres, see Kerber, "Separate Spheres."

65. Bruce, *The Making of a Race* (New York: n.p., 1922), 3–4, in JBP.

66. Bruce, Address to "Rev. Judd, Mrs. Judd, Ladies and Gentlemen," n.d., File B.8-109, JBP.

67. Bruce, "Present Tendencies," address, Jersey City, N.J., 20 June 1915, pp. 16–17, File B.7-89, JBP.

68. Taylor, *Veiled Garvey*, esp. 77–81.

69. Brooks quoted in typed transcript of Washington, D.C., UNIA meeting, 24 July 1920, RG 65, FBI Records, File OG329359, National Archives, in Hill, *Marcus Garvey and UNIA Papers*, 2:452.

70. Bruce, *Making of a Race*, 7–8.

71. Frederickson, *Black Image in the White Mind*, 256–82; Gossett, *Race*, 160–66, 378–82; Williamson, *Rage for Order*, 78–116; Pascoe, "Miscegenation Law."

72. Garvey, *Aims and Objects*.

73. Garvey, "Race Purity: A Desideratum," in Amy Jacques Garvey, *Philosophy and Opinions*, 2:62; Garvey, "Miscegenation," in ibid., 1:18. Not all supporters of Garveyism were as unequivocally opposed to miscegenation. A. H. Maloney, for example, argued that "cross-breeding" was a "natural thing" although he felt that it impeded "group consciousness." Maloney, *Some Essentials*, 80–87, 93.

74. Garvey quoted in report by Special Agent S-A-I-I, 9 November 1920, RG 65, FBI Records, File BS202600-667, National Archives, in Hill, *Marcus Garvey and UNIA Papers*, 3:85. In at least two instances, Garveyites used violence to chastise white men and black women who engaged in sexual relations. See Mitchell, "Adjusting the Race," 307–8.

75. Stein, *World of Marcus Garvey*, 154–70.

76. "Declaration of Rights of the Negro Peoples of the World," in Amy Jacques Garvey, *Philosophy and Opinions*, 2:139. Garvey referred to the document as "manly" in an editorial in the 21 August 1920 issue of the *Negro World*, reprinted in Hill, *Marcus Garvey and UNIA Papers*, 2:600.

77. "Declaration of Rights," 2:136; P. L. Burrows, "Black Man's Duty to His Women," *Negro World*, 16 August 1924.

78. For an example of the ways in which black women interpreted the argument for family wages as a woman's issue, see Melinda Chateauvert's discussion of the Ladies' Auxiliary to the Brotherhood of Sleeping Car Porters and Maids in *Marching Together*, 84–88.

79. "Universal Fashion Show and Historical Ball," advertisement in *Negro World*, 22 September 1923; Invitation from "Her Majesty Candace and Provisional Ladies of the Royal Court of Ethiopia" to Arthur Schomburg, n.d., Box 10, Fol. 1, ASP.

80. Robert A. Hill notes: "In terms of social-class status, female members of the Black Cross Nurses ranked well below the social elite of black women who occupied pride of place inside the UNIA court reception." Hill, "Making Noise," 194.

81. Bair, "True Women, Real Men"; Satter, "Marcus Garvey, Father Divine."

82. *New York Age*, 7 August 1920; *Negro World Convention Bulletin*, 3 August 1920, in Hill, *Marcus Garvey and UNIA Papers*, 2:493; *Negro World*, 9 August 1924.

83. Full-page advertisement in *Negro World*, 5 July 1924; "Garveyites Instal a 'Black Christ,'" *New York Times*, 1 September 1924, p. 24, col. 2.

84. Van Deburg, *New Day in Babylon*, 236–47. For discussions on motherhood and the Garvey movement, see Ford-Smith, "Women and the Garvey Movement," 73–83; Mitchell, "Adjusting the Race," esp. 328–31; Satter, "Marcus Garvey, Father Divine," 49–51; Taylor, *Veiled Garvey*, esp. 73–78.

85. UNIA, "Rules and Regulations Governing the Universal African Motor Corps," CBL.

86. Hine, *Black Women in White*, 14–15. Also see Satter, "Marcus Garvey, Father Divine," and Gilkes, "Roles of Church and Community Mothers," 48–50, for discussions of the multiple meanings of motherhood within the UNIA and black community as a whole.

87. Amy Jacques Garvey, "Women as Leaders, Nationally and Racially," typescript, 24 October 1925, Box 5, Fol. 9, MGMC. Also see Amy Jacques Garvey, "Woman's Function in Life," typescript, 19 December 1925, Box 5, Fol. 9, MGMC.

88. Taylor, *Veiled Garvey*, 73–74. Other female contributors to the *Negro World* discussed the public roles of women without reference to their potential capacity as mothers. See, for example, Saydee E. Parham, "The New Woman," *Negro World*, 2 February 1924.

89. Amy Jacques Garvey, "Listen Women!", typescript, 9 April 1927, Box 5, Fol. 9, MGMC. She went on to write that it was the black woman's "duty to bear children, and to care for those children, so that our race may have good and capable men and women, through whom they can achieve honor and power."

90. "The Kingston, Jamaica, U.N.I.A. Starts Co-operative Bank and Celebrates Ladies' Night," *Negro World*, 30 June 1923.

91. Amy Jacques Garvey, *Garvey and Garveyism*, 46.

92. *Negro World*, 9 September 1922, in Hill, *Marcus Garvey and UNIA Papers*, 4:1037–38. Also see Bair, "True Women, Real Men," 160–61; James, *Holding Aloft the Banner*, 138–40.

93. "Kingston, Jamaica, U.N.I.A. Starts Co-operative Bank."

94. Carter, "Will Women Neglect Race Propagation for Public Life?" *Negro World*, 14 June 1924. For an opposite view by a male Garveyite, see E. Elliott Rawlins, M.D., "Politics Purified by Women's Entry," ibid. Both cited in Taylor, *Veiled Garvey*, 79–80.

95. "Look Out for Mud," *Negro World*, 14 July 1923. Amy Jacques Garvey replied in the following week's issue: "with my unusual general knowledge and experience for a young woman, may I not ask if the word 'helpless' is not misapplied?" Both cited in Taylor, *Veiled Garvey*, 66–67. Also see James, *Holding Aloft the Banner*, 145–46.

96. "Message of Marcus Garvey to Membership of Universal Negro Improvement Association from Atlanta Prison," 1 August 1925, in Amy Jacques Garvey, *Philosophy and Opinions*, 2:327. On Amy Jacques Garvey's role in the production and distribution of the book, see Hill's introduction to it (xxviii–xxix, lxvi).

97. Sue M. Wilson Brown, *History of the Order*, 41.

98. For a detailed history, see United Grand Chapter, O.E.S., Missouri and Jurisdiction, *Brief Genealogical History and Present Difficulties* (n.p., 1924), 5, in "Order of Eastern Star-Printed Material, Missouri," HWC.

99. "True Status of the United Grand Chapter Order of the Eastern Star, of Missouri," letter from Lottie J. Gamble to *St. Paul Appeal*, 21 March 1922, "Order of Eastern Star-Printed Material, Missouri"; Open letter from Crittenden E. Clark, 8 January 1921, "O.E.S. Legal Papers—Prince Hall v. Eastern Star, 1921"; both in HWC.

100. Crittenden Clark, "Proclamation No. 3," 27 October 1921, "O.E.S. Legal Papers—Prince Hall v. Eastern Star, 1921," HWC; *Brief Genealogical History*, 9. It is not clear why the OES committee agreed to a plan that, in retrospect, they deemed as "obnoxious."

101. Open letter from Lottie J. Gamble, 18 August 1921; Clark, "Proclamation No. 1," n.d.; both in "O.E.S. Legal Papers—Prince Hall v. Eastern Star, 1921," HWC. Gamble, "True Status of the United Grand Chapter."

102. *Mary F. Woods et. al. v. Crittenden E. Clark, Lottie J. Gamble et. al.*, No. 161117, Jackson County Circuit Court (September 1921); Open letter from Mary Frances Woods, 1 October 1921; both in "O.E.S. Legal Papers—Prince Hall v. Eastern Star, 1921," HWC. Also see *Brief Genealogical History*, 10.

103. Gamble, "Proclamation No. 3," 29 September 1921; Open letter from Clark, 3 October 1921; both in "O.E.S. Legal Papers—Prince Hall v. Eastern Star, 1921," HWC. Gamble, "True Status of the United Grand Chapter."

104. Clark, "Proclamation No. 3."

105. Gamble, "Proclamation No. 4," 11 October 1921; Open letter from Gamble, 26 October 1921; both in "O.E.S. Legal Papers—Prince Hall v. Eastern Star, 1921," HWC.

106. See, for example, *Mary F. Woods v. Laura A. Smith, et al.*, No. 162118, Jackson County Circuit Court (November 1921), "O.E.S. Legal Papers—Prince Hall v. Eastern Star, 1921," HWC; *Maggie Merritt et. al. v. Josephine Trueheart et. al.*, No. 170660, Jackson County Circuit Court (n.d.), "O.E.S. Legal Papers—Merritt v. Trueheart," HWC.

107. Gamble, "True Status of the United Grand Chapter"; *Brief Genealogical History*, 4.

108. "Internal Strife Injurious to Fraternities," *Call* (Kansas City), 5 August 1922, 3.

109. *Eighty-fifth Grand Annual Session Proceedings of the Most Worshipful Grand Lodge of the Most Ancient and Honorable Fraternity of Free and Accepted Masons Prince Hall of the State of New York for the Year 1930* (n.p., 1930), 24, "Printed Material-New York," HWC.

110. Sue M. Wilson Brown, *History of the Order*, 30–31. Added emphasis.

111. Williamson to Officers and Members, Grand Lodge, F. & A.M. of New York (Prince Hall), copy, 1 August 1938, Box 7, Fol. 3, HWC (original emphasis). Williamson was writing in the midst of a controversy between New York Prince Hall Freemasons and Eastern Stars that resembled the Missouri conflict.

112. Higginbotham, *Righteous Discontent*.

Part Two

1. Mae Gwendolyn Henderson, "Portrait of Wallace Thurman," in Bontemps, *Harlem Renaissance Remembered*, 147–54; Wallace Thurman to William Jourdan Rapp, "Thursday," Box 1, Fol. 7, JWJ Small Collections (Thurman).

2. Henderson, "Portrait of Wallace Thurman," 151–55; Thurman to McKay, 3 February 1928, Box 5, CMC; West, "Elephant's Dance," 80.

3. Hughes, *Big Sea*, 234–35; Thurman to Harold Jackman, "Thursday" [30 August 1930], Box 1, Fol. 4, JWJ Small Collections (Thurman).

4. Henderson, "Portrait of Wallace Thurman," 149. Although she does not provide any concrete evidence of his early family life, Henderson suggests that Thurman's life paralleled the life of the female protagonist of his first novel, *The Blacker the Berry* (1929): "It deals with the problems of a dark-skinned girl, Emma Lou, among

her own people of lighter skin. Like Thurman, Emma Lou came from a middle-class family in a small Midwestern town. Again, recalling the author's own experiences, Emma Lou leaves the Midwest, going first to Los Angeles, then to New York's Harlem in a vain effort to escape the scorn and discrimination she has suffered among her own people because of her dark skin" (155–56).

5. For overviews of American society during the Jazz Age, see Dumenil, *Modern Temper*; Douglas, *Terrible Honesty*.

Chapter Four

1. Jean Toomer, "Book X," second typescript draft of unpublished autobiography, February 1935, Box 11, Fol. 362, JTP. Quotes on pp. 68–69.

2. On the changing nature of masculinity, see Rotundo, *American Manhood*, esp. 248–51, 282–86. On entertainment and the changing attitudes toward leisure among the upper and middle class, see Erenberg, *Steppin' Out*, esp. xi–xv, 233–38; Peiss, *Cheap Amusements*, 185–88. For a discussion of the entrance of middle-class women into the public sphere and the impact it had on gender conventions, marriage, and youth culture, see Cott, *Groundings of Modern Feminism*, 145–74, and Fass, *Damned and the Beautiful*. On queer identities, see Chauncey, *Gay New York*, 99–127. On the relationship between motion pictures, leisure, and changing attitudes toward sexuality, see Ullman, *Sex Seen*.

3. The literature on consumer culture is vast. Some of the works that I have found most useful include: Fox and Lears, *Culture of Consumption*; de Grazia and Furlough, *Sex of Things*; Dumenil, *Modern Temper*, esp. 56–97; Pendergast, "Consuming Questions." On the consumption patterns, including leisure practices, of white ethnic and black workers in the early twentieth century, see Susan Porter Benson, "Living on the Margin: Working-Class Marriages and Family Survival Strategies in the United States, 1919–1941," in de Grazia and Furlough, *Sex of Things*, 212–43; Cohen, *Making a New Deal*, 99–158; Tera Hunter, *To 'Joy My Freedom*, 145–86; Kelley, "'We Are Not What We Seem.'"

4. Quote is from Susman, "'Personality' and the Making of Twentieth-Century Culture," in *Culture as History*, 280. Also see Pendergast, *Creating the Modern Man*; Studlar, *This Mad Masquerade*.

5. There has been little work on the effects of consumer culture in the lives of middle-class African Americans. The work of Cohen, Hunter, and Kelley focuses on black workers and looks at consumption and leisure as working-class resistance. A recent work on blacks and consumer culture treats consumption from a business history perspective, examining marketing and retail strategies directed toward black consumers rather than the role that consumption may have played in the identities of African Americans. See Weems Jr., *Desegregating the Dollar*. Two works that do begin to do this are Mullins, "Race and the Genteel Consumer" and Pendergast, *Creating the Modern Man*.

6. Cooper, *Claude McKay*, 2–10; Claude McKay, *Long Way from Home*, 36; Claude McKay, "A Negro Poet," *Pearson's Magazine* (September 1918), 275–76, reprinted in Cooper, *Passion of Claude McKay*, 49. Thomas Francis was thought to be of Asante origin, and Hannah Edwards's family originated from Madagascar.

7. Claude McKay, *Long Way from Home*, 12–14; Cooper, *Claude McKay*, 11–34, 47–48, 56–59; Claude McKay, "A Negro Poet," 50. During this period, McKay wrote two volumes of poetry, *Songs of Jamaica* and *Constab Ballads*.

8. Claude McKay, "A Negro Poet," 50; Claude McKay, *Long Way from Home*, 4–5; Cooper, *Claude McKay*, 66–73, 84. Eulalie gave birth to a daughter, Hope Virtue, whom Claude never saw.

9. Claude McKay, *Long Way from Home*, 60, 67–70; Cooper, *Claude McKay*, 86–99, 105–7, 110, 112–13, 125–26. He published *Spring in New Hampshire* in 1920.

10. Claude McKay, *Long Way from Home*, 63 (quote), 97; Cooper, *Claude McKay*, 132, 157–61, 168–69.

11. Kerman and Eldridge, *Lives of Jean Toomer*, 19–24; Foner, *Reconstruction*, 353–54.

12. Quote from Nellie McKay, *Jean Toomer*, 13–14; Kerman and Eldridge, *Lives of Jean Toomer*, 25–26. For a discussion of the Pinchbacks within the larger context of the Washingtonian black elite, see Gatewood, *Aristocrats of Color*, esp. 42–43.

13. Toomer, "Book X," Box 11, Fol. 359, 11–12, JTP.

14. Kerman and Eldridge, *Lives of Jean Toomer*, 26–28, 33–34; Nellie McKay, *Jean Toomer*, 13; Toomer, "Book X," Box 11, Fol. 359, 7, JTP.

15. Toomer, "Book X," Box 11, Fol. 361, 41, 52, JTP; Kerman and Eldridge, *Lives of Jean Toomer*, 49–50.

16. Toomer, "Book X," Box 11, Fols. 358 and 363, 5–6, 82, JTP. For an excellent discussion of the importance of the frontier and production in early-twentieth-century literary constructions of black manhood, see Jayna Brown, "Black Patriarch on the Prairie."

17. Toomer, "Book X," Box 11, Fol. 364, 106, 108, JTP; Kerman and Eldridge, *Lives of Jean Toomer*, 50–51, 64.

18. Toomer, "Book X," Box 11, Fol. 364, 125, 127, JTP; Kerman and Eldridge, *Lives of Jean Toomer*, 64.

19. Toomer, "Book X," Box 12, Fol. 367, 202, JTP; Kerman and Eldridge, *Lives of Jean Toomer*, 65–71; Nellie McKay, *Jean Toomer*, 23–28. The Rand School was a socialist-supported institution that provided academic courses for students and workers. See Bender, *New York Intellect*, 300.

20. Nellie McKay, *Jean Toomer*, 44.

21. Kerman and Eldridge, *Lives of Jean Toomer*, 71–73; Bender, *New York Intellect*, 228–32, 241.

22. Kerman and Eldridge, *Lives of Jean Toomer*, 75, 79–83; Nellie McKay, *Jean Toomer*, 45–47.

23. Kerman and Eldridge, *Lives of Jean Toomer*, 85–88, 91–92.

24. Waldo Frank to Jean Toomer, 25 April 1922, Box 3, Fol. 83, JTP.

25. Toomer to Mrs. Wright, 18 August 1922, Box 9, Fol. 283, JTP.

26. Hughes, *Big Sea*, 13–17; Rampersad, *I, Too, Sing America*, 10–11.

27. Hughes, *Big Sea*, 17–18, 23, 26–34; Rampersad, *I, Too, Sing America*, 23–26.

28. Hughes, *Big Sea*, 35–40; Rampersad, *I, Too, Sing America*, 32–33.

29. Hughes, *Big Sea*, 39–44.

30. Ibid., 44–47.

31. Hughes to Carl Van Vechten, 12 January 1926, Box 5, Fol. 10, CVVP, NYPL; Rampersad, *I, Too, Sing America*, 34–35; Hughes, *Big Sea*, 48–49.

32. Hughes, *Big Sea*, 56–67, 69–71, 77–79; Rampersad, *I, Too, Sing America*, 48–49.

33. Hughes to Alain Locke, 6 April 1923, Box 164-38, Fol. 5, ALP; Hughes, *Big Sea*, 83–98 (quote on p. 98).

34. Fauset to Hughes, "Monday" [ca. 1920–26?], Box 57; Van Vechten to Hughes, 11 May [1927?], Box 154; both in LHP. Also see David Levering Lewis, *Harlem Renaissance Reader*, 757; Hughes, *Big Sea*, 216; Rampersad, *I, Too, Sing America*, 106, 113–15.

35. Nugent to Van Vechten, 26 February and 1 March 1942, no Box #, CVVP-Black.

36. Kirschke, *Aaron Douglas*, 1–11, 66–67 (Douglas's quotes on 4); Douglas to Locke, [1925–26?], Box 164-25, Fol. 36, ALP.

37. Douglas to Locke, n.d., Box 164-98, Fol. 2, ALP.

38. Quotes are from Fisher to Peterson, 12 November 1919 and "Wednesday" [October 1919], Box 1, Fol. 15, JWJ Small Collections (Peterson). For biographical information, see letters from his sister Pearl Fisher to Van Vechten, 29 July 1942 and 1 May 1951, no Box #, CVVP-Black. Also see Lewis, *Harlem Renaissance Reader*, 746. Fisher's novels were *The Walls of Jericho* (1928) and *The Conjure Man Dies* (1932).

39. For biographical information, see Lewis, *Harlem Renaissance Reader*, 764–65, and Locke, *New Negro*, 415–16. On Atlanta, see Walrond to Countee Cullen, 8 December 1923, Box 6, CCP. On Babbitt, see Kimmel, *Manhood in America*, 215, where he argues that the character, George Babbitt, became "a synonym for disaffected suburban manhood."

40. See introduction to Early, *Soul's High Song*, esp. 6–21. Also see Lewis, *Harlem Renaissance Reader*, 742.

41. Cullen to Jackman, 1 July 1923, Box 2, Fol. 19, JWJ Small Collections (Cullen).

42. See, for instance, Jervis Anderson, *This Was Harlem*, 128–33; Lawrence Levine, "Jazz and American Culture," in Levine, *Unpredictable Past*, 172–88. On jazz in Los Angeles, see Arna Bontemps, "The Awakening: A Memoir," in *Harlem Renaissance Remembered*, 7–8.

43. Johnson, *Black Manhattan*, 160–69.

44. Rogers, "Jazz at Home," in Locke, *New Negro*, 216–24. The ambiguity of the essay was most likely the result of Locke's editorial corrections. In a letter to Locke that generally praised his editorial skills, Rogers raised mild opposition to the final published draft: "Nevertheless I am inclined to say in all good nature that there was

injected into it a tinge of morality and 'uplift' alien to my innermost convictions" (Rogers to Locke, 7 March 1925, Box 164-81, Fol. 13, ALP). Locke's influence on the final draft is supported by his own letter to the publishers of *New Negro*: "I so largely rewrote the Rogersarticle [sic] on Jazz that it is practically my own." (Locke to Charles and Albert Boni, [1925], Box 164-10, Fol. 7, ALP).

45. Cullen to Jackman, 25 August 1923, Box 2, Fol. 19, JWJ Small Collections (Cullen).

46. Rogers, "Jazz at Home," 223–24. In his autobiography, Claude McKay recalls the "decorous cabarets," where visiting between tables was prohibited. See *Long Way from Home*, 47. For an excellent discussion of the class dynamics of leisure in early-twentieth-century Atlanta, see Hunter, *To 'Joy My Freedom*, 145–86.

47. Johnson, *Black Manhattan*, 169; Hughes, *Big Sea*, 244, 247–49; Bontemps, "The Awakening," 12, 18–19.

48. Hughes, *Big Sea*, 244–45, 248, 252–55; David Levering Lewis, *When Harlem Was*, 183–84, 212–13.

49. For a discussion of "slumming," see Mumford, *Interzones*, 133–56.

50. Wallace Thurman, "Harlem House-Rent Parties," handwritten draft, n.d., Box 3, Fol. 46; Thurman, "Harlem," typescript draft, n.d., Box 3, Fol. 45, 9; Thurman, "Terpsichore in Harlem," typescript draft, n.d., Box 1, Fol. 16; all in JWJ Small Collections (Thurman). On rents in Harlem, see Lewis, *When Harlem Was*, 108. On throwing a rent party in a rented hall, see Taylor Gordon to Carl Van Vechten, 6 June 1931, Box G, Fol. "Taylor Gordon, 1930–1934," CVVP-Black.

51. Hughes, *Big Sea*, 229–33; Thurman, "Harlem House-Rent Parties"; Thurman, "Terpsichore in Harlem."

52. Thurman, "Harlem," 9–10.

53. "Sweetbacks," typescript, n.d., Box 3, Fol. 47, JWJ Small Collections (Thurman). This draft was a combination of a description of the sweetback and publicity piece for Thurman and William Jourdan Rapp's play, *Harlem*. Although the author refers to Thurman in the third person, there is no reason to believe that, given the draft is in his collection, the author was not Thurman himself. The sociologist Charles S. Johnson also wrote of the economic situation in New York, the surplus of women to men, and the resulting relationship of working women and unemployed men, although he did not specifically refer to sweetbacks. See Johnson, "The New Frontage on American Life," in Locke, *New Negro*, 290.

54. Claude McKay, *Long Way from Home*, 120.

55. Johnson, *Black Manhattan*, 179–80; Rogers, "Jazz at Home," 223. Again, Rogers's interpretation of the cabaret was most likely modified by Locke. In a letter to Locke, Rogers expounded upon what he felt were the social benefits of the cabaret: "after a careful weighing of the matter I am inclined to think that of the two evils the church and the cabaret, the latter so far as the progress of the Negro group is concerned, is less of a mental drag." Rogers to Locke, 7 March 1925, Box 164-81, Fol. 13, ALP.

56. Fisher, "The Caucasian Storms Harlem," *American Mercury* (August 1927), reprinted

in Lewis, *Harlem Renaissance Reader*, 110–17; Mumford, *Interzones*, 153. Also see Tamara Brown, "It Don't Mean a Thing."

57. Hughes, *Big Sea*, 225–26; Fisher, "Caucasian Storms Harlem," 112–14.

58. Jones, *Labor of Love*, 161–62; Osofsky, *Harlem*, 136–37; Naison, *Communists in Harlem*, 32.

59. Committee of Fourteen report quoted in Chauncey, *Gay New York*, 248. On heteronormativity, see ibid., 105. On buffet flats, see Garber, "Spectacle in Color," 323.

60. Chauncey, *Gay New York*, 249–63.

61. Chauncey, *Gay New York*, 257; Hughes, *Big Sea*, 273–74; Jackman to Cullen, 19 April 1929, CCP, reel 1.

62. Lewis, *Harlem Renaissance Reader*, 758–59; Rampersad, *I, Too, Sing America*, 165; Locke to Louise Thompson Thurman, 8 October 1928, copy, Box 164-89, Fol. 44, ALP; Thurman to McKay, 4 October 1928, Box 5, CMC.

63. Lewis, *Harlem Renaissance Reader*, 763; Rampersad, *I, Too, Sing America*, 171–72; West, "Elephant's Dance," 80–81. West claimed that Thurman's marriage was ultimately a result of his desire to have a child, to "reproduce himself." The longer he remained childless, the more he felt less masculine: "He wanted to be thoroughly male and was afraid that he was not" (80).

64. Thurman to Rapp, 1 June 1929 and 7 May [1929?], Box 1, Fol. 7, JWJ Small Collections (Thurman); Lewis, *When Harlem Was*, 278–79. For a discussion of the significance of public washrooms in the "sexual topographies" of New York City, see Chauncey, *Gay New York*, 195–201.

65. Thurman to McKay, 4 October 1928, Box 5, CMC; Thurman to Hughes, "Friday," Box 150, Fol. "Thurman," LHP; Thurman to Rapp, 7 May [1929?], Box 1, Fol. 7, JWJ Small Collections (Thurman). Although Thurman resisted identifying himself as gay, he was actively involved in a gay subculture and also had at least one long-term relationship with a man prior to his marriage. See Henderson, "Portrait of Wallace Thurman," 160–61; Rampersad, *I, Too, Sing America*, 137. Louise Thompson Patterson, in an interview with Rampersad, claimed his sexual ambivalence was part of what destroyed their marriage: "He took nothing seriously . . . And he would never admit that he was a homosexual. *Never, never*, not to me at any rate" (172, original emphasis).

66. Hurston to Hughes, 8 March 1928 and n.d., Box 76, LHP; Hurston to Godmother [Charlotte Osgood Mason], 23 July 1931, Box 164-99, Fol. 6, ALP. Also see Hemenway, *Zora Neale Hurston*.

67. Robeson to Van Vechten and Fania M., 11 October 1925, no Box #, CVVP-Black; Robeson to Carl Van Vechten, 19 December 1930, 20 April 1931, 13 July 1932. All in Fol. "E. Robeson, 1930–33," CVVP-Black. Also see Duberman, *Paul Robeson*, 34–37 and passim.

68. May, *Great Expectations*, 1–11, 156–63; Cott, *Groundings of Modern Feminism*, 147–48; 179–93; Ullman, *Sex Seen*, 72–102.

69. Wilson to McKay, 12 October 1929, Box 5, CMC. Wilson's attitude toward marriage may have been the result of an ambivalent sexual identity. Regarding homosexuals, she wrote to McKay, "Some of my best friends are such people and I find them stimulating when they aren't too neurotic. I have often wondered about myself. . . . [U]p to now I have had no experience with that sort of thing and have avoided it, mainly because I am half-afraid and because I have studied enough psychology [and] psycho-analysis to be able to see it more as a psychopathic disease than as an experience to be hoped for." Wilson to McKay, 2 January 1930, Box 5, CMC.

70. Ann Rucker to Arthur Schomburg, 21 June 1933 and 11 July 1933, Box 6, Fol. 45, ASP (original emphasis).

71. Cott, *Groundings of Modern Feminism*, 157.

72. Reverend F. A. Cullen to Alain Locke, 29 January 1924, Box 164-22, Fol. 41, ALP; Cullen to Jackman, 20 July, 10 August, and 18 August 1923, Box 2, Fol. 19, JWJ Small Collections (Cullen); Lewis, *When Harlem Was*, 202.

73. Cullen to Jackman, 20 July 1923 and 7 October 1925, Box 2, Fol. 19, JWJ Small Collections (Cullen).

74. Cullen to Locke, 26 August and 30 September 1923, Box 164-22, Fol. 36, ALP.

75. Early, *Soul's High Song*, 19 n. 21. For works that claim that Cullen was homosexual, see Chauncey, *Gay New York*, 264–65; Garber, "Spectacle in Color," 327; Rampersad, *I, Too, Sing America*, 66; Lewis, *Du Bois: The Fight*, 224–28.

76. Cullen to Locke, 3 March 1923, Box 164-22, Fol. 36, ALP. On *Iölaus*, see Chauncey, *Gay New York*, 284. There are surviving letters from Locke to Cullen but few discuss homosexuality or, as Cullen termed it, "that friendship beyond understanding." One possible explanation may be that Cullen threw away letters from Locke that he felt were too explicit. Cullen was very cautious about his personal life and wished to keep any possible hint of homosexual inclinations from becoming public. He ended his letter to Locke with the following advice: "Sentiments expressed here would be misconstrued by others, so this letter, once read, is best destroyed." For a discussion of self-censorship, the "historical silences" around sexual subjectivity, and the problems these present to historians, see Freedman, " 'The Burning of Letters Continues.' "

77. Cullen to Locke, 1 April and 4 May 1924, Box 164-22, Fol. 37, ALP.

78. Cullen to Hughes, 13 June 1924, Box 44, LHP.

79. Cullen to Locke, 27 October 1924, Box 164-22, Fol. 37, ALP (original emphasis). Although Cullen only referred to this mysterious person by initials, it is clear that "L. R." was a man. See ibid. and Cullen to Locke, 31 October 1924.

80. Cullen to Locke, 20 September 1924, Box 164-22, Fol. 37, ALP.

81. Yolande Du Bois to Cullen, 27 September 1926 and 4 January 1927, Box 1, Fols. 9 and 11, JWJ Small Collections (Cullen).

82. Brenda Ray Moryck to Cullen, 3 April 1928, Box 3, Fol. 20, CCP, reel 2.

83. Yolande Du Bois to Cullen, 18 August 1927, Box 1, Fol. 13, JWJ Small Collections (Cullen).
84. Guillaume Brown to Cullen, 21 July 1927, Box 1, CCP, reel 1.
85. Yolande Du Bois to Cullen, 18 October, 25 October, 6 November 1927, Box 1, Fol. 13, JWJ Small Collections (Cullen), (original emphasis). I have not been able to locate any surviving letters from Cullen to Du Bois so it is difficult to get the entire picture of what created the initial break and the eventual reconciliation. It was most likely Yolande's deliberate flirting and attempts to make Countee jealous by discussing her male friends and acquaintances.
86. Hughes, *Big Sea*, 274–75; David Levering Lewis, *Du Bois: The Fight*, 220–23.
87. Yolande Du Bois to Cullen, 19 and 22 April 1928, Box 1, Fol. 15, JWJ Small Collections (Cullen); David Levering Lewis, *Du Bois: The Fight*, 223–27.
88. See the following letters from W. E. B. Du Bois to Cullen, 11 September, 9 October, 11 October 1928, Box 2, Fol. 12, CCP, reel 1; Lewis, *When Harlem Was*, 203.
89. W. E. B. Du Bois to Cullen, 11 October 1928, Box 2, Fol. 12, CCP, reel 1. On the companionate marriage, see Cott, *Groundings of Modern Feminism*, 156–59.
90. W. E. B. Du Bois to Cullen, 18 September 1928, Box 2, Fol. 12, CCP, reel 1; Early, *Soul's High Song*, 52.
91. Thurman to Rapp, 7 May [1929?], Box 1, Fol. 7, JWJ Small Collections (Thurman). On Powell's crusade, see Chauncey, *Gay New York*, 254–56.
92. Garber, "Spectacle in Color," 326. Also see Schwarz, *Gay Voices*, which promises to become the definitive queer history of the Harlem Renaissance. Unfortunately, it was published after I already completed this manuscript.
93. Toomer, "The Psychology of the Homosexual," handwritten draft, n.d.; "Homosexuals," typescript, n.d.; both in Box 49, Fol. 1036, JTP. For a discussion of Toomer's own sexuality, see Guterl, *Color of Race*, 177–79.
94. Duberman, *Paul Robeson*, 93–94; Aaron Douglas to Alta Sawyer, n.d., Fol. 3, #21 and #29, ADP.
95. Garber, "Spectacle in Color," 326; Rampersad, *I, Too, Sing America*, 46, 69. Cf. Douglas, *Terrible Honesty*, 97.
96. Claude McKay, *Long Way from Home*, 312; Cooper, *Claude McKay*, 30, 75, 149–51. On the term "pussyfoot" as a charge aimed at demasculinizing men, see Chauncey, *Gay New York*, 114–15.
97. McKay to Charles Henri Ford, 20 July 1938, copy, Box 6, Fol. "D–Kz," CMC; Claude McKay, *Long Way from Home*, 337–38; Chauncey, *Gay New York*, 191, 242–43.
98. Chauncey, *Gay New York*, 5, 99–127.
99. Hughes, *Big Sea*, 237; Nugent to Locke, 24 January 1929 and "Monday," Box 164-75, Fol. 18, ALP.
100. Locke to McKay, 13 March 1930, Box 3, CMC.

Chapter Five

1. Charles S. Johnson to Alain Locke, 7 March 1924, Box 164-40, Fol. 25, ALP. Also see David Levering Lewis's introduction to *Harlem Renaissance Reader*, xvi–xvii.

2. Locke to Langston Hughes, 10 February 1922 and 22 May 1924, Box 97, LHP. On Locke's credentials, see Arnold Rampersad's introduction to Locke, *New Negro*, xi.

3. *Survey Graphic* 6, no. 6 (March 1925); David Levering Lewis, *When Harlem Was*, 115–17. The list of contributors to the special number is by no means comprehensive.

4. Locke, "The New Negro," in Locke, *New Negro*, xxv, 3–4.

5. Ibid., 6–11, 15. For an overview of American modernism and its emphasis on "authenticity," the integration of the earlier Victorian dichotomies of civilization and savagery, and the sundering of barriers based on race, class, and gender, see Singal, "Towards a Definition." Although modernists strove to overturn the absolute "truths" of Victorian thought, "truths" that were based largely on nineteenth-century positivism and scientific objectivity, they nevertheless did not abandon Western epistemology. As Singal notes, American modernists, in particular, were still preoccupied with a "pragmatic empiricism" along with a "democratic pluralism." Also see Douglas, *Terrible Honesty*, 108–48.

6. Wood's comment is in the promotional brochure for "Harlem: Mecca of the New Negro," in Box 164-115, Fol. 20, ALP.

7. Locke, "New Negro," 15.

8. Rotundo, *American Manhood*, 169–72. Also see Dubbert, *Man's Place*, 31–32; Lears, *No Place of Grace*, 251–57. Ann Douglas argues that one aspect of modernism, particularly the modernism of Hemingway and Fitzgerald, was the overthrow of the Victorian matriarch through the masculinization of literature. Although her discussion of the masculinist ethos of New York modernists is persuasive, it also seems that it was directed not only at the matriarch but at the Victorian patriarch (i.e., nineteenth- and early-twentieth-century constructions of manhood) as well. See Douglas, *Terrible Honesty*, esp. 239–46.

9. Torgovnick, *Gone Primitive*, 17–18, 85–104, 141–58. Torgovnick also suggests, persuasively, that the "primitive" is associated with other "subordinated segments of a population," including Jews, blacks, and the working class. For another discussion of the complex interrelatedness of the "primitive," women, blacks, and Jews, see Gilman, *Difference and Pathology*, 109–27. On the feminine qualities of black culture as they were articulated by early-twentieth-century black intellectuals, see Paul Gilroy, "'Cheer the Weary Traveler': W. E. B. Du Bois, Germany, and the Politics of (Dis)placement," in *Black Atlantic*, esp. 135.

10. Hammer, *Hart Crane and Allan Tate*, 4, 12–13. Hammer argues that the "cult of production" was a way of negotiating the connoisseur's commitment to the "feminine" sphere of taste and the professional artists' adherence to the "masculine" sphere of technique. Hammer suggests that the masculine-coded "cult of production" elevated the skill of writing to an elite status, removed "true" literature from

the domain of mass culture, and contributed to the professionalization of cultural production.

11. Johnson to Carl Van Vechten, 6 March 1927, Fol. "JWJ 1927–9," CVVP-Black.

12. It should be stressed that, in focusing on male artists and the meanings that cultural production held for their sense of masculinity, I do not mean to diminish the contributions of female artists in the Harlem Renaissance or the role of gender in determining how we remember them. Writers and artists such as Zora Neale Hurston, Jessie Fauset, Nella Larsen, Gwendolyn Bennett, and Anne Spencer struggled over similar questions of black representation and the capacity of culture to improve the status of blacks. The significance of these questions and their attempts to resolve them, however, held different meanings for men and women in terms of their gender identities. On art and black women's identity in the Renaissance, see Hull, *Color, Sex and Poetry*; Wall, *Women of the Harlem Renaissance*.

13. Last quote is from Carl Van Vechten's response in "The Negro in Art: How Shall He Be Portrayed: A Symposium," *Crisis* 31 (March 1926): 219. Also see Julia Peterkin's response in *Crisis* 32 (September 1926): 238–39.

14. "Negro in Art," *Crisis* 32 (June 1926): 72.

15. "Negro in Art," *Crisis* 32 (August 1926): 194.

16. See, for instance, Singh, "Black-White Symbiosis"; Anderson, *This Was Harlem*, 223.

17. Locke, "Negro Youth Speaks," in Locke, *New Negro*, 48–49.

18. Hammer, *Hart Crane and Allan Tate*, 9 and passim. Hammer writes that modernism is "forward-looking in its manifold forms because it attacks the genteel monopoly on culture" while it "looks backward too, because it institutes and enforces its own monopolies of cultural prestige, reasserts hierarchies of sexual and racial difference, and reconstructs traditional authority in restrictive ways." Locke's discussion of the artistic genealogy of the New Negro bears out Hammer's point. In his discussion of the older poets' influence on the younger, he differentiated Grimké, Spencer, and Douglas Johnson from the older male poets without giving an explanation in terms of either the form or content of their verse. In part, this can be attributed to Locke's genteel, but pervasive, chauvinism that characterized his interaction with women; I would also argue that it was his attempt to establish a male "tradition" in black arts and letters.

19. Locke, "A Decade of Negro Self-Expression," *Trustees of the John F. Slater Fund Occasional Papers No. 26* (1928), 7, in Box 164-105, Fol. 2, ALP.

20. Johnson, *Black Manhattan*, 283–84.

21. "Negro in Art," *Crisis* 31 (April 1926): 279–80.

22. Johnson was born in Jacksonville, Florida, in 1871. Locke was born in Philadelphia in 1885.

23. Although fiction, Carl Van Vechten, who wrote the 1927 introduction, felt that it was "a composite autobiography of the Negro race in the United States in modern times." In his introduction to the 1989 Vintage Books edition, Henry Louis

Gates Jr. remarks that, despite *Autobiography*'s first-person narration, several review-
ers surmised that the work was a piece of fiction. See Johnson, *Autobiography of an
Ex-Coloured Man*, vi–vii, xv, xxxiv.

24. Johnson's assessment of the creation of this "desperate" class certainly was influenced by the changing ideas on the connection between race and culture in the early
twentieth century. Settlement house workers and sociologists began by arguing that
poverty, crime, and illiteracy were the results of environment and historical circumstances, such as slavery, rather than innate moral weakness. These ideas were scientifically buttressed in the 1920s and 1930s, as cultural anthropologists successfully
challenged the "conceptual links between race and character, morality, psychology,
and language." See Pascoe, "Miscegenation Law," 52–55. Also see Lasch-Quinn,
Black Neighbors, 9–23.

25. Johnson did not assume that the relational axis of masculinity only operated in one
direction. Black men were not alone in using another racial group as a reference
point in the construction of their gender identity: "The same thing may be said of
the white man of the South; most of his mental efforts run through one narrow
channel; his life as a man and a citizen, many of his financial activities, and all of
his political activities are impassably limited by the ever present 'Negro question'"
(75–76).

26. Hayes to Johnson, 23 April 1923, Box 9, Fol. 199, JWJP.

27. Fullinwinder, *Mind and Mood*, 87. Also see Huggins, *Harlem Renaissance*, 144–53.

28. White perceptively dealt with black women's marginalization in liberation politics through tragicomic critiques of male privilege. Even though the cooperative
is Jane's idea, she steps aside and allows people to think it is Kenneth's: "It was
amusing to see men, vain creatures that they are, preen themselves on what they
had done. It was not so amusing when they, in their pride, sought to belittle what
the women had done and take all the credit to themselves. Oh, well, what did it
matter? The end was the all-important thing—not the means" (167).

29. Toomer, Untitled manuscript draft, n.d., Box 51, Fol. 1111, JTP.

30. Toomer to Mae Wright, 4 August 1922, Box 9, Fol. 283, JTP; Kerman and Eldridge,
Lives of Jean Toomer, 87–88.

31. Toomer, Notes for untitled manuscript, n.d., Box 51, Fol. 1106; Toomer to John
McClure, 30 June 1922, Box 2, Fol. 46; both in JTP.

32. Toomer to Wright, 4 August 1922, Box 9, Fol. 283, JTP.

33. Toomer to Anderson, 29 December 1922, Box 1, Fol. 5; Toomer to Frank, [1923?],
Box 3, Fol. 84; both in JTP.

34. For a recent treatment of Toomer's resistance to being racially classified, see Guterl,
Color of Race, 154–83.

35. Although interpretations vary widely, most scholars agree that Toomer was attempting to work out his own relationship to his African American heritage in *Cane*.
In doing so, he achieved a temporary "unity" of self although he would later turn to

mysticism and other forms of spirituality to maintain the "unity" of a race-less self. Moreover, there is consensus that, in general, the symbolism in *Cane* is extremely ambiguous and, therefore, allows for multiple interpretations. See, for instance, Kerman and Eldridge, *Lives of Jean Toomer*, esp. 79–100; Nellie McKay, *Jean Toomer*, 85, 87, and passim; Lewis, *When Harlem Was*, 64–71; Huggins, *Harlem Renaissance*, 179–87; Singh, *Novels of the Harlem Renaissance*, 64–69; Fullinwinder, *Mind and Mood*, 133–44. Also see Darwin T. Turner's introduction to Toomer, *Cane*. I am using the 1993 reissue of this work.

36. Nellie McKay, *Jean Toomer*, 91.

37. Kabnis was clearly Toomer himself, an acknowledgment he made to his friend Waldo Frank and to Kenneth MacGowan, editor of *Theater Arts Magazine*. See Toomer to MacGowan, 15 March 1923, Box 5, Fol. 164, JTP.

38. On Lewis as a foil to Kabnis, see Nellie McKay, *Jean Toomer*, 166.

39. McKay, "He Who Gets Slapped," *Liberator* 5 (May 1922): 24–25, reprinted in Cooper, *Passion of Claude McKay*, 69–73.

40. McKay to Jackman, 9 May 1928, Box 6, CMC.

41. McKay, "A Black Man Replies," letter to *Daily Herald* published in *Worker's Dreadnought*, 24 April 1920, reprinted in Cooper, *Passion of Claude McKay*, 56. McKay's letter was in response to the *Daily Herald*'s raising of the specter of black barbarism. The race-baiting was a strategy used by the British government and newspaper to undermine France's proposal to use African colonial troops to occupy the Ruhr after World War I.

42. McKay to Jackman, 1 April [31 March] 1928, Box 6, CMC.

43. McKay to Jackman, 9 May 1928, Box 6, CMC.

44. Claude McKay, *Long Way from Home*, 304. Few whites have any place or role in these black working-class environments. Even when an Irish policeman, who McKay implies is also "primitive," visits the Philadelphia buffet flat—to enjoy the space rather than raid it—he is descriptively differentiated from the black revelers: "'Raided!' A voice screamed. Standing in the rear door, a policeman, white, in full uniform, smilingly contemplated the spectacle. There was a wild scramble for hats and wraps" (*Home to Harlem*, 197). The image one is left with is a fully clothed European adventurer or missionary observing the ritual "savagery" of half-naked Africans.

45. Douglas, *Terrible Honesty*, 31–40.

46. For intelligent discussions on these issues, see Singh, *Novels of the Harlem Renaissance*, 42–53; Lewis, *When Harlem Was*, 226–28.

47. Carby, "Policing the Black Woman's Body," 747.

48. "Zeddy discovered that in his own circles in Harlem he had become something of a joke. It was known that he was living sweet. . . . He had to fight a fellow in Dixie Red's pool-room, for calling him a 'skirt-man.'" Claude McKay, *Home to Harlem*, 87.

49. Lively, "Continuity and Radicalism," 228–34.

50. One exception is Agatha, Ray's girlfriend in *Home to Harlem*, who is a beautician's

assistant and, as Ray himself notes, a "slave of civilization." She does not command as much attention in these novels, however, as Felice, a prostitute who Jake eventually marries, and Latnah, a Middle Eastern woman who hangs out with the beach bums in *Banjo*.

51. A similar sentiment is expressed in the character of Billy Biasse in *Home to Harlem*. Biasse, a gay man, is a major character within the novel. He proudly proclaims that he is a "Wolf" because "he eats his own kind" (92). Biasse is also one of the toughest characters in the book, living his life by an urban, gangster-like code of ethics. He carries around a gun when others only carry knives. When Jake informs Biasse that he does not like to carry guns, he responds, " 'Youse a punk customer, then, I tell you . . . and no real buddy o'mine' " (287).

In urban, working-class gay subcultures of the early twentieth century, "wolf" referred to men who "abided by the conventions of masculinity and yet exhibited a decided preference for male sexual partners," usually younger, effeminate males who were labeled as "punks." See Chauncey, *Gay New York*, 86–88.

52. Hughes, "Negro Artist."

53. Hughes, *Big Sea*, 324–25; Hughes, "Negro Artist," 693.

54. Kirschke, *Aaron Douglas*, 9–10, 26–30.

55. Douglas [Daddy] to Alta Sawyer [Sweetheart], n.d., Fol. 3, #29, ADP (original emphasis). Douglas alluded to the power of cubism in strikingly masculine terms: "For Cubism no longer exists as an active artistic force. It has long since posited its germ plasma in the womb of art where it has come to life as modern art."

56. Douglas to Sawyer, n.d., Fol. 2, #13, ADP.

57. Douglas, open letter on *Fire!!* letterhead, n.d., Fol. 9, ADP.

58. Douglas to Hughes, 21 December 1925, Box 51, LHP. There was only one edition of *Fire!!* The irreverent magazine was lambasted by the older Harlem literati as well as the critics of the leading black newspapers. Furthermore, the editorial staff could not secure financial backing for any more issues. Ironically, the bulk of the copies of the first issue burned up in a basement fire. See Lewis, *When Harlem Was*, 194–97.

59. Douglas to Hughes, 21 December 1925, Box 51, LHP.

60. Douglas to Sawyer, n.d., Fol. 7, #66, ADP.

61. Woodruff to Locke, 24 March 1932, Box 164-94, Fol. 46, ALP.

62. See, for example, Gail Bederman's discussion of the cultural importance of Tarzan in modern definitions of masculinity in *Manliness and Civilization*, 218–32.

63. Lewis, *When Harlem Was*, 99–102; David Levering Lewis, "Parallels and Divergences," 560–64; Price, "In Search of a People's Spirit."

64. Hughes, *Big Sea*, 316; Lewis, *When Harlem Was*, 151–55.

65. Godmother to Locke, 16 August 1927, Box 164-68, Fol. 18, ALP. Also see her letters to Locke from March to July 1927, Box 164-68, Fol. 17, ALP. On the infantile and feminine interchangeability of what she calls "primitive tropes," see Torgovnick, *Gone Primitive*, esp. 8–9, 17–18.

66. Locke to Godmother, 7 June 1928, Box 164-68, Fol. 23; Hurston to Godmother, 20 December 1930, Box 164-99, Fol. 4; Johnson to Mrs. R. Osgood Mason, 25 May 1928, Box 164-99, Fol. 13. All letters are in ALP.

67. On obsequence as a tactic, see Lewis, *When Harlem Was*, 154–55, and Hemenway, *Zora Neale Hurston*, 139. For somewhat negative assessments of patronage and philanthropy, see Douglas, *Terrible Honesty*, 100, and Huggins, *Harlem Renaissance*, 128–36.

68. Hughes to Godmother, draft of unsent letter, 15 June [ca. 1930], Box 75, LHP; Rampersad, *I, Too, Sing America*, 147–201. Also see Chapter 4 above.

69. Hughes to Godmother, draft of unsent letter, 6 June [1930], Box 75, LHP; Rampersad, *I, Too, Sing America*, 175–84.

70. Hughes, *Big Sea*, 324–25. Shortly after Hughes officially broke with Godmother, he and Hurston became embroiled in a controversy surrounding their collaborative efforts on the play, *Mule Bone*. The dispute has been covered in detail elsewhere. Suffice it to say that, at its root, the fight concerned who was the actual author. During the controversy, Hurston—with Locke's support—pled her case to Godmother with particularly malicious letters about Hughes. See, for example, letters from Hurston to Godmother dated 20 January 1931, 14 August 1931, and 14 May 1932; all in ALP. For discussions of the *Mule Bone* controversy, see Hemenway, *Zora Neale Hurston*, 136–58, and Rampersad, *I, Too, Sing America*, 194–200.

71. Hughes, *Big Sea*, 3, 98.

72. Thurman, "Marcus Garvey," typescript draft of *Aunt Hagar's Children*, n.d., Box 1, Fol. 15, 11–12, JWJ Small Collections (Thurman).

73. Locke to Van Vechten, 21 December 1925, Fol. "Locke," CVVP-Black.

74. Claude McKay, *Long Way from Home*, 342–45; McKay to Cunard, copy, 25 January 1933, Box 6, CMC.

75. McKay to Jackman, 1 August 1927, Box 6, CMC. Also see McKay to Hughes, 22 September 1924, Box 102, LHP.

76. Ivy to McKay, 23 April 1928, Box 3, CMC. McKay was living in Marseilles at the time.

77. McKay to Locke, 27 July 1926, Box 164-67, Fol. 8, ALP; McKay to Hughes, 9 May 1925, LHP, Box 102.

78. McKay to Locke, 7 October 1924, Box 164-67, Fol. 8, ALP (original emphasis). On "pussyfoot" as a term aimed at demasculinizing men, see Chauncey, *Gay New York*, 114–15.

79. McKay to Locke, 1 August 1926 and 18 April 1927, Box 164-67, Fols. 8 and 9, ALP (original emphasis). McKay discussed his relationship with Locke and the flap over "The White House" in his autobiography. He ended his assessment of Locke: "I couldn't imagine such a man as the leader of a renaissance, when his artistic outlook was so reactionary." See McKay, *Long Way from Home*, 312–14.

80. Thurman, preface to typescript draft of *Aunt Hagar's Children*, n.d., Box 1, Fol. 11, JWJ Small Collections (Thurman).

81. Lewis, *When Harlem Was*, xvi; Huggins, *Harlem Renaissance*; Cruse, *Crisis of the Negro Intellectual*.

82. See, for instance, Douglas, *Terrible Honesty*; Houston Baker, *Modernism*; Hutchinson, *Harlem Renaissance in Black and White*.

Chapter Six

1. Wolters, *New Negro on Campus*; Lamon, "Black Community in Nashville."

2. Aptheker, "Negro College Student in the 1920s," 153–54.

3. All quotes are from Locke, "Negro Education Bids for Par." Also see Du Bois, "Negroes in College."

4. Howard was named after General Oliver Otis Howard, the commissioner of the Freedmen's Bureau, while Fisk took its name from General Clinton B. Fisk, assistant commissioner of the Freedmen's Bureau for Tennessee and Kentucky. The American Missionary Association was involved in the founding of both schools although it played a larger role in the daily functioning of Fisk. See Wolters, *New Negro on Campus*, 70–71; Richardson, *History of Fisk*, 2–4.

5. Richardson, *History of Fisk*, 4–15; Dyson, *Howard University*, 44–48.

6. Both universities foundered financially until they were bailed out by, in the case of Fisk, the successful fund-raising of the Fisk Jubilee Singers and, in the case of Howard, congressional support. See Richardson, *History of Fisk*, 22–39; Wolters, *New Negro on Campus*, 71, 78–82.

7. The definitive scholarly work on industrial versus liberal arts education in the South is Anderson, *Education of Blacks in the South*.

8. Dyson, *Howard University*, 109–16; "Report of Acting President Teunis S. Hamlin to the Board of Trustees of Howard University," 26 May 1903, Minutes of Board of Trustees Meeting, BOT/HU.

9. *Catalogue of the Officers and Students of Fisk University for 1900–1901* (Nashville, Tenn., 1901), 15, 20, in FUSC. Also see Richardson, *History of Fisk*, 59.

10. Richardson, *History of Fisk*, 59–63.

11. Du Bois and Dill, *College-Bred Negro American*, 12–18.

12. Anderson, *Education of Blacks in the South*, 250–51. Also see Du Bois, "Negro Education."

13. Wolters, *New Negro on Campus*, 29, 70.

14. For an excellent discussion of industrial, liberal arts, and Christian education in the context of higher education of black women, see Higginbotham, *Righteous Discontent*, 19–46.

15. Quote is from ibid., 30; Anderson, *Education of Blacks in the South*, 240–44. For discussions of social science approaches to the conditions of blacks around the turn of the century, see Lasch-Quinn, *Black Neighbors*, esp. 11–23; Gaines, *Uplifting the Race*, 152–78.

16. *Catalogue of the Officers and Students of Fisk University for 1900–1901*, 6, 22; *Fisk University News* 7, no. 9 (Catalogue No. 1915–16): 17.

17. *Catalogue of Officers and Students from March, 1899, to March, 1900* (Washington, D.C., 1900), 60; Howard University Record, *Catalogue: Howard University, 1909–10* (Washington, D.C., 1910), 32–33; both in Howardiana Collection, HUA.

18. *Catalogue of Officers and Students from March, 1899, to March 1900*, 13, 29; Howard University Record, *Catalogue: Howard University, 1909–10*, 165.

19. *Catalogue of the Officers and Students of Fisk University for 1900–1901*, 15.

20. Dr. Lyman P. Powell, "The By-Products of Fisk," *Fisk University News* 12, no. 3 (December 1921): 9–10. One article in a 1906 Howard University publication captured the tension around the transformation from a culture of character to a culture of personality that Warren I. Susman and others have identified as a major development in modern America. The author articulated a concern over a similar transformation when he or she wrote: "Character is a great deal more important than reputation. We are personally responsible for our character, but we are not personally responsible for our reputation. Our character depends on what we are; our reputation depends on what others think we are. If we will take good care of our character, we need not trouble ourselves about our reputation. Our reputation may change with the changes of popular opinion and feeling, but our character will not change so long as we are what we are. Yet as a practical matter we are more likely to worry over our reputation than our character. How foolish is this!" See "Character More Important Than Reputation," *University Journal* 3, no. 10 (26 January 1906): 1, in Howardiana Collection, HUA. Also see Susman, " 'Personality' and the Making of Twentieth-Century Culture," in *Culture as History*, 271–85.

21. Frederic J. Haskin, "Can College Be Civilized," *Atlanta Journal*, 18 November 1920, reprinted in "Are College Students Barbarians?" *Fisk University News* 11, no. 3 (December 1920): 12. Haskin invoked G. Stanley Hall's recapitulation theory in arguing that young men were essentially savages: "It has been stated many times that each individual in the course of his development repeats all the stages through which the race has passed. Probably the idea has been overworked, but it is certainly suggestive. Thus boys under sixteen are undoubtedly savages in many ways. They band loosely together like savages; they go adventuring like savages; and they often show savage cruelty both to each other and to animals." For a gendered interpretation of recapitulation theory, see Bederman, *Manliness and Civilization*, 77–120.

22. "Copy of fund-raising letter by Assistant to President," n.d., Box 18, Fol. 10, FMC. On the Houston mutiny, see Reich, "Soldiers of Democracy."

23. "Fisk University Opens with Impressive Flag-Raising," *Fisk University News* 9, no. 2 (October 1918): 18.

24. The number of African Caribbean men and women in historically black colleges and universities paled in comparison to the number of African Americans. To be

sure, there was an African Caribbean presence in higher educational institutions in the United States, although a contemporaneous report indicated that many tended to attend predominantly white universities. Howard attracted African Caribbean immigrants more than any other historically black institution. African Caribbean students were an important fixture on Howard's campus, evident in the presence of West Indian student associations and the fact that the institution prided itself on the fact that it conducted "official examinations" on the islands in an effort to recruit students. There is very little evidence of Fisk having a similar relationship with students from the Caribbean. See Alfred Edgar Smith, "West Indian on the Campus," *Opportunity* 11, no. 8 (August 1933): 238–41. Also see Howard University Record, *Catalogue: Howard University, 1909–10*, 218; Howard University Bulletin, *Annual Catalogue of Howard University for 1920–1921 with Announcements for 1921–1922* 1, no. 1 (June 1921), n.p.; *Report of President Durkee to the Board of Trustees, Howard University, Washington, D.C., 1925–26*, 11. All in Howardiana Collection, HUA.

25. A. C. Richey, "The Value of Athletics," *Fisk University News* 6, no. 6 (March 1916): 13–14; "Howard and Athletics," *University Journal* 3, no. 7 (5 January 1906): 1.

26. "Cricket," *University Journal* 3, no. 17 (16 March 1906): 3; "Cricket Match," *University Journal* 3, no. 25 (11 May 1906): 5; "Cricket," *Howard University Journal* 6, no. 27 (30 April 1909): 5; "Cricket Game Saturday," *Howard University Journal* 7, no. 29 (29 April 1910): 6; "Athletics," *Howard University Journal* 8, no. 21 (10 March 1911): 6.

27. McKenzie, "The President's Report to the Board of Trustees, Fisk University, for the Year Ending June 30, 1920 (1 January 1921)," *Fisk University News* 11, no. 4 (January 1921): 6–7; *Fisk University News* 7, no. 9 (Catalogue no. 1915–16): 22–23. On problems of player eligibility and professionalism in college sports, see Richardson, *History of Fisk*, 157–58; Little, "Extra-Curricular Activities," 143–44. For an example of a college team traveling in order to recruit new students—in this case Howard's baseball team's tour through West Virginia—see "Base Ball 1906," *University Journal* 3, no. 13 (16 February 1906): 1.

28. Oriard, *Reading Football*, 25–56.

29. Dyson, *Howard University*, 51–54. Dyson points out that "girls attending the University were not so restricted in their movements" (54).

30. Richardson, *History of Fisk*, 16–17.

31. "Report of Acting President Hamlin to the Board of Trustees of Howard University," 26 May 1903, Minutes of the Board of Trustees Meetings; Minutes of 31 May 1904 meeting of the Board of Trustees; both in BOT/HU.

32. Professors Lightfoot, Locke, and MacLear, "Howard University in the War—A Record of Patriotic Service," *Howard University Record* 13, no. 4 (April 1919): 159–65, in Box 164-115, Fol. 27, ALP. On the NAACP and the Camp Des Moines situation, see Lewis, *Du Bois: Biography of a Race*, 528–32.

33. Lightfoot, Locke, and MacLear, "Howard University in the War," 168–71; "Atten-

tion, All Colored Youth of High School and Colleges Age Not Yet Drafted," *Fisk University News* 9, no. 1 (September 1918): 1–3; "The President's Report," *Fisk University News* 9, no. 5 (January 1919): 2.

34. Lightfoot, Locke, and MacLear, "Howard University in the War," 172–77.

35. Miss Belle Ruth Parmenter, "Reorganization of Fisk Campus for War Purposes," *Fisk University News* 9, no. 1 (September 1918): 4–5; McKenzie's letter reprinted in *Fisk University News* 9, no. 1 (September 1918).

36. Lightfoot, Locke, and MacLear, "Howard University in the War," 172–73; Minutes of Semi-Annual Meeting of Board of Trustees, 7 February 1919, BOT/HU; Smith, "West Indian on the Campus," 240.

37. "The President's Report," *Fisk University News* 9, no. 5 (January 1919): 4–5; McKenzie, "Educational Efficiencies through the Military Idea," *Fisk University News* 9, no. 4 (December 1918): 20.

38. Quote is from Howard University, *Student Manual* (July 1922), pamphlet, 3, in Howardiana Collection, HUA.

39. *Catalogue of the Officers and Students of Fisk University for 1900–1901*, 26; Howard University, *Student Manual*, 7.

40. Howard University, *Student Manual*, 5. This practice undoubtedly assisted upperclasspersons in identifying first-year students for hazing purposes, which, interestingly, was prohibited by university policy.

41. *Catalogue of the Officers and Students of Fisk University . . . 1904–1905*, 22–23; *Fisk University News* 7, no. 9 (Catalogue no. 1915–16): 20–21.

42. "Special Note Regarding the 1919 Pictorial Catalogue," *Fisk University News* 9, no. 8 (April 1919): 11; McKenzie, "President's Report to the Board of Trustees of Fisk University, 1919–1920 (15 January 1920)," *Fisk University News* 10, no. 5 (January 1920): 9; *Catalogue of the Officers and Students of Fisk University . . . 1904–1905*, 23.

43. "Simplicity in College Dress," *Fisk University News* 12, no. 3 (December 1921): 23.

44. Alphonse D. Phillipse, "Analysis of Fisk University," typescript, Spring 1924, in WEBDP (microfilm), Alexander Library, Rutgers University, New Brunswick, N.J., reel 13.

45. McKenzie, "The Sign of the Scholar," *Fisk University News* 11, no. 4 (January 1921): 22–23 (original emphasis).

46. "Report of Committee on Class Ring," 10 January 1923, Box 13, Fol. 8, FMC. The chair of the committee, A. W. Partch, was critical of women wearing rings as well, but the committee ultimately agreed that standardization was desirable as long as the costs were kept low so as to make rings and pins affordable for all students.

47. For a general history of men and fashion, see Wilson, *Adorned in Dreams*, esp. 27–30.

48. *Fisk Herald* 32, no. 1 (November 1914): 16–17, 22. "The fact that the young men and women," the newspaper counseled, "have permission from time to time to play tennis together, and that this privilege has not been abused, thus far, shows signs

of progress. Let us not curtail this advancement by visiting courts for purely social purposes."

49. "The Social Life," Fisk University News 6, no. 2 (November 1915): 31–32. On Fisk's "Dance Law," see Herbert Shaw, "Dancing at Fisk," Greater Fisk Herald 2, no. 1 (October 1926): 12. Also see Little, "Extra-Curricular Activities," 139, where he points out that prior to the twentieth century, socials consisted of students marching to the music in unison instead of dancing.

50. Louise C. Berry, "Christmas Presents," Fisk Herald 32, no. 2 (December 1914): 5.

51. Phillipse, "Analysis of Fisk University," 3.

52. McKenzie to William McDaniel, copy, 23 October 1923, Box 13, Fol. 15, FMC.

53. Howard University, Student Manual, 7, 8–9, 16; Minutes of Board of Trustees meeting, 6 February 1913, BOT/HU. The prohibition on student marriage also existed at Fisk. See Fisk University News 7, no. 9 (Catalogue no. 1915–16): 23.

54. "Gladys on the Campus Rules," Howard University Journal 6, no. 26 (23 April 1909): 7.

55. Phillipse, "Analysis of Fisk University," 3. On pseudoscientific ideas of black sexuality in the early twentieth century, see Fredrickson, Black Image in the White Mind, 256–82.

56. Dr. and Mrs. A. W. Davis to F. A. McKenzie, 12 February 1925; D. W. Sherrod, '92, to F. A. McKenzie, 7 February 1925; S. W. and Cecele Jefferson to F. A. McKenzie, 8 February 1925; all reprinted in Letters and Telegrams from Parents of Fisk Students, Alumni, Students and Friends-at-Large together with Certain Statements relative to the Recent Disturbances at Fisk University, February 4, 1925, pamphlet, FUSC.

57. Fisk University News 7, no. 9 (Catalogue no. 1915–16): 23; Howard University, Student Manual, 7.

58. "The War and Alcohol," Fisk Herald 32, no. 1 (November 1914): 11; "Church," Fisk Herald 32, no. 2 (December 1914): 7.

59. "Report of the Secretary," handwritten copy in Minutes of Board of Trustees meeting, 3 June 1913; "Report of the President," handwritten copy in Minutes of Board of Trustees meeting, 2 June 1914; "Report of Secretary," handwritten copy in Minutes of Board of Trustees meeting, 2 June 1914; Minutes of Board of Trustees Executive Committee meeting, 20 June 1913; all in BOT/HU. There were also occasional articles supporting prohibition in the school newspaper. See, for instance, J. Francis Vanderhorst, "Strong Drink," University Journal 4, no. 13 (21 December 1906): 4; Uzziah Miner, "Intemperance," Howard University Journal 8, no. 14 (13 January 1911): 2.

60. On a student's suspension due to the use of alcohol, see correspondence between McKenzie and W. E. Newsom, March–October 1918, Box 13, Fol. 18; on a student's suspension because, in part, of smoking, see McKenzie to Nathaniel Fearonce, copy, 26 December 1921, Box 13, Fol. 6; both in FMC. Howard did not expressly prohibit smoking but, due to the occurrence of fires on campus in 1914, the Board

of Trustees instituted a no smoking inside policy, along with a prohibition of "matches, lamps, candles, gasoline, kerosene or other inflammable material." See Minutes of Board of Trustees Executive Committee meeting, 13 November 1914, BOT/HU.

61. Work, "Ragtime," *Fisk Herald* 32, no. 6 (April 1915): 18; *Fisk University News* 7, no. 9 (Catalogue no. 1915–16): 22.

62. McKenzie, "The President's Report to the Board of Trustees, Fisk University, for the Year Ending June 30, 1920 (1 January 1921)," *Fisk University News* 11, no. 4 (January 1921): 7.

63. "President-Elect F. A. McKenzie," *Fisk Herald* 32, no. 4 (February 1915): 13; Richardson, *History of Fisk*, 71–72.

64. Richardson, *History of Fisk*, 73–76, 79–82; Wolters, *New Negro on Campus*, 32–33.

65. Richardson, *History of Fisk*, 78; Lamon, "Black Community in Nashville," 225–31.

66. *Fisk University News* 6, no. 3 (December 1915): 23; "Editorials," *Fisk University News* 6, no. 6 (March 1916): 2–3.

67. Lamon, "Black Community in Nashville," 232; Wolters, *New Negro on Campus*, 34.

68. DeBerry to W. E. B. Du Bois, 1 July 1924, WEBDP, reel 13. Although DeBerry was not specific as to the makeup of the committee, particularly in terms of a gender breakdown, it is safe to say that the committee was all male. During the same week, DeBerry met with a group of female students who also registered their complaints with the administration.

69. Du Bois, "Diuturni Silenti," 2 June 1924, reprinted in *Fisk Herald* 33, no. 1 (1924): 1–11, in Fiskiana File, FUSC. The "new" *Fisk Herald* was actually an "outlaw" publication. The circumstances of its publication were printed below the masthead: "Formally a monthly college journal published by the Literary Societies of Fisk University. Suppressed by Fayette A. McKenzie in 1916. Re-established in 1924 by the Associated Fisk Clubs and dedicated to the emancipation of the Fisk Spirit from its present slavery. Published occasionally at 2339 Seventh Avenue, New York City." Also see Wolters, *New Negro on Campus*, 35–36.

70. Ortman's letter is an enclosure in A. D. Phillipse to Du Bois, 4 September 1924, WEBDP, reel 13 (original emphasis). Also see Wolters, *New Negro on Campus*, 36–39, for a discussion of more letters written to Du Bois.

71. Richardson, *History of Fisk*, 93; Wolters, *New Negro on Campus*, 44.

72. Streator to A. D. Phillipse, 9 August 1924, WEBDP, reel 13.

73. "A Statement of Grievances against Fayette A. McKenzie as President of Fisk University," typescript, n.d., Box 13, Fol. 18, FMC.

74. "Undergrad" to Du Bois, 11 November 1924; Streator to Phillipse, 6 November 1924. Both in WEBDP, reel 13 (original emphasis).

75. "Statement of Grievances"; Lamon, "Black Community in Nashville," 235–36.

76. W. N. DeBerry to Du Bois, 20 November 1924, WEBDP, reel 13; W. E. B. Du Bois,

"Fisk," *Crisis* 29, no. 6 (April 1925): 248. The modification of the dress code was limited to female students. See Dean of Women to Parent, copy of form letter, 26 December 1924, WEBDP, reel 13.

77. McKenzie quoted in Du Bois, "Fisk," 248; Lamon, "Black Community in Nashville," 236.

78. Du Bois, "Fisk," 248–49; Lamon, "Black Community in Nashville," 236–37, 242; Wolters, *New Negro on Campus*, 47–51, 59–61; Richardson, *History of Fisk*, 96–99.

79. Trawick to Frances S. Prentiss, copy, 12 March 1925, Box 4, Fol. 12; Trawick to W. C. Graves, copy, 12 March 1925, Box 4, Fol. 12. Du Bois's "evil influence" is quoted in F. J. Anderson to McKenzie, 30 August 1924, Box 13, Fol. 1. All in FMC.

80. McKenzie to Cravath, copy, [ca. June 1924]; Streator to Phillipse, 14 October 1924; both in WEBDP, reel 13.

81. See, for instance, Du Bois, "Fisk." Also see Wolters, *New Negro on Campus*, 42–44.

82. F. B. Coffin to McKenzie, 13 February 1925, reprinted in *Letters and Telegrams from Parents of Fisk Students*.

83. Dr. and Mrs. A. W. Davis to McKenzie, 12 February 1925; W. W. Sumlin to McKenzie, 5 February 1925; both reprinted in *Letters and Telegrams from Parents of Fisk Students*.

84. Four black Greek-letter organizations were founded at Howard: sororities Alpha Kappa Alpha (1908), Delta Sigma Theta (1913), and Zeta Phi Beta (1922), and Omega Psi Phi Fraternity (1912). The other major black fraternities were Alpha Phi Alpha, founded at Cornell in 1906, and Kappa Alpha Psi, founded in 1907 at Indiana University. See Little, "Extra-Curricular Activities," 141.

85. Dyson, *Howard University*, 396–97; "Inaugural Address of President Durkee," *Inauguration of J. Stanley Durkee*, pamphlet, 1919, in Howardiana Collection, HUA.

86. Dyson, *Howard University*, 63–66; Wolters, *New Negro on Campus*, 93–112.

87. Wolters, *New Negro on Campus*, 73–77.

88. Smith, "West Indian on the Campus," 240.

89. "602 Howard Students Strike on 20-Cut Rule," *Washington Post*, 8 May 1925, 1, 4; "Faculty at Howard Stands By Cut Rule," *Washington Post*, 9 May 1925, 2; Wolters, *New Negro on Campus*, 113–14. On the larger campaign against ROTC, see Cohen, *When the Old Left Was Young*; Fass, *Damned and the Beautiful*, 339–43.

90. "602 Howard Students Strike," 4; Wolters, *New Negro on Campus*, 110–11, 125–26.

91. "Howard U. Alumni Take Steps to End Strike of Students," *Washington Post*, 10 May 1925, 22; "800 Howard U. Strikers to Demand Arbitration," *Washington Post*, 11 May 1925, 3.

92. Wolters, *New Negro on Campus*, 114–15; "Durkee Tells Strikers Police May Be Called," *Washington Post*, 12 May 1925, 2; "Howard U. Faculty Threatens to Oust Striking Students," *Washington Post*, 13 May 1925, 2.

93. "Durkee Tells Strikers Police May Be Called," 2; "Howard U. Faculty Threatens to Oust Striking Students," 2; "Students' Strike Ended at Howard University," *Washington Post*, 15 May 1925, 11.

94. "Students' Strike Ended," 11.

95. General Alumni Association of the Howard University of Washington, D.C. to the Board of Trustees of Howard University, copy, 14 October 1925, in Minutes of the Special Meeting of the Board of Trustees, 10 December 1925, BOT/HU.

96. Minutes of the Special Meeting of the Board of Trustees, 10 December 1925, BOT/HU; Wolters, *New Negro on Campus*, 127–29.

97. Richardson, *History of Fisk*, 102–3, 106–7; "Our Student Body," *Greater Fisk Herald* 2, no. 5 (February 1927): 11.

98. Harry Overton Schell ('27), "Impressions," *Greater Fisk Herald* 2, no. 7–8 (April–May 1927): 13. On the dress committee, see Richardson, *History of Fisk*, 106–7.

99. John D'Emilio and Estelle B. Freedman define "sexual liberalism" as "an overlapping set of beliefs that detached sexual activity from the instrumental goal of procreation, affirmed heterosexual pleasure as a value in itself, defined sexual satisfaction as a critical component of personal happiness and successful marriage, and weakened the connections between sexual expression and marriage by providing youth with room for some experimentation as preparation for adult status." See D'Emilio and Freedman, *Intimate Matters*, 241.

100. "Modern Youth and the Sex Problem," *Greater Fisk Herald* 2, no. 5 (February 1927): 7–8.

101. On the use of lights at student socials, see Minutes of Executive Committee Meeting, 9 March 1928, BOT/HU.

102. Herbert Shaw ('28), "Dancing at Fisk," *Greater Fisk Herald* 2, no. 1 (October 1926): 12–13; "Dancing," *Greater Fisk Herald* 2, no. 3 (December 1926): 8.

103. Hewlett, "Shall We Tolerate Jazz at Fisk," *Greater Fisk Herald* 3, No. 7 (April–May 1928): 8–9; "Music," *Greater Fisk Herald* 2, no. 6 (March 1927): 22.

104. "Jazzing the Alma Mater," *Hilltop* 4, no. 7 (2 December 1925): 2; "King Jazz," *Hilltop* 1, no. 3 (15 February 1924): 4; both in Howardiana Collection, HUA.

105. For two opposing views, see "Prohibition," *Greater Fisk Herald* 1, no. 7 (June 1926): 7, and "Youth and the Liquor Problem," *Greater Fisk Herald* 4, no. 6 (April 1929): 5.

106. "Fire," *Greater Fisk Herald* 2, no. 6 (March 1927): 16; Nathaniel M. Martin ('29), "The Present Smoking Rule," *Greater Fisk Herald* 2, no. 7–8 (April–May 1927): 28; "Ladies and Cigarettes," *Greater Fisk Herald* 5, no. 2 (November 1929): 7; Richardson, *History of Fisk*, 107.

107. "Free Lance," *Greater Fisk Herald* 1, no. 1 (January 1926): 22; "Free Lance," *Greater Fisk Herald* 1, no. 7 (June 1926): 27.

108. "Scandal," *Hilltop* 4, no. 10 (11 March 1926): 2; "Feminist" to the Editor, *Hilltop* 4, no. 11 (20 March 1926): 2.

109. "Greek Letter Fraternity Organized," *University Journal* 5, no. 7 (10 January 1908): 1; "Fraternities," *University Journal* 5, no. 11 (10 March 1908): 4. On the administration's early position on Greek-letter organizations, see Minutes of Board of Trustees meeting, 21 January 1908, BOT/HU.

110. Richardson, *History of Fisk*, 107–8; "Fraternities," *Greater Fisk Herald* 2, no. 7–8 (April–May 1927): 7–8; *Greater Fisk Herald* 4, no. 7 (June 1929): 28–35.

111. "Modern Educational Tendencies," *Greater Fisk Herald* 1, no. 4 (March 1926): 8.

112. Ted R. Rowan ('27), "Fraternally Speaking," *Greater Fisk Herald* 2, no. 1 (October 1926): 20. Also see E. Cicero Horton ('28), "Free Lance," *Greater Fisk Herald* 2, no. 2 (November 1926): 20; "Fraternities," *Greater Fisk Herald* 3, no. 7 (April–May 1928): 5.

113. "Fraternity Progress," *Hilltop* 3, no. 4 (4 November 1925): 2. Also see "The Scrollers," *Hilltop* 4, no. 6 (25 November 1925): 6.

114. Taylor, "Hell-Week," *Hilltop* 4, no. 6 (25 November 1925): 3. On fraternity entertainment, see Bristow C. Meyers, "Impressions of the Year," *Greater Fisk Herald* 3, no. 8 (June 1928): 41.

115. Du Bois quoted in Anderson, *Education of Blacks in the South*, 276.

116. Other critics included Dean Kelly Miller, Alain Locke, and sociologist E. Franklin Frazier. See Wolters, *New Negro on Campus*, 88–89.

117. *Greater Fisk Herald* 4, no. 7 (June 1929): 14.

118. "Here and There," *Greater Fisk Herald* 3, no. 1 (October 1927): 5.

Conclusion

1. Frazier, "Durham: Capital of the Black Middle Class," in Locke, *New Negro*, 333–34.

2. Frazier, *Black Bourgeoisie*, 80–83, 122–29.

3. Du Bois quoted in Anderson, *Education of Blacks in the South*, 276.

4. Grimké to Johnson, 29 April 1929, Box 8, Fol. 175, JWJP.

5. Thurman, "This Negro Literary Renaissance," typescript draft from *Aunt Hagar's Children*, n.d., Box 1, Fol. 12, JWJ Small Collections (Thurman). Others that Thurman included in the "damned" were Langston Hughes, Rudolph Fisher, and Claude McKay.

6. "Farewell Address of Rodney L. Curtis," 27 December 1930, typescript, "Masonic Writings," Box 11, Fol. 1; Hall of Carthaginian Record Book, 4 September 1928, "Masonic Records," vol. 6; both in HWC.

7. On the importance of examining the role of power and difference in black community formations, see Earl Lewis, "To Turn as on a Pivot," and Higginbotham, "African-American Women's History."

Bibliography

Primary Sources

MANUSCRIPT COLLECTIONS
Nashville, Tennessee
   Fisk University, Franklin Library, Special Collections
      Fiskiana File
      Marcus Garvey Memorial Collection
      Fayette A. McKenzie Presidential Collection

New Brunswick, New Jersey
   Rutgers University, Alexander Library
      W. E. B. Du Bois Papers (microfilm)

New Haven, Connecticut
   Yale University, Beinecke Rare Book and Manuscript Library,
         James Weldon Johnson Memorial Collection
      Langston Hughes Papers
      James Weldon Johnson Papers
      JWJ Small Collections
      Claude McKay Correspondence
      Jean Toomer Papers
      Carl Van Vechten Papers (Black Correspondence)

New York, New York
   New York Public Library
      New York State Census, Kings County, 1905 and 1925
      Carl Van Vechten Papers
      Schomburg Center for Research in Black Culture
         John E. Bruce Papers
         J. R. Ralph Casimir Papers
         Countee Cullen Papers (microfilm)
         Aaron Douglas Papers
         Writers' Program, "The Negro of New York"

Arthur Schomburg Papers

Universal Negro Improvement Association Central Division Records

Harry A. Williamson Collection on Negro Masonry

Washington, D.C.

Howard University, Moorland-Spingarn Research Center

Alain Leroy Locke Papers

Howard University Archives

Howardiana Collection

Records of the Meetings of the Board of Trustees of Howard University

NEWSPAPERS AND JOURNALS

Call (Kansas City)	Howard University Journal
Crisis	Negro World
Fisk Herald	New York Age
Fisk University News	New York Times
Greater Fisk Herald	University Journal
Hilltop	Washington Post

PUBLISHED PRIMARY SOURCES

Brown, Sue M. Wilson. *The History of the Order of the Eastern Star among Colored People.* Des Moines, Iowa: The Bystander Press, 1924.

Cooper, Wayne F., ed. *The Passion of Claude McKay: Selected Poetry and Prose, 1912–1948.* New York: Schocken, 1973.

Du Bois, W. E. B. "Fisk." *Crisis* 29, no. 6 (April 1925): 247–51.

———. "Negro Education." *Crisis* 15 (February 1918): 173–78.

———. "Negroes in College." *Nation* 122 (3 March 1926): 228–30.

———. *The Souls of Black Folk.* 1903. Reprint, with an introduction by Henry Louis Gates Jr., New York: Bantam Books, 1989.

Du Bois, W. E. Burghardt, and Augustus Granville Dill, eds. *The College-Bred Negro American.* Atlanta University Publications, no. 15. Atlanta, Ga.: Atlanta University Press, 1910.

Early, Gerald, ed. *My Soul's High Song: The Collected Writings of Countee Cullen, Voice of the Harlem Renaissance.* New York: Anchor Books, 1991.

Garvey, Amy Jacques, ed. *Philosophy and Opinions of Marcus Garvey.* 2 vols. 1923–5. Reprint, 2 vols. in 1, with an introduction by Robert A. Hill, New York: Atheneum, 1992.

Garvey, Marcus. *Aims and Objects of Movement for Solution of Negro Problem Outlined.* New York: Press of the Universal Negro Improvement Association, 1924.

Gilbert, Peter, comp. and ed. *The Selected Writings of John Edward Bruce: Militant Black Journalist.* New York: Arno Press, 1971.

Hill, Robert A., ed. *The Marcus Garvey and Universal Negro Improvement Association Papers.* 10 projected vols. Berkeley: University of California Press, 1983.

Hill, Robert A., and Barbara Bair, eds. *Marcus Garvey: Life and Lessons.* Berkeley: University of California Press, 1987.

Hughes, Langston. *The Big Sea.* 1940. Reprint, with an introduction by Arnold Rampersad, New York: Hill and Wang, 1993.

———. "The Negro Artist and the Racial Mountain." *Nation* 122 (23 June 1926): 692–94.

Johnson, James Weldon. *The Autobiography of an Ex-Coloured Man.* 1927 [1912]. Reprint, with a new introduction by Henry Louis Gates Jr., New York: Vintage Books, 1989.

———. *Black Manhattan.* 1930. Reprint, with a new introduction by Sondra Kathryn Wilson, New York: Da Capo Press, 1991.

Locke, Alain. "Negro Education Bids For Par." *Survey* 54 (1 September 1925): 569–70.

———, ed. *The New Negro: Voices of the Harlem Renaissance.* 1925. Reprint, with an introduction by Arnold Rampersad, New York: Atheneum, 1992.

Longsdorf, George F., comp. and ed. *Abbott's Digest of All New York Reports, Supplement in Eight Volumes.* Vol. 1. New York: Baker, Voorhis, 1914.

Maloney, A. H. *Some Essentials of Race Leadership.* Xenia, Ohio: Aldine Publishing House, 1924.

McKay, Claude. *Banjo: A Story without a Plot.* 1929. Reprint, San Diego, Calif.: Harcourt, Brace, Jovanovich, 1957.

———. *Home to Harlem.* 1928. Reprint, with a new foreword by Wayne F. Cooper, Boston: Northeastern University Press, 1987.

———. *A Long Way from Home: An Autobiography.* 1937. Reprint, with an introduction by St. Clair Drake, San Diego, Calif.: Harcourt, Brace, Jovanovich, 1970.

"The Negro in Art: How Shall He Be Portrayed: A Symposium." *Crisis* 31–33 (March–November 1926).

Scott, Emmett J. *Negro Migration during the War.* New York: Oxford University Press, 1920.

Sheppard, Wheeler. *Mistakes of Dr. W. E. B. Du Bois: Being an Answer to Dr. W. E. B. Du Bois' Attack upon the Honorable Marcus Garvey.* 2 vols. Pittsburgh: Goldenrod Print, 1921.

Smith, Alfred Edgar. "West Indian on the Campus." *Opportunity* 11, no. 8 (August 1933): 238–41.

Smith-Irvin, Jeanette, ed. *Footsoldiers of the Universal Negro Improvement Association: Their Own Words.* Trenton, N.J.: Africa World Press, 1989.

Toomer, Jean. *Cane.* 1923. Reprint, with an introduction by Darwin T. Turner, New York: Liveright, 1975.

U.S. Bureau of the Census. *Abstract of the Fourteenth Census of the United States, 1920.* Washington, D.C.: Government Printing Office, 1923.

———. *Fourteenth Census of the United States Taken in the Year 1920.* Vol. 2, *Population 1920:*

General Report and Analytical Tables. Washington, D.C.: Government Printing Office, 1922.

White, Walter. *The Fire in the Flint.* 1924. Reprint, with a foreword by R. Baxter Miller, Athens: University of Georgia Press, 1996.

Williamson, Harry A. *The Story of Carthaginian Lodge, No. 47, F. & A.M.* Brooklyn, N.Y.: Carthaginian Study Club, 1949.

Secondary Sources

Aron, Cindy Sondik. *Ladies and Gentlemen of the Civil Service: Middle-Class Workers in Victorian America.* New York: Oxford University Press, 1987.

Anderson, James D. *The Education of Blacks in the South, 1860–1935.* Chapel Hill: University of North Carolina Press, 1988.

Anderson, Jervis. *This Was Harlem, 1900–1950.* New York: Farrar, Strauss, Giroux, 1981.

Aptheker, Herbert. "The Negro College Student in the 1920s—Years of Preparation and Protest: An Introduction." *Science and Society* 33, no. 2 (Spring 1969): 150–67.

Bair, Barbara. "True Women, Real Men: Gender, Ideology, and Social Roles in the Garvey Movement." In *Gendered Domains: Rethinking Public and Private in Women's History,* edited by Dorothy O. Helley and Susan M. Reverby, 154–66. Ithaca, N.Y: Cornell University Press, 1992.

Baker, Donald G. "Black Images: The Afro-American in Popular Novels, 1900–1945." *Journal of Popular Culture* 7 (Fall 1973): 326–46.

Baker, Houston A. *Modernism and the Harlem Renaissance.* Chicago: University of Chicago Press, 1987.

Baker, Paula. "The Domestication of Politics: Women and American Political Society, 1780–1920." *American Historical Review* 89 (June 1984): 620–47.

Barkley Brown, Elsa. "Negotiating and Transforming the Public Sphere: African American Political Life in the Transition from Slavery to Freedom." In *The Black Public Sphere: A Public Culture Book,* edited by The Black Public Sphere Collective, 111–50. Chicago: University of Chicago Press, 1995.

Barkley Brown, Elsa, and Gregg D. Kimball. "Mapping the Terrain of Black Richmond." *Journal of Urban History* 21 (March 1995): 296–346.

Baron, Ava. "An 'Other' Side of Gender Antagonism at Work: Men, Boys, and the Remasculinization of Printers' Work, 1830–1920." In *Work Engendered: Toward a New History of American Labor,* edited by Ava Baron, 47–69. Ithaca, N.Y.: Cornell University Press, 1991.

Bederman, Gail. *Manliness and Civilization: A Cultural History of Gender and Race in the United States, 1880–1917.* Chicago: University of Chicago Press, 1995.

Beito, David T. "To Advance the 'Practice of Thrift and Economy': Fraternal Societies and Social Capital, 1890–1920." *Journal of Interdisciplinary History* 29, no. 4 (Spring 1999): 585–612.

Belton, Don, ed. *Speak My Name: Black Men on Masculinity and the American Dream*. Boston: Beacon Press, 1995.

Bender, Thomas. *New York Intellect: A History of Intellectual Life in New York City, from 1750 to the Beginnings of Our Own Time*. Baltimore, Md.: Johns Hopkins University Press, 1987.

Black, Daniel P. *Dismantling Black Manhood: An Historical and Literary Analysis of the Legacy of Slavery*. New York: Garland Publishing, 1997.

Blake, Wayne M., and Carol A. Darling. "The Dilemmas of the African American Male." *Journal of Black Studies* 24 (June 1994): 402–15.

Blount, Marcellus, and George P. Cunningham, eds. *Representing Black Men*. New York: Routledge, 1996.

Bogle, Donald. *Toms, Coons, Mulattoes, Mammies, and Bucks: An Interpretive History of Blacks in American Films*. New York: Viking Press, 1973.

Bolster, W. Jeffrey. " 'To Feel like a Man': Black Seamen in the Northern States, 1800–1860." *Journal of American History* 76 (March 1990): 1173–99.

Bontemps, Arna, ed. *The Harlem Renaissance Remembered: Essays Edited with a Memoir*. New York: Dodd, Mead, 1972.

Booker, Christopher B. *"I Will Wear No Chain!" A Social History of African American Males*. Westport, Conn.: Praeger, 2000.

Boyle, Kevin. "The Kiss: Racial and Gender Conflict in a 1950s Automobile Factory." *Journal of American History* 84 (September 1997): 496–523.

Brereton, Bridget. "Society and Culture in the Caribbean: The British and French West Indies, 1870–1980." In *The Modern Caribbean*, edited by Franklin W. Knight and Colin A. Palmer, 85–110. Chapel Hill: University of North Carolina Press, 1989.

Bridenthal, Renate, Atina Grossman, and Marion Kaplan, eds. *When Biology Became Destiny: Women in Weimar and Nazi Germany*. New York: Monthly Review Press, 1984.

Brown, Jayna. "Black Patriarch on the Prairie: National Identity and Black Manhood in the Early Novels of Oscar Micheaux." In *Oscar Micheaux and His Circle: African-American Filmmaking and Race Cinema of the Silent Era*, edited by Pearl Bowser, Jane Gaines, and Charles Musser, 132–46. Bloomington: Indiana University Press, 2001.

Brown, Tamara. "It Don't Mean a Thing If It Ain't Got That Harlem Swing: Social Dance and the Harlem Renaissance." *Afro-Americans in New York Life and History* 22 (January 1998): 41–66.

Bullock, Steven C. *Revolutionary Brotherhood: Freemasonry and the Transformation of the American Social Order, 1730–1840*. Chapel Hill: University of North Carolina Press, 1996.

Burkett, Randall K. *Black Redemption: Churchmen Speak for the Garvey Movement*. Philadelphia: Temple University Press, 1978.

———. *Garveyism as a Religious Movement: The Institutionalization of a Civil Religion*. Metuchen, N.J.: Scarecrow Press, 1978.

Burton, Richard D. E. *Afro-Creole: Power, Opposition, and Play in the Caribbean*. Ithaca, N.Y.: Cornell University Press, 1997.

Butler, Judith. *Gender Trouble: Feminism and the Subversion of Identity*. New York: Routledge, 1990.

Byrd, Rudolph P., and Beverly Guy-Sheftall, eds. *Traps: African American Men on Gender and Sexuality*. Bloomington: Indiana University Press, 2001.

Carbado, Devon, ed. *Black Men on Race, Gender, and Sexuality: A Critical Reader*. New York: New York University Press, 1999.

Carby, Hazel. "Policing the Black Woman's Body in an Urban Context." *Critical Inquiry* 18 (Summer 1992): 738–55.

———. *Race Men*. Cambridge: Harvard University Press, 1998.

Carnes, Mark C. *Secret Ritual and Manhood in Victorian America*. New Haven, Conn.: Yale University Press, 1989.

Carnes, Mark C., and Clyde Griffen, eds. *Meanings for Manhood: Constructions of Masculinity in Victorian America*. Chicago: University of Chicago Press, 1990.

Cawelti, John G. *Apostles of the Self-Made Man*. Chicago: University of Chicago Press, 1965.

Chateauvert, Melinda. *Marching Together: Women of the Brotherhood of Sleeping Car Porters*. Urbana: University of Illinois Press, 1998.

Chauncey, George. *Gay New York: Gender, Urban Culture, and the Making of the Gay Male World, 1890–1940*. New York: Basic Books, 1994.

Chudacoff, Howard P. *The Age of the Bachelor: Creating an American Subculture*. Princeton, N.J.: Princeton University Press, 1999.

Clark, David Anthony Tyeeme, and Joane Nagel. "White Men, Red Masks: Appropriations of 'Indian' Manhood in Imagined Wests." In *Across the Great Divide: Cultures of Manhood in the American West*, edited by Matthew Basso, Laura McCall, and Dee Garceau, 109–30. New York: Routledge, 2001.

Clawson, Mary Ann. *Constructing Brotherhood: Class, Gender, and Fraternalism*. Princeton, N.J.: Princeton University Press, 1989.

Coben, Stanley. *Rebellion against Victorianism: The Impetus for Cultural Change in 1920s America*. New York: Oxford University Press, 1991.

Cohen, Lizabeth. *Making a New Deal: Industrial Workers in Chicago, 1919–1939*. Cambridge: Cambridge University Press, 1990.

Cohen, Robert. *When the Old Left Was Young: Student Radicals and America's First Mass Student Movement, 1929–1941*. New York: Oxford University Press, 1993.

Collins, Patricia Hill. *Black Feminist Thought: Knowledge, Consciousness, and the Politics of Empowerment*. New York: Routledge, 1991.

Connell, R. W. "The Big Picture: Masculinities in Recent World History." *Theory and Society* 22 (October 1993): 597–623.

———. *Masculinities*. Berkeley: University of California Press, 1995.

Connolly, Harold X. *A Ghetto Grows in Brooklyn.* New York: New York University Press, 1977.

Coontz, Stephanie. *The Social Origins of Private Life: A History of American Families, 1600–1900.* London: Verso, 1988.

Cooper, Wayne F. *Claude McKay: Rebel Sojourner in the Harlem Renaissance.* Baton Rouge: Louisiana State University Press, 1987; New York: Schocken Books, 1990.

Cott, Nancy F. *The Groundings of Modern Feminism.* New Haven, Conn.: Yale University Press, 1987.

Cronon, E. David. *Black Moses: The Story of Marcus Garvey and the Universal Negro Improvement Association.* Madison: University of Wisconsin Press, 1966.

Cruse, Harold. *The Crisis of the Negro Intellectual: A Historical Analysis of the Failure of Black Leadership.* 1967. Reprint, with a foreword by Bazel E. Allen and Ernest J. Wilson, New York: Quill, 1984.

Cullen, Jim. " 'I's a Man Now': Gender and African American Men." In *Divided Houses: Gender and the Civil War,* edited by Catherine Clinton and Nina Silber, 76–91. New York: Oxford University Press, 1992.

Curry, Leonard P. *The Free Black in Urban America, 1800–1850: The Shadow of the Dream.* Chicago: University of Chicago Press, 1981.

Davis, Harry E. *A History of Freemasonry among Negroes in America.* N.p., 1946.

De Grazia, Victoria. *How Fascism Ruled Women: Italy, 1922–1945.* Berkeley: University of California Press, 1992.

De Grazia, Victoria, with Ellen Furlough, eds. *The Sex of Things: Gender and Consumption in Historical Perspective.* Berkeley: University of California Press, 1996.

D'Emilio, John, and Estelle B. Freedman. *Intimate Matters: A History of Sexuality in America.* New York: Harper and Row, 1989.

Denning, Michael. *Mechanic Accents: Dime Novels and Working-Class Culture in America.* London: Verso, 1987.

Dollard, John. *Caste and Class in a Southern Town.* 1937. Reprint, with a foreword by Daniel Patrick Moynihan, Madison: University of Wisconsin Press, 1988.

Donaldson, Mike. "What Is Hegemonic Masculinity?" *Theory and Society* 22 (October 1993): 643–57.

Dorsey, Bruce. "A Gendered History of African Colonization in the Antebellum United States." *Journal of Social History* 34 (Fall 2000): 77–103.

Douglas, Ann. *The Feminization of American Culture.* New York: Knopf, 1977. Reprint, with a new preface, New York: Anchor Books, 1988.

———. *Terrible Honesty: Mongrel Manhattan in the 1920s.* New York: Farrar, Strauss, Giroux, 1995.

Draper, Theodore. *The Rediscovery of Black Nationalism.* New York: Viking Press, 1970.

Duberman, Martin Bauml. *Paul Robeson.* New York: Knopf, 1988.

Dubbert, Joe L. *A Man's Place: Masculinity in Transition.* Englewood Cliffs, N.J.: Prentice-Hall, 1979.

Dumenil, Lynn. *Freemasonry and American Culture, 1880–1930.* Princeton, N.J.: Princeton University Press, 1984.

———. *Modern Temper: American Culture and Society in the 1920s.* New York: Hill and Wang, 1995.

Duneier, Mitchell. *Slim's Table: Race, Respectability, and Masculinity.* Chicago: University of Chicago Press, 1992.

Dyson, Walter. *Howard University, The Capstone of Negro Education: A History: 1867–1940.* Washington, D.C.: Graduate School of Howard University, 1941.

Erenberg, Lewis A. *Steppin' Out: New York Nightlife and the Transformation of American Culture, 1890–1930.* Chicago: University of Chicago Press, 1981.

Estes, Steve. "'I AM A MAN!': Race, Masculinity, and the 1968 Memphis Sanitation Strike." *Labor History* 41 (May 2000): 153–70.

Fass, Paula S. *The Damned and the Beautiful: American Youth in the 1920s.* New York: Oxford University Press, 1977.

Ferguson, Ann Arnett. *Bad Boys: Public Schools in the Making of Black Masculinity.* Ann Arbor: University of Michigan Press, 2000.

Fiske, John. "Surveilling the City: Whiteness, the Black Man and Democratic Totalitarianism." *Theory, Culture and Society* 15 (May 1998): 67–88.

Foner, Eric. *Reconstruction: America's Unfinished Revolution, 1863–1877.* New York: Harper and Row, 1988.

Ford-Smith, Honor. "Women and the Garvey Movement in Jamaica." In *Garvey: His Work and Impact,* edited by Rupert Lewis and Patrick Bryan, 73–83. Trenton, N.J.: Africa World Press, 1991.

Fox, Richard Wightman, and T. J. Jackson Lears, eds. *The Culture of Consumption: Critical Essays in American History, 1880–1980.* New York: Pantheon Books, 1983.

Fox-Genovese, Elizabeth. *Within the Plantation Household: Black and White Women of the Old South.* Chapel Hill: University of North Carolina Press, 1988.

Franklin, Clyde W., II. "Surviving the Institutional Decimation of Black Males: Causes, Consequences, and Intervention." In *The Making of Masculinities: The New Men's Studies,* edited by Harry Brod, 155–69. Boston: Allen and Unwin, 1987.

Frazier, E. Franklin. *Black Bourgeoisie: The Rise of a New Middle Class.* New York: Free Press, 1957.

Fredrickson, George M. *The Black Image in the White Mind: The Debate on Afro-American Character and Destiny, 1817–1914.* New York: Harper Row, 1971.

Freedman, Estelle B. "'The Burning of Letters Continues': Elusive Identities and the Historical Construction of Sexuality." *Journal of Women's History* 9 (Winter 1998): 181–200.

Fullinwinder, S. P. *The Mind and Mood of Black America: Twentieth Century Thought.* Homewood, Ill.: Dorsey Press, 1969.

Gaines, Kevin K. "Rethinking Race and Class in African American Struggles for Equality, 1885–1941." *American Historical Review* 102 (April 1997): 378–87.

————. *Uplifting the Race: Black Leadership, Politics, and Culture in the Twentieth Century.* Chapel Hill: University of North Carolina Press, 1996.

Garber, Eric. "A Spectacle in Color: The Lesbian and Gay Subculture of Jazz Age Harlem." In *Hidden from History: Reclaiming the Gay and Lesbian Past*, edited by Martin Duberman, Martha Vicinus, and George Chauncey Jr., 318–31. New York: Meridian, 1990.

Garvey, Amy Jacques. *Garvey and Garveyism.* Kingston, Jamaica: n.p., 1963.

Gatewood, Willard B. *Aristocrats of Color: The Black Elite, 1880–1920.* Bloomington: Indiana University Press, 1990.

Giddings, Paula. *When and Where I Enter: The Impact of Black Women on Race and Sex in America.* New York: Quill, 1984.

Gilkes, Cheryl Townsend. "The Roles of Church and Community Mothers: Ambivalent American Sexism or Fragmented African Familyhood." *Journal of Feminist Studies in Religion* 2 (Spring 1986): 41–59.

Gill, Tiffany Melissa. "'Never Wanted to Do Anything but Hair': Beauty Salons, Hairdressers, and the Formation of African American Female Entrepreneurship." Paper presented at the Rutgers Center for Historical Analysis, "The Black Atlantic: Race, Nation, and Gender," New Brunswick, N.J., 13 April 1999.

Gilman, Sander L. *Difference and Pathology: Stereotypes of Sexuality, Race, and Madness.* Ithaca, N.Y.: Cornell University Press, 1985.

Gilmore, Glenda Elizabeth. *Gender and Jim Crow: Women and the Politics of White Supremacy in North Carolina, 1896–1920.* Chapel Hill: University of North Carolina Press, 1996.

Gilroy, Paul. *The Black Atlantic: Modernity and Double Consciousness.* Cambridge: Cambridge University Press, 1993.

Gorn, Elliott J. *The Manly Art: Bare-Knuckle Prize Fighting in America.* Ithaca, N.Y.: Cornell University Press, 1986.

Gossett, Thomas. *Race, The History of an Idea in America.* Dallas, Tex.: Southern Methodist University Press, 1963.

Grimshaw, William H. *Official History of Freemasonry among the Colored People in North America.* 1903. Reprint, New York: Negro Universities Press, 1969.

Grossman, James. *Land of Hope: Chicago, Black Southerners and the Great Migration.* Chicago: University of Chicago Press, 1989.

Guterl, Matthew Pratt. *The Color of Race in America, 1900–1940.* Cambridge: Harvard University Press, 2001.

Haeberle, Erwin J. "Swastika, Pink Triangle, and Yellow Star: The Destruction of Sexology and the Persecution of Homosexuals in Nazi Germany." In *Hidden From History: Reclaiming the Gay and Lesbian Past,* edited by Martin Duberman, Martha Vicinus, and George Chauncey Jr., 365–79. New York: Meridian, 1990.

Hammer, Langdon. *Hart Crane and Allan Tate: Janus-Faced Modernism.* Princeton, N.J.: Princeton University Press, 1993.

Harper, Phillip Brian. *Are We Not Men? Masculine Anxiety and the Problem of African-American Identity*. New York: Oxford University Press, 1996.

Harris, William H. *The Harder We Run: Black Workers since the Civil War*. New York: Oxford University Press, 1982.

Hatt, Michael. "'Making a Man of Him': Masculinity and the Black Body in Mid-Nineteenth Century Sculpture." *Oxford Art Journal* 15 (1992): 21–35.

Hemenway, Robert E. *Zora Neale Hurston: A Literary Biography*. Urbana: University of Illinois Press, 1977.

Henri, Florette. *Black Migration: Movement North, 1900–1920*. Garden City, N.Y.: Anchor Press, 1975.

Higginbotham, Evelyn Brooks. "African-American Women's History and the Metalanguage of Race." *Signs: Journal of Women in Culture and Society* 17 (Winter 1992): 251–74.

———. *Righteous Discontent: The Women's Movement in the Black Baptist Church, 1880–1920*. Cambridge: Harvard University Press, 1993.

Hilkey, Judy. *Character Is Capital: Success Manuals and Manhood in Gilded Age America*. Chapel Hill: University of North Carolina Press, 1997.

Hill, Robert A. "Making Noise: Marcus Garvey Dada, August 1922." In *Picturing Us: African American Identity in Photography*, edited by Deborah Willis, 181–205. New York: New Press, 1994.

Hine, Darlene Clark. *Black Women in White: Racial Conflict and Cooperation in the Nursing Profession, 1890–1950*. Bloomington: Indiana University Press, 1989.

———. "Rape and the Inner Lives of Black Women in the Middle West: Preliminary Thoughts on the Culture of Dissemblance." *Signs: Journal of Women in Culture and Society* 14 (Summer 1989): 912–20.

Hine, Darlene Clark, and Earnestine Jenkins, eds. *A Question of Manhood: A Reader in U.S. Black Men's History and Masculinity*. 2 vols. Bloomington: Indiana University Press, 1999–2001.

Hobsbawm, Eric. *Primitive Rebels: Studies in Archaic Forms of Social Movement in the 19th and 20th Centuries*. New York: Praeger, 1959.

Hobsbawm, Eric, and Terence Ranger, eds. *The Invention of Tradition*. Cambridge: Cambridge University Press, 1983.

Hoffnung-Garskof, Jesse. "The Migrations of Arturo Schomburg: On Being Antillano, Negro, and Puerto Rican in New York, 1891–1938." *Journal of American Ethnic History* 21 (November 2001): 3–49.

Hoganson, Kristin L. *Fighting for American Manhood: How Gender Politics Provoked the Spanish-American and Philippine-American Wars*. New Haven, Conn.: Yale University Press, 1998.

Holt, Thomas C. *The Problem of Freedom: Race, Labor, and Politics in Jamaica and Britain, 1832–1938*. Baltimore, Md.: Johns Hopkins University Press, 1992.

hooks, bell. "Reconstructing Black Masculinity." In *Black Looks: Race and Representation*. Boston: South End Press, 1992.

Horton, James Oliver. *Free People of Color: Inside the African American Community*. Washington, D.C.: Smithsonian Institution Press, 1993.

Huggins, Nathan I. *Harlem Renaissance*. New York: Oxford University Press, 1971.

Hull, Gloria T. *Color, Sex and Poetry: Three Women Writers of the Harlem Renaissance*. Bloomington: Indiana University Press, 1987.

Hunter, Andrea G., and James Earl Davis. "Constructing Gender: An Exploration of Afro-American Men's Conceptualization of Manhood." *Gender and Society* 6 (September 1992): 464–79.

———. "Hidden Voices of Black Men: The Meaning, Structure, and Complexity of Manhood." *Journal of Black Studies* 25 (September 1994): 20–40.

Hunter, Tera W. *To 'Joy My Freedom: Southern Black Women's Lives and Labors after the Civil War*. Cambridge: Harvard University Press, 1997.

Hutchinson, George. *The Harlem Renaissance in Black and White*. Cambridge: Belknap Press of Harvard University Press, 1995.

Jacobs, Margaret C. *Living the Enlightenment: Freemasonry and Politics in Eighteenth-Century Europe*. New York: Oxford University Press, 1991.

James, Winston. *Holding Aloft the Banner of Ethiopia: Caribbean Radicalism in Early Twentieth-Century America*. London: Verso, 1998.

Jones, Jacqueline. *Labor of Love, Labor of Sorrow: Black Women, Work and the Family, from Slavery to the Present*. New York: Basic Books, 1985. Reprint, New York: Vintage Books, 1986.

Kaplan, Amy. "Black and Blue on San Juan Hill." In *Cultures of United States Imperialism*, edited by Amy Kaplan and Donald E. Pease, 219–36. Durham, N.C.: Duke University Press, 1993.

Kelley, Robin D. G. "The Riddle of the Zoot: Malcolm Little and Black Cultural Politics during World War II." In *Race Rebels: Culture, Politics, and the Black Working Class*. New York: Free Press, 1994.

———. "'We Are Not What We Seem': Rethinking Black Working-Class Opposition in the Jim Crow South." *Journal of American History* 80 (June 1993): 75–112.

Kerber, Linda. "Separate Spheres, Female Worlds, Woman's Place: The Rhetoric of Women's History." *Journal of American History* 75 (June 1988): 9–39.

Kerman, Cynthia Earl, and Richard Eldridge. *The Lives of Jean Toomer: A Hunger for Wholeness*. Baton Rouge: Louisiana State University Press, 1987.

Kessler-Harris, Alice. *Out to Work: A History of Wage-Earning Women in the United States*. Oxford: Oxford University Press, 1982.

———. "Treating the Male as 'Other': Redefining the Parameters of Labor History." *Labor History* 34 (Spring–Summer 1993): 190–204.

Kimmel, Michael. *Manhood in America: A Cultural History*. New York: Free Press, 1996.

Kirschke, Amy Helene. *Aaron Douglas: Art, Race, and the Harlem Renaissance.* Jackson: University of Mississippi Press, 1995.

Lamon, Lester C. "The Black Community in Nashville and the Fisk University Student Strike of 1924–1925." *Journal of Southern History* 40 (May 1974): 225–44.

Lasch-Quinn, Elisabeth. *Black Neighbors: Race and the Limits of Reform in the American Settlement House Movement, 1890–1945.* Chapel Hill: University of North Carolina Press, 1993.

Lears, T. J. Jackson. "The Concept of Cultural Hegemony: Problems and Possibilities." *American Historical Review* 90 (June 1985): 567–93.

———. *No Place of Grace: Antimodernism and the Transformation of American Culture, 1880–1920.* Chicago: University of Chicago Press, 1981.

Lemons, J. Stanley. "Black Stereotypes as Reflected in Popular Culture, 1880–1920." *American Quarterly* 29 (1977): 102–16.

Levine, Lawrence. *The Unpredictable Past: Explorations in American Cultural History.* New York: Oxford University Press, 1993.

Lewis, David Levering. "Parallels and Divergences: Assimilationist Strategies of Afro-American and Jewish Elites from 1910 to the Early 1930s." *Journal of American History* 71 (December 1984): 543–64.

———. *W. E. B. Du Bois: Biography of a Race, 1868–1919.* New York: Henry Holt, 1993.

———. *W. E. B. Du Bois: The Fight for Equality and the American Century, 1919–1963.* New York: Henry Holt, 2000.

———. *When Harlem Was in Vogue.* New York: Oxford University Press, 1981.

———, ed. *The Portable Harlem Renaissance Reader.* New York: Penguin Books, 1994.

Lewis, Earl. "Expectations, Economic Opportunities, and Life in the Industrial Age: Black Migration to Norfolk, Virginia, 1910–1945." In *The Great Migration in Historical Perspective: New Dimensions of Race, Class, and Gender,* edited by Joe William Trotter Jr., 22–45. Bloomington: Indiana University Press, 1991.

———. *In Their Own Interests: Race, Class, and Power in Twentieth-Century Norfolk, Virginia.* Berkeley: University of California Press, 1991.

———. "To Turn As on a Pivot: Writing African Americans into a History of Overlapping Diasporas." *American Historical Review* 100 (June 1995): 765–87.

Lewis, Rupert. *Marcus Garvey: Anti-Colonial Champion.* Trenton, N.J.: Africa World Press, 1988.

Little, Monroe H. "The Extra-Curricular Activities of Black College Students, 1868–1940." *Journal of Negro History* 65 (Spring 1980): 135–48.

Lively, Adam. "Continuity and Radicalism in American Black Nationalist Thought, 1914–1929." *Journal of American Studies* 18 (August 1984): 207–35.

Lott, Eric. *Love and Theft: Blackface Minstrelsy and the American Working Class.* New York: Oxford University Press, 1993.

Majors, Richard, and Janet Mancini Billson. *Cool Pose: The Dilemmas of Black Manhood in America.* New York: Touchstone, 1992.

Mangan, J. A., and James Walvin, eds. *Manliness and Morality: Middle-Class Masculinity in Britain and America, 1800–1940*. New York: St. Martin's Press, 1987.

Marks, Carole. *Farewell—We're Good and Gone: The Great Black Migration*. Bloomington: Indiana University Press, 1989.

Martin, Tony. *Race First: The Ideological and Organizational Struggles of Marcus Garvey and the Universal Negro Improvement Association*. Westport, Conn.: Greenwood Press, 1976.

May, Elaine Tyler. *Great Expectations: Marriage and Divorce in Post-Victorian America*. Chicago: University of Chicago Press, 1980.

Maynard, Steven. "Rough Work and Rugged Men: The Social Construction of Masculinity in Working-Class History." *Labour/Le Travail* 23 (Spring 1989): 159–69.

McClintock, Anne. *Imperial Leather: Race, Gender and Sexuality in the Colonial Conquest*. New York: Routledge, 1995.

McKay, Nellie. *Jean Toomer, Artist: A Study of His Literary Life and Work, 1894–1936*. Chapel Hill: University of North Carolina Press, 1984.

Meier, August. *Negro Thought in America, 1880–1915: Racial Ideologies in the Age of Booker T. Washington*. Ann Arbor: University of Michigan Press, 1963.

Mercer, Kobena. *Welcome to the Jungle: New Positions in Black Cultural Studies*. London: Routledge, 1994.

Mitchell, Michele. "Adjusting the Race: Gender, Sexuality, and the Question of African American Destiny, 1877–1930." Ph.D. diss., Northwestern University, 1998.

———. " 'The Black Man's Burden': African Americans, Imperialism, and Notions of Racial Manhood, 1890–1910." *International Review of Social History* 44, suppl. (1999): 77–99.

———. "Silences Broken, Silences Kept: Gender and Sexuality in African-American History." *Gender and History* 11 (November 1999): 433–44.

Mjagkij, Nina. "True Manhood: The YMCA and Racial Advancement, 1890–1930." In *Men and Women Adrift: The YMCA and YWCA in the City*, edited by Nina Mjagkij and Margaret Spratt, 138–59. New York: New York University Press, 1997.

Montgomery, David. *The Fall of the House of Labor: The Workplace, the State, and American Labor Activism, 1865–1920*. Cambridge: Cambridge University Press, 1987.

Moore, Richard B. "The Critics and Opponents of Marcus Garvey." In *Marcus Garvey and the Vision of Africa*, edited by John H. Clark and Amy Jacques Garvey, 210–35. New York: Vintage Books, 1974.

Moore, William D. "Structures of Masculinity: Masonic Temples, Material Culture, and Ritual Gender Archetypes in New York State, 1870–1930." Ph.D. diss., Boston University, 1999.

Moses, Wilson. *Black Messiahs and Uncle Toms: Social and Literary Manipulations of a Religious Myth*. Rev. ed. University Park: Pennsylvania State University Press, 1993.

———. *The Golden Age of Black Nationalism, 1850–1925*. New York: Oxford University Press, 1978.

Mosse, George. *Nationalism and Sexuality: Respectability and Abnormal Sexuality in Modern Europe*. New York: H. Fertig, 1985.

Mullins, Paul R. "Race and the Genteel Consumer: Class and African American Consumption, 1850–1930." *Historical Archaeology* 33 (1999): 22–38.

Mumford, Kevin J. *Interzones: Black/White Sex Districts in Chicago and New York in the Early Twentieth Century*. New York: Columbia University Press, 1997.

Muraskin, William A. *Middle-Class Blacks in a White Society: Prince Hall Freemasonry in America*. Berkeley: University of California Press, 1975.

Naison, Mark. *Communists in Harlem during the Depression*. Urbana: University of Illinois Press, 1983. Reprint, New York: Grove Press, 1985.

Nash, Gary B. *Forging Freedom: The Formation of Philadelphia's Black Community, 1720–1840*. Cambridge: Harvard University Press, 1988.

Neilson, David Gordon. *Black Ethos: Northern Urban Negro Life and Thought, 1890–1930*. Westport, Conn.: Greenwood Press, 1977.

Oriard, Michael. *Reading Football: How the Popular Press Created an American Spectacle*. Chapel Hill: University of North Carolina Press, 1993.

Osofsky, Gilbert. *Harlem: The Making of a Ghetto: Negro New York, 1890–1930*. New York: Harper and Row, 1966.

Pascoe, Peggy. "Miscegenation Law, Court Cases, and Ideologies of 'Race' in Twentieth-Century America." *Journal of American History* 83 (June 1996): 44–69.

Peiss, Kathy. *Cheap Amusements: Working Women and Leisure in Turn-of-the-Century New York*. Philadelphia: Temple University Press, 1986.

Pendergast, Tom. "Consuming Questions: Scholarship on Consumerism in America to 1940." *American Studies International* 36 (June 1998): 23–43.

———. *Creating the Modern Man: American Magazines and Consumer Culture, 1900–1950*. Columbia: University of Missouri Press, 2000.

Price, Clement Alexander. "In Search of a People's Spirit: The Harmon Foundation and American Interest in Afro-American Artists." In *Against the Odds: African American Artists and the Harmon Foundation*, edited by Gary A. Reynolds and Beryl J. Wright, 71–87. Newark, N.J.: Newark Museum, 1990.

Rampersad, Arnold. *1902–1941: I, Too, Sing America*. Vol. 1 of *The Life of Langston Hughes*. New York: Oxford University Press, 1986.

Reich, Steven A. "Soldiers of Democracy: Black Texans and the Fight for Citizenship, 1917–1921." *Journal of American History* 82 (March 1996): 1478–1504.

Reid, Ira DeA. *The Negro Immigrant: His Background, Characteristics and Social Adjustment, 1899–1937*. New York: Columbia University Press, 1939.

Richardson, Joe M. *A History of Fisk University, 1865–1946*. Tuscaloosa: University of Alabama Press, 1980.

Rodgers, Daniel T. *The Work Ethic in Industrial America, 1850–1920*. Chicago: University of Chicago Press, 1979.

Roediger, David R. *The Wages of Whiteness: Race and the Making of the American Working Class*. London: Verso, 1991.

Rotundo, E. Anthony. *American Manhood: Transformations in Masculinity from the Revolution to the Modern Era*. New York: Basic Books, 1993.

Ryan, Mary P. *Women in Public: Between Banners and Ballots, 1825–1880*. Baltimore, Md.: Johns Hopkins University Press, 1990.

Rydell, Robert W. *All the World's a Fair: Visions of Empire at American International Expositions, 1876–1916*. Chicago: University of Chicago Press, 1984.

Sale, Maggie Montesinos. *The Slumbering Volcano: American Slave Ship Revolts and the Production of Rebellious Masculinity*. Durham, N.C.: Duke University Press, 1997.

Satter, Beryl. "Marcus Garvey, Father Divine and the Gender Politics of Race Difference and Race Neutrality." *American Quarterly* 48 (March 1996): 43–76.

Schwarz, A. B. Christa. *Gay Voices of the Harlem Renaissance*. Bloomington: Indiana University Press, 2003.

Scott, Joan W. "Gender: A Useful Category of Historical Analysis." *American Historical Review* 91 (December 1986): 1053–75.

————. "Women in *The Making of the English Working Class*." In *Gender and the Politics of History*. New York: Columbia University Press, 1988.

Segal, Lynne. "Changing Men: Masculinities in Context." *Theory and Society* 22 (October 1993): 625–41.

————. *Slow Motion: Changing Masculinities, Changing Men*. New Brunswick, N.J.: Rutgers University Press, 1990.

Shaw, Stephanie J. *What a Woman Ought to Be and to Do: Black Professional Women Workers During the Jim Crow Era*. Chicago: University of Chicago Press, 1996.

Singal, Daniel Joseph. "Towards a Definition of American Modernism." *American Quarterly* 39 (Spring 1987): 7–26.

Singh, Amritjit. "Black-White Symbiosis: Another Look at the Literary History of the 1920s." In *The Harlem Renaissance Re-examined*, edited by Victor A. Kramer, 31–42. New York: AMS Press, 1987.

————. *The Novels of the Harlem Renaissance: Twelve Black Writers, 1923–1933*. University Park: Pennsylvania State University Press, 1976.

Sonenshein, Raphael J. *Politics in Black and White: Race and Power in Los Angeles*. Princeton, N.J.: Princeton University Press, 1993.

Stecopoulos, Harry, and Michael Uebel, eds. *Race and the Subject of Masculinities*. Durham, N.C.: Duke University Press, 1997.

Stein, Judith. *The World of Marcus Garvey: Race and Class in Modern Society*. Baton Rouge: Louisiana State University Press, 1986.

Stoler, Ann Laura. *Race and the Education of Desire: Foucault's History of Sexuality and the Colonial Order of Things*. Durham, N.C.: Duke University Press, 1995.

Stuckey, Sterling. *Slave Culture: Nationalist Theory and the Foundations of Black America*. New York: Oxford University Press, 1987.

Studlar, Gaylyn. *This Mad Masquerade: Stardom and Masculinity in the Jazz Age*. New York: Columbia University Press, 1996.

Summers, Martin. "'This Immoral Practice': The Prehistory of Homophobia in Black Nationalist Thought." In *Gender Nonconformity, Race, and Sexuality: Charting the Connections*, edited by Toni Lester, 21–43. Madison: University of Wisconsin Press, 2002.

Susman, Warren I. *Culture as History: The Transformation of American Society in the Twentieth Century*. New York: Pantheon Books, 1984.

Taylor, Ula Yvette. *The Veiled Garvey: The Life and Times of Amy Jacques Garvey*. Chapel Hill: University of North Carolina Press, 2002.

Testi, Arnaldo. "The Gender of Reform Politics: Theodore Roosevelt and the Culture of Masculinity." *Journal of American History* 81 (March 1995): 1509–33.

Thompson, E. P. *The Making of the English Working Class*. 1963. Reprint, London: V. Gollancz, 1980.

Tolbert, Emory J. *The UNIA and Black Los Angeles: Ideology and Community in the American Garvey Movement*. Los Angeles: Center for Afro-American Studies and University of California Press, 1980.

Torgovnick, Marianna. *Gone Primitive: Savage Intellects, Modern Lives*. Chicago: University of Chicago Press, 1990.

Trotter, Joe William, Jr. *Black Milwaukee: The Making of an Industrial Proletariat, 1915–45*. Urbana: Illinois University Press, 1985.

Ullman, Sharon R. *Sex Seen: The Emergence of Modern Sexuality in America*. Berkeley: University of California Press, 1997.

Van Deburg, William L. *New Day in Babylon: The Black Power Movement and American Culture, 1965–1975*. Chicago: University of Chicago Press, 1992.

Vincent, Theodore. *Black Power and the Garvey Movement*. San Francisco: Ramparts Press, 1971.

Wade, Melvin. "'Shining in Borrowed Plumage': Affirmation of Community in the Black Coronation Festivals of New England, ca. 1750–1850." In *Material Life in America, 1600–1860*, edited by Robert Blair St. George, 171–81. Boston: Northeastern University Press, 1988.

Walkowitz, Daniel J. *Working with Class: Social Workers and the Politics of Middle-Class Identity*. Chapel Hill: University of North Carolina Press, 1999.

Wall, Cheryl. *Women of the Harlem Renaissance*. Bloomington: Indiana University Press, 1995.

Wallace, Maurice. "'Are We Men?': Prince Hall, Martin Delany, and the Masculine Ideal in Black Freemasonry, 1775–1865." *American Literary History* 9 (Fall 1997): 396–424.

———. *Constructing the Black Masculine: Identity and Ideality in African American Men's Literature and Culture, 1775–1995*. Durham, N.C.: Duke University Press, 2002.

Watkins-Owens, Irma. *Blood Relations: Caribbean Immigrants and the Harlem Community, 1900–1930*. Bloomington: Indiana University Press, 1996.

Weems, Robert E., Jr. *Desegregating the Dollar: African American Consumerism in the Twentieth Century*. New York: New York University Press, 1998.

Wesley, Charles H. *Prince Hall: Life and Legacy*. Washington, D.C.: United Supreme Council, Southern Jurisdiction, Prince Hall Affiliation, 1977.

West, Dorothy. "Elephant's Dance: A Memoir of Wallace Thurman." *Black World* 20 (November 1970): 77–85.

Westwood, Sallie. "Racism, Black Masculinity and the Politics of Space." In *Men, Masculinities and Social Theory*, edited by Jeff Hearn and David Morgan, 55–71. London: Unwin Hyman, 1990.

White, Deborah Gray. *Too Heavy a Load: Black Women in Defense of Themselves, 1894–1994*. New York: W. W. Norton, 1999.

Wilder, Craig Steven. *A Covenant with Color: Race and Social Power in Brooklyn*. New York: Columbia University Press, 2000.

———. *In the Company of Black Men: The African Influence on African American Culture in New York City*. New York: New York University Press, 2001.

Williams, Loretta J. *Black Freemasonry and Middle-Class Realities*. Columbia: University of Missouri Press, 1980.

Williams, Raymond. *Marxism and Literature*. Oxford: Oxford University Press, 1977.

Williamson, Joel. *A Rage for Order: Black-White Relations in the American South since Emancipation*. New York: Oxford University Press, 1986.

Wilson, Elizabeth. *Adorned in Dreams: Fashion and Modernity*. Berkeley: University of California Press, 1985.

Wolcott, Victoria. *Remaking Respectability: African American Women in Interwar Detroit*. Chapel Hill: University of North Carolina Press, 2001.

Wolters, Raymond. *The New Negro on Campus: Black College Rebellions of the 1920s*. Princeton, N.J.: Princeton University Press, 1975.

Young, R. J. *Antebellum Black Activists: Race, Gender, and Self*. New York: Garland Publishing, 1996.

Index

Page numbers in italics refer to photographs.

91–92; and homosexuality, 194–95; and Prince Hall Freemasonry, 116; and Universal Negro Improvement Association, 105–6, 314 (n. 111). *See also* Religion

Black colleges, 244–62; background of, 244–45, 336 (nn. 4, 6); and industrial education, 245–47; and missionary philosophy, 247–48. *See also* Black college student life policies; College unrest

Black college student life policies: alcohol/tobacco, 260–61, 279–80, 340–41 (nn. 59, 60); character, 248–50, 337 (nn. 20, 21); and consumption ethos, 152, 244, 269, 284–85; dress codes, 256–58, 276, 339 (n. 46); Greek-letter organizations, 270, 281–85, 289, 342 (n. 84); male-female interaction, 258–60, 276–78, 280–81, 339–40 (nn. 48, 49, 53); military training, 251–56, 271, 272; and modern masculinity ideals, 244, 264–65, 285–86; music, 261, 278–79; physical culture, 250–51, 272, 280; religion, 248, 270–71

Black Cross Nurses, 123, 138, 320 (n. 80)

The Blacker the Berry (Thurman), 150, 322–23 (n. 4)

Black manhood: precarious sense of, 3; scholarly approaches to, 10–14, 293–94 (n. 20). *See also* Black masculinity ethos transformation; Harlem Renaissance—masculinity ideals; Modern masculinity ideals; Prince Hall Freemasonry—manliness ideals; Universal Negro Improvement Association—manliness ideals

Black masculinity ethos transformation, 155–56, 292–93 (n. 15); ambiguities in, 9, 281; critiques of, 287–89; and culture of personality, 292 (n. 15), 337 (n. 20); and hegemonic masculinity theory, 14; overviews, 8–9, 152–53

Black messianism, 103–4

Black middle class status: and elite uplift ideology, 34–35; Frazier on, 287; and Harlem Renaissance, 151, 172, 204; in Harlem Renaissance literature, 211–12, 218–19; and Jazz Age leisure, 175, 179–80, 326 (n. 46); and post–World War I career choices, 170, 171, 172–73; and post–World War I marriage, 187, 191, 192, 194; and Prince Hall Freemasonry, 20–21, 46; and Prince Hall Freemasonry manliness ideals, 27, 28, 34, 35–36, 58, 65; and Prince Hall Freemasonry membership, 29, 30, 33–34; and Prince Hall Freemasonry public performance, 53–54, 58; and respectability, 42–43; and separate sphere ideology, 115, 119; and spurious Masonry charges, 59, 62–63; subjective nature of, 6–7, 28; Toomer on, 214–15; and Universal Negro Improvement Association, 70, 87, 95, 306 (n. 9); and women's public sphere roles, 119, 317 (n. 35)

Black nationalism, 137–38, 201–2; and Universal Negro Improvement Association, 61, 78, 89, 98, 99–100, 121, 139. *See also* Cultural nationalism

Black Star Line, 21, 104

Black women's club movement, 113–14, 117, 132. *See also* Women's public sphere roles

Black youth. *See* Manhood/boyhood distinctions; Youth training

Bledsoe, Jules, 176

"Blood-Burning Moon" (Toomer), 216–18

Blues, 278

Body. *See* Physicality

Boyhood/manhood distinctions. *See* Manhood/boyhood distinctions

Boy Scouts, 126

Braithwaite, William Stanley, 205, 215

Brawley, Benjamin, 204

Brereton, Bridget, 7

Briggs, Cyril, 142, 159
Brooks, J. D., 84, 104, 134
Brotherhood of Sleeping Car Porters and
    Maids, 243
Brown, Guillaume, 192
Brown, Harold S., 275
Brown, Sue M. Wilson: and domesticity,
    132, 317 (n. 23); on mutual aid/charity,
    131; on OES membership, 117; and
    women's challenges to male authority,
    142–43, 146; on women's suffrage, 132,
    319 (n. 61); and youth training, 128,
    130
Bruce, John Edward: on African origins
    of Freemasonry, 61; on clergy, 106;
    funeral of, 17–18, 19, 152; and Liberia,
    81–82; on producer ideals, 109; on self-
    made man ideology, 84; and social
    Darwinism, 78; on women, 133–34
Buffet flats, 181–82
Bulmer, Benjamin, 46
Burton, Richard D. E., 313 (n. 97)
Business. See Entrepreneurship; Producer
    values
Butler, Judith, 293 (n. 16)
Buxton, Travers, 66

Cabarets, 179–80, 326 (n. 55)
Cane (Toomer), 165, 216–21, 332–33
    (nn. 35, 37)
Carby, Hazel, 226
"Carma" (Toomer), 216
Carpenter, Edward, 190
Carter, George Emonei, 18, 141
Casimir, J. R. Ralph, 69
Character: and black college student life
    policies, 248–50, 337 (nn. 20, 21); and
    Prince Hall Freemasonry manliness
    ideals, 27, 41–42; and UNIA manliness
    ideals, 85, 94, 95; and Universal Negro
    Improvement Association, 69, 85–86;
    and Victorian manliness ideals, 1, 292
    (n. 15)
Charity. See Mutual aid/charity

Chauncey, George, 182, 197
Chestnutt, Charles W., 205, 215
Church. See Black clergy; Religion
Circle of Constantine, 129
Citizenship, 2, 119
Civilization: and Harlem Renaissance
    masculinity ideals, 214–15, 216, 221–
    22; and UNIA manliness ideals, 102–3,
    314 (n. 101). See also Primitivism
Civil service, 26, 79–80. See also Black
    middle class status
Clark, Crittenden E., 143, 144–45
Clark, Homer, 166
Clarke, Edward, 136
Clarke, Lizan, 140
Class status: and black college dress
    codes, 256–57; and consumption
    ethos, 152, 156; early twentieth cen-
    tury scholarship on, 332 (n. 24); and
    Harlem Renaissance artist role de-
    bate, 203–4; in Harlem Renaissance
    literature, 207–8, 332 (n. 24); and
    Jazz Age leisure, 174, 175, 177–78,
    179–80, 326 (n. 46); and Prince Hall
    Freemasonry membership, 25–26, 29–
    30, 33–34, 298 (nn. 15, 16, 17); and
    UNIA attitudes towards women, 137,
    320 (n. 80); and UNIA membership,
    70, 72–74, 76–78, 306 (n. 9); and
    UNIA/PCNIA split, 74–76; and Uni-
    versal African Legion, 95–97. See also
    Black middle class status
Clawson, Mary Ann, 27
Clothing. See Attire
Club movement, 113–14, 117
Coleman, J. W., 74, 76
College unrest, 152, 262–75, 285; course
    of, 262–67, 270–75, 341 (nn. 68, 69);
    delegitimization of, 268–69
Collins, Patricia Hill, 316–17 (n. 22)
Color (Cullen), 172
Color consciousness, 107, 322–23 (n. 4)
Companionate marriage, 194
Connell, R. W., 10

consumption ethos: and black college
student life policies, 152, 244, 269,
284–85; and Jazz Age, 151, 156, 157;
and modern masculinity ideals, 8, 152,
156–57, 287–88; scholarship on, 323
(n. 5); and Universal Negro Improve-
ment Association, 89–92
Cook, John F., 26
Cooper, Anna Julia, 113
Corporatization, 79–80, 155, 308 (n. 37)
Court receptions, 97–99, 136–37
Cravath, Paul, 268
Creativity, 165
Crime, 44–45
Crisis, 165, 264
Cubism, 232, 334 (n. 55)
Cullen, Carolyn, 172
Cullen, Countee: and artist role debate,
204–5; career choices of, 172–73;
and homosexuality, 189–91, 196, 328
(nn. 76, 79); and jazz culture, 175;
marriage of, 188–94, 328 (nn. 76, 79),
329 (n. 85)
Cullen, Frederick A., 172
Cultural nationalism: and Prince Hall
Freemasonry, 60–61, 304 (n. 101)
Culture of personality, 292 (n. 15), 337
(n. 20)
Cunard, Nancy, 237–38
Currin, G. I., 132
Curtis, Rodney L., 288–89

Dali, Salvador, 176
D'Alverez, Margarita, 176
Daugherty, Harry M., 72
Davis, A. W., 260, 269
Davis, Henrietta Vinton, 82, 121, 133
DeBerry, William N., 264, 265, 341
(n. 68)
Declaration of the Rights of the Negro
Peoples of the World, 136, 320 (n. 76)
D'Emilio, John, 343 (n. 99)
Diggs, James Robert Lincoln, 104
Divorce. See Post–World War I marriage

Dobbs, John Wesley, 41–42, 131
Domesticity: and citizenship, 119, 317
(n. 23); and Prince Hall Freemasonry
manliness ideals, 112, 130–31; and
UNIA manliness ideals, 112, 125–26,
130–31, 133, 138; and women's chal-
lenges to male authority, 138–40, 321
(n. 89); and women's public sphere
roles, 132–33, 138–40. See also Separate
sphere ideology
Domingo, W. A., 159
Dossen, J. J., 81, 97
Douglas, Aaron, 170–71, 176, 195, 232–
33, 334 (n. 55)
Douglas, Alta Sawyer, 176, 232, 233
Douglas, Ann, 330 (n. 8)
Douglass, Frederick, 299 (n. 29)
Drag balls, 182–83
Dress. See Attire
Dress codes, 256–58, 276, 339 (n. 46)
Dubbert, Joe L., 309 (n. 42)
Du Bois, W. E. B.: and artist role de-
bate, 203–4, 205; and civilization,
215; and college unrest, 264–65, 266,
267, 268; on consumption ethos, 284–
85, 287–88; and Cullen/Yolande Du
Bois marriage, 188, 193–94; and The
New Negro, 200, 201; and patronage,
238; on racism, 4; and Talented Tenth
model, 67–68; and Universal Negro
Improvement Association, 107–8
Du Bois, Yolande, 175; marriage of, 188–
94, 329 (n. 85)
Dudley, James B., 25
Dumenil, Lynn, 32
Dunbar, Paul Laurence, 205
Durkee, James Stanley, 262, 270, 272,
274
Dyer, Constantine, 310 (n. 58)

Early, Gerald, 189–90
Eason, J. W. H., 81, 86, 306 (n. 13), 310
(n. 58)
Eastman, Crystal, 159

67, 107–8; and Harlem Renaissance, 237, 239; incarceration of, 21, 109, 139, 142; and Liberia, 83; and PCNIA split, 74–75; and Prince Hall Freemasonry, 18; on racial purity, 135; on religion, 104–5; and Talented Tenth model, 68; and UNIA establishment, 66; on women, 121, 133, 141, 318 (n. 41). *See also* Universal Negro Improvement Association

Gaskin, Irene, 100

Gates, Henry Louis, Jr., 331–32 (n. 23)

Gay subculture: in Harlem Renaissance literature, 334 (n. 51); and Jazz Age leisure, 181–83; and modern masculinity ideals, 157; and post–World War I marriage, 190, 327 (n. 65). *See also* Homosexuality

Gender: and class, 299 (n. 33); social constructionist approach to, 9–11, 293–94 (nn. 16, 20). *See also* Gender roles; Separate sphere ideology

Gender roles: and elite uplift ideology, 34; and post–World War I marriage, 187, 188; and UNIA youth training, 124–26. *See also* Black middle class status; Domesticity; Prince Hall Freemasonry—attitudes towards women; Separate sphere ideology; Universal Negro Improvement Association—attitudes towards women; Victorian manliness ideals; Women's public sphere roles

German expressionism, 232

Gibson, Joseph D., 86, 106

Gilmore, Glenda, 65

Gleaves, Richard H., 25

Godmother. *See* Mason, Charlotte Osgood

Gordon, Hugh, 74

Gordon, John D., 74, 80–81

Gordon, Taylor, 176

Gramsci, Antonio, 10

Grant, U. A. Leo, 141

Great Migration. *See* Migration/immigration

Greek-letter organizations, 270, 281–85, 289, 342 (n. 84)

Griffen, Clyde, 308 (n. 37)

Griffith, D. W., 100

Grimké, Angelina, 205, 331 (n. 18)

Grimké, Francis J., 288

Grimshaw, William, 26, 36, 49, 53, 64–65, 295 (n. 6), 301 (n. 58), 302 (n. 77), 304 (n. 100)

Hall, G. Stanley, 337 (n. 21)

Hall, Prince, 19–20, 295 (n. 6)

Hamilton Lodge Ball, 182

Hamlin, Teunis S., 246, 252

Hammer, Langdon, 330–31 (nn. 10, 18)

Harlem (Thurman & Rapp), 150, 184, 326 (n. 53)

Harlem Renaissance, 200–241; and artistic genealogy of modernism, 205–6, 331 (n. 18); and artist role debate, 203–7; and college unrest, 243; female participation in, 237, 331 (n. 12); and Hughes, 168; and Nugent, 169, 170; and struggles against racism, 201–2, 240–41; and Thurman, 149, 151, 288, 344 (n. 5); Toomer's rejection of, 215. *See also* Jazz Age—leisure; Jazz culture; Post–World War I career choices; Post–World War I marriage; *and specific artists*

—cult of production, 330–31 (n. 10); Douglas on, 233–34; in literature, 209–10, 219–20, 227–29; and masculinity ideals, 203; McKay on, 224, 227–29; and patronage, 238, 239

—masculinity ideals, 152, 202–3; in *The Autobiography of an Ex-Coloured Man*, 207–11, 213–14, 332 (nn. 24, 25); and civilization, 214–15, 216, 221–22; in *The Fire in the Flint*, 207, 211–14; and industrialization, 214, 215, 216–18; McKay on, 179, 224, 226–31; and patronage,

203, 231–32, 234, 237, 240; and rural culture, 220–21
Harrison, Hubert, 81, 159
Harvey, Thomas, 97, 99
Haskin, Frederic J., 337 (n. 21)
Hayes, Roland, 209
Haynes, George E., 200, 263
He, The One Who Gets Slapped (Andreyev), 221–22
Hedgeman, Marie A., 143, 145
Hegemony theory, 10–11, 13–14, 42–43
Helps, Mary, 114
Hemingway, Ernest, 202, 330 (n. 8)
Henderson, Mae Gwendolyn, 322–23 (n. 4)
Hewlett, John, 278
Higginbotham, Evelyn Brooks, 42, 147
Hill, Robert A., 67, 98, 101, 317 (n. 30), 320 (n. 80)
Hine, Darlene Clark, 138, 317 (n. 35)
Hobsbawm, Eric, 22, 302 (n. 70)
Holzworth, Fred M., 32
Home to Harlem (McKay), 224–31, 238, 333–34 (nn. 48, 50, 51)
Homosexuality, 156, 169, 170, 194–98; in Harlem Renaissance literature, 225, 226–27, 229–30, 334 (n. 51); and Jazz Age leisure, 181–83; and modern masculinity ideals, 157, 196–98, 231; opposition to, 194–95; and post–World War I marriage, 184–85, 189–91, 327 (n. 65), 328 (nn. 69, 76, 79); UNIA disapproval of, 91. *See also* Gay subculture
Hood, J. W., 117
Hopkins, A. A., 74, 75–76
Howard University: African Caribbean students, 338 (n. 24); background of, 244–45, 336 (nn. 4, 6); and industrial education, 245–46; unrest, 270–75. *See also* Black colleges; Black college student life policies
Hughes, Carrie Langston, 166, 168
Hughes, James Nathaniel, 166–68

Hughes, Langston, 150, 181; career choices of, 166–69; and Douglas, 233; and homosexuality, 196; on Jazz Age leisure, 176, 177, 182; and *The New Negro*, 200; on Nugent, 197; and patronage, 235–37, 238, 335 (n. 70); on primitivism, 231–32; and Thurman, 150–51, 344 (n. 5)
Hurston, Zora Neale, 185–86, 235, 331 (n. 12), 335 (n. 70)
Hyatt, Ada, 140

Imperialism, 2–3, 80, 113. *See also* Frontier manliness
Independent, 149
Indian iconography, 102
Indian Wars, 2
Individualism, 79–80, 155
Industrial education, 245–47
Industrialization, 84–85, 214, 215, 216–18
Infants of the Spring (Thurman), 151
International Socialist Club, 159
Interracial relationships. *See* Racial purity
Iölaus (Carpenter), 190
Ivy, James W., 238

Jackman, Harold, 181; and Cullen, 173, 175, 189; on drag balls, 182; and McKay, 222, 224, 238
Jackson, Robert P., 145
Jackson, Rosa, 39
Jackson, Thornton A., 116
Jacobs, William, 143
Jacques Garvey, Amy, 76, 100, 139–40, 142, 321 (nn. 89, 95)
James, Winston, 70
Jazz Age: and homosexuality, 194–98; and nihilism, 150–51; overviews, 151, 155–56, 198–99. *See also* College unrest; Harlem Renaissance; Jazz culture; Modern masculinity ideals; Post–World War I career choices; Post–World War I marriage

—leisure, 173–83; and cabarets, 179–80, 326 (nn. 46, 55); in Harlem Renaissance literature, 179, 225–26, 333 (n. 44); and homosexuality, 181–83; and jazz culture, 173–75; and modern masculinity ideals, 152, 175, 178–79, 180–81, 182–83, 326 (n. 53); and private parties, 176–78; and sweetbacks, 178–79, 326 (n. 53). See also Black college student life policies

Jazz culture, 173–75; ambivalence about, 174–75, 325–26 (n. 44); and black college student life policies, 278–79; and class status, 174, 175, 326 (n. 46), and consumption ethos, 157; and primitivism, 174, 175, 231; UNIA critique of, 90–91. See also Jazz Age—leisure

Jekyll, Walter, 158, 159
Jenkins, Weldon Victor, 3
Jeppe, Louis Alexander, 28
Jim Crow. See Segregation
John F. Slater Fund, 246, 247
Johnson, Charles S., 200, 238, 326 (n. 53)
Johnson, Georgia Douglas, 169, 205, 331 (n. 18)
Johnson, Hall, 235
Johnson, James Weldon, 210; and artist role debate, 205, 206; and Harlem Renaissance masculinity ideals, 203, 207–11, 213–14, 332 (nn. 24, 25); on Jazz Age leisure, 174, 176, 179; "Lift Every Voice and Sing," 288
Joiner, W. Devoe, 64
Jones, J. W., 93
Jones, Jacqueline, 125, 292 (n. 6)
Jones, Thomas Elsa, 275, 281–82
Jones, Thomas Jesse, 265
Judeo-Christian tradition. See Religion

"Kabnis" (Toomer), 216, 219–21, 333 (n. 37)
"Karintha" (Toomer), 216

Kellogg, Paul Underwood, 200
Kenderdine, G. A., 60
Kerman, Cynthia Earl, 162
Kessler-Harris, Alice, 125
Kimmel, Michael, 11, 325 (n. 39)
King, C. D. B.: and Prince Hall Freemasonry, 58, 303 (n. 93); and Universal Negro Improvement Association, 81, 82, 83
King, C. D. B., Mrs., 117
Knights Templar, 56–58, 303 (n. 93)
Ku Klux Klan, 136

Labor unions, 27, 96
Ladies' auxiliaries, 114–15. See also Universal African Black Cross Nurses
Lane, Winthrop D., 200
Larsen, Nella, 176, 331 (n. 12)
Lawrence, Isabella, 98
Leadett, Carrie Mero, 88–89
Legionnaires. See Universal African Legion
Leisure. See Jazz Age—leisure
Lewars, Eulalie, 159
Lewis, David Levering, 241
Lewis, Earl, 299 (n. 24)
Lewis, Herbert Fitz, 37
Lewis, Sinclair, 172, 325 (n. 39)
Liberator, 159, 160, 165, 166, 221–22
Liberia, 81–83, 309 (n. 48)
"Lift Every Voice and Sing" (Johnson), 288
Locke, Alain: and artist role debate, 205, 206; and college unrest, 242–43, 274; and Cullen, 189, 190, 328 (n. 76); and Douglas, 234; and homosexuality, 195, 196, 328 (n. 76); on Jazz Age leisure, 326 (n. 55); and jazz culture, 325–26 (n. 44); on marriage, 183; The New Negro, 200–202, 205, 239, 287; and patronage, 235, 237, 238, 239, 335 (n. 79); on respectability, 198
Loeb, Ralph, 190
Lynching, 3, 135

MacGowan, Kenneth, 333 (n. 37)

Macoy, Robert, 116, 120

Maloney, A. H.: on frontier manliness, 79, 80, 308 (n. 33); on mainstream leaders, 106–7; on racial purity, 320 (n. 73); on women, 113

Manhood/boyhood distinctions: and Prince Hall Freemasonry manliness ideals, 27, 112, 126–27, 130, 148; and racism, 127–28; and UNIA manliness ideals, 112, 125–26, 148

Manhood in America (Kimmel), 11

Manliness. *See* Black masculinity ethos transformation; Prince Hall Freemasonry—manliness ideals; Universal Negro Improvement Association—manliness ideals; Victorian manliness ideals

Marinoff, Fania, 176

Marketplace. *See* Industrialization; Producer values

Marriage. *See* Post–World War I marriage

Martin, Charles D., 17–18, 40

Marxism, 159

Marxism and Literature (Williams), 13–14

Masculinity. *See* Black masculinity ethos transformation; Harlem Renaissance—masculinity ideals; Modern masculinity ideals

Mason, Charlotte Osgood ("Godmother"), 231–32, 235, 236–37, 335 (n. 70)

Mass culture, 151, 155. *See also* Jazz Age—leisure; Jazz culture

Masturbation, 162

Materialism. *See* consumption ethos; Producer values

Matisse, Henri, 232

Maugham, Somerset, 176

McClintock, Anne, 299 (n. 33)

McGuire, George Alexander, 106

McKay, Claude, 221–31, 223; and artist role debate, 224, 238–39; background of, 158, 324 (n. 6); career choices of, 158–60; and homosexuality, 196–97, 225, 226–27, 229–30, 334 (n. 51); on jazz culture, 326 (n. 46); and Locke, 196, 239; on masculinity, 179, 224, 226–31; and *The New Negro*, 200; and patronage, 237–39, 335 (n. 79); on primitivism, 222–24, 225–26, 227, 229, 333 (n. 44); on producer values, 224, 227–29; and racial essentialism, 222–24; and racism, 221–22, 333 (n. 41); and respectability, 198; on sweetbacks, 179, 228, 333 (n. 48); and Thurman, 149, 185, 344 (n. 5); and Wilson, 187, 328 (n. 69)

McKay, Hannah Edwards, 158, 324 (n. 6)

McKay, Nellie, 164, 216

McKay, Thomas Francis, 158, 324 (n. 6)

McKenzie, Fayette A., 261–62; on attire, 257–58; on character, 250; and college unrest, 262–64, 265–66, 267, 268; on male-female interactions, 259; and military training, 254, 255; on physical culture, 251

Messenger, 238

Migration/immigration, 5–6; extent of, 31; and Jazz Age, 151, 174; and Prince Hall Freemasonry, 27; and spurious Masonry charges, 63; and UNIA manliness ideals, 88, 95

Militarism: and black college student life policies, 251–56, 271, 272; and Prince Hall Freemasonry manliness ideals, 56–58; and Universal African Legion, 93–94, 100, 136–37

Miller, Kelly, 200, 274

Miller, Thomas S. F., 46–48

Mims, R. R., 34–35, 41, 42

Minor, Uzziah, 80

Minstrelsy, 102

Miscegenation. *See* Racial purity

Missionary educational philosophy, 247–48

Mitchell, Michele, 311 (n. 70)

Modernism: artistic genealogy of, 205–6,

New Woman: and Jazz Age, 151, 175; and Universal Negro Improvement Association, 91, 139; and youth training, 124

Northern Migration, 5–6. *See also* Migration/immigration

Not without Laughter (Hughes), 236

Nugent, Richard Bruce, 169–70, 195, 196, 197–98

Nursing, 123, 138, 317 (n. 35)

Occupational status. *See* Black middle class status; Class status; Post–World War I career choices

OES. *See* Order of the Eastern Star

Opportunity, 172, 200

Order of Bees for Boys and Girls, 128–29, 318 (n. 50)

Order of the Builders for Boys, 129

Order of the Eastern Star (OES), 114, 115–20; and adoption, 117, 316 (n. 13); functions of, 117–18; governing structure of, 119–20; and mutual aid/charity, 117, 131–33; origins of, 115–17; and struggles against racism, 131, 319 (n. 57); symbolism of, 118–19; and women's challenges to male authority, 139, 142–47, 321 (n. 100); and women's public sphere roles, 131, 319 (nn. 57, 61); and youth training, 128–29, 318 (n. 50)

Orphanages, 39, 300 (n. 45). *See also* Mutual aid/charity

Ortman, Elmer J., 265

"Overcivilization," 79, 126–27

Pacific Coast Negro Improvement Association (PCNIA), 74–76

Pankhurst, Sylvia, 159

Parades: Prince Hall Freemasonry, 56; Universal Negro Improvement Association, 99–101, 137–38

Parker, Lafayette, 44–45

Partch, A. W., 339 (n. 46)

"Passing," 208, 209, 211

Patriarchal role: difficulty in blacks obtaining, 3, 136; and Prince Hall Freemasonry manliness ideals, 26–27, 36–37, 39, 112; and UNIA attitudes towards women, 136; and women's roles in Prince Hall Freemasonry, 112, 114; and women's UNIA roles, 114, 122. *See also* Separate sphere ideology

Patronage, 234–40, 335 (n. 70); and Harlem Renaissance masculinity ideals, 203, 231–32, 234, 237, 240

PCNIA (Pacific Coast Negro Improvement Association), 74–76

Peabody, George Foster, 245

Peart, Indiana Garvey, 121

Performative gender identity: and Prince Hall Freemasonry manliness ideals, 48–59, 302 (n. 77); and UNIA attitudes towards women, 136–38. *See also* Attire; Public rituals; Universal African Legion

Peterkin, Julia, 204

Peterson, Dorothy, 171

Phillipse, Alphonse D., 260

Philosophy and Opinions (Jacques Garvey), 107

Physical culture, 79, 162, 250–51, 272, 280

Physicality: and Harlem Renaissance masculinity ideals, 203, 224, 228; and modern masculinity ideals, 152, 178, 179, 180, 244, 285; and UNIA manliness ideals, 79, 80

Piano players, 178, 179

Picasso, Pablo, 232

Pickens, William, 306 (n. 13)

Pinchback, Bismarck, 160, 162, 163

Pinchback, Nina Hethorn, 160

Pinchback, P. B. S., 160, 163, 165

Poole, R., 46

Poston, Robert L., 104

Post-Victorian masculinity ideals. *See* Modern masculinity ideals

Post–World War I career choices, 152, 157–73; Cullen, 172–73; Douglas, 170–71; Fisher, 171–72; and Harlem

Renaissance, 202; Hughes, 166–69; McKay, 158–60; and modern masculinity ideals, 163, 164, 165, 169, 171; Nugent, 169–70; Toomer, 160–65, 324 (n. 19); Walrond, 172

Post–World War I marriage, 156, 157, 183–94; Cullen/Du Bois, 188–94, 328 (nn. 76, 79), 329 (n. 85); Hurston/Sheen, 185–86; and modern masculinity ideals, 185, 191, 327 (n. 63); Robesons, 186–87; Rucker, 188; Thurman/Thompson, 183–85, 327 (nn. 63, 65); Wilson, 187–88, 328 (n. 69)

Powell, Adam Clayton, 194

Powell, Lyman P., 249

Primitivism: feminization of, 202, 205, 330 (n. 9); and Harlem Renaissance artist role debate, 205; in Harlem Renaissance literature, 215, 216, 222–24, 225–26, 227, 229, 333 (n. 44); and Harlem Renaissance masculinity ideals, 152, 202, 203, 224, 234; Hughes on, 231–32; and Jazz Age leisure, 174, 175, 178, 231; McKay on, 222–24, 225–26, 227, 229, 333 (n. 44); and modernism, 151, 202, 205, 330 (n. 5); and patronage, 231–32, 235; and UNIA manliness ideals, 102–3. *See also* Civilization

Prince Hall Freemasonry, 25–65; African Caribbean membership of, 29, 31–32, 297 (n. 14); and Bruce funeral, 17–18, 19, 152; class demographics of, 25–26, 29–30, 33–34, 298 (nn. 15, 16, 17); and critiques of modern masculinity ideals, 288–89; diasporic character of, 25, 33; and elite uplift ideology, 34–35, 64; and gatekeeping, 51–52, 302–3 (n. 80); history of, 19–20; importance of, 20–21, 26; Knights Templar, 56–58, 303 (n. 93); lodge rooms, 51, 302 (n. 77); meeting procedure, 52–53; membership numbers, 26, 296 (n. 5);

membership selection process, 30–31; and mutual aid/charity, 36–39, 299–300 (nn. 41, 42, 45), 302–3 (n. 80); organizational structure of, 36, 295 (n. 7); public rituals, 17–18, 56–59, 303 (n. 93); racial/ethnic inclusiveness of, 29, 31–32, 65, 298–99 (n. 24); and racial solidarity, 32–33; and religion, 43, 49, 300–301 (n. 56), 302 (n. 77); and sovereignty, 46–48, 301–2 (nn. 66, 67); and spurious Masonry charges, 59, 61–64; temple construction, 39–41; and Universal Negro Improvement Association, 18–19, 21–22; and white Masonic nonrecognition policy, 27, 31, 59–61, 304 (n. 100); youth training, 27, 126–30, 318 (n. 50). *See also* Women's roles in Prince Hall Freemasonry
—attitudes towards women, 27, 35, 148; and Order of the Eastern Star symbolism, 118; and producer values, 36; and separate sphere ideology, 112, 116, 131–33; and women's challenges, 112, 113, 142–47, 321 (n. 100), 322 (n. 111)
—manliness ideals, 26–28; and attire, 54–56; and black middle class status, 27, 28, 34, 35–36, 58, 65; and character, 27, 41–42; and entrepreneurship, 39–41; and intraorganizational relationships, 48–53, 302 (n. 77); and manhood/boyhood distinctions, 27, 112, 126, 127, 130, 148; and militarism, 56–58; and mutual aid/charity, 36–37, 39; and older men, 41–42; and patriarchal role, 26–27, 36–37, 39, 112; and producer values, 27, 28, 35–36, 39–42; and public rituals, 58–59; and respectability, 27, 42–46, 53, 58, 64, 301 (n. 58); and self-made man ideology, 37; and spurious Masonry charges, 63–64; and UNIA manliness ideals, 18–19, 22–23, 68, 92–93, 109–10; and women's roles, 39–40, 111–13, 130–31

Producer republicanism, 20, 36, 295–96 (n. 9)

Producer values: and Black Christ/Black Madonna, 138; and black college student life policies, 248; and industrial education, 246; and Prince Hall Freemasonry manliness ideals, 27, 28, 35–36, 39–42; and producer republicanism, 20, 36, 295–96 (n. 9); and religion, 104, 105; and self-made man ideology, 83; and UNIA manliness ideals, 68, 83, 84–85, 95–97, 101, 103, 105, 109–10; and Victorian manliness ideals, 1. See also Artisanship; Harlem Renaissance—cult of production; Separate sphere ideology

—post–World War I rejection of, 157; and career choices, 163; in Harlem Renaissance literature, 214, 221, 227; and Harlem Renaissance masculinity ideals, 202; and homosexuality, 196; and Jazz Age leisure, 179, 180; and jazz culture, 174; and modern masculinity ideals, 152–53

Prohibition, 174, 279

Property ownership, 27

Protector role. See Patriarchal role

Provider role. See Patriarchal role

Public-private organization of gender roles. See Separate sphere ideology

Public rituals: and Prince Hall Freemasonry, 17–18, 56–59, 303 (n. 93); and UNIA attitudes towards women, 136–38, 139; and Universal African Legion, 97–101, 313 (n. 97)

Puritanism, 214–15

Queer identities, 156. See also Homosexuality

Race riots, 44–45

Racial essentialism: and black messianism, 103–4; and Douglas, 232–33; and Harlem Renaissance artist role debate, 204–5, 206; and jazz culture, 174, 278; and McKay, 222–24. See also Cultural nationalism; Primitivism

Racial purity, 122, 134–36, 317 (n. 30), 320 (nn. 73, 74)

Racial solidarity, 32–33, 34–35

Racism: and manhood/boyhood distinctions, 127–28; and McKay, 221–22, 333 (n. 41); and Northern migration, 6; and racial purity, 134–36

—struggles against: and civilization, 102; and college unrest, 263–64, 268; and criticisms of segregation, 3; and Harlem Renaissance, 201–2, 211–13, 240–41; McKay on, 221–22; and Order of the Eastern Star, 131, 319 (n. 57); and Prince Hall Freemasonry, 38–39, 40–41, 44–45, 60–61; and respectability, 42–43; and Universal African Legion, 100–101; and women's roles, 114, 133–34, 332 (n. 28)

Ragtime, 261

Rampersad, Arnold, 196

Ramus, Esau, 310 (n. 58)

Rapp, William Jourdan, 184, 326 (n. 53)

Rawlins, E. Elliot, 98

Recapitulation theory, 337 (n. 21)

Reiss, Weinold, 232

Religion: black college policies on, 248, 270–71; and critiques of modern masculinity ideals, 288; and homosexuality, 194–95; and Jazz Age leisure, 326 (n. 55); and post–World War I career choices, 167; and Prince Hall Freemasonry, 43, 49, 300–301 (n. 56), 302 (n. 77); and Prince Hall Freemasonry attitudes towards women, 146–47; and self-made man ideology, 84; and suspicion of Freemasonry, 116; and UNIA attitudes towards women, 137–38; UNIA feminization of, 84, 105–6, 314 (n. 111); and Garvey's social Darwinist thought, 78, 104–5

Rent parties, 177–78, 182

policies, 247; and racial purity, 135; and UNIA manliness ideals, 85, 107–8

Smith, Bessie, 176

Smith, G. L., 37

"Smoke, Lilies and Jade" (Nugent), 197

Smoking, 260–61, 340–41 (n. 60)

Social constructionist approach, 9–11, 293–94 (nn. 16, 20)

Social Darwinism, 2, 78, 104, 167

Social discipline, 256–62

Socialist Call, 166

Society of Christian Endeavor, 248

Sororities. *See* Greek-letter organizations

Sovereignty, 46–48, 301 (n. 66)

Spanish-American-Cuban-Filipino War, 2–3, 32

Speakeasies, 179–80

Spencer, Anne, 200, 205, 331 (nn. 12, 18)

Spencer, Harry, 45, 47

Spingarn, Amy, 236

Sports, 92

Spurgeon, James Robert, 57

Spurious Masonry charges, 59, 61–64

Stein, Judith, 76, 306 (n. 9), 310 (n. 58)

Stereotypes. *See* Racism—struggles against

Streator, George, 265–66, 280, 281

Student Army Training Corps (SATC), 253–54, 255

Student strikes. *See* College unrest

Success manual genre, 1–2

Sullivan, Joseph, 40

Survey Graphic, 200, 239. See also *The New Negro*

Susman, Warren I., 292 (n. 15), 337 (n. 20)

Sweetbacks, 178–79, 228, 326 (n. 53), 333 (n. 48)

Talbert, Mary, 117

Talented Tenth model, 67–68

Talliaferro, Lillie, 132

Taylor, Charles, 46

Taylor, Ula, 119, 140

Taylor, Van, 283–84

Teagle, Daniel T., 146, 147

Terrell, Mary Church, 113

Terrell, Robert H., 25

"Theater" (Toomer), 218–19

Thomas, Norton G. G., 91

Thompson, Louise, 183–85, 195, 236, 327 (n. 65)

Thompson, Noah, 74, 75, 76

Thurman, Wallace, 149–51, 150; and Harlem Renaissance, 149, 151, 288, 344 (n. 5); and homosexuality, 184, 185, 195, 196, 327 (n. 65); on Jazz Age leisure, 178; and marriage, 183–85, 327 (nn. 63, 65); and patronage, 237; on sweetbacks, 179, 326 (n. 53)

Tobacco, 260–61, 279–80, 340–41 (n. 60)

Toomer, Jean, 161, 214–21, 333 (n. 37); career choices of, 160–65, 324 (n. 19); on civilization, 214–15, 216; on class, 218–19; on homosexuality, 195; on industrialization, 214, 215, 216–18; on Jazz Age, 155, 157; and *The New Negro*, 200; on producer values, 214; on rural culture, 220–21; and unity of self, 332–33 (n. 35)

Transvestism, 182–83

Trawick, Mrs. Arch, 268

Torgovnick, Marianna, 330 (n. 9)

Turner, Victoria W., 140

Tuskegee model, 67

Tyler, George, 313 (n. 99)

Tyler, Parker, 197

Uebel, Michael, 293 (n. 16)

UNIA. *See* Universal Negro Improvement Association

Universal African Black Cross Nurses, 123, 138, 320 (n. 80)

Universal African Legion, 93–101; and character, 94, 95; and militarism, 93–94, 100, 136–37; organization of, 94; and public rituals, 97–101, 313 (n. 97); and UNIA manliness ideals, 94–97, 99; vs. Universal African Black Cross Nurses, 123

Gender and American Culture

Manliness and Its Discontents: The Black Middle Class and the Transformation of Masculinity, 1900–1930, by Martin Summers (2004).

Citizen, Mother, Worker: Debating Public Responsibility for Child Care after the Second World War, by Emilie Stoltzfus (2003).

Women and the Historical Enterprise in America: Gender, Race, and the Politics of Memory 1880–1945, by Julie Des Jardins (2003).

Free Hearts and Free Homes: Gender and American Antislavery Politics, by Michael D. Pierson (2003).

Ella Baker and the Black Freedom Movement: A Radical Democratic Vision, by Barbara Ransby (2003).

Signatures of Citizenship: Petitioning, Antislavery, and Women's Political Identity, by Susan Zaeske (2003).

Love on the Rocks: Men, Women, and Alcohol in Post–World War II America, by Lori Rotskoff (2002).

The Veiled Garvey: The Life and Times of Amy Jacques Garvey, by Ula Yvette Taylor (2002).

Working Cures: Health, Healing, and Power on Southern Slave Plantations, by Sharla Fett (2002).

Southern History across the Color Line, by Nell Irvin Painter (2002).

The Artistry of Anger: Black and White Women's Literature in America, 1820–1860, by Linda M. Grasso (2002).

Too Much to Ask: Black Women in the Era of Integration, by Elizabeth Higginbotham (2001).

Imagining Medea: Rhodessa Jones and Theater for Incarcerated Women, by Rena Fraden (2001).

Painting Professionals: Women Artists and the Development of Modern American Art, 1870–1920, by Kirsten Swinth (2001).

Remaking Respectability: African American Women in Interwar Detroit, by Victoria W. Wolcott (2001).

Ida B. Wells-Barnett and American Reform, 1880–1930, by Patricia A. Schechter (2001).

Taking Haiti: Military Occupation and the Culture of U.S. Imperialism, 1915–1940, by Mary A. Renda (2001).

Before Jim Crow: The Politics of Race in Postemancipation Virginia, by Jane Dailey (2000).

Captain Ahab Had a Wife: New England Women and the Whalefishery, 1720–1870, by Lisa Norling (2000).

Civilizing Capitalism: The National Consumers' League, Women's Activism, and Labor Standards in the New Deal Era, by Landon R. Y. Storrs (2000).

Rank Ladies: Gender and Cultural Hierarchy in American Vaudeville, by M. Alison Kibler (1999).

Strangers and Pilgrims: Female Preaching in America, 1740–1845, by Catherine A. Brekus (1998).

Sex and Citizenship in Antebellum America, by Nancy Isenberg (1998).

Yours in Sisterhood: Ms. Magazine and the Promise of Popular Feminism, by Amy Erdman Farrell (1998).

We Mean to Be Counted: White Women and Politics in Antebellum Virginia, by Elizabeth R. Varon (1998).

Women Against the Good War: Conscientious Objection and Gender on the American Home Front, 1941–1947, by Rachel Waltner Goossen (1997).

Toward an Intellectual History of Women: Essays by Linda K. Kerber (1997).

Gender and Jim Crow: Women and the Politics of White Supremacy in North Carolina, 1896–1920, by Glenda Elizabeth Gilmore (1996).

Delinquent Daughters: Protecting and Policing Adolescent Female Sexuality in the United States, 1885–1920, by Mary E. Odem (1995).

U.S. History as Women's History: New Feminist Essays, edited by Linda K. Kerber, Alice Kessler-Harris, and Kathryn Kish Sklar (1995).

Common Sense and a Little Fire: Women and Working-Class Politics in the United States, 1900–1965, by Annelise Orleck (1995).

How Am I to Be Heard?: Letters of Lillian Smith, edited by Margaret Rose Gladney (1993).

Entitled to Power: Farm Women and Technology, 1913–1963, by Katherine Jellison (1993).

Revising Life: Sylvia Plath's Ariel Poems, by Susan R. Van Dyne (1993).

Made From This Earth: American Women and Nature, by Vera Norwood (1993).

Unruly Women: The Politics of Social and Sexual Control in the Old South, by Victoria E. Bynum (1992).

The Work of Self-Representation: Lyric Poetry in Colonial New England, by Ivy Schweitzer (1991).

Labor and Desire: Women's Revolutionary Fiction in Depression America, by Paula Rabinowitz (1991).

Community of Suffering and Struggle: Women, Men, and the Labor Movement in Minneapolis, 1915–1945, by Elizabeth Faue (1991).

All That Hollywood Allows: Re-reading Gender in 1950s Melodrama, by Jackie Byars (1991).

Doing Literary Business: American Women Writers in the Nineteenth Century, by Susan Coultrap-McQuin (1990).

Ladies, Women, and Wenches: Choice and Constraint in Antebellum Charleston and Boston, by Jane H. Pease and William H. Pease (1990).

The Secret Eye: The Journal of Ella Gertrude Clanton Thomas, 1848–1889, edited by Virginia Ingraham Burr, with an introduction by Nell Irvin Painter (1990).

Second Stories: The Politics of Language, Form, and Gender in Early American Fictions, by Cynthia S. Jordan (1989).

Within the Plantation Household: Black and White Women of the Old South, by Elizabeth Fox-Genovese (1988).

The Limits of Sisterhood: The Beecher Sisters on Women's Rights and Woman's Sphere, by Jeanne Boydston, Mary Kelley, and Anne Margolis (1988).